POSITIVE ACCOUNTING THEORY

**Prentice-Hall
Contemporary Topics in Accounting Series**

ALFRED RAPPAPORT, SERIES EDITOR

POSITIVE ACCOUNTING THEORY

ROSS L. WATTS
JEROLD L. ZIMMERMAN

University of Rochester

PRENTICE-HALL, INC., ENGLEWOOD CLIFFS, NEW JERSEY 07632

Library of Congress Cataloging in Publication Data

WATTS, ROSS L., (date)
  Positive accounting theory.

  Bibliography: p.
  Includes index.
  1. Accounting. I. Zimmerman, Jerold L.,
(date). II. Title.
HF5625.W35 1986   657'.01   85-3567
ISBN 0-13-686171-7

To Helen and Dodie

Editorial/production supervision: *Barbara Grasso*
Manufacturing buyer: *Ray Keating*

PRINTED IN THE UNITED STATES OF AMERICA

10 9 8 7 6 5 4 3 2 1

ISBN 0-13-686171-7   01

Prentice-Hall International (UK) Limited, *London*
Prentice-Hall of Australia Pty. Limited, *Sydney*
Prentice-Hall Canada Inc., *Toronto*
Prentice-Hall Hispanoamericana, S.A., *Mexico*
Prentice-Hall of India Private Limited, *New Delhi*
Prentice-Hall of Japan, Inc., *Tokyo*
Prentice-Hall of Southeast Asia Pte. Ltd., *Singapore*
Editora Prentice-Hall do Brasil, Ltda., *Rio de Janeiro*
Whitehall Books Limited, *Wellington, New Zealand*

Contents

---

v

Foreword

Accounting, broadly conceived as the measurement and communication of economic information relevant to decision makers, has undergone dramatic changes during the past decade. Recent advances in quantitative methods, the behavioral sciences, and information technology are influencing current thinking in financial as well as managerial accounting. Leasing, pension plans, the use of convertible securities and warrants in mergers and acquisitions, inflation, and corporate diversification are but a few of the challenging problems facing the accountant.

These developments and the very pervasiveness of accounting activity make it difficult for teachers, students, public accountants, and financial executives to gain convenient access to current thinking on key topics in the field. Journal articles, while current, must often of necessity give only cursory treatment or present a single point of view. Many of the important developments in the field have not crystalized to a point where they can be easily incorporated into textbooks. Further, because textbooks must necessarily limit the space devoted to any one topic, key topics often do not get the attention they properly deserve.

The Contemporary Topics series attempts to fill this gap by covering significant contemporary developments in accounting through brief, but self-contained, studies. These independent studies provide the reader with up-to-date coverage of key topics. For the practitioner, the series offers a succinct overview of developments in research and practice in areas of special interest to him. The series enables the teacher to design courses with maximum flexibility and to expose his students to authoritative analysis of controversial problems.

ALFRED RAPPAPORT

Preface

This book reviews the theory and methodology underlying the large and growing economics-based empirical literature in accounting. Theory does not present a rule for choosing among alternative accounting procedures (e.g., choose the one that better matches revenue and expense). Rather, theory provides an explanation for accounting and auditing practice. For example, a theory explains *why* some firms use accelerated depreciation methods and others use straight line and why some firms use Big Eight auditors and others do not. Such a theory is important to accounts and managers; it helps them to make better decisions when conditions change and they are confronted with unfamiliar situations.

The theory, as it currently exists, is far from complete. In fact, the investigation into the factors affecting accounting and auditing practice is just beginning, and the causes of the empirical regularities that have been observed are still debated. This is expected because the world is complex and continually changing. Complexity and change ensure that we will never have a complete theory of accounting.

Interpretation of associations between variables requires a theory. Hence, empirical research is not a question of discovering facts about accounting and auditing. A researcher explicitly specifies a hypothesis from a theory and tests it. If the hypothesized relation is substantiated, the theory is used to interpret the findings. However, often the researcher's evidence causes the theory to be revised and new hypotheses to be generated and tested. The result is that theory evolves over time, and a current survey of the state of the research often interprets an early study in a fashion very different from the original researcher.

Presenting the empirical research with only current-day interpretations of the results is misleading and does not give the student an understanding of how research evolves. Consequently, the literature is analyzed chronologically in this book. In Chapters 3–6 we analyze the early applications of empirical work in financial economics to accounting. These studies addressed hypotheses underlying the existing accounting literature. Evidence provided by those studies (combined with theoretical developments in finance) led to the formulation of a new accounting theory presented in Chapters 8–10 and 14. The development of the new theory was also spurred by an ongoing debate over the desirability of government regulation of financial disclosure, a debate that is analyzed in Chapter 7. Studies empirically testing hypotheses of the new theory are summarized and evaluated in Chapters 11, 12, and 13.

Our chronological approach has its costs. Studies addressing the same question appear in different chapters. For example, investigations of the stock price effect of changes in accounting procedures appear in both Chapters 4 and 12. However, we think that cost is offset by the benefit the student receives in understanding the research process.

In analyzing important studies in the development of the literature, we try to explain the methodology underlying the literature. That methodology is rarely taught, even in economics and finance Ph.D. programs. It is learned by hands-on experience in conducting empirical studies and is passed on to colleagues and Ph.D. students in workshops and seminars, the refereeing process, and published reviews of past research. We discuss empirical methodology explicitly in Chapter 1. Our purpose is to give students the benefit of the accumulated years of experience of researchers in producing useful theories.

The single-period capital asset pricing model (CAPM) is used throughout the book as the valuation model. The CAPM is simple, yet as powerful as more complicated models in yielding an underlying framework for deriving testable implications.

The prerequisites for this book include an elementary knowledge of accounting, price theory (microeconomics), finance, and statistics (including multivariate regression analysis). Some knowledge of the material in standard intermediate and advanced financial accounting texts is helpful but not necessary.

The book is written and has been used for a second-year M.B.A. and Ph.D. audience. While our students are well prepared, they still find the level of sophistication and rigor challenging. Several chapters are difficult for M.B.A. students. Subtle methodological or theoretical points are addressed rather than ignored or glossed over. The process of discussing the issue illustrates that it is far from being understood.

Some students prefer to know just "the bottom line." Unfortunately, a tidy "bottom line" does not exist at the present time. We are dealing with the shifting sands of a body of research. Our purpose is not so much with presenting a map of the current sands as with providing students with the tools and understanding to draw their own maps of, and contribute to, future literature.

An important and well-received supplementary teaching aid used in the M.B.A. course has been a term paper analyzing current proposed or recently adopted accounting standards (e.g., deferred taxes). In particular, the assignment requires student teams to analyze the cash flow effects of various standards, the parties benefited and harmed by the standards, and the circumstances causing the standards to be placed on the standard board's agenda. This project illustrates how the book's theory can be used to explain current accounting controversies and pulls together the various theoretical issues raised in the book. Time permitting, these projects provide students with useful experience making class presentations and expose students to applications of the theory to other recent controversies.

There are two points of style that should be explained. Each chapter finishes with a summary. And whenever important concepts are introduced, they are set in **boldface** type.

Students have provided (often involuntary) "consumer" feedback, thereby helping us to discover some hidden land mines. Comments and editorial assistance from Susan Thomas, Jan Baker Pass, and Chris Surrette were particularly useful. Several colleagues provided helpful discussions and insightful and critical remarks on earlier versions: Andrew Christie, Linda DeAngelo, Michael Jensen, Martin Geisel, William Meckling, G. William Schwert, Clifford Smith, Lee Wakeman, and Jerold Warner. And most important, Pat Baldeck and Chris Haszlauer supplied large inputs of document processing. Daniel Collins, George Foster, Robert Holthausen, Richard Leftwich, and Alfred Rappaport reviewed earlier versions of the manuscript. Financial assistance was provided by the Center for Research in Government Policy in Business and the Managerial Economics Research Center, both at the Graduate School of Management, University of Rochester. To all these individuals and institutions we offer our sincere gratitude.

Ross L. Watts
Jerold L. Zimmerman

CHAPTER ONE

The Role of Accounting Theory

This book is about accounting theory. The accounting literature includes many different views of theory, so we begin by giving our view. The concept of theory we describe is broader and has a different focus from that given in financial accounting texts. Nevertheless, it underlies a large and growing body of empirical literature in accounting. In this chapter we explain the concept's evolution and why that type of theory is important.

The theory concept we describe has an accompanying research methodology. That methodology is the result of the accumulated years of experience of empirical researchers in producing useful theories and also is outlined in this chapter.

The book's objective is to provide an understanding of the theory and methodology underlying the economics-based empirical literature in accounting. Knowledge of the impact of methodology on the evolution of theory is crucial to that understanding. For that reason, the structure of the book, which is summarized at the end of this chapter, is chronological.

NATURE OF THEORY

The objective of accounting theory is to *explain* and *predict* accounting practice. Our definition of accounting practice is broad. Because the development and nature of accounting is closely tied to auditing, auditing practice is included as part of accounting practice.

Explanation means providing reasons for observed practice. For example, an accounting theory should explain *why* certain firms use the last-in, first-out (LIFO) method of inventory rather than the first-in, first-out (FIFO) method.

Prediction of accounting practice means that the theory predicts unobserved accounting phenomena. Unobserved phenomena are not necessarily future phenomena; they include phenomena that have occurred but on which systematic evidence has not been collected. For example, an accounting theory can provide hypotheses about the attributes of firms that use LIFO versus the attributes of firms using FIFO. Such predictions can be tested using historical data on the attributes of firms using the two methods.

The preceding view of theory, explicitly or implicitly, underlies most empirical studies in economics. It is also the view of theory in science (e.g., Poincaré, 1905; Popper, 1959; Hempel, 1965).

WHY ACCOUNTING THEORY IS IMPORTANT

Many individuals have to make decisions about external accounting reports. Corporate managers have to decide which particular accounting procedures to use to calculate the numbers given in the reports. For example, they have to decide whether to use straight-line or an accelerated method of calculating depreciation. Corporate managers also make representations to bodies determining the accounting procedures used in external accounting reports (i.e., accounting standards). Managers have to decide when to make such representations and which procedures to support and which to oppose. Managers also have to choose an audit firm.

Public accountants are frequently called on by managers for advice concerning the use of accounting procedures in reports. Also, the public accountants themselves have to decide whether to make representations on a proposed accounting standard and, if so, which position to take.

Officers of lending institutions (e.g., banks and insurance companies) have to assess the creditworthiness of corporations that use different accounting procedures. As lenders or investors, they have to weigh the implications of the different accounting procedures in making decisions to extend credit or invest. In addition, loan agreements generally specify that the corporations must meet requirements based on accounting numbers or the loans will be in default. The officers of the lending institutions have to decide what accounting procedures to specify (if any) for the calculation of such numbers.

Investors and financial analysts employed by brokerage houses, pension funds, and the like interpret accounting numbers as an input to investment decisions. In particular, they assess investments in corporations that use different procedures and auditors. Like public accountants and corporate executives, financial analysts also make representations on potential accounting standards.

Finally, individuals in accounting standard–setting bodies such as the Financial Accounting Standards Board (FASB) and the Securities and Exchange Commission (SEC) are responsible for setting accounting standards. They decide which procedures to sanction, thereby restricting accounting procedures available to individual firms. They also decide issues such as how frequently corporations should report (e.g., monthly, quarterly, semiannually, or annually) and what must be audited.

We assume that all these various parties in selecting or recommending accounting and auditing procedures act so as to maximize their own welfare (i.e., their expected utility). To make a decision on accounting reports, individuals want to know how the alternative reporting methods affect their welfare. For example, in choosing among alternative depreciation methods, corporate managers want to know how straight-line depreciation affects their welfare vis-à-vis accelerated depreciation. If the corporate manager's welfare is dependent on the market value of the corporation (as it is via stock option plans, debt agreements, and other mechanisms), the corporate manager wants to know the effect of the accounting decisions on stock and bond prices. The manager wants a theory that explains the relation between accounting reports and stock and bond prices.

Stock and bond prices are not the only variables by which accounting reporting decisions affect an individual's welfare. An individual at the SEC is concerned with the effect of an accounting standard on the attitude of members of Congress toward the SEC because that affects the SEC's budget and the resources under that individual's control.

Determining the relation between accounting reporting decisions and variables affecting individual welfare is difficult. The relation between the accounting procedures and stock market values is complex and cannot be determined just by observing whether stock prices change when accounting procedures change. Likewise, the effects of alternative accounting procedures and alternative reporting and auditing methods on bond prices, on the SEC budget, on profits from accounting practices, and so on, are complex and cannot be determined by mere observation.

The public accountant or corporate manager may observe an association between variables such as changes in procedures and changes in stock prices, but cannot tell whether the association is causal. The stock price change might not be *caused* by the procedure change; that is, both changes could be the result of some other event. In that case, changing procedures would not necessarily produce a stock price effect. To make the causality interpretation, the practitioner requires a theory that explains the relation between the variables. The theory enables the practitioner to attach causality to a particular variable, such as a procedure change.

Of course, based on their own experience public accountants, lending officers, and so on will develop implicit theories to assess the effects of different accounting procedures or changes in accounting procedures when making decisions. However, practitioners' theories will be conditioned by their specific experiences. This may cause them to develop a theory such as that developed by the small child who observed that men who attended burlesque shows tend to be old and bald and concluded that burlesque shows caused one to become old and bald. By using large numbers of observations and carefully constructed empirical tests, it is hoped that researchers can develop theories that provide explanations of the world that are more intuitively appealing and have better predictive power than the child's theory. In essence, researchers should be able to provide theories that are more useful to decision makers in maximizing their welfare.

EVOLUTION OF ACCOUNTING THEORY

In the late nineteenth and early twentieth centuries, accounting writers were primarily concerned with describing observed practices and with providing pedagogical rules for classifying those practices. While they did, at times, provide insight into the reasons for a particular practice, the early writers did not attempt to structure sets of principles to explain accounting practice in general.

Later, after the U.S. securities acts of 1933 and 1934, which regulated disclosure by corporations with securities listed on stock exchanges and which established the SEC, accounting theorists became much more concerned with prescribing how firms should report. For example, there was a debate over the basis of valuation of assets, some saying that old assets should be valued on a replacement cost basis, others that they should be valued on a current cost basis. Accounting theorists became more concerned with policy recommendations; they became more **normative**—concerned with what should be done. Very little concern was exhibited for the empirical validity of the hypotheses on which the normative prescriptions rested. These theorists thought the nature of accounting, its role, the effects of different procedures on stock prices, and so on were self-evident, so deriving prescriptions was only a matter of assuming an objective for accounting and applying logic.

The introduction of the concept of theory used in this book came as the result of developments in finance, which inherited the concept from economics. In the 1950s Joel Dean (1951) and others, for example, Modigliani and Miller (1958), made significant advances in finance by applying economic analysis to financial problems. Empirical tests of hypotheses arising from the analysis were facilitated by the creation of a large computer data base of security prices by the Center for Research into Security Prices (CRSP). The data, combined with the availability of the computer, led to numerous studies on the behavior of stock prices and the effect of information on stock prices (see Fama, 1976, for a summary of some of these studies). The results of these early empirical studies led to the development of the **efficient markets hypothesis** (see Chapter 2).

The introduction of large-scale empirical testing of hypotheses in economics and finance, particularly the efficient markets hypothesis, eventually had a major impact on accounting research. In the mid-1960s, tests of the efficient markets hypothesis produced results contrary to the hypotheses underlying accountants' normative prescriptions. In particular, the results imply that the stock market is not systematically misled by accounting methods. The contradictions were noticed by accounting researchers who were trained in the new research methods in finance. In explaining the contradictions to accountants, those researchers introduced the research methods of finance and its accompanying concept of theory and methodology to accounting. While other finance-based articles preceded it in the literature, the article that had the biggest impact on the accounting literature was Ball and Brown (1968).[1]

The alien concept of theory and methodology was not understood by most accounting researchers of the time and was met with resistance. Dyckman and Zeff (1984) document the difficulty Ball and Brown encountered in publishing their paper. However, over time the approach gained popularity, and papers based on it now constitute a large fraction of papers published by the leading academic journals.[2]

The early economics-based empirical studies in accounting (late 1960s and early 1970s) tested hypotheses in the existing accounting literature and investigated the relation between accounting numbers

---

[1] Examples of earlier finance-based articles are Beaver (1966) and Benston (1967).

[2] See Dyckman and Zeff (1984, p. 278) for a summary of the content of recent volumes of the *Journal of Accounting Research*.

and economic variables and the time series of accounting numbers. Most of those papers did not attempt to explain accounting practice. For example, they did not provide an explanation for the time series and cross-sectional variation in the accounting procedures adopted by corporations. Indeed, many of the early studies assumed that the choice of accounting techniques was irrelevant to the valuation of the firm (see Chapter 4).

The concern with testing previously existing theory and lack of concern with developing a theory of accounting practice can be partially explained by the desire of those applying the new methodology to address what were regarded as important hypotheses in the existing literature. It can also be explained by the influence of the research in finance at the time. That research had also concerned itself with investigating the logic and empirical support for traditional explanations of financial practice (e.g., explanations for variations in debt/equity ratios).

By the mid-1970s researchers in finance realized that after demolishing the old explanations, they were left with no explanation for financial practice, no theory. For example, they could not explain the systematic variation in debt/equity ratios across firms. This realization led to the development of theories of finance that had the potential to explain financial practice such as the systematic variation in debt/equity ratios.

Also by the mid-1970s accounting researchers had observed systematic behavior in accounting practice. For example, they observed whole industries changing from one method of accounting to another at one point in time (e.g., the switch by the steel industry from accelerated depreciation to straight line in 1968). This suggested that a theory could be developed to explain accounting practice. The developments in finance aimed at explaining financial practice provided a ready basis for such a theory.

Another basis for the emerging accounting theory was the ongoing debate over the desirability of government regulation of financial disclosure. The early empirical studies had questioned the existing rationales for regulation, but researchers found new rationales in economic theory. The debate over those new rationales, in turn, led to the recognition that the rationales relied on simplistic models of the behavior of politicians and bureaucrats that were inconsistent with the evidence emerging in economics. This realization caused accounting researchers to adopt the assumption that politicians and bureaucrats, like managers and accountants, act to maximize their own welfare and to use that assumption to model the effect of regulation on accounting practice.

Today the literature contains many studies using the finance-based theory and/or the theory of regulation to explain accounting and auditing practice. Other approaches exist in the literature (e.g., the behavioralist approach), but in this book we explain only the development and methodology of the economics-based empirical approach.

POSITIVE AND NORMATIVE PROPOSITIONS

As described, after the securities acts the accounting literature became normative in the sense that it sought to prescribe the contents of accounting reports. For example, Chambers (1966) advocates current cash equivalents, and Edwards and Bell (1961) advocate current costs as the basis for the valuation of assets. Financial accounting texts also tend to adopt normative (i.e., prescriptive) positions.

By itself, theory, as we describe it, yields no prescriptions for accounting practice. It is concerned with explaining accounting practice. It is designed to explain and predict which firms will and which firms will not use a particular method of valuing assets, but it says nothing as to which method a firm should use. The situation is well described by Passmore (1953, p. 676):

> Such a theory (a theory in social science) will have the limitations characteristic of the physical sciences. It will not tell us what we ought to do, any more than physics tells us whether to build a bridge or to be content with a ferry.

Prescription requires the specification of an **objective** and an **objective function**. For example, to argue that current cash equivalents should be the method of valuing assets, one might adopt the objective of **economic efficiency** (i.e., the size of the economic pie available) and specify how certain variables affect efficiency (the objective function). Then one could use a theory to argue that adoption of current cash equivalents will increase efficiency. Theory provides a method for assessing this *conditional* statement (i.e., do we observe that adoption of current cash equivalents increases efficiency?). But theory does not provide a means for assessing the appropriateness of the objective. The decision on the objective is subjective, and we have no method for resolving differences in individual decisions.

Economic efficiency is frequently used as an objective in economics and accounting. However, support for that objective is not unanimous. Economic efficiency does not rank alternative cross-sectional distributions of wealth (i.e., the division of the pie), and many are concerned with the "equity" of those distributions. This attitude is reflected in statements on accounting theory. For example, the American Institute of Certified Public Accountants (AICPA) Study Group on the Objectives of Financial Statements (1973, p. 17) argues that "financial statements should meet the needs of those with the least ability to obtain information." Unfortunately, individuals do not agree on what is "equitable"; they have different preferences for different wealth distributions. And we cannot be assured that those preferences can be combined in a fashion that will yield consistent results or unanimity (Arrow, 1963). Choosing an objective, other than economic efficiency, amounts to choosing among individuals and, therefore, necessarily entails a subjective value judgment.

We should add that researchers are subjective in developing theory. The topics researchers choose to work on and the models they develop are affected by the researcher's own values. However, in evaluating that research, the contentious issues become less subjective. They involve questions as to whether the development of a model's implications are logical and whether hypotheses are or are not consistent with the evidence.

In economics the concept of theory used in science (the concept we describe) has traditionally been called **positive theory** to discriminate it from prescription or normative arguments. This terminology, which was popularized by Friedman (1953), often leads to the concept of positive theory (the concept used in science) being confused with another, different view in the philosophy of science, logical positivism.[3] Despite this confusion, in this book we use the term positive theory because of its common usage in economics and recently in accounting.

Theorists have to be very careful in discriminating between positive and normative propositions. Positive propositions are concerned with how the world works. They take the form "If A then B" and are refutable. For example, the following is a positive proposition: "If a firm switches from FIFO to LIFO and the stock market has not anticipated the change, the stock price will rise." This statement is a

---

[3] In logical positivism, statements are either true by definition or through practical experience. Verification of nondefinitional statements is emphasized (Blaug, 1980, p. 11). Scientific laws are "no more than a conceptual reflection on *facts*" (emphasis added; Kockelmans, 1968, p. 171).

In positive or scientific theory there are no brute facts. The interpretation of facts depends on theories (e.g., assignment of causation requires a theory). Further, we cannot prove a hypothesis correct; all that is possible is to disprove a hypothesis. Hence, there is an emphasis on criticizing theories and attempting to falsify them rather than verifying them (see Blaug, 1980, Ch. 1, pp. 1–28; Popper, 1963, pp. 228–229).

The emphasis on verification in logical positivism leads to a distrust of nonobservable concepts such as absolute space and time in mechanics and natural selection in evolution theory (Blaug, 1980, p. 11). There is not the same distrust in positive economics. Indeed, abstract concepts such as economic Darwinism play an important role in positive economics. In attempting to explain existing economic institutions, empiricists typically assume that efficient institutions survive (see Chapter 8).

prediction that can be refuted by evidence. Normative propositions are concerned with prescriptions. They take the form "Given the set of conditions C, alternative D should be chosen." For example, a normative proposition is, "Since prices are rising, LIFO should be adopted." This proposition is not refutable. Given an objective, it can be made refutable. For example, the statement "If prices are rising choosing LIFO will maximize the value of the firm," is refutable by evidence. Thus, given an objective, a researcher can turn a prescription into a conditional prediction and assess the empirical validity. However, the choice of the objective is not the theorist's, it is the theory user's.

As a final note on the relation between positive and normative propositions, we emphasize that positive theory does not make normative propositions unimportant. The demand for theory arises from the users' demands for prescriptions, for normative propositions (see the preceding discussion of theory's importance). However, theory only supplies one of the two necessary ingredients for a prescription: the effect of certain actions on various variables. The user supplies the other ingredient: the objective and the function that provides the effect of variables on that objective (the objective function).

AN OUTLINE OF METHODOLOGY

Development of a Theory

A theory consists of two parts: the assumptions, including the definitions of variables and the logic that relates them, and the set of substantive hypotheses. The assumptions, definitions, and logic are used to organize, analyze, and understand the empirical phenomena of interest, while the hypotheses are the predictions generated from the analysis.

The development of a theory begins with the researcher thinking of an explanation for some phenomena. For example, an explanation for the use of LIFO or FIFO might be that the manager chooses the method that minimizes the tax liability.

Whether he spells it out formally or not, the researcher is making certain assumptions. In our example, he is assuming that the manager's objective is to minimize the present value of taxes and maximize the value of the firm. From the assumptions, the researcher explicitly or implicitly derives implications that can be empirically tested. For example, our researcher might derive the conditions under which the manager will choose LIFO or FIFO. Given some further assumptions, our researcher may show that the choice depends on the behavior of the prices of firms' products and prices of material inputs. This provides an hypothesized relation between the behavior of those prices and the LIFO/FIFO choice. After gathering data on those prices and the firms' inventory methods, the researcher can test the hypothesis.

The assumptions the researcher makes may be very simplistic. The logic employed may or may not take the form of math; the assumptions, logic, and hypothesis may not even be spelled out in detail in the paper. However, the researcher must implicitly take those steps before conducting any empirical work. The reason is that he must have an hypothesis and theory to collect the data. Without an hypothesis, the researcher does not know which facts or data to investigate. As Popper (1959, p. 59) puts it, "Theories are nets cast to catch what we call 'the world'; to rationalize, to explain, and to master it." Theories tell us which facts are relevant and which are not—that is, where to fish. Physics provides an excellent example of directed fishing. In investigating the structure of matter, physicists predicted the existence of quarcks and then successfully looked for them. Similarly, stars are often "proved" to exist and then a search is conducted.

If the phenomena the research addresses and/or the empirical results are interesting, other researchers will try to improve the original researcher's methodology, apply it to different phenomena, find and test alternative explanations for his results, and so on, and a literature will develop. The theory itself will change and evolve as a result of those efforts, often to the point that current-day interpretation of the original researcher's result is totally different from the original interpretation.

The Nonexistence of Perfect Theories and the Role of Anomalies

We cannot find a theory that explains and predicts all accounting phenomena. The reason is that theories are simplifications of reality and the world is complex and changing. Theorists try to explain and predict a class of phenomena and, as a consequence, try to capture in their assumptions the variables common to that class. The result is that facts particular to a given observation or subset of observations and not common to the whole class are ignored and are not incorporated into the theory's assumptions. Ignoring these facts (or omitted variables) necessarily leads to a theory not explaining or predicting every observation.[4] Hence, the mere fact that a theory does not predict perfectly does not cause researchers or users to abandon that theory.

---

[4] Even in the physical sciences, theories do not explain all phenomena, so the problem is not unique to the social sciences. For example, until recently, the theories of aerodynamics predicted that the bumble bee would not fly. Also, at the present time, theories of physics cannot explain the existence of black holes.

While prediction errors may not cause abandonment of a theory, those errors are important. In fact, they are very important, because investigation of them frequently leads to improvements in the accepted theory—they suggest ways a "better" theory can be developed. In fact, systematic prediction errors or anomalies in an extant theory often lead to development and acceptance of a completely new theory.

The Nature of Evidence

Because they are concerned with predictions for a class of phenomena and realize that prediction errors will necessarily exist, researchers are skeptical of anecdotal evidence. They are afraid that the event described may be atypical—a prediction error. Consequently, researchers prefer large samples that they can use to test their hypotheses for statistical significance.

The concern with anecdotal evidence being atypical does not mean that such evidence should be ignored. First, in some circumstances, that evidence is the only evidence available, and some evidence is better than none. Second, as noted, if that anecdotal evidence contradicts the results of carefully designed studies using larger numbers of observations (more powerful tests), it can suggest ways to improve the theory that are consistent with the more powerful tests. (See Beaver, 1976, pp. 69–70, for a discussion of the role of anecdotal evidence.)

The Criterion for a Theory's Success

If there is no perfect theory, how do we choose among imperfect theories? What determines the success and survival of a theory? One important determinant is the value of the theory to users. As we have seen, users want to predict the effects of decisions. The value of a theory for this purpose depends on the cost of prediction errors to the user and the cost of using the model. For example, suppose that we have two theories that predict future credit card account defaults. Both theories make mistakes. Some customers who would not default on their accounts are predicted to default and are denied credit. Some who will default are predicted not to default and are granted credit. One model might produce fewer errors, but if its errors are more costly (e.g., predicting someone will not default when in fact they will), the model that makes more errors is the better model in this application. In some other application, the other model might be better.

The cost of developing the theory's predictions is also considered by users in choosing theories. In our example, the model with the most costly errors would be chosen if the increased cost of errors is more than offset by lower costs of calculating the prediction. For this reason, we still observe Newtonian physics being used for many purposes.

The value of a theory's predictions explains why we do not abandon a theory even if it has a lot of prediction errors. If there is only one theory available, it will be used if the cost of its errors and implementation is less than the cost of naïve guesses.

While the value of the predictions of a theory to users influences its use, it does not solely determine its success. Because the costs of errors and implementation vary, several theories about the phenomena can exist simultaneously for predictive purposes. However, only one will be generally accepted by theorists. In accepting one theory over another, theorists will be influenced by the intuitive appeal of the theory's explanation for phenomena and by the range of phenomena it can explain and predict as well as by the usefulness of its predictions to users. There is a competition between alternative theories on these dimensions for general acceptance. As Popper (1959, p. 108) writes, "We choose the theory which best holds its own in competition with other theories; the one which, by natural selection, proves itself the fittest to survive."

The Important Role of Competing Theories

Competing theories arise because theories are imperfect and we cannot *prove* a theory correct. All we do is test a theory's hypotheses. An hypothesis is tested by comparing it with observed phenomena. If the hypothesis is consistent with the phenomena, the hypothesis is confirmed. However, as Friedman (1953, p. 9) writes, "If there is one hypothesis that is consistent with the available evidence, there are always an infinite number that are." The result is that there is often competition among alternative theories about the same phenomena for general acceptance.

Competing theories are important in testing an hypothesis of a particular theory. If no competing theory has been advanced, there is no obvious way of deciding which variables to investigate other than those indicated by the theory being tested because, as indicated, there are an infinite number of alternative possible variables that could be important. In that case, there is no necessity to investigate the effect of variables other than those suggested by the theory being tested. However, if competing theories exist, we have to investigate the variables that those competing theories suggest are important. Typically in that situation the researcher attempts to find circumstances where the competing theories give different predictions so that we can test each theory and discriminate among them.

STRUCTURE OF THIS BOOK

The structure of this book follows the evolution of economics-based accounting theory. The next chapter explains the two developments in finance that led to the introduction of the scientific concept of theory (the efficient markets hypothesis and the **capital asset pricing model**).[5] That chapter also describes the effect of those two developments on accounting research.

Chapters 3–7 analyze the literature that developed before researchers concentrated on explaining and predicting accounting practice. Chapter 3 analyzes studies of the relation between accounting earnings and stock prices. Chapter 4 traces attempts to use the stock price effects of changes in accounting procedures to discriminate between the efficient markets hypothesis and an hypothesis underlying the earlier literature's prescriptions. Studies on the usefulness of accounting numbers for valuing securities are analyzed in Chapter 5 and studies on the time series of earnings are analyzed in Chapter 6. Chapter 7 describes and analyzes the empirical studies' effect on previously existing rationales for regulation and analyzes new rationales that subsequently arose.

The second half of the book (Chapters 8–14) covers the theory that evolved from attempts to explain and predict accounting and auditing practice. Chapters 8 and 9 describe the part of the theory that is based on attempts to explain financial practice. Chapter 10 outlines the part that emerged from the theory of regulation. The empirical studies testing the theory are analyzed in Chapters 11, 12, and 13. Chapter 14 presents a theory of the accounting literature.

An important element of a theory's success is its usefulness to users. Chapter 15 evaluates the usefulness of the economics-based accounting theory that evolved from the use of the scientific concept of theory.

SUMMARY

This book presents the theory and methodology underlying the economics-based empirical literature in accounting. The concept of theory underlying that literature is the scientific concept of theory; the objective of theory is to explain and predict phenomena (in this case,

---

[5] Other advances in finance and economics, in particular, information economics and welfare economics, have been introduced into the accounting literature. While such topics are beyond the scope of this book, the interested reader is referred to Beaver (1981) for a review and discussion of this literature.

accounting practice). In economics, that concept has come to be called "positive theory."

Positive accounting theory is important because it can provide those who must make decisions on accounting policy (corporate managers, public accountants, loan officers, investors, financial analysts, regulators) with predictions of, and explanations for, the consequences of their decisions. An important test of an accounting theory is how useful it is. A user will use the theory that increases his or her welfare the most until a more useful theory is developed.

The concept of positive theory was introduced into the accounting literature relatively recently (1960s). Previously the literature was normative, emphasizing prescriptions and not being concerned with empirically testing the hypotheses underlying the prescriptions. Advances in the theory of financial economics in the 1950s and 1960s eventually led to application of those advances to accounting. This led to the introduction of positive research and the concept of positive theory.

Scientific methodology was introduced into accounting from finance along with positive theory. Under that methodology, there is no true or perfect theory. Because theory tries to explain general class of phenomena, it may not explain and predict all observations. Further, many theories can explain a given set of observations; hence, there exists a competition among theories for general acceptance. Variables affecting the success of a theory in that competition are the utility of the theory to users, the intuitive appeal of the theory's explanations, and the range of phenomena the theory can explain.

Theory tends to evolve over time. Errors in the predictions of existing theories are examined and the theories modified. Hence, to understand the current theory, one has to understand its evolution. For that reason, this book examines the empirical studies in the positive tradition in a chronological sequence. We begin with the introduction of the concept of positive theory and scientific methodology from finance and end with the studies in which researchers ask the crucial question for an accounting theorist: Why is accounting and auditing practice like it is?

CHAPTER TWO

The Efficient Markets Hypothesis and Capital Asset Pricing Model

As indicated in Chapter 1, the efficient markets hypothesis (EMH) played an important role in the evolution of accounting research. The conflict between the EMH and hypotheses underlying many accounting prescriptions led to the introduction and popularization of positive theory and methodology in the accounting literature. The EMH spawned an empirical literature on the relations between accounting earnings and stock prices (see Chapter 3) and between changes in accounting procedures and stock prices (see Chapter 4). It also caused changes in the rationales for regulation of corporate disclosure (see Chapter 7).

The capital asset pricing model (CAPM) was introduced from finance in the late 1960s, and it also had a significant impact on the accounting literature. It identified factors that affect the market values of securities, specifically the firm's expected cash flows and their risk. Also, the CAPM influenced the specification of the relation between earnings and stock prices tested in Ball and Brown (1968) and other studies reported in Chapter 3.

A reasonable characterization of the objective of the economics-based empirical literature that evolved in the 10 years following Ball and Brown (1968) (Chapters 3–7) is that it sought to investigate the implications of the EMH and the CAPM for the role of accounting numbers in supplying information to the capital markets for valuation purposes. The capital markets studies in Chapter 3 were concerned with the extent to which reported earnings conveyed information to the capital markets *vis-à-vis alternative sources of information.* The pricing model–based studies in Chapter 5 explored the extent to which accounting numbers conveyed information on factors that (according to the CAPM) affect value.

The primary focus of the early literature was exploring the role of accounting information in capital markets, not explaining and predicting existing accounting practice.[1] The early studies using the EMH did criticize and test existing explanations of accounting practice (see Ball, 1972, and Kaplan and Roll, 1972, reported in Chapter 4), but they did not attempt to build theories to replace those already existing. This lack of emphasis on explaining existing practice was due partially to the natural desire of proponents of a new set of theories and methodology (of a new *paradigm*) to demolish the existing paradigm's theories. It was also due partially to the early researchers' having been trained in finance. With that training, it was natural for them to concentrate on explaining and predicting security price behavior and not on explaining and predicting accounting practice.

When positive theory researchers turned to explaining accounting practice (see Chapters 8–13), they did not abandon the EMH and the CAPM or the evidence generated in the early empirical studies. Instead, the EMH was generally accepted and assumed valid in attempts to explain practice. Also, the evidence gathered in the early EMH and CAPM studies was used to generate hypotheses. Consequently, a knowledge of both the EMH and the CAPM is still crucial to current researchers and those wanting to understand and perform accounting research.

The objective of this chapter is to explain the EMH and the CAPM and how they influenced the questions accounting researchers asked. We begin with the EMH and the interest it generated in the relation between accounting earnings and stock prices and in the effects of changes in accounting procedures on stock prices. Then follows an explanation of the CAPM and how it led accounting researchers to hypothesize that accounting numbers provided information on the variables in the pricing model; to hypothesize that, in the absence of tax effects, changes in accounting procedures would not affect stock prices; and to specify a particular relation between accounting earnings

---

[1] Some studies did attempt to use the relation between accounting earnings numbers and stock prices to assess the desirability of alternative accounting procedures, for example, Beaver and Dukes (1972), but they did not attempt to explain and predict the use of such practices.

and stock prices. Finally, the chapter introduces the market model that is frequently used in empirical studies of the relation between accounting numbers and stock prices.

THE EFFICIENT MARKETS HYPOTHESIS

Competition in the classical certainty world of price theory (microeconomics) drives **economic profits** to zero. Economic profits are calculated after deducting a market rate of return (interest) on capital. The EMH is essentially the extension of that zero profits equilibrium condition to the dynamic behavior of prices in competitive markets under uncertainty.

Jensen (1978, p. 96) defines an efficient market as follows:

> A market is efficient with respect to information set θ_t if it is impossible to make economic profits by trading on the basis of information set θ_t.

The idea is that if some set of information θ_t (e.g., corporate accounting earnings published in *The Wall Street Journal*) is widely known to participants in a market (e.g., the stock market) competition drives prices in that market to be such that on average participants can only earn the market risk–adjusted rate of return from trading on that information (i.e., on average the economic profits are zero).

In an uncertain world there is not one market rate of return. Instead, there is a market rate of return for each level of risk. To compare rates of return on investments of different risk, we have to adjust for risk; hence the use of the term "risk-adjusted rate of return." The commonly used definition of risk and its effect on the market rate of return is explained later when we discuss the CAPM.

We use the term "on average" in describing the zero economic profits condition because in a world of uncertainty a participant can be lucky and may earn a risk-adjusted rate of return on an investment that is greater than the market risk–adjusted rate of return. However, the participant will not be consistently lucky so that over time his average realized risk-adjusted return will be close to the market risk–adjusted rate of return.

Economic profits are net of all costs. So in assessing the zero profit condition (i.e., whether a market is efficient with respect to some information), all costs should be considered. This includes costs of storage of the good, transaction costs, and costs of obtaining the information. However, if storage, transaction, and information costs are zero, in a market that is efficient with respect to an information set at time t (θ_t), the expected price of asset i in the market at time $t + 1$ given $\theta_t[E(P_{i,t+1} \mid \theta_t)]$ is

$$E(P_{i,t+1} \mid \theta_t) = P_{i,t}[1 + E(r_{i,t+1} \mid \theta_t)] \qquad (2.1)$$

where $P_{i,t}$ is the price of asset i at time t and $E(r_{i,t+1} \mid \theta_t)$ is the market's required **expected rate of return** for period $t + 1$ for asset i and other assets of the same risk as asset i, given θ_t.

If the actual price of asset i at time $t + 1$ $(P_{i,t+1})$ is greater than expected given the information set θ, $P_{i,t+1} > E(P_{i,t+1} \mid \theta_t)$, an investor in the asset would earn a **realized rate of return** $(r_{i,t+1})$ greater than the market's expected rate of return, $E(r_{i,t+1} \mid \theta_t)$.[2] If the actual price is less than the expected price given the information set, an investor in the asset would earn a realized rate of return less than expected. Defining the **abnormal rate of return** on asset i for period $t + 1$ $(v_{i,t+1})$ as the difference between the realized rate of return for asset i and the expected (or normal) rate of return for asset i,

$$v_{i,t+1} \equiv r_{i,t+1} - E(r_{i,t+1} \mid \theta_t) \qquad (2.2)$$

an investor can earn an abnormal rate of return on asset i in any given period t. However, across many periods (T) we would expect the abnormal rates of return from using a particular set of information (e.g., published earnings reports) to average zero:

$$\frac{1}{T} \sum_{t=1}^{T} v_{i,t+1} \cong 0 \qquad (2.3)$$

The EMH has been tested with respect to particular sets of information by determining whether on average nonzero abnormal rates of return can be earned by trading on the particular information set. The tests typically ignore the costs of obtaining the information. Those costs vary with information sets. For example, the cost of obtaining information on the past series of prices of a security is low relative to the cost of obtaining information available only to the management of the firm issuing the security (**insider information**). Hence, one would expect the average abnormal rate of return from trading on the past time series of prices to be approximately zero but not necessarily expect the average abnormal rate of return from trading on inside information to be zero.

---

[2] The rate of return on asset i for period $t + 1$ $(r_{i,t+1})$ assuming no cash distributions, such as dividends, is defined as

$$r_{i,t+1} = \frac{P_{i,t+1} - P_{i,t}}{P_{i,t}}.$$

Since

$$E(r_{i,t+1} \mid \theta_t) = \frac{E(P_{i,t+1} \mid \theta_t) - P_{i,t}}{P_{i,t}},$$

if $P_{i,t+1} > E(P_{i,t+1} \mid \theta_t)$, $r_{i,t+1} > E(r_{i,t+1} \mid \theta_t)$.

The tests of the EMH are usually classified into three broad categories. Those categories reflect the cost of the information set (θ_t) used to test the efficiency of the market. The categories are

1. **Weak form tests.** In these tests the information set (θ_t) contains only past security prices and/or past trading volume. These data are readily available to many people at very low cost, so we expect no systematic abnormal rates of return to be observed in these tests.

2. **Semistrong form tests.** The information set (θ_t) in these tests contains all published information at time t (e.g., it contains earnings reported in *The Wall Street Journal*). These data are also readily available at low cost so we expect no systematic abnormal rates of return to be observed in these tests.

3. **Strong form tests.** In these tests, the information set (θ_t) includes all information known to anyone at time t (e.g., the management's future investment production plans, pricing policies). Few people expect this form of the EMH to be consistent with the data.

In general, the evidence is consistent with the semistrong form of the hypothesis (the weak form is a restricted version of the semistrong form) and is generally accepted by researchers as descriptive (see Fama, 1976, Ch. 5). Usually, unqualified references to the EMH are references to the semistrong form. There is evidence inconsistent with the strong form, but that evidence is surprisingly scarce.

THE EFFICIENT MARKETS HYPOTHESIS AND THE PREVIOUS LITERATURE

A common hypothesis underlying the prescriptions in the early 1960s accounting literature is that corporate accounting reports are the only source of information on the corporation.[3] A typical argument is that because the reports are the only information source and because managers are allowed flexibility in choosing accounting procedures, those managers are able to report the results they want and mislead the stock market. By inflating reported earnings, managers can cause their corporations' shares to be overvalued (e.g., Briloff, 1972, Ch. 2). The result is that the stock market cannot discriminate between efficient and less efficient corporations and price their shares appropriately.[4] The argument leads to the prescription that all corporations should be required to use the same accounting procedures.

---

[3] See Ball (1972) for examples and a discussion of the hypothesis.

[4] The interested reader is referred to Leftwich (1981) who catalogs most of the criticisms of current accounting practice and describes the inconsistencies of those criticisms with the theory and evidence of economics and finance.

The hypothesis that accounting reports are the sole source of information to stock and bond markets (capital markets) led to criticisms of the calculation of accounting earnings. It was asserted that earnings should measure changes in the value of the firm, so stock prices could be good signals for the allocation of resources. This assertion in turn led to the criticism that earnings are not calculated consistently in terms of some formal definition of changes in value or income. Earnings are calculated under several different bases. In some cases, historical cost is used to estimate revenues and expenses, and in others, current market value is used. The result is, it was alleged, that earnings are meaningless numbers, like the difference between eight apples and six oranges. Because earnings are meaningless numbers, the argument went, they could not be useful in investment/production decisions, and, furthermore, the stock prices based on them could not be useful signals for the allocation of resources among competing investments.[5]

The EMH has important implications for the arguments that the lack of uniformity in accounting procedures enabled managers systematically to mislead capital markets and that accounting earnings are meaningless. Both arguments rest on the hypothesis that accounting reports are the only source of information on the firm. The EMH suggests that this sole source hypothesis is unlikely to be descriptive and that the stock market is not systematically misled by accounting earnings. Further, the EMH implies that if there is an empirical association between earnings and stock prices, earnings can be useful even if they are not calculated consistently in terms of a formal definition of income.

Underlying the EMH is competition for information. Competition drives investors and financial analysts to obtain information on the firm from many sources outside the firm's accounting reports and even outside the firm itself. For example, analysts obtain weekly production data on automobile firms and interview management. Analysts also interview competitors about a corporation's sales and creditors about the corporation's credit standing.

In a world with such information being generated, capital markets (including the stock, bond, and trade credit markets) eventually learn if a firm is having cash flow problems; it cannot be hidden forever by accounting subterfuge. If cash flow difficulties become known and the stock markets are semistrong form efficient, the current stock price includes an assessment of earnings' implications for future cash flow difficulties that is on average correct. The price is such that investors

---

[5] Ball and Brown (1968, p. 159, fn. 1) provide a list of prominent accounting writers who make this assertion. The list includes Canning (1929), Gilman (1939), Paton and Littleton (1940), Vatter (1947), Edwards and Bell (1961), and Chambers (1964, 1966, 1967).

on average earn a risk-adjusted market rate of return. On average, losses in bankruptcies do not cause a below-market rate of return. In other words, in a semistrong efficient market, the market is not systematically misled by accounting earnings.

On average, in an efficient market stock prices adjusted for the market's expected rate of return are correct estimates of future stock values (i.e., they are **unbiased** estimates of future value). So if accounting earnings are empirically related to stock prices or changes in stock prices, those earnings could be useful indices of value or changes in value despite not being calculated using one concept of income. In the absence of observed market values, accounting earnings could be used to estimate value.

The implications of the efficient market clearly contradict the hypothesis that accounting reports are the sole source of information and its implications. These contradictions led to researchers' addressing two questions: Do changes in accounting methods and their earnings effects systematically mislead the stock market? and Are accounting earnings associated with stock prices or changes in stock prices?

Investigating both these questions requires a model that shows how accounting earnings are related to stock prices. While researchers did not formally specify the model underlying the earnings/stock price relation they tested, they did know the CAPM and the relation tested is consistent with that model. Undoubtedly, the researchers were influenced by the CAPM.

THE CAPITAL ASSET PRICING MODEL

The CAPM is essentially a generalization of the perfect certainty Fisher, or present value, model that is probably familiar to readers. That perfect certainty model assumes that

1. All present and future cash flows to individuals and firms can be perfectly foreseen by all (i.e., perfect certainty).
2. Capital markets are perfect. That means that
   a. No individual borrower or lender in the capital market is wealthy enough to have an effect on market interest rates (no one individual can influence the market price of loans).
   b. Each individual can borrow or lend up to the limit of his or her resources at the market rate of interest.
   c. Information is free, costless, and available to everyone.
   d. There are no transactions costs or taxes.
   e. All assets are infinitely divisible.

3. Investors are rational and prefer more consumption in any period to less and are indifferent as to the form of the cash flows which finance that consumption.

4. Investors assume that other individuals also act rationally.

Under these assumptions, the market value of a firm can be written as the discounted present value of future cash flows of the firm (for a derivation, see Hirshleifer, 1958; Fama and Miller, 1972; Brealey and Myers, 1984). If $V_{i,0}$ denotes the market value of firm i at the present (time 0) after all the cash flows of time 0 have occurred, r_t denotes the market rate of return for the period t (i.e., time $t - 1$ to time t), $C_{i,t}$ denotes the net cash flows of firm i for period t (received at time t), and T is the life of the firm, then

$$V_{i,0} = \sum_{t=1}^{T} \frac{C_{i,t}}{\prod_{\tau=1}^{t} (1 + r_\tau)} \tag{2.4}$$

Note that we call the present value ($V_{i,0}$), the *market* value. Under the foregoing assumptions, it is the value of the claims on the firm (shares and bonds earn the same rate of return under perfect certainty) in the capital market. For convenience in this chapter, it is assumed that the firm is fully financed by equity (i.e., has no debt). Also note that in equation (2.4) the market rate of return does not have an i subscript because with perfect certainty all assets are riskless and earn the same rate of return.

An important result of Fisher's analysis is that regardless of individuals' preferences for current versus future consumption, they invest so as to maximize the present value of cash flows (see Hirshleifer, 1958; Fama and Miller, 1972; or Brealey and Myers, 1984). Regardless of whether owners of firms are misers or spendthrifts, they invest so as to maximize the market value of the firm. Hence, if the manager of a firm wants to maximize the shareholder's interests, individual stock-holders' time preferences for consumption need not be known. All the manager must do is invest to maximize the market value. In essence, the investment decision is separated from the consumption decision (this is called a separation theorem).

A substantial portion of the finance literature assumes that the manager maximizes the market value of the firm and acts in the stockholders' interests. However, in recent years that assumption has been relaxed and the interaction between the firm's manager and claimholders (stockholders and bondholders) analyzed. That analysis has important implications for a theory of accounting (see Chapters 8 and 9).

The Fisherian model assumes perfect certainty about cash flows. Clearly the returns from most investments are anything but certain. The CAPM introduced by Sharpe (1964) and Lintner (1965) is essentially the Fisher model extended to uncertainty. There are many versions of the CAPM (see the introduction of Jensen, 1972, and Fama, 1976, for a summary of some of these versions). This chapter describes only the original or standard CAPM. Later in the book, studies that use other versions of the CAPM are examined. At that time any important differences in the versions are described.

The original CAPM is a one-period model. Investments are made at the beginning of the period and cash flows are received at the end. The model is based on the following assumptions:

1. The rates of return on assets have distributions that can be fully described by the expected rate of return $E(r_i)$ and some measure of dispersion such as the variance $\sigma^2(r_i)$. Alternatively, the preferences of individuals are such that $E(r_i)$ and $\sigma^2(r_i)$ are the only parameters of the distribution of rates of return that are of interest to those individuals.

2. Markets are perfect, meaning that
   a. No investor is wealthy enough to have an effect on the market price of any asset and no firm is large enough to have an effect on the opportunity set available to investors.
   b. No transactions costs or taxes are levied.
   c. All assets are infinitely divisible.

3. Investors are rational and risk averse and maximize the expected utility of consumption.

4. Investors assume that other individuals also act rationally.

5. All individuals in the market have the same costless access to information and hold the same views of expected rates of returns on assets and of the variances of those returns. That is, the investors have homogeneous expectations.

6. There exists a riskless asset f (i.e., $\sigma^2(r_f) = 0$) and all individuals can borrow and lend at the riskless rate r_f.[6]

With these assumptions, in equilibrium the price of asset i at the beginning of the period is such that the expected rate of return on the asset $E(r_i)$ is a function of (1) the riskless rate of return, r_f; (2) the expected rate of return on the market portfolio of assets,[7] $E(r_m)$; (3) the covariance between the rate of return on asset i and the rate of

[6] This assumption is not crucial. There are versions of the CAPM without this assumption.

[7] The market portfolio of assets consists of all risky assets in the economy and the proportion of each asset in the portfolio is the ratio of the total market value of that asset to the total market value of all risky assets.

return on the market, $\text{cov}(r_i, r_m)$; and (4) the variance of the rate of return on the market, $\sigma^2(r_m)$.[8]

$$E(r_i) = r_f + [E(r_m) - r_f] \frac{\text{cov}(r_i, r_m)}{\sigma^2(r_m)} \tag{2.5}$$

There are no time subscripts (*t*'s) on the variables in equation (2.5) because there is only *one* period.

In equation (2.5), the expected rate of return on a risky asset is equal to the rate of return on the riskless asset plus a *risk premium*:

$$[E(r_m) - r_f] \frac{\text{cov}(r_i, r_m)}{\sigma^2(r_m)}$$

The risk premium in turn is composed of two parts: the level of risk, $\text{cov}(r_i, r_m)/\sigma^2(r_m)$, which varies across assets, and the price per unit of risk, $E(r_m) - r_f$, which is the same for all assets. Since the expected rate of return on the market portfolio (which is risky) is greater than the riskless rate, the larger the risk of asset i, $\text{cov}(r_i, r_m)/\sigma^2(r_m)$, the larger the expected rate of return on the asset.

While the Fisher perfect certainty model has only one rate of interest or return, the CAPM allows many expected rates of return. There is a different expected rate for every level of risk.

Readers unfamiliar with portfolio theory will wonder why asset i's risk measure is $\text{cov}(r_i, r_m)/\sigma^2(r_m)$. The first assumption of the CAPM probably causes you to expect the risk measure to be the variance of the rate of return, $\sigma^2(r_i)$. The explanation is that individuals are concerned with the variance of the rate of return on their *portfolios* of assets not on any *single* asset. The fluctuations in the rates of return on the assets in the portfolio can be offsetting, so variances of the individual asset's rates of return can give a misleading impression of the overall variance for the portfolio. The issue is how much does an asset add to the risk of the individual's portfolio (i.e., to the variance of the portfolio rate of return)?

The answer to the question can be seen intuitively if we assume that an individual has a portfolio of N assets with proportion x_i invested in asset i. The variance of the rate of return on the portfolio, $\sigma^2(r_p)$, is

$$\sigma^2(r_p) = \sum_{i=1}^{N} \sum_{j=1}^{N} x_i x_j \text{cov}(r_i, r_j) \tag{2.6}$$

The component parts of the variance can be illustrated as

[8] For a derivation of the equation, see Fama and Miller (1972).

$$\sigma^2(r_p) = \begin{bmatrix} x_1^2\sigma^2(r_1) + x_1x_2 \ \text{cov}(r_1, \ r_2) + x_1x_3 \ \text{cov}(r_1, \ r_3) + \cdots \\ \qquad\qquad\qquad\qquad\qquad + x_1x_N \ \text{cov}(r_1, \ r_N) \\ + x_2x_1 \ \text{cov}(r_2, \ r_1) + x_2^2\sigma^2(r_2) + x_2x_3 \ \text{cov}(r_2, \ r_3) + \cdots \\ \qquad\qquad\qquad\qquad\qquad + x_2x_N \ \text{cov}(r_2, \ r_N) \\ + x_3x_1 \ \text{cov}(r_3, \ r_1) + x_3x_2 \ \text{cov}(r_3, \ r_2) + x_3^2\sigma^2(r_3) + \cdots \\ \qquad\qquad\qquad\qquad\qquad + x_3x_N \ \text{cov}(r_3, \ r_N) \\ \qquad\vdots\qquad\qquad\vdots\qquad\qquad\vdots \\ + x_Nx_1 \ \ \text{cov}(r_N, \ \ r_1) + x_Nx_2 \ \ \text{cov}(r_N, \ \ r_2) + x_Nx_3 \ \ \text{cov}(r_N, \\ \qquad\qquad r_3) + \cdots + x_N^2\sigma^2(r_N) \end{bmatrix} \quad (2.7)$$

The contribution of asset i to the risk of the portfolio, $\sigma^2(r_p)$, comes via the ith row and ith column of the block (primarily via covariance terms):

ith row:

$$x_ix_1 \ \text{cov}(r_i, \ r_1) + x_ix_2 \ \text{cov}(r_i, \ r_2)$$
$$+ \cdots + x_i^2\sigma^2(r_i^2) + \cdots + x_ix_N \ \text{cov}(r_i, \ r_N)$$

ith column:

$$x_1x_i \ \text{cov}(r_1, \ r_i) + x_2x_i \ \text{cov}(r_2, \ r_i)$$
$$+ \cdots + x_i^2\sigma^2(r_i^2) + \cdots + x_Nx_i \ \text{cov}(r_N, \ r_i)$$

The effect on the risk of the portfolio, $\sigma^2(r_p)$, of marginally varying the proportion invested in asset i (x_i), holding other variables constant, is determined by taking the partial derivative of the contribution of asset i to the variance with respect to x_i:

$$\frac{\partial\sigma^2(r_p)}{\partial x_i} = \sum_{\substack{j=1 \\ i \neq j}}^{N} x_j \ \text{cov}(r_j, \ r_i) + \sum_{\substack{j=1 \\ i \neq j}}^{N} x_j \ \text{cov}(r_i, \ r_j) + 2x_i\sigma^2(r_i) \quad (2.8)$$

Since $\text{cov}(r_j, \ r_i) = \text{cov}(r_i, \ r_j)$, $\sigma^2(r_i) = \text{cov}(r_i, \ r_i)$, and $\sum_{j=1}^{N} x_j \ \text{cov}(r_i, \ r_j) = \text{cov}(r_i, \ r_p)$, equation (2.8) yields

$$\frac{\partial\sigma^2(r_p)}{\partial x_i} = 2 \ \text{cov}(r_i, \ r_p) \quad (2.9)$$

The *marginal* contribution of asset i to the portfolio's risk is directly proportional to the covariance of the rate of return on asset i with the rate of return on the individual's portfolio.

In equilibrium all individuals, to the extent that they hold a risky portfolio, hold the market portfolio. Hence, the relevant measure of the marginal contribution of individual asset i to the risk of an individual's portfolio is $\text{cov}(r_i, \ r_m)$. The risk measure for the market portfolio is $\sigma^2(r_m)$, so $\text{cov}(r_i, \ r_m)/\sigma^2(r_m)$ is a proportional measure of risk, measuring the proportion of the risk of the market portfolio contributed by asset i. The term $\text{cov}(r_i, r_m)/\sigma^2(r_m)$ is usually called β_i. β takes the value 1 for the market portfolio. Assets with $\beta > 1$ are relatively more risky than the market portfolio, and assets with $\beta < 1$ are relatively less risky.

Equation (2.5) is expressed in terms of rates of return, but the CAPM is a pricing model and equation (2.5) can be rewritten in terms of prices. Such rewriting helps to explain why researchers thought accounting numbers could convey information to the market and used the earnings/price relation specified in studies such as Ball and Brown (1968).

Letting $C_{i,1}$ be firm i's cash flows at the end of the period and $V_{i,0}$ the market value of firm i at the beginning of the period, the expected rate of return on investment in firm i is

$$E(r_i) = \frac{E(C_{i,1}) - V_{i,0}}{V_{i,0}} \tag{2.10}$$

Substituting the CAPM (equation (2.5)) for $E(r_i)$ in equation (2.10) and rearranging yields an equation for the value of the firm ($V_{i,0}$) analogous to the discounted present value of the Fisherian model:[9]

$$V_{i,0} = \frac{E(C_{i,1}) - [E(r_m) - r_f]\left[\dfrac{\text{cov}(C_{i,1}, r_m)}{\sigma^2(r_m)}\right]}{1 + r_f} \tag{2.11}$$

In a perfectly certain world, the equivalent equation for one period is

$$V_{i,0} = \frac{C_{i,1}}{1 + r} \tag{2.12}$$

The difference between equations (2.11) and (2.12) is that, while it is the cash flows at time 1 ($C_{i,1}$) that are discounted in the Fisherian world (equation (2.12)), in the uncertain world (equation (2.11)) it is the certainty equivalent of the cash flows at time 1, $E(C_{i,1}) - \{[E(r_m) - r_f] \cdot [\text{cov}(C_{i,1}, r_m)/\sigma^2(r_m)]\}$, that is discounted at the riskless rate, r_f. The certainty equivalent consists of the expected cash flows at time 1, $E(C_{i,1})$, minus a risk adjustment, $E(r_m - r_f) [\text{cov}(C_{i,1}, r_m)/\sigma^2(r_m)]$. The risk adjustment is the price of risk, $E(r_m) - r_f$, multiplied by a risk measure, $\text{cov}(C_{i,1}, r_m)/\sigma^2(r_m)$.

In a one-period world the value of the firm can also be expressed as the expected future cash flows of the firm i, $E(C_{i,1})$, discounted at the expected rate of return for the risk of the firm's cash flows, $E(r_i)$:

$$V_{i,0} = \frac{E(C_{i,1})}{1 + E(r_i)} \tag{2.13}$$

where $E(r_i)$ is obtained from equation (2.5).

[9] See Fama and Miller (1972, pp. 295–298).

The CAPM can be applied to a multiperiod world if some additional stringent assumptions about investor utilities and the returns on investments are made (see Fama and Miller, 1972, Ch. 8). If those assumptions are made, a multiperiod version of equation (2.11) can be derived. If, in addition, it is assumed that the riskless rate and the expected rate of return on the firm, $E(r_i)$, are constant over time, a multiperiod version of equation (2.13) can be derived and the value of the firm written in an analogous fashion to the Fisherian world's equation (2.4):

$$V_{i,0} = \sum_{t=1}^{T} \frac{E(C_{i,t})}{[1 + E(r_i)]^t} \tag{2.14}$$

where $E(C_{i,t})$ is the expected cash flows of firm i for period t (see Brealey and Myers, 1984, p. 182). A comparison of equations (2.4) and (2.14) makes it apparent that the CAPM is the Fisher model expanded to allow for uncertainty. In essence, under the multiperiod version of the CAPM, the market value of the firm is the discounted expected future cash flows. The separation theorem applies and managers will maximize their shareholders' expected utility of consumption if they maximize the market value of the firm.

Having given a brief explanation of the CAPM, our next tasks are to explain (1) why, under the CAPM, researchers thought that accounting numbers could convey information and (2) the earnings/price relation researchers specified.

THE CAPM AND ACCOUNTING NUMBERS

The Potential for Information in Accounting Numbers

The multiperiod CAPM (equation (2.14)) values an asset based on its expected cash flows and the expected rate of return the market requires for the risk of those cash flows. How can accounting numbers convey information about those two variables?

Empirically, accounting earnings can be associated with cash flows. *If* they are associated, then accounting earnings of a firm for the current period can provide information on the firm's current cash flows and (if current cash flows provide information on future cash flows) on expected future cash flows.

To see the potential for a firm's accounting earnings to convey information and thereby affect the firm's market value, consider a simple example. Assume that the information set available to investors does not include the firm's cash flows, but does include knowledge of the firm's accounting earnings. Assume that firm i will last for T periods where T is large. At the end of period t the firm's cash flows are $C_{i,t}$, and it invests $I_{i,t}$. The expected rate of return on the firm in the capital market is $E(r_i)$. The only accounting accrual is depreciation, and the depreciation for period t is $D_{i,t}$. The accounting earnings of period t ($A_{i,t}$) are

$$A_{i,t} = C_{i,t} + I_{i,t} - D_{i,t} \qquad (2.15)$$

and expected earnings of period t are

$$E(A_{i,t}) = E(C_{i,t}) + E(I_{i,t}) - E(D_{i,t}) \qquad (2.16)$$

Using equations (2.14) and (2.16), the market value of the firm at time 0 can be written

$$V_{i,0} = \sum_{t=1}^{N} \frac{E(A_{i,t}) + E(D_{i,t}) - E(I_{i,t})}{[1 + E(r_i)]^t} \qquad (2.17)$$

If depreciation is approximately equal to the investment each year, then accounting earnings would approximate cash flows and the market value of the firm in equation (2.17) would be approximately equal to the present value of the firm's expected future earnings. In this example, earnings could supply information on cash flows and affect the value of the firm.

While the preceding example suggests that accounting earnings can affect the market value of the firm, it does *not* imply that in the absence of taxes and tax effects managers can affect the market value by varying accounting procedures. The reason is that the example assumes information on the firm's accounting procedures is costlessly available to all investors. As a result, the market value of the firm will vary with the present value of earnings only to the extent that those variations imply variations in cash flows.

Assume the firm represented by equation (2.17) has a life of two periods ($T = 2$) and that all investments have been made. Then equation (2.17) becomes

$$V_{i,0} = \frac{E(A_{i,1}) + E(D_{i,1})}{1 + E(r_i)} + \frac{E(A_{i,2}) + E(D_{i,2})}{[1 + E(r_i)]^2} \qquad (2.18)$$

If a manager adopts a depreciation method to increase the expected earnings for period 1 (e.g., straight-line as opposed to accelerated depreciation) and that adoption is known, all that happens in equation (2.18) is that $E(A_{i,1})$ increases and is offset by a decrease in $E(D_{i,1})$.

Apart from providing information on expected cash flows, accounting numbers can supply information on the other variable in the multiperiod CAPM (equation (2.14)), the expected rate of return on the asset. That expected rate of return depends on the risk of the asset,

$cov(r_i, r_m)/\sigma^2(r_m)$ or β_i, and that risk is likely to be empirically associated with accounting numbers. For example, equation (2.11) demonstrated that the risk measure can be written in terms of the covariance of future cash flows with the market rate of return. If accounting earnings are a surrogate for those cash flows, then information on the extent that accounting earnings vary with fluctuations in business activity could supply information on a firm's risk. It is possible that the use of accounting ratios as measures of risk has developed because they are empirical surrogates for risk. Chapter 5 investigates this possibility.

The Specified Relation Between Earnings and Stock Prices

In testing whether accounting earnings convey information to the stock market, most researchers do not use specifications such as equation (2.14) to test whether the levels of firms' market values vary cross sectionally with the level of their earnings. The reason is that many factors affect the expected future cash flows and are likely to make the relation between the levels of earnings and stock prices difficult to observe. Instead, following Ball and Brown (1968), most researchers concentrate on the relation between *changes* in earnings and *changes* in stock prices around the time of announcement of those earnings changes. More specifically, they concentrate on changes in earnings and the rate of return on stock prices around the earnings change announcement. It is hoped that by concentrating on the rate of return around earnings announcements and pooling those rates of return over time, other factors affecting future cash flows and the level of stock prices will average out to zero.

If accounting earnings are surrogates for cash flows, the CAPM has specific implications for the relation between changes in earnings and the rate of return on the firm's market value. In particular, the CAPM implies that changes in accounting earnings *are not* related to the *expected* rates of return on the firm (unless accounting earnings changes are related to risk changes). It also implies that changes in accounting earnings *are* related to the *realized* rate of return on the firm.

To see the relations between changes in earnings and expected and realized rates of return, assume a two-period CAPM world and a firm with a constant expected rate of return. Then let's look at the relation between changes in cash flows (for which earnings are assumed to surrogate) and rates of return. The value of firm i at time 0 is

$$V_{i,0} = \frac{E_0(C_{i,1})}{1 + E(r_i)} + \frac{E_0(C_{i,2})}{[1 + E(r_i)]^2} \qquad (2.19)$$

where the subscript 0 has been added to the expected cash flows of periods 1 and 2 to indicate that the expectation is formed at time 0. The value of the firm at time 1, assuming $C_{i,1}$ has been paid out in dividends, is

$$V_{i,1} = \frac{E_1(C_{i,2})}{1 + E(r_i)} \tag{2.20}$$

The realized rate of return on the firm for period 1 ($r_{i,1}$) is

$$r_{i,1} = \frac{V_{i,1} + C_{i,1} - V_{i,0}}{V_{i,0}} \tag{2.21}$$

Adding and subtracting the expected rate of return on the firm, $E(r_i)$, to the right-hand side of equation (2.21) gives

$$r_{i,1} = E(r_i) + \frac{V_{i,1} + C_{i,1} - V_{i,0}[1 + E(r_i)]}{V_{i,0}} \tag{2.22}$$

Substituting equations (2.19) and (2.20) for $V_{i,0}$ and $V_{i,1}$ in the numerator of the second term on the right-hand side of equation (2.22) yields

$$r_{i,1} = E(r_i) + \frac{[C_{i,1} - E_0(C_{i,1})] + \left[\dfrac{E_1(C_{i,2}) - E_0(C_{i,2})}{1 + E(r_i)}\right]}{V_{i,0}} \tag{2.23}$$

Equation (2.23) shows that the extent to which the realized rate of return for the firm for period 1 differs from the expected rate is a function of the **unexpected cash flows** for period 1, $C_{i,1} - E_0(C_{i,1})$, and any revision in the market's expected cash flows for period 2, $E_1(C_{i,2}) - E_0(C_{i,2})$. In words, equation (2.23) is

Realized rate of return = expected rate of return

$+ \kappa \times$ unexpected cash flows for period 1

$+ \lambda \times$ change in expected cash flows for period 2

where

$$\kappa = \frac{1}{V_{i,0}}$$

$$\lambda = \frac{1}{V_{i,0}[1 + E(r_i)]}$$

Whether or not the revisions in expected cash flows for future periods are related to the unexpected cash flows of the current period depends on the process generating the cash flows. If the process is a **martingale** (i.e., $E_t(C_{i,t+1}) = C_{i,t}$) then expected future cash flows would be revised to equal the most recent observation of cash flows. In our example $E_0(C_{i,2})$ would be revised to $E_1(C_{i,2}) = C_{i,1}$. If the process is such that expected future cash flows are always equal to a constant regardless of observed cash flows (i.e., $E_t(C_{i,t+1}) = E_t(C_{i,t+1}) = C$), current unexpected cash flows cause no revision of expected cash flows. In our example $E_1(C_{i,2}) = E_0(C_{i,2})$, and the change in expected cash flows for period 2 is zero. The studies reported in Chapter 6 investigating the time series process generating earnings are motivated partially by this issue. They assume that earnings are a surrogate for cash flows and investigate the impact of current earnings on expected future earnings.

It seems likely that the revision in expected cash flows for period 2 is related to the unexpected cash flows of period 1. If so, then the extent to which the realized rate of return for period 1 differs from its expectation is a function of the unexpected cash flows for period 1 ($V_{i,0}$ and $E(r_i)$ are determined at the beginning of period 1). For expository purposes, let the market's expectation at time 0 of the cash flows of periods 1 and 2 be the same (i.e., $E_0(C_{i,1}) = E_0(C_{i,2})$) and the market's expectation at time 1 of cash flows for period 2 be the realized cash flows of period 1 (i.e., $E_1(C_{i,2}) = C_{i,1}$). Substituting these relations in equation (2.23) and also substituting for $V_{i,0}$ gives

$$r_{i,1} = E(r_i) + \frac{[1 + E(r_i)][C_{i,1} - E_0(C_{i,1})]}{E_0(C_{i,1})} \tag{2.24}$$

Under our assumptions of a stationary expected rate of return, expected cash flows of all future periods equal to the most recently realized cash flows, and all cash flows paid out in dividends, equation (2.24) holds in a three- or greater-period world as well as a two-period world.

Equation (2.24) implies that the abnormal rate of return for the period ($v_{i,1}$, see equation (2.2)) is directly proportional to the unexpected cash flows of the period. Rearranging equation (2.24) gives

$$v_{i,1} = r_{i,1} - E(r_i) = \pi_i[C_{i,1} - E_0(C_{i,1})] \tag{2.25}$$

where $\pi_i = [1 + E(r_i)]/[E_0(C_{i,1})]$. In words,

Abnormal rate of return of period 1 = $\pi_i \times$ unexpected cash flows of period 1

With positive interest rates, $E(r_i) > 0$ and $E_0(C_{i,1}) > 0$, so $\pi_i > 0$.[10] Thus, the larger the unexpected cash flows of the period, the larger the abnormal rate of return of the period.

---

[10] If expected rates of return are positive, $E_0(C_{i,1}) < 0$ in our model implies a negative market value. Since we don't observe negative market values, if the model is descriptive, $E_0(C_{i,1})$ must be positive.

If accounting earnings are a surrogate for realized cash flows, it is likely that the portion of accounting earnings *unexpected by the market* is related to the market's unexpected cash flows and hence to the abnormal rate of return and the realized rate of return on the firm. Such a relation between **unexpected earnings** and the abnormal rate of return is specified by Ball and Brown (1968) and others in investigating the relation between accounting earnings and stock prices (see Chapter 3). Ball and Brown do not formally derive the relation from the CAPM, but it is certain that their specification was influenced by the CAPM.

Note that equation (2.25) explains why we say researchers concentrate on the relation between *changes* in earnings and *changes* in stock prices. Extending equation (2.25) to a multiperiod world in which the market's expectations at time t of cash flows at times $t + 1, t + 2, \ldots,$ are equal to the cash flows of period t, equation (2.25) becomes

$$v_{i,t} = \pi_{i,t}(C_{i,t} - C_{i,t-1}) \tag{2.26}$$

The abnormal rate of return for firm i for period $t(v_{i,t})$ is the unexpected *change* in firm i's stock price for period t, adjusted for dividends, relative to firm i's stock price at the beginning of period t. The term in parentheses on the right-hand side of equation (2.26) is the *change* in the firm's cash flows in period t. If earnings are a surrogate for cash flows, we expect changes in earnings to be a surrogate for changes in cash flows and related to changes in stock prices.

If information on the firm's accounting procedures is costlessly available to everyone, the relation between unexpected earnings and the abnormal rate of return exists only to the extent the unexpected earnings reflect unexpected cash flows. Unexpected accounting earnings that are solely the result of accounting procedures will not be associated with the abnormal rate of return. If the individual firms' specific procedures are unknown, an efficient market makes an unbiased prediction about the procedures used and an unbiased assessment of the extent to which unexpected earnings are the result of accounting procedures. Then, *on average* the abnormal rate of return is zero for unexpected earnings that are the result of accounting procedures and not the result of unexpected cash flows. Researchers test this prediction using accounting procedure changes that do not affect taxes (see Chapter 4).

Once the assumption of a constant expected return is dropped, unexpected earnings may also be related to the abnormal rate of return *if* those unexpected earnings changes are associated with unexpected changes in the risk of the firm. However, if the firm changes accounting procedures, thereby changing reported earnings, those accounting changes will not be related to the abnormal rate of return and the realized return unless they are *also* related to unexpected changes in risk or cash flows (e.g., the accounting change to LIFO is related to cash flows because it affects taxes).

Empirical tests of the relation between abnormal rates of return and unexpected earnings require estimates of normal rates of return and expected earnings. Expected earnings are often determined using evidence on the process generating the time series of earnings (see Chapter 6). Normal rates of return are typically determined using the **market model**.

THE MARKET MODEL

The market model is a statistical description of the relation between the rate of return on asset i ($r_{i,t}$) and the rate of return on a market portfolio of assets ($r_{m,t}$) when the joint distribution of the rate of return on the asset and the market portfolio is bivariate normal. It is

$$r_{i,t} = \alpha_i + \beta_i r_{m,t} + \epsilon_{i,t} \tag{2.27}$$

where $\beta_i = \text{cov}(r_{i,t}, r_{m,t})/\sigma^2(r_{m,t})$ and $\alpha_i = E(r_{i,t}) - \beta_i E(r_{m,t})$ and $\epsilon_{i,t}$ is a disturbance term with $E(\epsilon_{i,t} | r_{m,t}) = E(\epsilon_{i,t}) = 0$ and $\sigma^2(\epsilon_{i,t} | r_{m,t}) = \sigma^2(\epsilon_{i,t})$.[11]

Equation (2.27) is purely the result of the assumption of bivariate normality. There is no requirement that the portfolio be the market portfolio; the same linear relation would hold between the rate of return on asset i and the rate of return on any portfolio p if the joint distribution of $r_{i,t}$ and $r_{p,t}$ were bivariate normal. In the accounting and finance empirical literature, however, the market model has an additional interpretation that does not come from the statistical assumption used to derive equation (2.27). The rate of return on the market portfolio ($r_{m,t}$) is presumed to capture the effect of variables that affect the rates of return of all assets, and the disturbance term $\epsilon_{i,t}$ is presumed to capture variables that only affect the rate of return on asset i ($r_{i,t}$) (e.g., earnings announcements). Like the difference between the realized rate of return and the expected rate of return ($\nu_{i,t}$), $\epsilon_{i,t}$ is called an abnormal rate of return.

To investigate the relation between the abnormal rate of return defined in equation (2.2) ($\nu_{i,t}$) and the abnormal rate of return defined using equation (2.27) ($\epsilon_{i,t}$), take expectations of both sides of the market model (equation (2.27)):

$$E(r_{i,t}) = \alpha_i + \beta_i E(r_{m,t}) \tag{2.28}$$

---

[11] See Fama (1976, Ch. 3, pp. 63–68) for a more complete discussion of the market model.

Let the difference between the realized and expected rates of return on the market portfolio be μ_t:

$$\mu_t = r_{m,t} - E(r_{m,t}) \tag{2.29}$$

Substituting equation (2.29) and equation (2.2) for $E(r_{m,t})$ and $E(r_{i,t})$, respectively, in equation (2.28) yields the following relation between the realized rates of return on asset i and the market:

$$r_{i,t} = \alpha_i + \beta_i r_{m,t} + v_{i,t} - \beta_i \mu_t \tag{2.30}$$

Comparing equations (2.30) and (2.27) we can see that

$$\epsilon_{i,t} = v_{i,t} - \beta_i \mu_t \tag{2.31}$$

The abnormal rate of return on asset i from the market model ($\epsilon_{i,t}$) is equal to the abnormal rate of return on asset i defined by equation (2.2) ($v_{i,t}$) minus the effect of the abnormal rate of return on the market (μ_t). So the abnormal rate of return from the market model is the abnormal rate of return due to factors specific to the firm and not to the market portfolio.

To obtain estimates of $\epsilon_{i,t}$, typically α_i and β_i are estimated using the following regression equation:

$$r_{i,t} = a_i + b_i r_{m,t} + e_{i,t} \tag{2.32}$$

The estimated constant ($\hat{a}_i$) is an estimate of market model's α_i, and the estimated coefficient of $r_{m,t}$ ($\hat{b}_i$) is an estimate of β_i. These estimated coefficients, together with the realized rate of return on the market portfolio for period t ($r_{m,t}$), provide the expected (or normal) rate of return for the stock for period t conditional on the market rate of return in period t, $E(r_{i,t} | r_{m,t})$:

$$E(r_{i,t} | r_{m,t}) = \hat{a}_i + \hat{b}_i r_{m,t} \tag{2.33}$$

The estimated abnormal rate of return for the stock for period t is then just the difference between the actual and expected rate of return for the period t conditional on the market rate of return in period t ($\hat{e}_t$):

$$\hat{e}_{i,t} = r_{i,t} - E(r_{i,t} | r_{m,t})$$

$$= r_{i,t} - \hat{a}_i - \hat{b}_i r_{m,t} \tag{2.34}$$

The market model can be interpreted using the CAPM. Assume a multiperiod CAPM and assume that β_i and r_f are constant over time and that the market portfolio we observe is the market portfolio in the CAPM. Then β_i in equation (2.27) is the measure of risk in the CAPM, and $\hat{b}_i$ from the estimation of equation (2.32) is an estimate of β_i. $\hat{a}$ is an estimate of $\alpha_i = r_f(1 - \beta_i)$. This interpretation supports the calculation of abnormal rates of return as equation (2.34). It also supports a different method of calculating abnormal rates of return. That method is illustrated next using an example.

Suppose that a researcher is interested in the unexpected rate of return accompanying a particular change in accounting standards for firms affected by the standard. Estimates of β for the portfolio of firms' stocks are generated by estimating equation (2.32) for the portfolio over some period. A portfolio of stocks of firms unaffected by the standard is constructed with the same estimated β as the portfolio of firms affected by the change. This is achieved by estimating the β's for the stock of each unaffected firm and appropriately weighting the stocks in the portfolio. Since both portfolios have the same β under the CAPM, each should earn the same rate of return over time. Hence any difference in the rates of return of the two portfolios (affected and unaffected) is attributed to the criteria on which the portfolios are formed (i.e., the effect of the accounting standard).

The portfolio approach to estimating abnormal rates of return is commonly used in the studies investigating the stock price effects of accounting standards that are reported in Chapter 12. The studies in Chapter 3 investigating the relation between abnormal rates of return and unexpected earnings use the market model to generate unexpected or abnormal rates of return.

SUMMARY

Conflicts between the EMH and hypotheses in the accounting literature in the 1960s led to studies popularizing positive theory and methodology (particularly Ball and Brown, 1968). Further, the EMH and the CAPM heavily influenced the nature of empirical studies in the 1970s.

The EMH states that competition for information drives the expected economic profits from the production and use of information to zero. It suggests the popular hypothesis in the 1960s that accounting reports are the only source of information on firms' stocks is unlikely to be descriptive. It also suggests that, if accounting earnings are associated with changes in stock prices, those earnings can be useful (contrary to arguments in the literature). This latter suggestion follows because stock prices are unbiased estimates of the stock's future value. These implications led accounting researchers to investigate the extent to which changes in accounting procedures mislead the stock market (see Chapter 4) and to investigate the relation between accounting earnings and stock prices (see Chapter 3).

Based on the CAPM, valuing the firm requires estimates of the firm's expected future cash flows and risk. Accounting numbers could convey information to the market about a firm's value if they convey information about the firm's expected future cash flows or risk. These implications led researchers to investigate the relation among accounting numbers, expected cash flows and risk (see Chapter 5), and the time series of accounting earnings (see Chapter 6).

The CAPM combined with the assumption that accounting earnings are a surrogate for cash flows led researchers to specify an association between unexpected changes in earnings and the unexpected rate of return on firms' stocks. That relation is investigated using the market model to estimate unexpected rates of return (see Chapter 3). The market model is the relation between the rate of return on an asset and the rate of return on a market portfolio that follows from the assumption that the joint distribution of those rates of return is bivariate normal. The estimates from the market model can be interpreted using the CAPM.

CHAPTER THREE

Accounting Earnings
and Stock Prices

In Chapter 2 we point out that the implications of the efficient markets hypothesis (EMH) conflict with popular arguments in the accounting literature of the 1960s. In particular, they conflict with the argument that managers can use accounting earnings for the purpose of systematically misleading the stock market. Further, *if* accounting earnings are related to stock prices, the EMH suggests that earnings can be useful measures or indices of value contrary to the 1960s argument that earnings numbers are useless because they are not measured using a single concept of income.

Based on our description of methodology in Chapter 1, one might expect early researchers to test the conflicting predictions of the EMH and the existing accounting literature (e.g., test whether changes in accounting procedures do or do not systematically mislead the stock market). Eventually attempts at such discriminatory tests did occur (see Chapter 4). However, the article that initially popularized positive research in accounting (Ball and Brown, 1968) does not attempt such a test. Instead, based on the evidence supporting it in finance, Ball and Brown assume that the EMH is descriptive. Then, given the EMH, Ball and Brown investigate whether accounting earnings are empirically related to stock prices and therefore potentially useful.

Finding an association between accounting earnings and stock prices, Ball and Brown also investigate whether accounting earnings merely reflect factors already incorporated in stock prices or whether earnings announcements convey information to the stock market (i.e., earnings announcements have **information content**).

The Ball and Brown article led to an extensive literature investigating the empirical association between earnings and stock prices and whether earnings have information content.[1] That literature is still developing. It is positive in that it investigates *why* accounting earnings and stock prices are related and *why* earnings convey information to the stock market. However, the literature does not explore why accounting earnings are calculated in their current fashion.

In this chapter, we examine the literature on the relation between accounting earnings and stock prices and the information content of earnings. For the reasons explained in Chapter 2, the earnings/stock price relation that is investigated in this literature and used to assess information content tends to be the relation between unexpected earnings and abnormal rates of return. Given the assumption of multivariate normality, the studies investigate both the mean abnormal rates of return and the variance of abnormal rates of return. The first set of studies we examine investigates the relation between unexpected earnings and mean abnormal rates of return. This set includes Ball and Brown. That is followed by the studies of the relation between earnings announcements and the variance of abnormal rates of return and the variance of rates of return implicit in stock and option prices. Then we examine studies that use trading volume to assess the information content of earnings announcements.

The basic conclusions from the studies of the relations among earnings, abnormal rates of return, and volume are that earnings and abnormal returns are associated and earnings convey information to the market. These conclusions led to studies of whether the relation between earnings and abnormal rates of return can be explained by earnings surrogating for cash flows. Those studies are examined next.

Then follows an analysis of studies of how the information content of earnings varies across firms. An example of such a study compares the information content of earnings of firms traded in the over-the-counter market (OTC) to firms traded on the New York Stock Exchange (NYSE).

The chapter ends with a summary of the evidence on the relation between accounting earnings and stock prices.

---

[1] Another paper on the information content of earnings (Benston, 1967) was published before Ball and Brown (1968). However, that paper did not have the same impact on the literature as did Ball and Brown's due to the former's methodological problems and consequent failure to find information content.

INFORMATION CONTENT OF EARNINGS

In the foregoing outline we distinguish between earnings *reflecting* factors that affect stock prices and earnings announcements *conveying* information to the stock market (i.e., having information content).[2] A firm's quarterly accounting earnings can reflect factors (such as the quarter's cash flows) that affect stock price and so be associated with the firm's abnormal rate of return for the quarter without their announcement conveying information and causing stock price changes. The reason is that, under the EMH, market participants may learn, from alternative sources, the firm's cash flows for a quarter, before the quarter's earnings are announced. Hence, while an observed relation between a firm's quarterly earnings changes and its quarterly abnormal rates of return indicates that earnings reflect factors affecting stock prices, it does not indicate that the earnings actually convey information to the market. To test that hypothesis, ideally one would want to observe the stock price change at the time the earnings are announced.

There are many alternative sources of information on a firm's cash flows that can reduce the information content of earnings announcements. Some of these are formal reports by the firm itself. For example, the number of automobiles produced by U.S. manufacturers is regularly reported in *The Wall Street Journal* (*WSJ*). These numbers, together with a knowledge of production costs, sales, and sale prices, enable analysts to predict U.S. automobile manufacturers' quarterly cash flows and earnings. Other sources are less formal. Financial analysts regularly interview officers about the firm's current and future performance. Also, outsiders observe changes in the firm's business. For example, distributors of a firm's products notice increases in sales and may trade on the information and affect stock prices or inform analysts. Finally, insiders in the firm who observe weekly sales (for example) may (illegally) trade on that knowledge and affect stock prices. The first studies of information content of earnings (e.g., Ball and Brown, 1968) were interesting because they provided evidence on the extent to which these alternative information sources preempted information in earnings.

---

[2] Ball and Brown (1968) use the term "information content" to refer to the relation between annual earnings and annual abnormal rates of return and call the issue of whether stock prices change on earnings announcements a "timeliness" question. Other researchers also refer to studies of relations between the distribution of annual (or quarterly) abnormal rates of return and annual (or quarterly) earnings as information content studies. We, however, reserve the term "information content" for the issue of whether an event such as an earnings announcement has a stock price effect at the time of the event. Our reason is that information by definition is something not previously known. If the stock price changes associated with an event have occurred before the event, the factors affecting stock price that are associated with that event are already known.

SIGN OF UNEXPECTED EARNINGS
AND MEAN ABNORMAL RETURNS

Ball and Brown (1968) investigate the relation between the *sign* of unexpected earnings and mean abnormal rates of return. Their study was followed by a series of studies of that relation. Only recently have researchers followed the suggestion of Ball and Brown (1968, p. 177) and investigated the relation between the magnitude of unexpected earnings and mean abnormal rates of return.

Ball and Brown

Ball and Brown (1968) predict that unexpected increases in earnings are accompanied by positive abnormal rates of return and unexpected decreases by negative abnormal rates of return. In Chapter 2 we saw that these predictions can be derived from the assumption that earnings are a surrogate for cash flows and that shares are valued under the multiperiod capital asset pricing model (CAPM).[3]

An example will help to clarify the Ball and Brown predictions. Suppose that a firm's earnings for the year are $2.00 per share and that the market expects them to be $2.00 for the coming year. The current stock price is $20 and the expected rate of return on the stock is 10 percent, so for $20 share, we would expect to receive $2 next year from the sale of the share and from its dividends. If accounting earnings next year turn out to be $2.10 per share (the unexpected earnings are positive), the sum of the firm's stock price and dividends should exceed $22. Also, the *realized* rate of return should exceed the *expected* rate of return, 10 percent (the abnormal rate of return is positive). However, if actual earnings are only $1.80 per share, the sum of the stock price and dividends should be less than $22 and the realized rate of return should be less than 10 percent (the abnormal rate of return is negative).

Ball and Brown investigate *annual* earnings announcements. To test whether annual earnings *reflect* factors affecting stock prices, they test whether a subsample of unexpected earnings announcements of a particular sign has a mean abnormal rate of return over the year ending with the earnings announcement of the same sign. The hypothesis that annual earnings announcements *convey* information to the market is tested using the mean abnormal rate of return for the *month* of announcement. If earnings announcements have information content, the subsample of positive unexpected earnings changes should have a

[3] The actual prediction derived in Chapter 2 is that the abnormal rate of return for firm *i* for period *t* is equal to the unexpected change in firm *i*'s cash flows for period *t* multiplied by a positive parameter (see equation (2.26)). Hence, if unexpected cash flows are positive, the abnormal rate of return is positive, and if unexpected cash flows are negative, the abnormal rate of return is negative.

positive mean abnormal rate of return in the announcement month and the negative subsample should have a negative mean abnormal rate of return.

In testing whether annual earnings *convey* information, the researcher wants to use the rate of return for the shortest period that includes the earnings announcement. Ideally, one would want to observe the rate of return from the transaction before the announcement to the transaction after the announcement.[4] Failing the availability of transactions data, daily rate-of-return data are used to see whether stock prices change on the day of the earnings announcement. However, at the time of the Ball and Brown study, the shortest period for which reliable rate-of-return data were available in computer-readable form was a month.

The monthly data test of the information content hypothesis is not a very powerful test. The reason is that the mean abnormal rate of return in the month of announcement could be nonzero, not due to price changes on the day of announcement but due to stock price changes occurring on days before the announcement.

ABNORMAL RETURN MEASURES

The foregoing tests require estimates of the abnormal rate of return for the *month* of an earnings announcement and the abnormal rate of return for the *year* ending with the month of announcement. Ball and Brown generate both from estimates of monthly abnormal rates of return. They regress monthly rates of return for each firm's stock on a market index over a period prior to the year for which monthly abnormal rates of return are being calculated to obtain estimates of the parameters of the market model ($\hat{a}_i$ and $\hat{b}_i$). These parameters are then used to predict the rate of return for each month in the year. The abnormal rate of return for each month is the difference between the actual and predicted rates of return. This **prediction error** is calculated using equation (2.34):

$$\hat{e}_{i,t} = r_{i,t} - \hat{a}_i - \hat{b}_i r_{m,t}$$

The prediction error is used as a measure of the abnormal rate of return instead of the estimated error term from a market model regression that includes the announcement year. The reason is that the latter procedure causes the estimated coefficients ($\hat{a}_i$ and $\hat{b}_i$) to incorporate some of the abnormal returns that should be included in the abnormal return measure.

[4] Also one would want the earnings to be the only number announced. Otherwise, any stock price effect could be the result of accompanying announcements.

The month of announcement is defined to be month 0. Thus the abnormal rate of return for firm i in the earnings announcement month is $\hat{e}_{i,0}$, the abnormal rate of return in the month before the announcement is $\hat{e}_{i,-1}$, and so on. The average of the $\hat{e}_{i,0}$ across the firm/years in the subsamples of positive and negative unexpected earnings announcements can then be used to test the information content hypothesis.

A measure of the annual abnormal rate of return is calculated from the monthly abnormal rates of return for each year for each firm. The measure is $(1 + \hat{e}_{i,-11})(1 + \hat{e}_{i,-10}) \cdots (1 + \hat{e}_{i,0})$ or $\prod_{t=-11}^{0} (1 + \hat{e}_{i,t})$. This measure has the dimension of 1 plus an annual rate of return. Intuitively, it measures the amount to which one dollar invested 12 months before the earnings announcement would grow if the investment carried a rate of return in the first month of $\hat{e}_{i,-11}$, in the second month $\hat{e}_{i,-10}$, and so on.

To obtain a measure of the mean annual abnormal rate of return for all firm/years in which earnings changes are of a particular sign, Ball and Brown average the measure of annual abnormal rates of return across all firm/years Q in which earnings changes have that sign. The resultant measure is called the **abnormal performance index** at time 0 (API_0):

$$API_0 = \frac{1}{Q} \sum_{q=1}^{Q} \prod_{t=-11}^{0} (1 + \hat{e}_{q,t}) \qquad (3.1)$$

where Q is the number of firm/years with earnings changes of the particular sign.

If annual earnings are related to stock prices, we expect $API_0 > 1$ for the subsample with positive unexpected earnings changes and $API_0 < 1$ for the subsample with negative unexpected earnings changes. If there is no relation, API_0 for all subsamples is expected to be approximately 1.[5]

Ball and Brown also calculate the API for varying periods beginning with month -11 (12 months before the announcement) and ending with months -11 to $+6$.

$$API_T = \frac{1}{Q} \sum_{q=1}^{Q} \prod_{t=-11}^{T} (1 + \hat{e}_{q,t}); \qquad T = -11, -10, \ldots, +6 \quad (3.2)$$

The path of the API_T as T varies from -11 to 0 provides evidence of the timing of release of information on factors reflected in annual earnings announcements.

---

[5] Note that the expected value of API in the absence of any association with earnings changes is not exactly 1 because there is slight negative dependence in stock rates of return (see Ball and Brown).

UNEXPECTED EARNINGS MEASURES

Ball and Brown estimate unexpected earnings in two ways. First, they use the change in earnings. If earnings are a surrogate for cash flows, this is consistent with the relation between abnormal rates of return and changes in cash flows specified in Chapter 2 in equation (2.26). Implicitly it assumes that earnings follow a martingale process (i.e., the expectation of next year's earnings is this year's earnings, see Chapter 2).

The second estimate of unexpected earnings is the change in earnings after removing the effect of the change in a market index of earnings. This estimate has the same underlying implicit assumptions as the change in earnings plus the recognition that Ball and Brown use an estimate of abnormal returns that has removed the effect of the abnormal rate of return on the market.[6] Consistency between the abnormal rate of return and unexpected earnings measures requires both to have the market effect removed.

Define the change in earnings for firm i for period t to be $\Delta A_{i,t} \equiv A_{i,t} - A_{i,t-1}$, where $A_{i,t}$ is the earnings of firm i for period t, and define the change in market earnings for period t to be $\Delta M_t \equiv M_t - M_{t-1}$, where M_t is a market index of earnings for period t. Then the change in earnings for firm i for period t adjusted for unexpected market earnings for period t ($\Delta A_{i,t}^M$) is

$$\Delta A_{i,t}^M = \Delta A_{i,t} - (\hat{g}_i + \hat{h}_i \Delta M_t) \tag{3.3}$$

where $\hat{g}_i$ and $\hat{h}_i$ are parameters estimated from a regression of the change in earnings ($\Delta A_{i,t}$) on the change in market earnings (ΔM_t).

Two measures of earnings are used in the two methods of estimating unexpected earnings, net income and earnings per share. Changes in earnings adjusted for changes in market earnings ($\Delta A_{i,t}^M$) are calculated using net income and earnings per share (Ball and Brown call these variables 1 and 2, respectively). Changes in earnings ($\Delta A_{i,t}$) are calculated using earnings per share only (Ball and Brown call this variable 3).

Ball and Brown investigate whether changes in earnings are serially correlated and find that they are serially uncorrelated. This implies that earnings follow a **random walk**, a particular kind of martingale

---

[6] Ball and Brown use the prediction error $\hat{e}_{i,t}$, which is an estimate of the abnormal rate of return adjusted for the effect of the market ($\epsilon_{i,t}$):

$$\epsilon_{i,t} = v_{i,t} - \beta_i \mu_t \tag{2.31}$$

where $v_{i,t}$ is the abnormal rate of return, β_i is the slope coefficient in the market model, and μ_t is the abnormal rate of return on the market (see Chapter 2).

process.[7] As we noted, earnings are implicitly assumed to follow a martingale process in using earnings changes as estimates of unexpected earnings.

The lack of serial correlation in earnings changes is a desirable attribute in interpreting the API_0. It means that the API_0 measures the extent to which current earnings changes reflect factors affecting stock prices *beyond* what is reflected in previous earnings changes. Suppose that earnings are correlated so that if the current year's earnings change is positive, it is likely the previous year's earnings change is positive. Then, if the two earnings announcements happen to be 11 months apart, the abnormal rate for month -11 in the current earnings' API_0 impounds information content of the previous year's earnings announcement. As a result, the API_0 overstates the potential information content of the current earnings announcement (i.e., the information the current earnings could convey if it had not been provided by alternative sources). If earnings changes are uncorrelated, the sign of earlier unexpected earnings (e.g., those of the previous year) is random across the firms in the sample or subsample and, on average, the earnings changes of prior years for the sample is zero. Hence, the sample API_0 does not impound any stock price effects of prior years.

SAMPLE

Ball and Brown select their sample of annual earnings announcements on the following basis:

1. The firm's earnings data must be available on the Standard & Poor's *Compustat* tapes for each of the years 1946–1965.
2. The firm's fiscal year must end on December 31.
3. The firm's stock rate of return data must be available on the Center for Research into Security Prices (CRSP) tapes for 100 months.
4. The earnings announcements must be available in *The Wall Street Journal* (*WSJ*).

These criteria yield a sample of earnings announcements of 261 NYSE firms.

The analysis of the relation between earnings and stock prices is limited to the annual earnings announcements for the nine fiscal years 1957–1965, because the earnings data prior to 1957 are used to *estimate* the parameters of equation (3.3) ($\hat{g}_i$ and $\hat{h}_i$). If the same data are used

---

[7] The simple random walk model for annual earnings is

$$A_{i,t} = A_{i,t-1} + \omega_{i,t}$$

where $E(\omega_{i,t}) = 0$, $\sigma^2(\omega_{i,t}) = $ constant for all t and covariance $(\omega_t, \omega_{t+\tau}) = 0$ for all $\tau \neq 0$. See Chapter 6 for a further discussion of this model.

to estimate the parameters and predict unexpected earnings, the predictions would be "too accurate" because they utilize data that were unavailable to the market when it formed its expectations of earnings. The greater accuracy would cause errors in the estimate of unexpected earnings.

RESULTS

The relation between abnormal rates of return and earnings changes is portrayed graphically in Figure 3.1. Variables 1 and 2 in that graph refer to earnings changes adjusted for market earnings changes where earnings are measured by net income and earnings per share, respectively. Variable 3 refers to changes in earnings per share. The figure shows the graph of API_T for positive and negative earnings changes from 12 months before the earnings announcement ($T = -11$) to 6 months after the announcement ($T = +6$).

The behavior of the abnormal rates of return (represented by API) is as predicted. At the end of the announcement month, the API for the sample of positive earnings changes is greater than 1 for all three variables (varying from 1.056 to 1.073). These observations imply mean annual abnormal rates of return of 5.6 and 7.3 percent. At month 0, the API for the sample of negative earnings changes is less than 1 under all three variables, implying negative mean annual abnormal rates of return of -11.3 to -9.5 percent. The difference in abnormal rates of return between the positive and negative samples over the year is substantial (approximately 16.5 percent for all three variables). Clearly it would be valuable to know next year's annual accounting earnings 12 months in advance.[8]

It is apparent in Figure 3.1 that much of the price adjustment to *annual* earnings changes occurs before the month of the earnings announcement. The APIs for the positive and negative earnings change samples move in the same direction as the sign of the earnings change in every month before the announcement, and as Ball and Brown point out, 85–90 percent of the stock price change associated with the unexpected earnings occurs before the month of announcement. This earlier movement is undoubtedly due to quarterly reports of earnings as well as to nonaccounting sources of information. Because of this large price movement before the earnings announcement, Ball and Brown conclude (p. 176) that annual earnings do not rate highly as a

---

[8] Recall that this 16.5 percent return is net of adjustment for the market and hence could be earned in both up and down markets, if one knew the firm's earnings one year in advance. To earn this 16.5 percent actual return before transaction costs, one would purchase one year in advance those stocks whose earnings will increase and sell short one year in advance those stocks whose earnings will fall. Both positions are liquidated 12 months later.

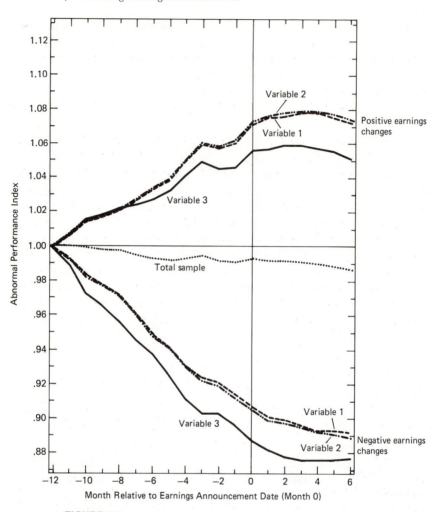

FIGURE 3.1

Abnormal performance indices by month relative to earnings announcement dates

Source: R. Ball and P. Brown, "An Empirical Evaluation of Accounting Income Numbers," *Journal of Accounting Research* 6 (Autumn 1968), Figure 1, p. 169.

timely source of information despite the evidence consistent with earnings conveying information. This conclusion is discussed further later in this chapter.

Ball and Brown do not report a significance test for the relation between the sign of annual earnings changes and the mean annual abnormal rate of return. However, later studies confirm that the mean abnormal rates of return associated with earnings announcements are significantly different from zero.[9] Hence, it is safe to conclude that annual earnings changes and stock price changes are related. Given the efficient markets hypothesis, this finding implies that reported accounting earnings reflect factors affecting stock prices and are potentially useful.

A significance test is reported by Ball and Brown for the association between the sign of the earnings change and the sign of the abnormal rate of return in the month of the earnings announcement ($\hat{e}_{i,0}$). They report χ^2 statistics for all three variables that are sufficient to reject the null hypothesis of no association at any reasonable probability level (Ball and Brown, 1968, Table 5, p. 170). This result is consistent with the hypothesis that earnings announcements convey information. However, a problem with this test is that the earnings changes are not cross sectionally independent even if the changes are adjusted for market changes. The χ^2 tables that Ball and Brown use to assess significance assume that the changes are independent.[10] The cross-sectional dependence is due to industry effects on earnings and rates of return. Subsequent studies using tests that take account of this cross-sectional dependence confirm a significant association between the sign of earnings changes and mean abnormal rates of return in the month of the earnings announcement (e.g., Benston and Watts, 1978). This association is consistent with the earnings announcement conveying information.

Other Studies of Annual Earnings

The Ball and Brown study has been replicated for annual earnings announcements by firms traded in U.S. markets other than the NYSE (e.g., Foster, 1975). It also has been replicated for annual earnings announcements for firms traded in other countries.[11] The replications suggest that the results are not unique to the NYSE.

Brown's (1970) results for Australian companies are summarized in Figure 3.2. The movements of the API in Figure 3.2 are similar to the movements of the API in Figure 3.1 and so are the levels of abnormal returns for positive and negative unexpected earnings changes at month 0.

---

[9] For example, Watts (1978) finds that portfolios formed on the basis of the sign of earnings changes have mean abnormal rates of return for the 6 months up to and including the week of an earnings announcement that are significantly different from zero.

[10] Gonedes and Dopuch (1974) expand on this and related points.

[11] These studies include Brown (1970) on Australia; Firth (1981) on the United Kingdom; Forsgardh and Hertzen (1975) on Sweden; and Knight (1983) on South Africa.

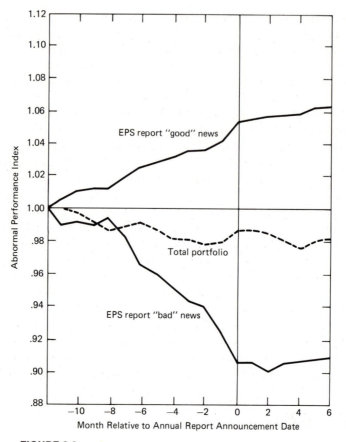

FIGURE 3.2

Annual earnings and rates of returns on stocks for Australian firms

Source: P. Brown, "The Impact of the Annual Net Profit Report on the Stock Market," *The Australian Accountant* (July 1970), Figure 1.

Differences between Ball and Brown and Brown are that the price adjustment during the year is less rapid on the Australian exchanges than on the NYSE and that there is more price adjustment in the announcement month on the Australian exchanges. This result could be due to the fact that Australian companies issue semiannual instead of quarterly reports, which suggests that annual accounting reports are more important sources of information in Australia. Another hypothesis is that the result is due to differences in the size of the Australian and NYSE firms. The Australian firms are, on average, much smaller, suggesting that there are fewer alternative sources of information about them. In turn, this suggests that accounting reports are relatively more important as a source of information for smaller than for larger firms. Evidence on this last hypothesis is presented later in the chapter.

Interim Earnings

The existence of interim earnings announcements creates some problems in interpreting Ball and Brown's results, in particular, the implication that only 10–15 percent of the potential information in annual earnings is conveyed to the market in the month of the annual earnings announcement. First, those interim reports could be responsible for some of the stock price adjustment to annual earnings that occurs in the year before the annual earnings announcement. Hence, all accounting reports (including quarterlies and annuals) could, in fact, convey more than 10–15 percent of the potential information.

Second, the abnormal rate of return in the month of announcement for positive and negative unexpected earnings could be understated and, hence, the information content of the earnings announcement understated. As interim earnings are announced, the market changes its expectation of annual earnings. Hence, the annual earnings expectation implicit in the stock price at the beginning of the month of announcement (at the end of month -1) is not the expectation implicit in the stock price at the beginning of the year (at the end of month -12). Consequently, separating the samples on positive and negative unexpected earnings based on expectations at month -12 incorporates error in unexpected earnings at month -1. Working with interim earnings reduces this understatement.

It should also be noted that Ball and Brown's 10–15 percent estimate could *overstate* the information content of accounting earnings because the stock price adjustment in the month of announcement could occur *before* the actual day of announcement. For example, if stock prices completely adjusted to unexpected earnings a *week before* the announcement, a significant relation will be observed between the abnormal rate of return in the month of announcement and the unexpected earnings. Using daily instead of monthly rates of return reduces this overstatement.

To address the preceding issues, Foster (1977) performs a study similar to Ball and Brown's, but uses quarterly earnings and daily rates of return. Foster uses time series analysis to develop expectation models for quarterly earnings. Some of those models have the desirable attribute of serially uncorrelated forecast errors. Chapter 6 discusses these models in detail.

Foster calculates abnormal rates of return in a slightly different fashion than did Ball and Brown. Each firm's risk measure (β) is estimated using the following regression equation:

$$(r_{i,t} - r_{f,t}) = b_i(r_{m,t} - r_{f,t}) + e_{i,t} \tag{3.4}$$

where $r_{f,t}$ is the rate of return on a risk-free security in *month* t. A portfolio of other firms is constructed such that the portfolio has the same estimated risk as $\hat{b}_i$. The rate of return on that portfolio on *day* t $(r_{p,t})$ is then deducted from the rate of return on security i on day t $(r_{i,t})$ to obtain an estimate of the abnormal returns for security i on day t $(\hat{e}_{i,t})$:[12]

$$\hat{e}_{i,t} = r_{i,t} - r_{p,t} \tag{3.5}$$

Instead of using the discrete daily rate of return, Foster uses the natural logarithm of the daily price relative (1 plus the discrete rate of return) to approximate the daily rate of return with continuous compounding.[13] The estimated abnormal rate of return for security i on day t, $\hat{e}_t$, has the dimension of a continuous rate of return. Hence, the abnormal rate of return over a longer period, the 60 trading days up to and including the earnings announcement day, for firm i in a particular quarter can be calculated as the *sum* of the 60-day abnormal returns. Specifically, the resultant measure, called the **cumulative abnormal return** (CAR_i) for firm i, is calculated as follows:

$$CAR_i = \sum_{t=-59}^{0} \hat{e}_{i,t} \tag{3.6}$$

The average CAR over the 60 days for all firm/quarters with unexpected earnings of a particular sign is obtained by averaging the CARs across all firm/quarters in which unexpected earnings have that sign.

$$CAR = \frac{1}{Q} \sum_{q=1}^{Q} CAR_q;$$
$$Q = \text{number of firm/quarters in the sample} \tag{3.7}$$

If earnings are unrelated to stock prices, the CAR should be zero.

The CARs that Foster estimates over the 60 trading days up to and including the announcement day for this earnings expectation model are 2 percent for positive unexpected earnings and -3 percent for negative unexpected earnings. The χ^2 statistic for the relation

---

[12] This approach to calculating abnormal returns is the portfolio approach described in Chapter 2. For a discussion of the use of prediction errors from the market model versus the portfolio approach, see Brown and Warner (1980).

[13] Continuously compounded returns are calculated as

$$r_{i,t} = \log_e \left(\frac{P_{i,t} + DPS_{i,t}}{P_{i,t-1}} \right)$$

where $P_{i,t}$ and $DPS_{i,t}$ denote price per share and dividends per share, respectively.

between the sign of the unexpected earnings and the abnormal rate of return is 130. That statistic would allow rejection of no association at any reasonable probability level. However, as we noted when discussing Ball and Brown, the test is flawed because of cross-sectional dependence in unexpected earnings and abnormal rates of return. Nevertheless, later tests show the relation to be significant (discussed shortly), and we can conclude that quarterly earnings, like annual earnings, reflect factors impounded in stock prices and are potentially useful (given the efficient markets hypothesis).

Foster also calculates CARs for various periods beginning 20 days before the earnings announcement. The ending dates for those periods range from 15 days before to 20 days after the announcement. Those CARs are provided in Table 3.1. The "Composite CAR" in that table is the average of the CAR for the positive and negative unexpected earnings where the negative earnings changes' CARs are multiplied by -1.

The evidence in Table 3.1 is consistent with the hypothesis that quarterly earnings convey information to the capital market. The day of announcement is defined as the day of announcement in the *WSJ*. However, the actual announcement often occurs the day before (after the *WSJ* is published). Hence, the stock price adjustment at the time of announcement is best estimated by using both days -1 and 0. The average stock price movement for those two days is .0080 (.0162 $-$ .0082), or approximately 1 percent ($CAR_0 - CAR_{-2}$). In other words, if earnings are unexpectedly positive (negative) at the time of the announcement, the stock price increases (decreases) by 1 percent, on average, over the two-day announcement period. The χ^2 statistic for testing the relation between the sign of the unexpected earnings and the abnormal rate of return is 55 for day -1 and 67 for day 0. These test statistics are significant at any reasonable level even after adjusting for cross-sectional dependence in unexpected earnings and stock price changes.

The composite CAR for the 60 trading days up to and including the announcement day (i.e., for approximately the quarter) is .0253. Hence, the abnormal rate of return associated with an unexpected earnings of a particular sign is approximately 2.53 percent over the quarter. If .80 of a percent is the abnormal rate of return at the time of announcement and 2.53 percent is the potential information in quarterly earnings, approximately 32 percent (.8/2.53) of that potential information is not impounded in the price before the announcement. That amount is a substantial increase from the 10–15 percent Ball and Brown estimate for annual earnings and indicates that accounting earnings are a timely source of information.

TABLE 3.1

Cumulative Abnormal Return for Trading Days Surrounding Quarterly Earnings Announcement

Trading Days Surrounding Announcement	All Four Quarters		First Quarter		Second Quarter		Third Quarter		Fourth Quarter	
	Composite CAR	χ^2	Composite CAR	χ^2	Composite CAR	χ^2	Composite CAR	χ^2	Composite CAR	χ^2
−20	.0004	7.07	.0005	5.05	.0009	3.27	.0006	1.82	−.0002	.00
−15	.0017	.85	.0030	.24	.0025	.00	.0034	.44	−.0022	2.96
−10	.0041	1.65	.0075	.50	.0025	1.27	.0059	1.82	.0003	4.66
−9	.0040	.96	.0074	1.33	.0020	.88	.0062	1.60	.0005	.83
−8	.0045	1.12	.0081	.01	.0029	.38	.0065	1.20	.0007	.27
−7	.0048	.49	.0081	1.22	.0022	.24	.0076	1.67	.0010	.50
−6	.0059	8.60	.0087	.70	.0036	1.85	.0091	7.09	.0020	.95
−5	.0062	.79	.0088	1.01	.0033	2.82	.0092	.14	.0037	1.56
−4	.0072	4.26	.0102	2.30	.0048	5.92	.0101	.00	.0038	.01
−3	.0075	1.05	.0110	2.31	.0058	1.64	.0099	.86	.0031	.02
−2	.0082	8.90	.0115	3.12	.0074	2.71	.0110	3.42	.0031	.41
−1	.0124	55.08	.0148	8.09	.0120	23.85	.0156	14.63	.0073	10.43
0	.0162	66.87	.0184	23.35	.0166	12.15	.0197	23.69	.0104	9.99
1	.0168	3.81	.0188	1.57	.0170	.72	.0204	.11	.0109	4.52
2	.0170	.91	.0192	1.80	.0171	.51	.0212	2.25	.0103	2.42
3	.0170	.17	.0201	1.97	.0163	1.70	.0216	.11	.0099	.35
4	.0173	1.31	.0210	.35	.0161	.00	.0215	.34	.0107	1.10
5	.0169	4.93	.0210	.25	.0152	.08	.0211	6.10	.0100	1.31
6	.0169	.34	.0210	.08	.0153	.13	.0209	.49	.0101	.02
7	.0169	.35	.0209	.20	.0149	.09	.0217	1.61	.0101	.02
8	.0174	5.67	.0216	.94	.0134	3.12	.0233	12.93	.0113	4.16
9	.0176	.51	.0219	.05	.0135	.17	.0233	.31	.0116	1.05
10	.0178	2.86	.0218	.29	.0148	2.04	.0229	1.12	.0117	.20
15	.0183	.09	.0215	.13	.0169	.13	.0235	2.14	.0111	.58
20	.0189	.29	.0201	.20	.0192	2.78	.0242	.39	.0122	.01

Source: G. Foster, "Quarterly Accounting Data: Time-Series Properties and Predictive-Ability Results," *Accounting Review* 52 (January 1977), p. 17.

MAGNITUDE OF UNEXPECTED EARNINGS
AND MEAN ABNORMAL RETURNS

Beaver, Clarke and Wright

The studies just discussed investigate the relation between the *sign* of unexpected earnings and the sign of abnormal rates of return. Such a relation is expected if earnings are a surrogate for cash flows and shares are valued under the multiperiod CAPM. However, under the same assumptions, we also expect a relation between the *magnitude* of unexpected earnings and the magnitude of the abnormal rate of return—the larger the unexpected earnings, the larger the abnormal rate of return.

The relation derived in Chapter 2 (equation (2.26)) between the abnormal rate of return for firm i in period t ($v_{i,t}$) and the unexpected cash flows for firm i in period t ($\Delta C_{i,t}$) can be written as follows,

$$v_{i,t} = [1 + E(r_i)] \left[\frac{C_{i,t} - E_{t-1}(C_{i,t})}{E_{t-1}(C_{i,t})} \right] \qquad (3.8)$$

where $E(r_i)$ is the expected rate of return for firm i's shares, $C_{i,t} - E_{t-1}(C_{i,t})$ is the unexpected cash flows for firm i in period t, and $E_{t-1}(C_{i,t})$ is the expected (at time $t - 1$) cash flows for firm i in period t. In equation (3.8), the abnormal rate of return ($v_{i,t}$) is proportional to the percentage unexpected cash flows. If earnings are a surrogate for cash flows, we expect a similar relation between abnormal rates of return and percentage unexpected earnings.

Beaver, Clarke, and Wright (1979) investigate such a relation. They define unexpected earnings for year t as the change in earnings for year t ($\Delta A_{i,t}$) minus a trend term (estimated as $1/Q \sum_{q=1}^{Q} \Delta A_{i,t-q}$, where Q is the number of changes used in the estimate). This definition assumes that earnings follow a martingale with a drift in the direction of the sign of the trend term. They deflate unexpected earnings of year t by expected earnings for year t ($A_{i,t-1} + 1/Q \sum_{q=1}^{Q} \Delta A_{i,t-q}$) to produce percentage unexpected earnings:

$$\frac{\Delta A_{i,t} - \dfrac{1}{Q} \sum_{q=1}^{Q} \Delta A_{i,t-q}}{A_{i,t-1} + \dfrac{1}{Q} \sum_{q=1}^{Q} \Delta A_{i,t-q}}$$

From equation (3.8), if earnings are surrogates for cash flows we expect the larger the percentage unexpected earnings, the larger the abnormal rate of return.

Using observations of annual earnings for 276 firms for the period 1965–1974, Beaver, Clarke, and Wright formed 25 portfolios of firm/

TABLE 3.2

Mean Percentage Unexpected Annual Earnings and Mean Annual Abnormal Rate of Return by Portfolio

Portfolio	No. of Observations	Mean Annual Abnormal Rate of Return	Mean Percentage Unexpected Annual Earnings
1	107	−.1751	−1.5478
2	107	−.1240	−.4469
3	106	−.1469	−.3123
4	106	−.1176	−.2292
5	106	−.1133	−.1747
6	106	−.0903	−.1273
7	106	−.0438	−.0874
8	106	−.0853	−.0510
9	106	−.0415	−.0203
10	106	−.0210	.0047
11	106	−.0011	.0213
12	106	.0198	.0381
13	106	.0117	.0543
14	106	−.0180	.0709
15	106	.0197	.0906
16	106	.0409	.1105
17	106	.0025	.1316
18	106	.0750	.1595
19	106	.0640	.1939
20	106	.1037	.2343
21	106	.1044	.2870
22	106	.1179	.3628
23	106	.1576	.4972
24	106	.2223	.7206
25	106	.2916	1.8508
	2,652		

Source: W. H. Beaver, R. Clarke, and W. Wright, "The Association Between Unsystematic Security Returns and the Magnitude of Earnings Forecast Errors," *Journal of Accounting Research* 17 (Autumn 1979), Table 3, p. 328.

years based on the magnitude of each observation's percentage unexpected earnings. They then calculated the mean annual abnormal rate of return for each portfolio using the observations' CARs for the 12 months ending three months after the firm's fiscal year. Table 3.2 lists each portfolio's mean annual abnormal rate of return and mean percentage unexpected earnings.

As can be seen from Table 3.2, the mean abnormal rate of return increases almost monotonically with the mean percentage unexpected earnings. The mean abnormal rate of return varies as the unexpected earnings vary. For portfolio 1, the mean percentage unexpected earnings are −154 percent and the mean annual abnormal rate of return is −17.5 percent. The equivalent numbers for portfolio 25 are 185 percent and 29.2 percent. The rank correlation between the two variables is significant at any reasonable probability level. Hence, it is apparent that there is a relation between the magnitude of the unexpected annual earnings change and the annual abnormal rate of return.

Equation (3.8) suggests that if earnings are approximately the same magnitude as cash flows, the abnormal rate of return should be approximately the same as the percentage unexpected earnings change (i.e., if we assume that a portfolio's mean adjusted rate of return $(E(r_i))$ is approximately .2, the relation would be approximately 1.2 to 1). In Table 3.2 this relation does not hold. The absolute value of the abnormal rate of return is usually less than the absolute value of the percentage unexpected earnings, particularly for extreme percentage unexpected earnings.

There are several possible reasons for the relation being less than one to one. One is that earnings measure cash flows with error. Hence, not every unexpected change in earnings implies an unexpected change in cash flows and an abnormal rate of return in the same direction. When portfolios are formed on the basis of the unexpected change in earnings, some abnormal rates of return are offsetting. Accounting accruals are one obvious potential source of measurement error.

The derivation of equation (3.8) assumes that cash flows follow a martingale process (see Chapter 2) and a particular multiperiod CAPM. It is possible that the relation between unexpected earnings and abnormal returns is less than one to one because those assumptions are not descriptive.

A third possible reason for the relation not being one to one is that the stock price adjustment to some factors reflected in annual earnings may have occurred in previous years. For example, while a government contract may have its initial earnings effect in the current year, the stock price capitalizes the cash flows from the contract in an earlier year when the award of the contract was announced.

Finally, stock prices may change even if earnings do not, because interest rates, and the rates at which earnings are capitalized, change.

Beaver, Lambert, and Morse

Beaver, Lambert, and Morse (1980) regress the percentage change in price on the percentage change in earnings per share across firms for each year in the 19-year period 1958–1976.[14] The average slope coefficient for the 19 regressions (the average sensitivity of the per-

---

[14] Percentage change in price is the same as the rate of return except dividends are excluded. They are able to replicate their results using rates of return (Beaver, Lambert, and Morse, 1980, p. 17) and, therefore, conclude that their results are robust to the choice of dependent variables. See Christie, Kennelley, King, and Schaefer (1984) for a discussion of valuation models and comments on Beaver, Lambert, and Morse.

centage change in price to the percentage change in earnings) is .12. This is consistent with the less than one-to-one relation observed by Beaver, Clarke, and Wright (1979).

When Beaver, Lambert, and Morse group the firms into portfolios based on percentage *price change* and rerun their regressions, the average slope coefficient increases. When all firms are assigned to one of 25 portfolios and the regression performed for 25 portfolios, the average coefficient is 1.80. This indicates a more than one-to-one relation between unexpected earnings and the *abnormal rate of return*.

The difference between the Beaver, Clarke, and Wright and Beaver, Lambert, and Morse results is at least partially due to the difference in method of portfolio formation. Beaver, Clarke, and Wright form their portfolios on the independent variable (percentage unexpected earnings) and Beaver, Lambert, and Morse form theirs on the dependent variable (percentage change in *price*). The Beaver, Clarke, and Wright procedure probably understates the sensitivity of rate of return to cash flows whereas the Beaver, Lambert, and Morse procedure probably overstates it.[15]

Regardless of the degree of sensitivity, it is apparent from both studies that there is a significant positive relation between abnormal rates of return and unexpected annual earnings. That association is consistent with annual earnings reflecting factors that affect stock prices (such as current and expected cash flows). But, because the focus is on unexpected earnings for a one-year period, the Beaver, Clarke, and Wright and Beaver, Lambert, and Morse studies do not provide evidence on the information content of earnings announcements.

EARNINGS ANNOUNCEMENTS AND VARIANCE OF ABNORMAL RETURNS

The preceding discussions summarized evidence on the relation between unexpected earnings and mean abnormal rates of return. However, the mean abnormal rate of return is not the only measure of

---

[15] Beaver, Lambert, and Morse (1980, fn. 9) recognize that their approach may overstate the estimated coefficients. Forming portfolios based on percentage price changes causes the high percentage price change portfolio to include stocks whose abnormal rate of return is high because of high unexpected cash flows and/or because of factors unrelated to current cash flows. On average, the high portfolio's rate of return is greater than expected given cash flows. Likewise, the low percentage price change portfolio is less than expected. The measurement error in earnings should not be related to either variable, so the estimated coefficient is greater than the true relation (see Wheatley, 1982).

By a similar set of arguments, the Beaver, Clarke, and Wright results understate the true relation. Beaver, Clarke, and Wright form portfolios based on unexpected earnings that cause the high unexpected earnings portfolio to have positive average measurement error and the low unexpected earnings portfolio to have negative measurement error. This procedure overstates high unexpected cash flows and understates low unexpected cash flows, thereby reducing the estimated coefficient.

stock price reaction to earnings announcements that is used. Researchers also use the variance of the abnormal rate of return as a measure of the information content of earnings announcements.

Beaver (1968a) was the first to use the variance of abnormal returns as a measure of the information content of annual earnings announcements. He uses the variance to avoid specifying a model for expected earnings. The idea is that information changes investors' estimates of the probability distributions of the firm's future cash flows and hence the firm's stock price. If an earnings announcement conveys information to the capital markets, it causes a price change. Thus, Beaver expects more and larger price changes on days of earnings announcements than on other days. Since, in an efficient market the expected abnormal rate of return on an earnings announcement day is expected to be zero, these price changes result in a larger variance of abnormal returns on earnings announcement days.[16] Hence, the hypothesis that earnings convey information to the market can be tested by observing whether the abnormal return variance increases at the time of earnings announcements. The variance test of earnings information content avoids errors in measuring the unexpected earnings (e.g., equation (3.3)) used to partition earnings announcements in mean abnormal rate-of-return tests. Because the variance tests obviate the need to specify an expectation model, they have been used frequently in studies of other types of information disclosures.

Beaver

To compare the abnormal return variance in report weeks (i.e., the 17 weeks around an earnings announcement, week -8 to week $+8$) and nonreport weeks, Beaver (1968a) forms the ratio $U_{q,t}$,

$$U_{q,t} = \frac{e^2_{q,t}}{\sigma^2(e_q)} \; ; \qquad t = -8, \ldots, +8 \qquad (3.9)$$

where $e^2_{q,t}$ is the square of the prediction error from the market model for announcement q in week t and $\sigma^2(e_q)$ is the residual variance from the estimated market model for announcement q. Since the expected abnormal return in an earnings announcement week is zero in an efficient market, $e^2_{q,0}$ is also the abnormal return variance for the announcement week ($e^2_{q,t}$ is the abnormal return variance for report week t). The residual variance, $\sigma^2(e_q)$, is an estimate of the abnormal return variance in nonreport weeks. If there is no information in an earnings announcement, the abnormal return variance should not change, and the ratio for the announcement week ($U_{q,0}$) should be

---

[16] See Christie et al. (1984) for a discussion of when the expected abnormal rate of return conditional on an announcement day is expected to be zero.

approximately $1.$[17] If there is information in earnings announcements the ratio $U_{q,0}$ should be greater than 1.

It is important to remember than the U ratio is only a test of change in the abnormal return variance *if* the expected abnormal return on announcement is zero. Since all listed firms have earnings announcements at relatively regular intervals, this is a reasonable assumption for a random sample of earnings announcements. On average, the fact that an earnings announcement is being made does not convey information in an efficient market.[18] On the other hand, a merger announcement per se does convey information, and it would not be reasonable to assume an expected abnormal return of zero for a sample of merger announcements. Hence, for merger announcements, the square of the abnormal rate of return on announcement (the numerator of the U ratio) is not an estimate of the abnormal return variance. It is affected by the mean abnormal return so that the U ratio can be greater than 1 because the merger announcement affects the mean abnormal return and/or the abnormal return variance.[19]

SAMPLE

Beaver's sample consists of annual earnings announcements of 143 firms in the period 1961–1965 that

1. Are on the *Compustat* tapes
2. Are listed on the NYSE
3. Have a fiscal year other than December 31
4. Have no dividends in the same week as earnings announcements
5. Have no stock splits in the report periods (17 weeks around announcement)
6. Have less than 20 news announcements per year in the *WSJ*

The fiscal year requirement is imposed to avoid the clustering of earnings announcements in a few weeks. Such a clustering increases the likelihood that variables other than earnings produce any observed abnormal stock price effect. The dividends and stock split restrictions are also imposed to reduce the potential impact of nonearnings variables. The restriction on the number of news announcements is imposed to compare earnings announcement weeks to weeks in which there are few other announcements. However, it may cause the selection of small firms that have relatively few alternative sources of information and so

---

[17] See Patell (1976) for a discussion of the Beaver U statistic.

[18] Note that the timing of the earnings announcement (i.e., whether it is earlier or later than normal) does convey information (see Chambers and Penman, 1984).

[19] See Patell (1976).

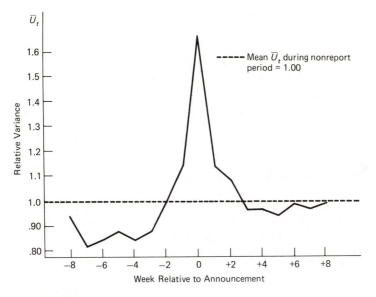

FIGURE 3.3

Relative variance of the unexpected rates of return around annual earnings announcements

Source: W. H. Beaver, "The Information Content of Annual Earnings Announcements," *Empirical Research in Accounting: Selected Studies 1968*, supplement to Vol. 6 of *Journal of Accounting Research* (1968), p. 91.

overstate the average information content of earnings announcements (see Grant, 1980). Not all 143 firms meet all the criteria in each year, so the final sample consists of 506 earnings announcements.

Beaver calculates $U_{q,t}$ for the report weeks for all 506 announcements and estimates an average ratio $\overline{U}_t$ for each week in the announcement period:

$$\overline{U}_t = \frac{1}{506} \sum_{q=1}^{506} U_{q,t}; \qquad t = -8, \ldots, 0, \ldots, +8 \qquad (3.10)$$

The estimate $\overline{U}_t$ is used to test whether the abnormal return variance increases in report weeks.

RESULTS

Figure 3.3 portrays the variation in $\overline{U}_t$ around the announcement week.

From the figure the average abnormal return variance is larger in the week of announcement of annual earnings. The ratio at time 0 is 1.67. In other words, the variance during the announcement week is

67 percent larger than normal. The increased variance is most pronounced at time zero, but weeks -1, $+1$, and $+2$ are also above average.

The conclusion from Figure 3.3 is that the announcement of annual earnings contains information relevant to the valuation of securities. While no significance tests are performed on the numbers in Figure 3.3, Beaver checks to see whether the reported increase is unusual. First, he investigates the frequency with which $\overline{U}_t$ exceeds 1.67 in the nonreport period. Out of 250 values, only 11 exceed 1.67, suggesting that a mean value of 1.67 is unusually high. The frequency of values above 1 is greatest in week 0 and the probability of chance occurrence of that frequency is less than .00001.

Even if greater than normal variances of abnormal rates of return in the two weeks following the earnings announcement (see Figure 3.3) were significant (which they almost certainly are not), they do not contradict the efficient markets hypothesis. Increased variances do not necessarily imply an opportunity to earn abnormal returns. This is apparent when one considers that half of the above-normal price changes in week $+1$ could be positive and half negative so that the mean abnormal return is zero.

Other Variance Studies

The variance measure of information content has been used for earnings announcements on exchanges other than the NYSE with similar results. May (1971) applies it to the quarterly earnings announcements of American Stock Exchange (ASE) firms over the period 1964–1968. Hagerman (1973) applies Beaver's methodology to earnings announcements of bank stocks on the OTC market. Both Hagerman's and May's results are similar to Beaver's.

In general, the results of the abnormal return variance tests of earnings information content are consistent with the results of tests that use the sign of unexpected earnings and mean abnormal returns. Both sets of results are consistent with earnings announcements conveying information to the capital market.

EARNINGS ANNOUNCEMENTS AND IMPLICIT RETURN VARIANCES

Firms tend to announce a particular quarter's earnings on approximately the same date each year (see Chambers and Penman, 1984). Hence, we would expect investors in an efficient market to anticipate both earnings announcement dates and the accompanying increase in rate of return variance. In other words we expect the market to anticipate the information release at the time of earnings announcements. Market prices cannot adjust to the information prior to the announcement because the earnings are not known, but the market should expect information to be released and the rate-of-return variance to increase.

The hypothesis that the market expects return variance increases on earnings announcements can be tested using **call option** prices. A call option is a right to buy a given number of shares of a particular firm at a specific price (the **exercise price**) within a stated period of time. These options are traded on the Chicago Board Options Exchange (CBOE), the ASE, the Philadelphia Stock Exchange, and the Pacific Stock Exchange. Call option prices vary with the underlying share's return variance.

Patell and Wolfson (1979, 1981) use call option prices to test whether the market anticipates the variance increase at the time of earnings announcements. They obtain estimates of the variance rate from the Black and Scholes (1973) option pricing model. In that model a call option price is a function of the contemporaneous price of the underlying share, the option's exercise price, the time to expiration of the option, the continuous risk-free interest rate, and the variance rate of the continuous return on the share per unit of time. If the variance rate is a deterministic function of time, the variance rate in the model can be defined as the *average* of the variance rates from the date of the option valuation to the expiration date (Merton, 1973). Given call option prices at a given date, the underlying share price, the exercise price, and the risk-free rate, Patell and Wolfson are able to solve the Black and Scholes model for the *average* variance rate implicit in the call and stock prices.

Based on the studies of the association between earnings announcements and return variances, Patell and Wolfson assume that the instantaneous variance of a share's return is a constant (k) except for a temporary increase (l) during an announcement period (t_3 to t_4 in Figure 3.4). Given that pattern, the constant k should be the average variance rate calculated using the prices, at time t_4, of options expiring at time t_5 and the underlying share. However, the average variance rate for prices at time t_1 and an expiration date of t_5 should be larger because it includes times when the variance rate is k (e.g., t_2) and times when the variance is $k + l$. In that case, the average variance rate is the average of k and $k + l$. Holding the expiration date constant at t_5 and varying the time of share and call price observation, the average variance rate will vary as in Figure 3.5.

Patell and Wolfson (1981) test whether the calculated variance rate behaves as predicted in Figure 3.5. In particular, using options with expirations following an announcement period, they test whether

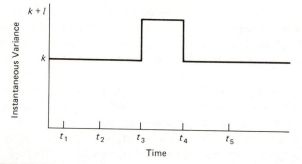

FIGURE 3.4

Assumed profile of instantaneous return variance around announcement period (t_3 to t_4)

Source: J. M. Patell and M. A. Wolfson, "The Ex Ante and Ex Post Price Effects of Quarterly Earnings Announcements Reflected in Option and Stock Prices," *Journal of Accounting Research* 19 (Autumn 1981), p. 437.

1. The average variance rate increases between two dates prior to the announcement period (e.g., between t_1 and t_2 in Figures 3.4 and 3.5)
2. The average variance rate drops during the announcement period (i.e., t_3 to t_4)
3. There is an ordinal correlation between the magnitude of average variance rate increases in (1) and the increase in share price variability in the announcement period

FIGURE 3.5

Average variance to expiration with variation in the time of observation of share and option prices given and expiration date of t_5

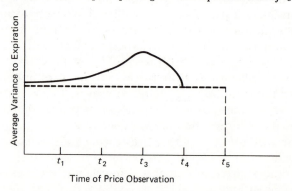

Source: J. M. Patell and M. A. Wolfson, "The Ex Ante and Ex Post Price Effects of Quarterly Earnings Announcements Reflected in Option and Stock Prices," *Journal of Accounting Research* 19 (Autumn 1981), p. 439.

The sample used by Patell and Wolfson (1981) consists of the 96 firms with options traded on the CBOE during any part of the period August 23, 1976, through October 21, 1977. Using the exact time of announcement on the Dow Jones New Service or "broad tape" whenever possible, Patell and Wolfson identify the announcement day for 333 quarterly earnings announcements by the 96 firms in that period.[20] They estimate the market model on the firm's share returns and calculate the ratio of the squared daily residual returns for days in announcement periods (days -1 to $+2$) to the average squared residual in nonannouncement periods.

The ratio is similar to Beaver's U_t statistic. The average ratios for days -1, 0, $+1$, and $+2$ are 1.72, 3.34, 2.01, and 1.24, respectively. The first three days' ratios are significant (at the .001 level). The ratios for days 0 and $+1$ are higher than the 1.67 reported by Beaver (1968a), but that can be explained by Beaver's use of weekly data (which include the lower ratios on days -2 and $+2$).

Based on the significance of the increase in variances for days -1, 0, and $+1$, Patell and Wolfson define the announcement period to include those three days. They test whether the average variance rate increases prior to the period using the average variance rates calculated 20 trading days before the earnings announcement (day -20) and the average variance rate calculated for day -2. The hypothesis that the average variance rate declines through the announcement period is tested using average variance rates estimated for days -2 and $+1$.

The increase in average variance rates from day -20 to day -2 is significant for short options (20–90 days to expiration), median options (90–180 days to expiration), and long options (180–270 days to expiration) and three different measures of the variance increase at probability levels ranging from .0001 to .072. The decline in average variance rates from day -2 to $+1$ is significant for all nine combinations of types of options and measures at probability levels ranging from .006 to .067.

Patell and Wolfson estimate the rank order correlation between the increase in the average variance rate in the period prior to the announcement period (inferred from option prices) and the relative increase in the ratio of squared daily residuals in the announcement period (inferred from stock prices). When the announcement period is defined as day -1 to $+1$, the rank order correlation is significant at the .03 probability level. Hence, not only is the direction of the change in implicit average variance in the preannouncement prices consistent

[20] Patell and Wolfson obtain the exact time for 290 of the 333 firms. The day preceding publication of the announcement in the *WSJ* is assumed to be the announcement day for the other 43 firms.

with the market expecting a variance increase on an earnings announcement, but the magnitude of the implicit average increase is related to the magnitude of the actual increase in variance on announcement. The evidence is consistent with the average variance rate following the time profile depicted in Figure 3.4 and consistent with the market anticipating the release of the information in earnings announcements.

EARNINGS ANNOUNCEMENTS AND TRADING VOLUME

In his article introducing the variance methodology, Beaver (1968a) also investigates changes in the volume of trading associated with earnings announcements. While Beaver interprets an increase in the volume of trading as evidence of information, there is a problem with this interpretation. Conceptually, information could be conveyed to the market and prices could change by large amounts without a single transaction (trade). For example, after the close of trading on a given day, a firm could announce a major, unanticipated loss. When trading on the stock opens again, the bid and ask prices will be substantially below the last transaction price. On the other hand, there could be substantial trading (e.g., due solely to portfolio rearrangement) without any information release. The problem is the lack of an economic theory of volume. Consequently, as Beaver recognizes, his volume measure of information is ad hoc.[21]

In his volume study, Beaver uses the same 506 earnings announcements used investigating the residual return variance at the time of an earnings announcement. Beaver measures the volume for firm i for week t as follows:

$$v_{i,t} = \frac{\text{number of shares of firm } i \text{ traded in week } t}{\text{number of shares outstanding for firm } i \text{ in week } t}$$
$$\text{x} \frac{1}{\text{number of trading days in week } t} \qquad (3.11)$$

This weekly average of the daily percentage of shares traded is then averaged across all 506 announcements for each week of the announcement period (week -8 to week $+8$) to obtain $\bar{v}_t$.

$$\bar{v}_t = \frac{1}{506} \sum_{q=1}^{506} v_{q,t}; \qquad t = -8, \ldots, 0, \ldots, +8 \qquad (3.12)$$

Figure 3.6 shows the average volume over the announcement

[21] Also see Verrecchia (1981).

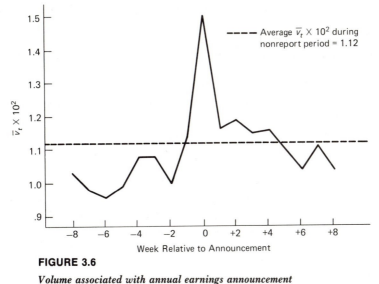

FIGURE 3.6

Volume associated with annual earnings announcement

Source: W. H. Beaver, "The Information Content of Annual Earnings Announcements," *Empirical Research in Accounting: Selected Studies 1968*, supplement to Vol. 6 of *Journal of Accounting Research* (1968), p. 91.

period. The dotted line represents the average in the nonannouncement period. As can be seen in Figure 3.6, the average volume in the announcement week (week 0) is much larger than in the nonreport period (33 percent larger) and in the other weeks of the report period.

Beaver also investigates trading volume after adjusting for the market volume. The results are very similar to those reported in Figure 3.6 (i.e., a large increase in volume in the earnings announcement week). Hence the observed trading volume reinforces the findings using the mean and variance of abnormal returns and the implicit average variance; earnings announcements convey information to the stock market.

EARNINGS AND CASH FLOWS

Underlying the tests of association between abnormal returns and unexpected earnings and the information content of earnings is the notion that earnings are measures of current and future cash flows. In Chapter 2 a firm's abnormal rate of return for a period is expressed as a positive function of the unexpected cash flows of the period and the change in that period in the expected cash flows for future periods (e.g., see equation (2.23)). Unexpected earnings could be associated with abnormal returns because they are an index of unexpected current cash flows and/or the change in expected future cash flows. If unexpected earnings are a better index of the change in expected future cash flows than unexpected current cash flows, unexpected earnings could have a higher association with abnormal returns than unexpected cash flows. It is possible that the accrual process, by which accountants convert current cash flows to accounting earnings, causes earnings to be a better index of "permanent" earnings or expected future cash flow than current cash flows.

Several studies address the issue of whether unexpected earnings or unexpected cash flows are more highly associated with abnormal returns. These studies use operating cash flows (cash flows minus investment cash flows) instead of total cash flows, presumably because the investment cash flows (outlays and salvage) are thought to be unstable over time. Ball and Brown replicate their study using cash flows instead of earnings (Ball and Brown, 1968, pp. 172–173). They use operating income as a surrogate for operating cash flows. The absolute abnormal returns for both positive and negative cash flow changes are slightly lower than those for earnings changes, suggesting that current cash flows are less highly associated with abnormal returns.

Beaver and Dukes (1972) support Ball and Brown's results. They approximate annual operating cash flows by adding back to earnings depreciation, depletion and amortization charges, and the change in the deferred tax account in the balance sheet. They find that unexpected earnings are more highly associated with abnormal returns than are unexpected operating cash flows.

Patell and Kaplan (1977) test whether operating cash flows provide any information beyond that in annual earnings. They conclude that cash flows do not have any such marginal information content. Patell and Kaplan use the *Compustat* variable "total funds from operations" as a surrogate for operating cash flow. That variable is defined as net income after extraordinary items plus deferred taxes and depreciation minus unremitted earnings of unconsolidated industries plus "other adjustments."

While the foregoing results suggest that accounting earnings are better predictors of future cash flows than are current cash flows (given models such as equation (2.23)), it should be noted that none of the studies actually uses operating cash flows. While they all "undo" some accruals in earnings to estimate operating cash flows, none of them undoes accruals such as changes in inventory and changes in accounts receivable. Undoing these accruals may increase the operating cash flows' association with abnormal returns, since there is some evidence that managers manipulate these accruals to affect their compensation (see Healy, 1985, and Chapter 11). Also, it would be interesting to use total net cash flows instead of operating cash flows. Eliminating investment cash flows could reduce the association between abnormal returns and cash flows.

VARIATION IN INFORMATION CONTENT

As we discuss at the beginning of this chapter, it was not obvious prior to Ball and Brown (1968) that earnings reports convey information. The reason is that under the EMH, there is competition for information so that other information sources could convey factors reflected in earnings to the market before earnings announcements occur. The evidence presented in previous subsections indicates that other sources do not convey all the factors reflected in earnings, that there is information content in earnings announcements in general. However, the amount of available public information varies across firms. There are more news stories on large firms than on small firms and more analysts study large firms than small firms. This suggests less alternative sources of information for smaller firms and that the information content of earnings announcements by those firms is larger. The hypothesis is tested by Grant (1980).

Given that earnings announcements convey information, the question arises whether more frequent earnings announcements lead to a given earnings announcement having less information content. For example, when a firm changes from reporting earnings annually to reporting earnings quarterly, does the information content of the annual earnings announcement drop? McNichols and Manegold (1983) test that hypothesis.

Grant

Grant (1980) investigates the relative information content of annual earnings announcements of NYSE and OTC firms. OTC firms are typically much smaller than NYSE firms. Grant observes that there are fewer news items reported in the *WSJ* for OTC firms than for NYSE firms and predicts that as a result, OTC firms' annual earnings announcements have more information content.

Information content is measured using Beaver's U statistic, the ratio of the squared prediction errors in the report period to the residual variance in the nonreport period. Grant calculates this statistic for samples of 747 annual earnings announcements by 211 OTC firms and 336 announcements by 101 NYSE firms in the period 1960–1964. The statistic is 2.60 and significant (at least at the .10 level) in the announcement week for the OTC firms, and 1.28 and insignificant for the NYSE firms. The NYSE statistic is lower than the 1.67 reported by Beaver for NYSE firms, probably because Beaver's sample selection process tends to pick the NYSE firms with the fewest number of *WSJ* news items. In other words, Beaver investigates the NYSE firms for which the earnings information content should be larger.

Grant is able to reject the hypothesis that there is no difference in the announcement week *U* statistic of the NYSE and OTC firms at the .001 probability level. Since OTC firms have fewer news items in the *WSJ*, this evidence is consistent with the hypothesis that the information content of earnings announcements varies with the number of alternative sources of information (as measured by *WSJ* news items).

McNichols and Manegold

In 1962 the ASE imposed a requirement that ASE firms report earnings quarterly. Prior to that time, many ASE firms reported earnings only annually. McNichols and Manegold (1983) investigate whether the return variance at the time of annual earnings announcements decreased after ASE firms began reporting quarterly earnings.

McNichols and Manegold define a relative variance measure similar to Beaver's *U* statistic. They calculate the mean and variance of daily rates of return for a nonannouncement period for each firm. Then they calculate the return variance for a given day of the announcement period as the square of the difference between mean nonannouncement return and the daily return. The ratio of the return variance on a given day in the announcement period to the daily return variance for the nonannouncement period is the relative variance measure.

Using a sample of 34 firms, McNichols and Manegold compare the average relative variance measures for annual earnings announcements before and after the firms began reporting quarterly earnings. They find that the relative variance measure for days -4, $+1$, and $+2$ is significantly lower at the .05 probability level after the commencement of quarterly reporting. When the averages of the relative variances over days -5 to $+2$ are compared, the average after quarterly reporting is significantly less at the .01 probability level. This evidence is consistent with a reduction in the relative information content of annual earnings announcements following the introduction of quarterly reporting.

SUMMARY

This chapter summarizes and analyzes the empirical literature on the relation between earnings and stock prices. That literature developed directly from Ball and Brown (1968), which popularized the use of positive theory and scientific methodology in accounting. The literature assumes that the EMH is descriptive and interprets the empirical results accordingly.

The evidence summarized in this chapter indicates that stock price changes for a given period (e.g., quarter or year) are associated with both the sign and magnitude of unexpected earnings for that period. Given the EMH, this evidence is consistent with the hypothesis that accounting earnings reflect factors that affect stock prices. The evidence also indicates that annual and quarterly earnings convey information to the stock market. Stock prices change at the time of earnings announcements. This finding is obtained under four measures of information: mean abnormal rates of return, variance or dispersion of abnormal rates of return, return variance implicit in stock and option prices, and trading volume.

The stock price change on the day of a quarterly earnings announcement is smaller than the total stock price change associated with the unexpected quarterly earnings. This indicates that alternative sources of information exist that allow the market to anticipate the accounting earnings. The evidence that the information content of earnings announcements varies inversely across firms with the frequency of news items in the *WSJ* is consistent with alternative information sources playing an important role in determining the information content of earnings. The information content of annual earnings announcements also varies with the presence or absence of interim earnings announcements. The information content of annual earnings is less if the firm reports quarterly earnings.

Studies conclude that abnormal returns are more highly associated with earnings than with operating cash flows. Given the EMH and the CAPM, this suggests that the accountants' accrual process makes accounting earnings the better predictor of future cash flows. However, those studies use surrogates for operating cash flows that contain accruals. Elimination of those accruals from the cash flow surrogates and/or use of actual rather than operating cash flows may change the conclusions.

The studies described in this chapter make no attempt to discriminate between the EMH and hypotheses underlying the previously existing accounting literature. Instead, following Ball and Brown, the studies assume that the EMH is descriptive and interpret their empirical results accordingly. In our opinion, the reason is that the studies are aimed at an audience of researchers who are trained in finance and economics and are aware of the evidence in finance consistent with the EMH. However, while this line of research was developing, studies were undertaken that tried to discriminate between the EMH and alternative hypotheses in the accounting literature. These studies seek to provide evidence to affect the opinions of accountants who accepted the hypotheses underlying the previously existing literature. The next chapter investigates those studies.

CHAPTER FOUR

Discriminating Between Competing Hypotheses

The efficient market hypothesis and the role of accounting earnings in stock valuation are discussed in Chapter 3. While that literature uses scientific methodology in the positive tradition, it makes no attempt to discriminate empirically between the EMH and a competing hypothesis. The competing hypothesis underlies much of the previous literature and posits a mechanical relation between accounting earnings and stock prices. It implies that the stock market is systematically misled by accounting procedures. The literature analyzed in this chapter attempts to discriminate between the two hypotheses. Circumstances are identified in which the competing hypotheses yield contradictory predictions and tests are conducted to determine which hypothesis is more consistent with the evidence.

The discrimination attempts raise a series of methodological issues that are discussed. The objective of the discussion, and of the chapter, is to improve the understanding of the scientific methodology of positive economics. The literature is an example of how theory progresses. Ambitious early studies have serious methodological problems. These problems are addressed by follow-up studies, which in turn, are criticized and improved by other studies. While the studies, in aggregate, do not discriminate between the hypotheses, they have moved us much closer to that goal by identifying problems and finding ways of addressing them. The evidence accumulated from the studies also leads to the development of new hypotheses about, and new perspectives on, accounting phenomena.

The chapter begins by outlining the competing hypotheses' contradictory predictions for stock price changes at the time of an accounting change. Then it describes one of the studies that began the literature, Kaplan and Roll (1972). That description is followed by an analysis of the methodological problems in accounting change studies using Kaplan and Roll as an example. The analysis is aided by a decade of hindsight. Another original study (Ball, 1972) is assessed in terms of how it handles the methodological problems.

After a review of the original studies, the development of the literature is traced through a series of studies of the stock price effects of changes between the LIFO and FIFO inventory accounting methods (Sunder, 1973, 1975; Ricks, 1982; Biddle and Lindahl, 1982). The chapter concludes with a summary of the evidence on the association between stock price changes and changes in accounting methods and the lessons for theory development.

THE COMPETING HYPOTHESES

The early positive accounting researchers use the relation between stock price changes and changes in accounting procedures to discriminate between the efficient markets hypothesis (EMH) and its competing hypothesis. In combination with the capital asset pricing model (CAPM) and assumptions of zero transaction, contracting, and information costs and no taxes, the EMH predicts that *no* stock price changes are associated with certain voluntary changes in accounting procedures. This is called the **"no-effects" hypothesis**. The competing hypothesis (i.e., the stock market is systematically misled by accounting procedures) predicts that stock price changes are associated with those particular accounting changes. This is called the **"mechanistic" hypothesis**.

The No-Effects Hypothesis

The semistrong form of the EMH implies only that following a publicly announced accounting change, it is not possible to make abnormal returns by trading on knowledge of the change. In other words, any stock price change accompanying the accounting change is unbiased (i.e., it reflects the implications of the accounting change for future value). By itself, the EMH provides no prediction for a stock price change at the time of a change in accounting procedure. For example, if a firm switches to accelerated depreciation, the stock price might go up or down. The EMH does not predict the direction of the change, only that the price will not drift up or down *after* the change is announced. Predicting the direction of the stock price change requires a valuation model and an hypothesis about the relation between accounting changes and factors affecting valuation. The early researchers use the CAPM as the valuation model.

Under the multiperiod CAPM, the market value of the firm is a function of the firm's expected future cash-flows and the expected rate of return. In the CAPM world outlined in Chapter 2, there is no reason to expect a change in an accounting procedure to carry any implications for cash flows. In that world there are no transaction costs, no costs of contracting, and no information processing costs. Information is assumed costless and available to all investors. Since it costs investors the same amount (zero) to process accounting earnings calculated under different methods, there is no reason for a firm's manager to prefer one accounting method over another. So, without additional assumptions, an accounting change has no implications for stock prices in the CAPM world.[1]

The proposition that accounting methods are irrelevant to a firm's value is analogous to the famous Modigliani and Miller (1958) proposition that capital structure is irrelevant. Both hold in the CAPM world. Capital structure only breaks the firm's cash flows into claims with different patterns of cash flows. Hence, with zero transactions costs, the investor can costlessly create any capital structure or costlessly "undo" any capital structure. Given this, capital structure is irrelevant (see Brealey and Myers, 1984, Ch. 17).

The capital structure irrelevance proposition is more than an analogy. It influenced the early accounting researchers' predictions of the stock price changes associated with accounting changes. Under the CAPM, capital structure and accounting procedures are just form and have no value effects. However, if taxes are introduced, both capital structure and accounting methods affect cash flows and firm value. Modigliani and Miller (1963) show that in a world with corporate taxes, where interest payments are tax deductible and dividend payments are not, capital structure affects the firm's cash flows and hence its value (see Brealey and Myers, 1984, Ch. 18). Some accounting changes (i.e., LIFO changes) affect corporate taxes and hence affect cash flows and firm values. At the time of the early studies attempting to discriminate between the competing hypotheses, the Modigliani and Miller tax analysis was the only rigorous analysis that allowed capital structure to

---

[1] The role of transaction costs, information costs, and contracting costs in the relation between accounting changes and stock prices is also explored in Holthausen and Leftwich (1983).

affect a firm's cash flows and value. Hence, it was natural for accounting researchers to predict that, unless an accounting change had implications for taxes, it would not have any effect on the stock price.

Tax implications are not sufficient for stock price changes to be associated with accounting changes in the EMH/CAPM world. The accounting change has to be unexpected by the market. If it is expected, the tax implications of an accounting change will be in the stock price already and no price change will occur at the time of the accounting change.

Tests of the "no-effects" hypothesis (the prediction that unless an accounting change affects taxes it has no effect on stock prices) are not tests of the EMH. They are tests of the *joint hypothesis* of the EMH, the CAPM, and zero transactions, contracting, and information costs. Hence failure to confirm the prediction does not necessarily imply failure of the EMH since the failure could be due to one of the other joint hypotheses (e.g., that transactions costs are zero).

The Mechanistic Hypothesis

Many accounting articles prior to the introduction of the EMH hypothesize that changes in accounting procedures affect stock prices even if those changes have no effect on, or implications for, the firm's cash flows. The hypothesis follows from an assumption that accounting reports are the sole source of information on the firm and that, as a consequence, investors use accounting earnings to value the firm's shares.[2]

Some accounting practitioners and financial investors adopting the mechanistic hypothesis allege that corporate managers change accounting procedures to inflate reported earnings and their corporation's stock price.[3] For example, Leonard M. Savoie (executive vice-president of the American Institute of Certified Public Accountants) argues:

> In corporate financial reporting . . . [t]he game plan is to show a steadily rising earnings-per-share, thus stimulating investor demand for shares, with consequent rise in their price, and creating a favorable atmosphere for the issuance of new securities in case additional capital is needed.
> Game plans come in two kinds—offensive and defensive. The offense predominated during the late 1960's when the stock market was high, conglomerate mergers were commonplace and prosperity reigned. Game plans then were designed with style and finesse, using "funny money," pooling of interests, deferral of research and development costs,

[2] See Ball (1972) for examples of academic papers in which the hypothesis is advanced.

[3] See Kaplan and Roll (1972, p. 226) for a list of articles in *Barron's* and the *Financial Analysts Journal*.

stretched-out depreciation, front-end loading on installment revenue of doubtful collectibility, and so on.

As take-overs by the offense became commonplace, even the defensive-minded game planners were forced into liberal accounting practices to make themselves a harder target. Witness the 1968 switch of the steel industry from declining-balance depreciation to straight-line depreciation, thus increasing earnings per share and asset values. (Savoie, 1970)

Managers also believe that the stock market can be misled by changes in accounting techniques. *The Wall Street Journal* editorial on October 1, 1974 states that:

A lot of executives apparently believe that if they can figure out a way to boost reported earnings their stock price will go up even if the higher earnings do not represent any underlying economic change. In other words, the executives think they are smart and the market is dumb.

Even those managers who switch to LIFO to increase cash flows (via reduced taxes) are concerned about the stock price effect of the resultant decrease in reported earnings per share. They try to convince directors and shareholders that the earnings drop does not affect stock prices. Thomas Bray writing in the *WSJ* (October 7, 1977) states as fact the consequence managers fear:

Because of the negative impact of earnings, LIFO conversions haven't always been welcome news to the stock market.

The foregoing statements suggest that some sophisticated individuals believe that the market is systematically misled by accounting procedures when the use of those procedures and their effects on earnings is publicly known. They believe that the market is inefficient. Their belief does not imply the market is inefficient. The EMH is an aggregate concept, and it does not require that *all* individuals believe the market is efficient. The EMH can be descriptive of aggregate market behavior even if some individual market participants believe otherwise.

The mechanistic hypothesis postulates a mechanical relationship between earnings and stock prices. The early positive researchers specified the mechanistic hypothesis as an alternative or competing hypothesis to the joint hypothesis of the EMH, the CAPM, and zero transactions costs. This competing hypothesis predicts that an earnings increasing accounting change is accompanied by a positive abnormal stock return and that an earnings decreasing change is accompanied by a negative abnormal stock return regardless of the effect of the change on the present value of cash flows.

The competing hypothesis is given various names. Ball (1972) calls it the "monopolistic hypothesis."[4] He argues that the literature assumes there are no alternative sources of information to accounting reports.

> Presumably, accountants possess a monopolistic influence over data used by the market, since it is assumed that either competing sources do not exist or (if they exist) they are not used. (Ball, 1972, p. 4)

Discriminating Between the Hypotheses

The early studies use three sets of accounting changes to discriminate between the competing hypotheses:

1. All accounting changes whether they affect taxes or not (e.g., Ball, 1972)
2. Accounting changes that do not affect taxes (e.g., Kaplan and Roll, 1972)
3. Accounting changes that affect taxes (e.g., Sunder, 1973, 1975)

One way in which to discriminate between the competing hypotheses is to examine the stock price changes associated with nontax-related accounting changes. Under the "no-effects" hypothesis, such changes should not have any stock price effects. The mechanistic hypothesis predicts that the accounting change affects the stock price in the direction it affects earnings. Kaplan and Roll (1972) test these contradictory predictions by examining stock price changes associated with accounting changes that do not affect taxes.

Ball (1972) takes a different approach. He argues that under the EMH and the CAPM, there is no observable stock price effect of an accounting change that affects taxes (specifically, the LIFO/FIFO change) at the time of announcement of the change. Thus, he investigates abnormal returns associated with all accounting changes and expects no abnormal returns. Ball implicitly assumes that, under the competing (mechanistic) hypothesis, accounting changes on average are accompanied by abnormal returns of a particular sign (presumably positive).

Sunder (1973, 1975) specifies contradictory predictions under the competing hypotheses for the stock price effects of changes in inventory methods. Clearly, a change from FIFO to LIFO affects future taxes and, hence, future cash flows. If LIFO is chosen for tax purposes, it also must be used for reporting purposes. Hence a change to LIFO for

---

[4] Another name is the "functional fixation" hypothesis.

reporting purposes generally implies a change for tax.[5] The LIFO switch usually decreases taxes and increases net cash flows. For this reason alone, ceteris paribus, LIFO increases the stock price. This increase is the opposite of the stock price effect predicted by the mechanistic hypothesis. That hypothesis predicts that the decreased earnings under LIFO will depress the stock price; in other words, the market ignores the effects on future cash flows.

The Kaplan and Roll, Ball, and Sunder studies led to numerous other studies that tried to discriminate between the competing hypotheses.[6] In sum the results of these studies provide no clear discrimination. Nevertheless, those studies are important because they demonstrate how theory progresses:

1. The studies and the literature that followed led to the development of a new theory. They showed that the assumption of zero transactions and information costs would not provide a descriptive theory of accounting practice. Transactions and information costs were then introduced to explain the manager's choice of accounting procedures (see Chapters 8 and 9).

2. The studies and subsequent literature uncovered many methodological problems and led to attempts to solve those problems.

The approach begun by Sunder (i.e., investigating the LIFO choice) has more potential for discriminating between the competing hypotheses. For that reason this chapter discusses later studies that attempt to discriminate using the LIFO change.

KAPLAN AND ROLL

The Changes Investigated

Kaplan and Roll (1972) investigate accounting changes that do not affect taxes. The particular changes Kaplan and Roll select are

1. The change, in 1964, by firms from a deferral method of accounting for the investment tax credit to the flowthrough method
2. The switchback, in the 1960s, by firms from accelerated depreciation to straight-line depreciation

[5] Prior to 1979 firms using LIFO for tax purposes had to use LIFO for external reporting and could not disclose in supplemental form earnings on any other basis. Beginning in 1979–80, companies were allowed to disclose what earnings and inventories would have been under some other inventory method.

[6] Space limitations preclude an exhaustive review of the literature, which includes Cassidy (1976), Harrison (1977), Archibald (1972), and Abdel-khalik and McKeown (1978). Also see Kaplan (1978) and Benston (1980) for literature reviews.

The investment tax credit was first introduced in 1962. It allowed companies purchasing certain new assets a direct reduction in taxes equal to 7 percent of the cost of those assets. For example, if a company purchased an eligible asset at a cost of $1,000, that company's income tax liability was reduced immediately by $70. When the credit was first introduced, the then existing accounting standard setting body, the Accounting Principles Board (APB) forbade firms from using the flow-through method and thereby reducing tax expense by the full amount of the credit in the year of acquisition. Rather, the APB allowed two methods of deferring the credit, both of which do not recognize the entire decrease in taxes ($70) as a reduction in expense in the year of acquisition. Under those two methods, either (1) the tax saving is brought into income over the life of the asset or (2) 48 percent of the tax saving is recognized in the year of acquisition and 52 percent is brought in over subsequent periods.

In 1964, the APB reversed its decision and allowed all the tax savings of the credit to be brought into income in the year of acquisition. While some companies remained on the deferral methods, many companies switched to flowthrough and thereby increased their reported earnings.[7] Note that the switch had no effect on taxes and that it was voluntary. In our example, the investment credit decreases taxes payable in the year of acquisition by $70 independent of the reporting method adopted.

The switchback to straight-line depreciation was popular in the 1960s, with entire industries switching in some years. In 1965 the paper companies switched back, and in 1968 the steel firms switched. The switchback has no effect on taxes. Between 1961 and 1972, 13 percent of the *Fortune* 500 and firms in *Accounting Trends and Techniques* switched back to straight-line depreciation (Holthausen, 1978, Table 1). (*Accounting Trends and Techniques* is issued by the AICPA and summarizes the reporting practices of 600 large and small companies.)

Sample

THE INVESTMENT TAX CREDIT

From *Accounting Trends and Techniques*, Kaplan and Roll identify 275 companies that changed from deferral to flowthrough and 57 that remained on deferral. The stock price behavior of the no-change sample is used as a control (comparison) for the stock price behavior of the sample of firms that change. Stock price behavior is investigated *at the time of announcement of the first annual earnings* that are affected by the change.

---

[7] Ball (1972, p. 31, fn. 33) reports that roughly 62 percent of firms on CRSP changed to the flowthrough method.

THE SWITCHBACK TO STRAIGHT-LINE DEPRECIATION

This sample is obtained from a survey of *Accounting Trends and Techniques* (1962–1968) and is cross-checked against other researchers' samples of switchback firms. The actual announcement dates of the switchback are obtained from the *WSJ*, as are the announcement dates of the first annual earnings affected by the switchback. In many cases they are the same date. Kaplan and Roll investigate the stock price changes associated with the switchback at both the earnings announcement date and the switchback announcement date.

Unlike the announcement dates for the investment tax credit change sample, those for the depreciation switchback sample are spread across quite a few years. Nevertheless, there is more clustering of events within years in the Kaplan and Roll sample than in the Ball and Brown or Foster samples of annual and quarterly earnings. Seventy percent of the announcements for the switchback sample occur in the three years: 1965, 1966, and 1968.

Methodology

Kaplan and Roll use abnormal rates of return to investigate the stock price changes at the time of accounting changes. They first estimate the following regression equation,

$$r_{i,t} = a_i r_{f,t} + b_i r_{m,t} + e_{i,t} \qquad (4.1)$$

where $r_{i,t}$ is the rate of return for firm i in week t, $r_{f,t}$ is the risk-free rate of return for week t, and $r_{m,t}$ is the market rate of return for week t. The 60 weeks around the earnings announcement are excluded from the estimation period because the competing hypothesis predicts non-zero abnormal returns during that period. If that prediction is true, and the observations are not excluded, some of that abnormal return is incorporated in the estimated parameters.

Abnormal rates of return are calculated as prediction errors from equation (4.1) for the weeks around the earnings announcement week. Average abnormal returns $(\bar{e}_t)$ and CARs are calculated for periods beginning week -30 and ending week $+29$. Defining CAR_T as the CAR for the period beginning with week -30 and ending with week T, the mechanistic hypothesis predicts $\bar{e}_0 > 0$ and $CAR_0 > 0$ (ceteris paribus) for the change and switchback samples because those firms have, in general, increased their earnings by changing. The no-effects hypothesis predicts $\bar{e}_0 = CAR_0 = 0$ for all samples (ceteris paribus).

Results

THE INVESTMENT TAX CREDIT

Figure 4.1 contains the results for the sample of firms that changed their accounting method for the investment tax credit. This figure is

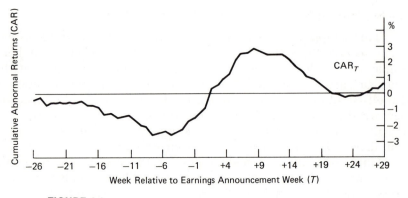

FIGURE 4.1

Cumulative abnormal rates of return (CAR$_T$) associated with investment tax credit changes

Source: R. Kaplan and R. Roll, "Investor Evaluation of Accounting Information: Some Empirical Evidence," *Journal of Business* 45 (April 1972), p. 237.

the graph of the cumulative abnormal rate of return, CAR$_T$. Figure 4.2 contains the same estimates for the control sample of firms that did not change their accounting method for the investment tax credit.

A striking aspect of Figures 4.1 and 4.2 is that CAR$_T$ is not as well behaved as the API and CAR graphs in Chapter 3 (Figures 3.1 and 3.2). The CARs do not move consistently in one direction prior to the earnings announcement date, and they are not flat after week 0. The lack of direction prior to the earnings announcement is consistent with the no-effects hypothesis.

At first glance, the movement in the CAR after the earnings announcement is inconsistent with the EMH. For example, the CAR for the control sample (Figure 4.2) increases from 1.96 percent in week 0 to 9.17 percent in week +29. That implies that an investor could earn an abnormal rate of return of 7.21 percent over those 29 weeks after the earnings announcement date. From the statistical tests presented by Kaplan and Roll, it appears that the postannouncement price movement is significant at least at the 20 percent probability level (two-tail test). This movement raises serious questions about the Kaplan and Roll methodology, questions that are addressed in the next subsection.

Ignoring the post announcement abnormal returns for the moment, Kaplan and Roll find that average abnormal returns in the week of the earnings announcement are 1.18 percent for the firms that change their investment tax credit method and .55 percent for the control sample. The 1.18 percent is significant at any reasonable

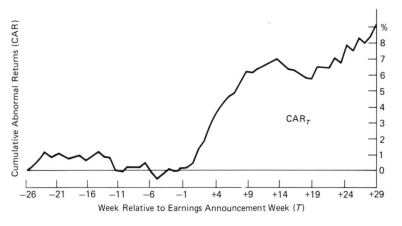

FIGURE 4.2

Cumulative abnormal rates of return (CAR$_T$) for the control sample

Source: R. Kaplan and R. Roll, "Investor Evaluation of Accounting Information: Some Empirical Evidence," *Journal of Business* 45 (April 1972), p. 237.

probability level consistent with the prediction that $\bar{e}_0 > 0$ for the investment tax credit change sample.[8] The .55 percent for the control sample is not significant at the .10 probability level.[9] Since neither the no-effects hypothesis nor the mechanistic hypothesis predicts $\bar{e}_0 \neq 0$ for the control group, this latter result is consistent with both hypotheses. Although Kaplan and Roll do not highlight the implication, on face value these two results—$\bar{e}_0 > 0$ for the change sample and $\bar{e}_0 = 0$ for the control sample—support the mechanistic hypothesis rather than the no-effects hypothesis.

The predictions for both the no-effects and mechanistic hypotheses rely on the ceteris paribus assumption. As we shall see in the next subsection, Kaplan and Roll's results raise serious doubts about the descriptive validity of the ceteris paribus assumption for the investment tax credit change and control samples.

---

[8] Kaplan and Roll calculate the 80 percent acceptance interval for $\bar{e}$ assuming abnormal returns have a symmetric stable distribution with a characteristic exponent of 1.6. The lower bound for that interval is .89 for $\bar{e}_0$ for the investment tax change sample indicating that $\bar{e}_0$ is significantly positive at the .10 probability level, given the prediction $\bar{e}_0 > 0$. Clearly, under those distributional assumptions, $\bar{e}_0$ would also be significant at much lower probability levels. It would be even more significant if abnormal returns are assumed to be normally distributed (i.e., the characteristic exponent is 2).

[9] Neither the no-effects hypothesis nor the mechanistic hypothesis predicts $\bar{e}_0 \neq 0$ for the control sample. Hence, we base this statement on a two-tail test.

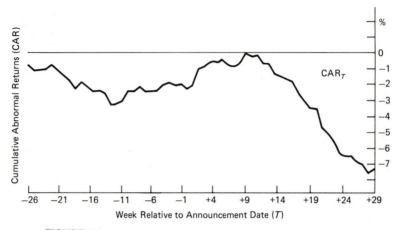

FIGURE 4.3

Cumulative abnormal rates of return associated with depreciation switchback

Source: R. Kaplan and R. Roll, "Investor Evaluation of Accounting Information: Some Empirical Evidence," *Journal of Business* 45 (April 1972), p. 239.

THE DEPRECIATION SWITCHBACK

Figure 4.3 presents the CARs for the depreciation switchback sample. Like the CAR graphs in Figures 4.1 and 4.2, the graph in Figure 4.3 is not well behaved. There is a pronounced downward trend in the CAR after the earnings announcement week, suggesting an ability to earn abnormal returns (a trading rule) after the earnings announcement. That implication is inconsistent with the EMH. Whether that trend is significant or not depends on distributional assumptions made for the abnormal returns. It is significant if the abnormal returns are assumed to be normal and insignificant if the returns are assumed to have a stable paretian distribution with a characteristic exponent of 1.6.

The average abnormal return in the week of announcement of the first annual earnings affected by the depreciation switch is .18 percent and is insignificantly different from zero. That result is inconsistent with the mechanistic hypothesis and consistent with the joint EMH, CAPM, and no transactions costs hypothesis.

Superficially Kaplan and Roll's results for the investment tax credit change and the depreciation switchback are contradictory. The investment tax credit results suggest the mechanistic hypothesis (i.e., the market is misled by the earnings effect of the change) is descriptive. But the depreciation switchback results are consistent with the no-effects hypothesis and suggest that the market is not misled by the switchback. Based on the CARs at week $+29$, Kaplan and Roll conclude that the market is not misled by either change. However, that conclusion is affected by methodological problems Kaplan and Roll discover in their study. The next section addresses those methodological problems and some others not discussed by Kaplan and Roll.

METHODOLOGICAL ISSUES IN THE KAPLAN AND ROLL STUDY

Throughout this discussion, the reader should keep in mind that we have the benefit of hindsight based on over a decade of research since the Kaplan and Roll study. For its time, Kaplan and Roll is an innovative and well-performed study.

For convenience we break the issues into two groups: (1) those arising from the specification of the hypotheses tested and (2) those relevant to the CAR or **event study** methodology. The break is not clean since some issues fit into both categories.

Specification of the Hypotheses Tested

The literature begun by Kaplan and Roll and by Ball (1972) aims to discriminate between the no-effects hypothesis and the mechanistic hypothesis that the market is misled by accounting procedures. However, most of the studies concentrate on testing one of the two hypotheses. In Kaplan and Roll and most other studies, the concentration is on the competing hypothesis—the hypothesis that the market is misled.

Kaplan and Roll present statistical tests of the **null hypothesis** that the average abnormal return in the week of announcement of the first annual earnings affected by the accounting change ($\bar{e}_0$) is zero. Thus, the **alternative hypothesis**, the hypothesis in which they are interested, is the hypothesis that the average stock price change is associated with the accounting change is not zero, $\bar{e}_0 \neq 0$ (i.e., the mechanistic hypothesis). Little effort is given to specifying and testing the no-effects hypothesis. Instead, the tendency is to accept the no-effects hypothesis if the null hypothesis is not rejected. This tendency is common in the literature and is inherited from tests of the EMH in finance. However, it is a tendency fraught with problems, as we shall see shortly.

Testing the mechanistic hypothesis is not easy. Most researchers who test the hypothesis are finance trained and are testing someone else's hypothesis. Those who advance the hypothesis that the market is misled are not empiricists and typically have not specified the hypothesis fully. For example, they don't specify exactly when the stock price reacts to the earnings effect of an accounting change. Hence, when Kaplan and Roll test the hypothesis by examining abnormal returns at the announcement of the first annual earnings affected by a change, a proponent of the mechanistic hypothesis could argue that the stock price is expected to react, but at some other time. Testing the mechanistic hypothesis is like trying to catch a slippery eel. We'll begin with a discussion of the problems of specifying the mechanistic hypothesis and then return to the issue of testing the no-effects hypothesis.

SPECIFYING THE MECHANISTIC HYPOTHESIS

Ideally, one would like to specify as **powerful** a **test** of the mechanistic hypothesis as possible. That is, holding the probability of a **Type 1 error** constant, one would like to minimize the probability of a **Type II error**. A Type I error occurs when the alternative hypothesis is accepted but the null hypothesis is correct. A Type II error occurs when the null hypothesis is accepted but the alternative hypothesis is correct. So in minimizing the probability of a Type II error, we are giving the alternative hypothesis the greatest possible chance to be accepted.

Because the proponents of the mechanistic hypothesis do not specify their hypothesis fully, it is difficult to specify a powerful test of that hypothesis. Nevertheless, if the hypothesis is to be tested, the attempt should be made. Kaplan and Roll fail to make their test as powerful as they could when they use a two-tail test on the abnormal returns. That implies an alternative hypothesis that the abnormal returns are not equal to zero. Given that Kaplan and Roll interpret the mechanistic hypothesis to imply that firms that change procedures increase reported earnings and stock prices (at least for the investment tax credit, see Kaplan and Roll, 1972, pp. 227–228), a more powerful test would be to specify the alternative hypothesis as $\bar{e}_0 > 0$ and the null hypothesis $\bar{e}_0 \leq 0$.

Another way to increase the power of the test is actually to calculate the earnings effect of the accounting change and then investigate the abnormal returns associated with the largest effects. For example, if they could obtain the data, Kaplan and Roll could investigate the abnormal returns associated with the firms for which the switch to the flowthrough method has the largest effect on earnings relative to firm value. Under the mechanistic hypothesis, those firms should have the largest abnormal returns, and so, if those returns exist, they are more likely to be observed.

Kaplan and Roll increase the power of their test using the earnings effects of the investment tax credit change. They investigate whether the change samples' abnormal rates of return vary with the firms' treatment of the deferred investment tax credit existing at the time of the change, that is, whether they include it in earnings or not. Half the firms transferred the deferred credit to current earnings, thereby inflating current earnings to the maximum extent. Ceteris paribus, under the mechanistic hypothesis, those firms should have the strongest stock price reaction. Thus, a more powerful test is to examine the abnormal returns for this subsample of firms. The other sample firms continued to amortize the deferred credit or transferred it to the income tax liability account and hence did not use it to increase current earnings. Kaplan and Roll find that this second group have patterns of CARs more consistent with the control group in Figure 4.2. In particular, their CARs prior to the earnings announcement, like those of the control group, exceed the CARs of the firms that took the deferred credit into current earnings. Kaplan and Roll interpret this result as indicating that poor performers change accounting methods to boost reported earnings.

As indicated, the timing of the stock price reaction to an accounting change is not specified under the mechanistic hypothesis. Kaplan and Roll choose the announcement of the first *annual* earnings affected by the change. This appears more appropriate for a test of the mechanistic hypothesis than the announcement of the accounting change itself if the change announcement is not accompanied by an earnings announcement. If the mechanistic hypothesis is correct and the stock market does not use available information to "undo" the effect of accounting change, why expect the market to react to an announced change in accounting method?

On the other hand, it would seem more appropriate to use the announcement date of the first earnings number affected by the change, whether it is a quarterly or annual earnings number. Kaplan and Roll use the first annual earnings number, which is not necessarily the first earnings disclosed using the changed accounting method. Suppose that the change affected all quarterly earnings by the same amount. Then under the mechanistic hypothesis we would expect a stock price change at the time of the first quarterly earnings affected by the change. Later quarterly earnings changes would be unaffected (see Chapter 6), so on average there would be no abnormal returns at those times. This suggests that Kaplan and Roll use the incorrect announcement date. Holthausen (1981) finds that of 75 depreciation switchbacks announced concurrently with earnings, 43 percent are concurrent with annual earnings and 57 percent with earlier quarterly earnings.

Kaplan and Roll separate the depreciation switchback firms into two subsamples based on whether or not the firms announce the switchback prior to, or at the time of, the year-end earnings report.

They find that the firms that announce the change prior to the year end have an increasing CAR prior to the earnings announcement. The other firms, which delay the announcement of the change until the year-end report, have a decreasing CAR prior to the announcement of earnings. This result is consistent with the hypothesis that the poorest performers try the hardest to hide that poor performance by changing accounting procedures.

TESTING THE NO-EFFECTS HYPOTHESIS

This is not emphasized in the early literature—Kaplan and Roll and Ball both test the mechanistic hypothesis only. This concentration on the mechanistic hypothesis is influenced by the evidence on the EMH in the finance literature. By 1972 the EMH was accepted by many finance researchers and finance-trained accounting researchers. Combined with the CAPM, the acceptance of the EMH led early accounting researchers to accept readily the no-effects hypothesis when, as the null hypothesis to the mechanistic hypothesis, it was not rejected.[10]

Acceptance of the null when it is not rejected in investigations of a particular alternative hypothesis can easily be a mistake. Such tests are not powerful tests of the null. To illustrate this point, consider the case of the drug thalidomide. Before its release, researchers investigated alternative hypotheses of particular types of side effects and tested the null hypothesis of no side effects. They designed powerful tests that minimized Type II errors for the particular alternative hypotheses investigated and failed to reject the null. If those particular side effects are the only possible side effects, the researchers also had powerful evidence for accepting the null. However, those particular side effects are not the only possible side effects of thalidomide. After acceptance of the null and release of thalidomide, it was discovered there was another side effect, another alternative hypothesis that had not been tested.

Clearly, there are an infinite number of alternative hypotheses to the null hypothesis of no stock price changes associated with an accounting change. We cannot test all of them. It is reasonable to accept the null after investigating the most obvious and plausible alternatives. However, failure to reject the null in investigations of one hypothesis (the mechanistic hypothesis) is a dangerous basis for acceptance of the null.

Given the tests of a multitude of alternative hypotheses to the EMH, the preceding criticism of researchers (including ourselves) seems

[10] This is not a statement about Kaplan and Roll (1972) and Ball (1972) who test the mechanistic hypothesis. Instead, it is a statement about the attitude of the researchers in the positive tradition of the time, as reflected in public policy discussions.

unjustified. However, the EMH alone does not imply the no-effects hypothesis. The no-effects hypothesis is due to the no-information or transactions costs assumptions.

Event Study Methodology

In event studies, observations are typically pooled across years and firms to generate CARs. The pooling is intended to average out stock price effects of variables other than the variable on which the CAR sample is constructed. For example, Ball and Brown (1968) calculate CAR equivalents for positive and negative unexpected earnings samples using 261 firms and nine years. In any one year the positive unexpected earnings sample does not include the same industry distribution of firms as the negative unexpected earnings sample. Earnings of firms in the same industry tend to fluctuate together. Hence, the CARs of the two samples for a particular year depend on industry variables. However, across the nine years industries are distributed randomly across both samples so that those industry variables are randomized and their average effects are removed in the pooled CARs.

There are two reasons to believe that the randomization of other variables has not been achieved in the CARs calculated by Kaplan and Roll and presented in Figures 4.1, 4.2, and 4.3. One reason is the *clustering* of observations in particular years and industries. The other is the evidence of a *selection bias* in the results.

CLUSTERING

Clustering of the investment tax credit changes and depreciation switches was noted when we described Kaplan and Roll's samples. Nearly all the investment tax credit changes occur in one year (1964) and the depreciation switches occur predominantly in three years (1965, 1966, and 1968) and are overrepresented in several industries (e.g., paper and steel).

The effect of the clustering is to cause cross-sectional dependence in the abnormal returns for the change samples. The variability of the abnormal returns for the announcement week is increased. As a result, the fluctuations that occur in the CAR following week 0 and the apparent abnormal returns on announcement of earnings affected by an investment tax credit change may be due to chance. Kaplan and Roll's significance tests assume cross-sectional independence in the abnormal returns and so overstate the significance of the CARs. Likewise, the significance of the positive average abnormal return on announcement of investment tax credit changes is overstated.

SELECTION BIAS

Kaplan and Roll argue that the evidence in Figures 4.1, 4.2, and 4.3 suggests that firms with poor stock price performance change accounting methods. The CAR of the investment tax credit change sample (Figure 4.1) is less than the CAR of the control sample (Figure 4.2) at the time of the earnings announcement. The CAR of the depreciation switch sample is negative at the earnings announcement. While it is not clear that the CAR difference and/or the negative CAR are significant, these observations raise questions about the CARs interpretations.

Consider the investment tax credit change and control samples. Their CARs are different prior to the earnings announcement. So separating the firms by whether they change the accounting method for the investment tax credit separates them on their stock price performance prior to the change. When a sample is selected on the basis of one variable (e.g., change in accounting method) and it is later found that the sample differs from the population of observations on the basis of some other variable (e.g., prior stock price performance), there is a **selection bias**. That other variable, or something related to it, could be responsible for the sample results. In other words, the ceteris paribus conditions are likely violated for these cross-sectional tests—other things are *not* constant.

If the accounting change firms have poor stock price performance prior to their announcement, it is likely that they have different quarterly earnings performance prior to the annual earnings announcement (given the evidence in Chapter 3). This suggests that the unexpected earnings announced in week 0 (adjusted for the accounting change) are not comparable for the change and control samples. If the earnings are not comparable, the interpretation of the abnormal returns in the announcement week is difficult. Given their discussion of selection bias, with hindsight Kaplan and Roll should have allowed for the unexpected earnings (adjusted for the change) in estimating the accounting change's effect on abnormal returns at the time of the annual earnings announcement.

Conclusion

Given the methodological problems of the Kaplan and Roll study, it is difficult to agree with Kaplan and Roll's conclusion that their study shows that earnings manipulation by accounting changes does not permanently affect stock prices.

Many of the methodological problems were not recognized immediately, so not all of them are addressed by the studies that followed the Kaplan and Roll study. The next study we discuss (Ball, 1972) was already in progress at the time of the Kaplan and Roll study, so it is not really a follow-up study. Nevertheless, it did attempt to solve the clustering problem.

BALL

The Changes Investigated

Ball (1972) investigates all types of accounting changes within a given time period. He does not restrict his sample to changes that do not affect taxes; changes to LIFO are included. Nevertheless, Ball argues that under the "no-effects" hypothesis, accounting changes have no observable effects on the stock price *at the time an accounting change is announced*.

Ball argues that there are no abnormal returns at the time of tax affecting accounting changes (e.g., LIFO) for three reasons. First, changes in the optimal tax inventory method are induced by changes in other variables affecting the manager's decisions (e.g., changes in factor prices). The net stock price effect of those other changes might offset the tax reduction under LIFO. Second, the tax effects are too small to be observed. Third, the changes in other variables occur before the accounting change enabling the market to predict the accounting change. Thus, the stock price reaction to the tax effects occurs before the accounting change, at the time of the other variable changes.

Ball's three arguments involve questions of fact (i.e., they are empirical issues). Such empirical questions can only be answered by investigating stock price changes at the time of procedure changes and observing whether they are consistent with expected cash flow effects of accounting changes. Hence, when we discuss Ball's results, we investigate the descriptive validity of his assumption that under the no-effect hypothesis, there are no tax effects of accounting changes on stock prices at the time of announcement.

Sample

Ball searches issues of *Accounting Trends and Techniques* from 1947 to 1960 (inclusive) for changes in accounting procedures. He finds 517 changes involving 365 firms. The requirement that the firms be on the CRSP file (so that rates of return are available) reduces the sample to 430 changes involving 300 firms. A further requirement that there be sufficient return data to estimate the market and other models reduces the final sample to 267 changes involving 197 firms. The first column

TABLE 4.1

Average Abnormal Return at Month Zero and Cumulative Abnormal Returns (CARs) by Subsample of Accounting Change After Allowing for Changes in Relative Risk

Category	Number of Changes	Average Error at 0	Cumulative from −109	Cumulative from −12
(a)	**Type of Accounting Change**			
Miscellaneous	3	.0215	.1111	−.0964
Inventory				
Miscellaneous	14	.0106	−.3904	−.0790
To LIFO	71	.0094	.0044	.0701
Depreciation				
Miscellaneous	12	−.0092	.0251	−.1073
To accelerated	46	−.0213	−.0918	−.0093
To straight line	5	.0157	.1897	−.0034
To replacement cost	12	.0050	−.3792	−.0054
Other expenses				
Miscellaneous	19	−.0036	.0449	.0217
To accrual	17	−.00021	−.1976	.0280
To cash	5	−.0019	−.1241	−.0206
Inclusion in net income	6	−.0059	−.4133	.0034
Revenue recognition	5	.0245	−.0068	.0430
Subsidiary accounting				
Miscellaneous	5	−.0018	−.1796	.0069
To inclusion in consolidation	26	.0072	.0646	−.0041
To exclusion from consolidation	15	.0132	.0749	−.0012
To equity for unconsolidated	3	.0132	.7270	.1098
To cash for unconsolidated	3	.0088	.1238	.0883
Average	267	.0012	−.0501	.0118
(b)	**Disclosure of Effect on Net Income**			
Effect disclosed				
Estimate given (in dollars)	108	.0068	−.1196	.0203
Described as immaterial, etc.	35	−.0094	.1789	.0193
Effect undisclosed	124	−.0001	−.0548	.0023

Source: R. J. Ball, "Changes in Accounting Techniques and Stock Prices," *Empirical Research in Accounting: Selected Studies 1972,* supplement to Vol. 10 of *Journal of Accounting Research* (1972), Table 6, p. 24.

in Table 4.1 summarizes the change samples by type of change and by whether or not the effect of the change on net income is disclosed.

Table 4.1 indicates that inventory changes (mainly LIFO changes) and depreciation changes (mainly to accelerated) are the most frequent changes in the sample. Both of these changes are likely to be associated with tax effects. The changes to accelerated depreciation methods for reporting purposes occur in the 1950s and are probably accompanied by changes for tax purposes.

The requirement that firms be on the CRSP file causes the most recent changes to be lost because of insufficient postchange stock price data. These are the changes whose effect on earnings had to be disclosed. The requirement truncates the sample from 430 to 267. That requirement also causes the omission from the final sample of most of the switchbacks from accelerated depreciation to straight line (the number falls from 25 to 5). Most of the changes *to* accelerated depreciation are retained in the 267 sample because they occur in the mid-1950s, so that sufficient postchange price data are available for these firms. Despite the loss of the more recent changes, the 267 sample is relatively uniformly spread over the 14-year period, reducing the clustering problem encountered by Kaplan and Roll. It should also be noted that Ball's sample does not overlap with Kaplan and Roll's sample so the results are independent of Kaplan and Roll's results.

Methodology and Results

Ball tests whether the average abnormal return in the announcement month of the annual earnings affected by a change is nonzero. To be a test of the null hypothesis for the mechanistic hypothesis, Ball must implicitly assume the *average* earnings effect of the change is nonzero. Ball's implicit assumption is consistent with the argument that managers tend to change accounting procedures to increase reported earnings. But including both earnings increasing and decreasing changes results in a weak test of the mechanistic hypothesis. Mixing the two types of changes reduces the average stock price effect and increases the probability of a Type II error.

To increase the power of the tests, Ball calculates abnormal rates of return by type of accounting change (i.e., for LIFO/FIFO changes, depreciation switches). Also, using the firms for which he is able to observe the earnings effect of the change, Ball calculates abnormal returns for changes that increase earnings and decrease earnings. These abnormal rates of return provide more powerful tests of the mechanistic hypothesis.

Ball also investigates whether an accounting change is associated with a change in the firm's risk. Finding an association, Ball calculates abnormal returns after adjusting for the change in risk.

Our discussion of Ball's methodology and results is broken into three parts:

1. Tests of the mechanistic hypothesis using the whole sample without adjustment for risk changes
2. Tests of the hypothesis that a risk change accompanies an accounting

change and tests of the mechanistic hypothesis using the whole sample with adjustment for risk changes and

3. Tests of the mechanistic hypothesis using subsamples with adjustment for risk changes

ABNORMAL RETURNS UNADJUSTED FOR RISK CHANGES FOR THE WHOLE SAMPLE

Ball estimates the market model regression over months -159 to -140 and $+20$ to $+90$. He excludes months -139 to $+19$ because monthly abnormal returns are systematically negative as early as month -139 (11 to 12 years before the earnings announcement). Ball finds that the change sample CAR drops continuously from month -140 to month -60 (approximately). The drop over that five- to six-year period is 30 percent (approximately). Given that the price drop finishes five years before the change, it is difficult to ascribe the price drop to the change itself. An alternative explanation is a selection bias similar to that observed in Kaplan and Roll; poor performers are more likely to change accounting techniques. However, if that explanation is correct, why do they wait five years to change procedures? There appears to be no price change associated with the earnings announcement, so the results are consistent with the no-effects hypothesis.

TESTS FOR RISK CHANGES AND ABNORMAL RETURNS ADJUSTED FOR RISK CHANGES

Ball hypothesizes that firms that change accounting procedures also experience risk changes. Ball's rationale for contemporaneous risk changes is plausible. We observe that firms in the same industry tend to follow the same procedures and that procedures vary across industries. Further, firms in the same industry tend to have similar β's. Thus, if a firm changes industries via mergers or spinoffs of divisions, it is likely to change both its accounting procedures and its β.

It is also plausible that some accounting changes, notably the change to LIFO, could themselves lead to changes in a firm's relative risk. For example, absent inventory stockouts, a firm's inventories and inventory prices are expected to increase in economic expansions. Thus, LIFO is likely to reduce taxes and increase cash flows in these periods. Also, the rate of return on the market is likely to be larger during expansions. On the other hand, in economic contractions, inventories are likely to be reduced so that under LIFO, inventory layers are "stripped." This causes the realization of holding gains and increased taxes (i.e., reduced cash flows relative to those under FIFO). At the same time, the market rate of return is likely to be below normal. The result is that LIFO could increase the covariance of the firm's cash flows with the market and increase the firm's β.[11]

Ball adjusts for risk changes by estimating a different β for each firm every month. To estimate the β of month t, the market model is estimated over the 50 months preceding month t, month t, and the 50 months succeeding month t. For example, the β for firm i for month -10 is estimated over the period month -60 to month $+40$.

Figure 4.4 plots the average β for the sample of accounting changes over the period -109 to month $+49$. As seen in that figure, the average β increases from .909 at month -109 to .995 at month 0 and to 1.028 at month $+49$. Ball doesn't report significance tests for this increase. However, this increase, if it is significant, occurs primarily between months -50 and $+49$. Other than that general observation, we cannot be more specific. The whole increase *could* occur at month 0 and be smoothed over the months between -50 and $+49$ by the method of estimation of the β. Alternatively, the increase could occur over several months beginning at month 0. (Remember, month -50 is the first month that month 0 enters the estimation of β).

Ball estimates β's by type of accounting change for months relative to the earnings announcement. The average estimated β for switches to LIFO increases from .990 in month -50 to 1.049 in month 0, consistent both with the hypothesis that firms changing to LIFO have become more risky and the hypothesis that a change to LIFO itself causes risk to increase. Further, the change in average β is not in the same direction for all types of accounting changes. For example, for the 12 miscellaneous depreciation changes, the average estimated β decreases, not increases, from month -50 to month $+49$.

Ball uses the β's estimated for each month to produce estimates of abnormal and cumulative abnormal rates of return adjusted for risk changes. Figure 4.5 graphs the resultant CARs. That figure illustrates that

1. Most of the stock price decrease accompanying an accounting change occurs by month -60, five years before announcement of the first annual earnings affected by the change. This result is consistent with the poor performers' selection bias. It does not suggest a stock price effect of the change, since it is unlikely the market price would fully incorporate the change five years in advance. While the selection bias relates to performance long before the change, it suggests that Ball (like Kaplan and Roll) should investigate the current unexpected earnings for the change sample.

2. The abnormal rate of return in month 0 is close to zero (and not statistically significant). *If* we accept Ball's assumption of no observable tax effects on stock price in month 0 and assume that the average

---

[11] See Biddle (1980) for a discussion of the factors affecting the LIFO-FIFO choice.

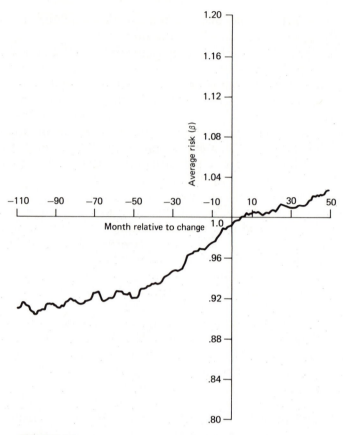

FIGURE 4.4

The average relative risk (β) surrounding changes in accounting procedures

Source: R. J. Ball, "Changes in Accounting Techniques and Stock Prices," *Empirical Research in Accounting: Selected Studies 1972*, supplement to Vol. 10 of *Journal of Accounting Research* (1972), Figure 4, p. 20.

unexpected annual earnings for the change sample is zero, the lack of any stock price effect in month 0 is consistent with the no-effects hypothesis.

The lack of a price change at month 0 being inconsistent with the mechanistic hypothesis depends on (a) the average effect of the accounting change on reported earnings and (b) the average unexpected earnings of the change sample. If the average effect is zero, and the average unexpected earnings for the change sample is zero, the observation of no price change at zero is also consistent with the mechanistic hypothesis. On the other hand, if the average earnings effect is positive and the

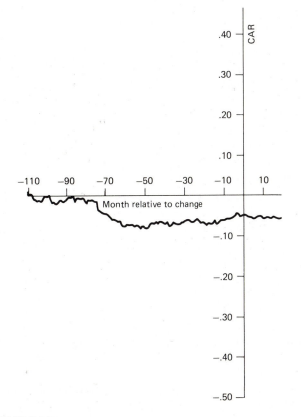

FIGURE 4.5

Cumulative abnormal rates of return (CARs) surrounding changes in accounting procedures after adjusting for changes in relative risk

> *Source:* R. J. Ball, "Changes in Accounting Techniques and Stock Prices," *Empirical Research in Accounting: Selected Studies 1972*, supplement to Vol. 10 of *Journal of Accounting Research* (1972), Figure 5, p. 22.

average unexpected earnings (adjusted for the earnings effect) is zero, the observation of no price change is inconsistent with the mechanistic hypothesis. Unfortunately, Ball cannot provide evidence on the average earnings effect for all 267 changes because this information is not available. He provides evidence on the stock price effect, after controlling for the sign of the earnings effect, for the changes where the earnings effect is disclosed. However, he does not produce any evidence on the average unexpected earnings (adjusted for the earnings effect) for the changes, even when the earnings effect is disclosed.

3. There is virtually no abnormal rate of return after zero, consistent with the EMH.

ABNORMAL RETURNS ADJUSTED FOR RISK CHANGES FOR PARTICULAR
ACCOUNTING CHANGES

Table 4.1 presents the abnormal rate of return at month 0 and
the CARs from month −109 to 0 and from −12 to 0 by type of
procedure change. The table suggests that either Ball's assumption of
no observable tax effects of procedure changes is incorrect or that the
average unexpected earnings (adjusted for the earnings effect of a
change) is not zero for the change sample.

Cash flow effects are associated with LIFO switches. For the 71
such switches, the CAR over the 12 months up to and including the
month of announcement is .0701 and is likely to be significant (Ball
does not provide significance tests). The abnormal rate of return at
month zero for LIFO switches is .0094 (.9 of 1 percent), which is positive
but almost certainly insignificant.

LIFO switches tend to reduce reported earnings. If we assume
that the average unexpected earnings (adjusted for the effect of the
switch) for LIFO switches is zero and no observable tax effects, the lack
of significant abnormal return in month 0 is consistent with the no-
effects hypothesis and inconsistent with the mechanistic hypothesis.
However, under the zero unexpected earnings assumption, how can
we explain the 7 percent abnormal return in the 12 months preceding
month 0? It is inconsistent with both hypotheses.

One plausible explanation consistent with the no-effects hypothesis
is that the abnormal returns are due to the reduction in taxes caused
by the LIFO switch. Another nonmutually exclusive, plausible explanation is that firms changing to LIFO have experienced improved
current and/or expected future earnings and, thus, their stock prices
have risen. This latter explanation implies a selection bias, that is, the
ceteris paribus conditions do not hold.

Brown (1980) provides evidence that firms switching to LIFO have
substantially improved earnings in the year of, or year following, the
switch. Firms switching to LIFO in 1974 would have experienced
earnings increases of 47 percent over 1973 levels had they not adopted
LIFO. Firms switching in 1975 had 1976 earnings (under LIFO) that
increased 66 percent over 1975 levels. This evidence indicates a selection
bias in the firms that switch to LIFO. Those firms have positive current
unexpected earnings and an increase in their expected future earnings.
Both would lead to an abnormal return in the 12 months preceding
month 0. This selection bias suggests that it is important to control for
contemporaneous unexpected earnings when investigating stock price
changes associated with accounting changes. Such control is also necessary to determine whether any of the 7 percent abnormal return is
due to tax benefits of the LIFO switch.

TABLE 4.2

Relation Between the Sign of the Cumulative Abnormal Rate of Return over the 12 Months up to and Including the Month of Announcement of an Accounting Change and the Sign of the Effect on Earnings of the Change

	Sign of Cumulative Abnormal Returns from Month -12 *to 0*		
Earnings Effect	$+$	$-$	Total
Positive	48	27	75
Negative	21	12	33
Total	69	39	108

Source: R. J. Ball, "Changes in Accounting Techniques and Stock Prices," *Empirical Research in Accounting: Selected Studies 1972*, supplement to Vol. 10 of *Journal of Accounting Research* (1972), Table 7a, p. 28.

As noted, Ball's tests using the whole sample of accounting changes assume that the average earnings effect of the changes is nonzero. A more powerful test of the competing hypothesis is whether stock prices increase when the accounting change increases reported earnings and decrease when the change decreases earnings. Ball investigates this relation for the 108 changes where the sign of the effect on earnings of the accounting change is revealed in the annual report.

Table 4.2 presents the contingency table for the relation between the sign of the earnings effect and the CAR over the 12 months ending in month 0. The χ^2 is .03 and insignificant, indicating no relation. The χ^2 for the relation between the sign of the earnings effect and the sign of the abnormal return in month 0 is .05, which is also insignificant. These results assume more importance when one recalls that Ball and Brown (1968) obtain a significant relation ($\chi^2 = 28$) between the sign of the annual earnings change and the sign of the average abnormal rate of return in the announcement month. The inference, given ceteris paribus, is that the stock market can discriminate between changes in reported earnings that do and do not reflect cash flow changes. The evidence indicates that the stock price reacts to annual earnings changes that reflect real economic changes (Ball and Brown) but does not react to earnings changes that result only from accounting changes that have no cash flow effects (Ball).

The absence of a relation between the sign of the earnings effect and the stock price change in Ball's study is inconsistent with the mechanistic hypothesis, *if* we assume ceteris paribus. The ceteris paribus is important because it is possible that the earnings effect of the accounting change is offset by earnings changes resulting from cash flow changes. Suppose that there is a selection bias such that firms that change procedures and increase (decrease) earnings would have had earnings declines (increases) otherwise. Then, if the market is misled by accounting changes, it is quite possible to observe no relation between the earnings effect of the change and the CAR for the 12 months ending in month 0.

Conclusion

The Ball study was in progress at the time of the Kaplan and Roll study, so it is not surprising that it has many of the same methodological problems. Like Kaplan and Roll, Ball concentrates on testing the mechanistic hypothesis and, hence, provides very weak evidence on the no-effects hypothesis.

Restricting the study to tests of the mechanistic hypothesis, Ball also fails to account for selection biases associated with accounting changes (e.g., that change firms' average unexpected earnings adjusted for the effects of accounting changes are not likely to be zero). The potential for such selection biases is revealed by Kaplan and Roll's *results* and by Ball's *results* for LIFO switches, so it is difficult to criticize Kaplan and Roll and Ball for failing to take account of it. We expect to, and do, observe later studies learning from the early studies and addressing the contemporaneous unexpected earnings problem.

Ball avoids the problem of accounting changes being clustered in time and industries by including all types of accounting changes in his sample. However, this procedure leads to weak tests of the mechanistic hypothesis when Ball uses the whole sample. The average earnings effect of the changes in the sample may be zero, so the mechanistic hypothesis could predict zero abnormal returns for the sample at the time of announcement of the first annual earnings affected by the change.

Restricting the study to the 108 procedure changes whose earnings effects are disclosed increases the power of Ball's tests. However, the inconsistency of the lack of association between the earnings effect and abnormal returns with the mechanistic hypothesis is undercut by the potential selection biases with respect to contemporaneous earnings.

Ball's and Kaplan and Roll's tests are not powerful tests of the no-effects hypothesis because they test predictions of no stock price effects. A more powerful test can be generated for the no-effects hypothesis by using nonzero stock price effect predictions. Such predictions can be derived for changes in inventory methods because they affect taxes. A third early study (Sunder, 1973, 1975) tests such predictions. The inventory method studies that follow Sunder's provide the best opportunities to discriminate between the no-effects hypothesis and the mechanistic hypothesis.

STUDIES OF CHANGES IN INVENTORY PROCEDURES

The mechanistic hypothesis predicts that firms switching to LIFO thereby lowering earnings have *negative* abnormal returns on announcement of the lower earnings. Under the no-effects hypothesis, the market "sees through" accounting changes that are publicly known, so the abnormal return associated with the change occurs when the market learns of the change, presumably on announcement of the change. That announcement can occur before, at the time of, or after the announcement of the first annual earnings affected by the change. Assuming the managers of firms switching to LIFO do so to reduce the present value of tax payments, there should be *positive* abnormal returns associated with the change announcement.

Sunder

Sunder (1973, 1975) realizes the potential of the LIFO changes to discriminate between the two hypotheses (no effects and mechanistic). He investigates the abnormal returns and risk changes associated with changes to and from LIFO. However, Sunder's tests are designed to test the mechanistic hypothesis and do not represent powerful tests of the no-effects hypothesis. He investigates CARs for the fiscal year in which the change occurs on the assumption that most annual earnings are known by the fiscal year end. He doesn't identify the switch's announcement date and investigate the abnormal returns at that time.

In addition, Sunder does not remedy some of the methodological problems present in the studies that precede his (Kaplan and Roll, 1972; Ball, 1972). In particular, Sunder does not allow for the contemporaneous earnings selection bias. He doesn't allow for the tendency of firms that switch to LIFO to have positive unexpected earnings in the year of the switch.

SAMPLE AND METHODOLOGY

Sunder's sample consists of 118 firms switching to LIFO and 21 firms abandoning LIFO in the 1946–1966 period. To estimate the market model, he uses a regression technique that allows β to change over time. Using this technique, Sunder obtains estimates of β for each of the 24 months surrounding the time of the procedure change ($t = -11, \ldots, +12$). He uses those β estimates to calculate a cross-sectional average estimated β by month relative to the announcement month ($\bar{b}_t$).

Abnormal returns for each month are the residuals from the estimation of the market model. The average abnormal return for each

TABLE 4.3

Average β of Stocks of Firms Switching to and from LIFO by Month Relative to End of Fiscal Year of the Switch

Month	118 Switches to LIFO	21 Switches from LIFO
−11	1.058	1.090
−5	1.086	1.111
0	1.102	1.065
+12	1.115	1.032

Source: S. Sunder, "Stock Price and Risk Related to Accounting Changes in Inventory Valuation," *Accounting Review* 50 (April 1975), Table 1, p. 312.

month relative to month 0 is the cross-sectional average $(\bar{e}_t)$. CAR_t is just the sum of the e_t's from month −11 to month t.

RESULTS—β CHANGE

Table 4.3 lists the $\bar{b}_t$'s for firms switching to and from LIFO by month. Month 0 is the last month of the fiscal year of the switch. The average estimated β for the firms switching to LIFO increases from 1.058 at month −11 to 1.115 at month +12, a 5.4 percent increase. Ball found that the average β's of his sample of LIFO switches increased from .99 in month −50 to 1.049 in month 0, a 6.0 percent increase. Thus, Sunder confirms the observation that risk increases contemporaneously with a switch to LIFO.[12]

The finding that β increases with a switch to LIFO is strengthened by the observation in Table 4.3 that risk *decreases* when LIFO is abandoned. In month −11 the average β for the 21 switches from LIFO is 1.090, and in month +12 it is 1.032, a drop of 5.3 percent.

As discussed previously, the LIFO accounting method could contribute to risk changes. The adoption of LIFO could cause relative risk to increase if inventory declines do not occur as frequently in economic expansions as in contractions. This evidence is consistent with that hypothesis.

RESULTS—ABNORMAL RATES OF RETURN

Figure 4.6 graphs the CARs for the switches to LIFO. The CAR is 4.7 percent over the 12 months up to and including the last month of the fiscal year of the change. The CAR obtained by Ball for the 12 months ending in the earnings announcement month is 7 percent.

[12] These are not independent tests since the two samples contain many of the same firms.

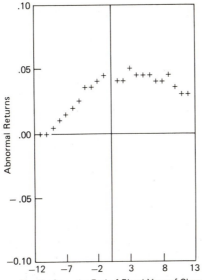

FIGURE 4.6

Cumulative abnormal rates of return around the time of a change to LIFO

> *Source:* S. Sunder, "Stock Price and Risk Related to Accounting Changes in Inventory Valuation," *Accounting Review* 50 (April 1975), Figure 1, p. 313.

Thus, Sunder's results replicate Ball's in that we observe abnormal price increases associated with switches to LIFO. There is an insufficient number of switches from LIFO to obtain any interpretable results from the CAR.

The results in Figure 4.6 are consistent with both the no-effects and mechanistic hypotheses. Given the contemporaneous earnings selection bias, earnings could increase in the switch year more than sufficiently to offset the earnings reduction due to the LIFO switch. Because they lack unexpected earnings control, these LIFO tests cannot discriminate between the no-effects and mechanistic hypotheses.

Many firms do not publicly announce LIFO switches. The first published information on the change (the annual report) is issued months after the fiscal year end. If the market learns of a switch on release of the annual report, the month 0 CAR of 4.7 percent does not incorporate the stock price effect of that switch.

Sunder also has a clustering problem similar to that of Kaplan and Roll. The last month of the fiscal year of the LIFO switch is between

December 1950 and December 1952 for 40 percent of the sample (see Sunder, 1973, Table 2c, p. 13).

CONCLUSION

In choosing inventory method changes, Sunder pinpoints accounting procedure changes that have greater potential for discriminating between the no-effects and mechanistic hypotheses. Unfortunately, not controlling for contemporaneous unexpected earnings prevents such discrimination. The studies of Ricks (1982) and Biddle and Lindahl (1982) address those methodological problems in their investigations of the abnormal returns associated with inventory procedure changes.[13]

Ricks

Ricks (1982) attempts to control for the unexpected increase in earnings associated with LIFO switches in his study of firms that switched to LIFO *in 1974*. The use of changes in only one year obviously introduces the clustering problem, but Ricks attempts to reduce that problem by using samples of change and no-change firms matched on industry as well as on unexpected earnings.

THE SELECTION BIAS

In 1974, there was a relatively high level of inflation, and over 400 firms on the NYSE and ASE switched to LIFO. The sample firms include those on *Compustat* that were listed on the NYSE or ASE and that had a ratio of inventories to total assets greater than 5 percent. After exclusions, Ricks has 354 firms changing to LIFO and 693 firms not changing. He compares the attributes of firms that did and didn't switch and finds that if the change firms had not switched, the average percentage increase in their earnings per share for 1974 would have been 47 percent. Earnings are calculated *as if* they had not switched. The average change in earnings per share for nonchange firms is −2 percent. The difference is statistically significant at the .05 level, so discrimination between the joint and competing hypotheses requires control of this selection bias.

CONTROL OF THE SELECTION BIAS

Ricks attempts to control for the earnings and the other unspecified selection biases by matching his change and no-change firms by industry (two-digit Standard Industrial Classification (SIC) code) and on the

---

[13] Other studies of the stock price changes associated with LIFO changes include Abdel-khalik and McKeown (1978) and Brown (1980). However, these studies do not deal with the methodological problems as well as Ricks (1982) and Biddle and Lindahl (1982) and are not discussed in this chapter.

percentage change in earnings.[14] Ricks matches on the latter variable using the 1974 earnings, assuming that those firms had not changed to LIFO ("as if" earnings). The matching procedure yields 275 matched pairs of change and no-change firms. The average percentage earnings change is 30 percent for the change firms (assuming they had not changed) and 28 percent for the no-change firms.

RETURN RESULTS

Ricks defines month 0 as either (1) the month of announcement of the LIFO change if the change was announced (40 percent of the sample) or (2) the month of the preliminary annual earnings announcement if the change was not announced. He calculates the difference in the CARs to month 0 for the change and no-change samples.

Figure 4.7 graphs the differences in CARs for the 275 pairs matched on as if earnings. The difference in cumulative returns fluctuates around zero prior to month −1 and then falls by approximately 8 percent over the next three months. During those three months information becomes available that the change firms will not report as if earnings, that lower earnings will be reported (only 5 percent of the firms announce the LIFO change prior to the fourth quarter). This difference in stock price behavior is significant and consistent with the mechanistic hypothesis. The market appears to be misled by the drop in earnings caused by the LIFO change.

Ricks repeats his stock price analysis using weekly rates of return, defining month 0 as the preliminary earnings announcement week. The CAR difference begins to drift downward six weeks before the earnings announcement. By week 0 the cumulative difference is −5 percent. The difference in week 0 is approximately −2 percent and is significant at the .005 level. Since the firms have been matched on "as if" earnings, the difference is presumably due to the earnings effect of the LIFO switch. The result is consistent with the mechanistic hypothesis. It is inconsistent with the no-effects hypothesis given the monthly results.[15]

The results are reinforced when Ricks correlates the earnings effect of the change for the change firms with the difference in returns. The earnings effect is calculated as the difference between the 1974 "as

[14] Ricks also matches on three-digit SIC codes and on reported earnings with similar results.

[15] If the market learns that the earnings drop is due to the LIFO switch *after* the earnings announcement, a negative abnormal return in week 0 could be consistent with the no-effects hypothesis. However, in that case the negative abnormal return would be completely recovered when the market learns of the LIFO switch. SEC filings would make that information publicly available by month +4, and negative returns are not recovered by month +4 in Figure 4.7

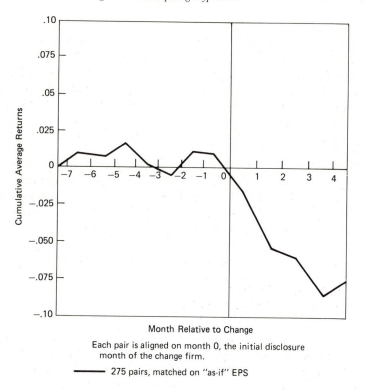

Each pair is aligned on month 0, the initial disclosure
month of the change firm.

——— 275 pairs, matched on "as-if" EPS

FIGURE 4.7

*Cumulative average monthly return differences (average raw return
for the change firms minus the average raw return for the no-change
firms)*

Source: W. Ricks, "The Market's Response to the 1974 LIFO Adoptions,"
Journal of Accounting Research 20 (Autumn 1982, Part 1), Figure 1, p.
375.

if" earnings and the 1974 reported earnings divided by the 1973
earnings. The return difference between the change and no-change
firms is calculated for periods as short as day 0 (the day of the
preliminary earnings announcement) and as long as the 11-week period
surrounding day 0. In every case, the correlation between the earnings
difference and the return difference is negative and significant at the
.05 probability level.[16]

---

[16] Ricks, like Ball and Sunder, tests for β changes around the LIFO switch. The
postchange β's for the change firms are insignificantly higher than the prechange β's (.94
versus .93). However, the no-change firms have a significant decrease in β's over the
same period (from 1.01 to .96). Hence, there is a relative increase in risk for the LIFO

CONCLUSION

The evidence presented by Ricks favors the mechanistic hypothesis over the no-effects hypothesis. The prime methodological problem is the clustering of changes in 1974. It is possible that because of this clustering, a variable related to the LIFO switch is not randomized out and could explain the different return behavior for the change and no-change firms.

If the market capitalizes the tax savings of the LIFO switch, we expect systematic differences between the change and no-change firms' abnormal returns. For example, the decision to change to LIFO is based on the expected rate of inflation for the goods in inventory. So the expected inflation rate is likely to be different for the two sets of firms. The managers of the firms self-select into the change and no-change samples based on economic variables such as relative price changes. Those economic variables could explain Ricks' results.

Biddle and Lindahl (1982) suggest such a self-selection bias. They suggest that the change and no-change firms are affected differently by the 1973–1975 recession. In Figure 4.7 the change firms have significantly lower returns than the no-change firms over the period from month −1 to month +3. Since most firms have December 31 fiscal years, that period corresponds to December 1974 to March 1975 for Ricks's sample. Although it isn't reported in Figure 4.7, Ricks's change firms have significantly higher returns than do his no-change firms in the eight months following month +4. That period would tend to be April 1975 to November 1975 (see Biddle and Lindahl, 1982, pp. 557–558). These differences in stock price performance for change and no-change firms coincide with a steep decline in industrial production from October 1974 to March 1975 and a steady increase in production thereafter (Biddle and Lindahl, 1982, p. 558). This evidence suggests that significant economic differences exist between the two samples and that an important variable is omitted from Ricks's explanation of the return difference for the two samples.

Biddle and Lindahl

Biddle and Lindahl (1982) use a different methodology to avoid the self-selection bias inherent in the use of a control sample of non-LIFO users to control for the unexpected earnings selection bias. Applying this methodology, they conclude that the evidence is consistent with the no-effects hypothesis.

---

change firms. Given the market return behavior in 1974, this difference would tend to reduce the difference in CARs found for the change and no-change samples. So the evidence for the mechanistic hypothesis cannot be explained by risk changes.

METHODOLOGY

Biddle and Lindahl adopt a direct approach to determining the extent to which the market reacts to tax savings associated with a LIFO change. They estimate the following regression using firms that change to or increase their use of LIFO:

$$\text{CAR}_i = c_0 + c_1 \log \frac{\text{TSAV}_i}{S_i} + c_2 \frac{\Delta A_i^*}{S_i} + u_i \qquad (4.2)$$

where CAR_i = the cumulative abnormal rate of return for firm i over the 15-month period ending in month $+3$ when month 0 is the end of the fiscal year in which the LIFO change takes place

TSAV_i = the tax savings from the LIFO change in the year of the change

S_i = the market value of equity at the beginning of the fiscal year of the change

ΔA_i^* = the change in earnings calculated as if the change had not been made (i.e., the "as if" change in earnings)

u_i = an error term

The abnormal returns are cumulated over 15 months because it isn't apparent when the information on the tax savings becomes available to the market. Lengthening the interval over which abnormal returns are calculated increases the likelihood that any abnormal returns associated with the tax savings are included. On the other hand, it increases measurement error because abnormal returns due to other factors are included.

Tax savings are estimated by taking the difference between the disclosed effect of the change on cost of goods sold and the disclosed effect on after-tax earnings. Obviously, the estimated tax savings varies negatively with the effect of the change in reported earnings.

Given that abnormal returns are measured over the time period in which annual earnings are determined and revealed to the market, Biddle and Lindahl control for unexpected annual earnings using the change in "as if" earnings($\Delta A_i^*/S_i$). The effect of risk changes are investigated by calculating abnormal returns using β's estimated both before and after the LIFO change.

The coefficient of unexpected earnings (c_2) is predicted to be positive as in Beaver, Clarke, and Wright (1979) (see Chapter 3). If the market capitalizes the tax savings, the coefficient of tax savings (c_1) is also predicted to be positive. However, the mechanistic hypothesis predicts that coefficient to be negative because the tax savings serve as a surrogate for the effect of the change on reported earnings.

SAMPLE AND RESULTS

Biddle and Lindahl's sample is 311 LIFO change firms and spans the years 1973 through 1980. But over half the sample, 183 firms, are clustered in 1974. They find that the c_1 and c_2 coefficients are positive and statistically significant. That is, the larger the tax savings, the larger the change in the value of the firm. Similarly, the larger the unexpected "as if" earnings, the higher the value of the firm. These results are consistent with the EMH and the capitalization of the tax savings and are inconsistent with the mechanistic hypothesis.

Over half of Biddle and Lindahl's sample have decreases in risk, a finding that is inconsistent with Ball, Sunder, and Ricks. The coefficient of tax savings is still positive and significant after accounting for the risk changes.

One methodological problem with the study is the clustering of the observations in time and in particular industries. The results are primarily due to 1974 changes. The clustering means that there is cross-sectional correlation in the data that will tend to understate the standard errors of, and overstate the significance of, the coefficients c_1 and c_2.

Perhaps a more important problem is discovered when Biddle and Lindahl estimate equation (4.2) using abnormal returns for the individual quarters of 1974. The coefficient of the tax savings variable is significantly positive only for the regressions estimated using the first and third quarters of 1974. It is significantly negative for the fourth quarter, a quarter in which the change tends to be announced. Biddle and Lindahl explain this result by suggesting that it could be due to measurement errors in abnormal returns (see Biddle and Lindahl, 1982, p. 581). Their measurement error explanation does not rule out the mechanistic hypothesis but rather is another competing hypothesis.

CONCLUSION

Biddle and Lindahl's argument that Ricks's results are influenced by a self-selection bias is plausible, and it is consistent with macroeconomic data. Their own results from using a 15-month cumulation period for abnormal returns (which confirm the joint hypothesis and reject the mechanistic hypothesis), combined with this argument, suggest that the no-effects hypothesis rather than the competing hypothesis is descriptive. However, the negative coefficient of tax savings for the fourth quarter of 1974 confuses the issue. More empirical research into the fourth quarter effect and the contradictory results of Ricks (1982) and Biddle and Lindahl (1982) will undoubtedly be forthcoming.

SUMMARY

A common hypothesis in the accounting literature prior to the introduction of the EMH, CAPM, and positive theory was that the stock market is misled by changes in accounting procedures. Such a hypothesis contradicts the EMH, which implies that the stock market reacts in an unbiased fashion to all information, including information that accounting procedures have changed. The natural outcome, given the early empiricists' adherence to scientific methodology, was an attempt to discriminate empirically between the two hypotheses.

The EMH has no predictions about the direction or sign of stock price changes associated with accounting changes. Its only prediction is that any stock price changes accompanying accounting changes are such that the resultant stock price is an unbiased estimate of the stock's future value. Prediction of stock price changes requires a valuation model. Influenced by the finance literature, the early researchers adopted the CAPM and its assumptions of no information and transaction costs. The only potential cash flow effect of accounting procedures was assumed to be taxes. Thus they predicted that no stock price changes would accompany accounting changes unless those changes affected taxes.

The competing hypothesis (the mechanistic hypothesis) has a contradictory prediction (i.e., that an accounting change that increases earnings increases stock prices). The earliest researchers attempted to discriminate between the two contradictory predictions. Kaplan and Roll (1972) investigated stock price changes associated with changes in procedures for the investment tax credit and depreciation switchbacks using the event study methodology introduced to accounting by Ball and Brown (1968). Ball (1972) investigated the stock price effects of all types of accounting changes, arguing that the stock price effect of any changes affecting taxes would not influence the predictions.

Both studies revealed methodological problems associated with using event studies to test the stock price effects of accounting changes. A problem observable in the results of both is a selection bias in terms of contemporaneous unexpected earnings that prevents the "averaging out" of variables other than accounting changes. A second problem present in the Kaplan and Roll study is the clustering of observations in time and industries. That clustering also leads to the result that variables other than accounting changes do not average out. A third problem Ball's study reveals also involves the violation of the ceteris paribus assumption—the risk of a firm's stock changes when accounting procedures change.

The early studies concentrate on testing the mechanistic hypotheses. However, failure to reject the null of that hypothesis provides very weak evidence on the no-effects hypothesis. This methodological problem and those in the preceding paragraph reduce the ability of the early studies to discriminate between the no-effects and mechanistic hypotheses.

A more powerful test of the no-effects hypothesis is a test of a nonzero stock price change prediction. Such a prediction can be generated from the no-effects hypothesis for accounting changes that affect taxes. Sunder (1973, 1975) led the literature in this direction by trying to discriminate between the two competing hypotheses using LIFO and FIFO changes. Sunder's study, however, is subject to the clustering and contemporaneous unexpected earnings selection bias problems.

Eventually, studies attempted to discriminate between the hypotheses using LIFO changes and controlling for the contemporaneous unexpected earnings selection bias. Ricks (1982) controls the selection bias problem by matching firms that change to LIFO with firms that do not change but have approximately the same earnings change. He finds evidence consistent with the mechanistic hypothesis and inconsistent with the no-effects hypothesis.

Biddle and Lindahl (1982) argue that Ricks's matching procedure introduces a self-selection bias that can explain Ricks's results. They concentrate on LIFO change firms, controlling the earnings selection bias using unexpected earnings as an explanatory variable when testing the effect of LIFO tax savings on abnormal rates of return. Biddle and Lindahl's results are consistent with the no-effects hypothesis and inconsistent with the mechanistic hypothesis. However, those results are not definitive because the stock price effects of the tax savings are concentrated in early quarters and because of clustering problems.

The way the discriminatory tests developed illustrates the way studies build on previous studies. Problems discovered in one study are addressed by a later study. The literature gradually iterates toward more powerful tests, tests that can better discriminate. No early study can hope to be definitive. The development process shows that progress is made by attempting to answer the questions. The more powerful tests used by Biddle and Lindahl are possible because of the efforts of the pioneers, Kaplan and Roll, Ball and Sunder.

The literature, the leading articles of which are summarized in this chapter, had an important effect that has not been discussed: it caused researchers to ask questions that led to a related, but different literature on the stock price effect of accounting changes. One of the questions raised is, Why do whole industries change accounting procedures (e.g., paper and steel in Kaplan and Roll's sample) when such changes are costly and have no beneficial effects on stock price? Those questions, in turn, led some researchers to drop the zero information and transaction costs assumptions used in the studies discussed in this chapter and use those costs to attempt to explain accounting changes.

The empirical studies of the effect of information and transaction costs on the manager's choice of accounting procedures are reported in Chapter 11. Studies of the stock price effects of changes in accounting procedures are summarized in Chapter 12. The thrust of that literature is to explain accounting procedures, *not* to discriminate between the EMH and the hypothesis that the market is misled by accounting changes.

CHAPTER FIVE

Accounting Data, Bankruptcy, and Risk

Chapter 3 found that accounting earnings reflect factors affecting stock prices and that earnings convey information on those factors to the stock market. However, earnings is not the only accounting number available to investors in the capital market. Corporations' annual reports and SEC filings provide much more accounting data (including balance sheet data and earnings components, such as revenues and expenses). Investors, financial analysts, and others appear to use these data in investment decisions. Such use suggests that these other data, like earnings, reflect factors affecting the market value of assets.

The apparent use of nonearnings accounting data for valuation purposes, the positive tradition of explaining such observed phenomena, and the influence of finance (the capital asset pricing model, CAPM) led early positive accounting researchers to investigate whether accounting data reflect factors affecting security valuation. The literature begins even before Ball and Brown (1968) (e.g., Horrigan, 1966) and investigates factors entering the CAPM. Under that model (see Chapter 2), an asset's market value is a function of its expected future cash flows, the risk of its future cash flows (β), the market price of risk, and the risk-free rate of return. The risk-free rate and the price of risk are determined in the capital market and are unlikely to be related to firm-specific variables. A firm's accounting data are likely to be more useful in estimating the firm's securities' expected cash flows and risk. So it is not surprising that studies provide evidence accounting data are useful for estimating these last two factors.

This chapter summarizes studies of nonearnings accounting data useful in security valuation. Three sets of studies are reviewed. First there is a review of studies of the use of accounting data to predict bankruptcy. Bankruptcy reduces the firm's future cash flows, so estimation of the firm's expected future cash flows involves assessing the probability of bankruptcy and its accompanying cash outflows. Next described are studies of the association between accounting data and the systematic risk of stocks. Finally, there is a review of studies involving accounting data, bond ratings, and bond prices. A bond's rating is a surrogate for its systematic risk.

ACCOUNTING DATA AND BANKRUPTCY

The Nature of Bankruptcy

Corporate bankruptcies are "proceedings which are undertaken under bankruptcy laws when a corporation is unable to pay or reach agreement with its creditors outside of court" (Warner, 1977, p. 241). Bankruptcy proceedings begin when the firm, or some other party, files for court assistance in settling the firm's claims. The creditors or trustees can file when the firm has committed an "act of bankruptcy" such as failing to meet a payment required under bond indentures (e.g., an interest payment). The court usually appoints a trustee who is then responsible for managing the firm.

When the firm initiates proceedings, it continues in operation while the management and creditors try to work out a plan for debt settlement. Such voluntary bankruptcies are presumably less costly than involuntary bankruptcies. However, neither type of bankruptcy implies that the firm will cease to exist (i.e., go into liquidation). The firm can still be a profitable operation with a market value of future operating cash flows that exceeds the sum of the market value of the firm's assets in liquidation (so that it is optimal to stay in operation). Bankruptcy does not imply that the firm should cease operations.

If the face value of debt claims exceeds the market value of the firm, the debtholders have an incentive to file for bankruptcy and eliminate the shareholders' claim. If the debtholders do not eliminate the shareholders' claim, at some future time the cash flows of the firm could, by chance, increase, and if the value of the firm exceeded the value of the debt, the shareholders would receive the difference, *not* the debtholders. Hence, by allowing the shareholders to continue as residual claimants of the firm's cash flows, the debtholders are giving the shareholders something of value—an option on the future cash flows of the firm—and are reducing their own wealth.

Debtholders will file for bankruptcy if the value of the shareholders' option is more than the following bankruptcy costs.

1. The fees of lawyers, accountants, trustees, and others.
2. Losses that result from the court's or trustee's failure to maximize the market value of the firm (see Warner, 1977). That is, trustees do not have the same incentive or comparative advantage at maximizing the firm's market value as management.

If these costs are greater than the value of the shareholders' option, then the claimants on the firm have incentives to make voluntary arrangements that avoid the court and still leave shareholders with some claims on the firm.

The expected value of the foregoing costs increase as the probability of bankruptcy increases. Ceteris paribus, the firm's expected future cash flows and market value fall as the probability of bankruptcy increases. As the value of the firm falls, so does the value of claims on the firm (stocks, bonds, creditors' claims, etc.). Thus, estimates of the value of stocks, bonds, and other claims on the firm depend on the probability that the firm will go bankrupt. It is not surprising that there is a large literature devoted to bankruptcy prediction models.

The Role of Accounting Data in Predicting Bankruptcy

Most bankruptcy prediction models use accounting data. The data are often expressed in ratio form (e.g., debt/total assets, the current ratio, times charges earned). One reason accounting data might be useful in predicting bankruptcy is that bond indentures and lending agreements often use accounting ratios to restrict managers' actions. For example, a firm may be required to maintain a minimum current ratio. Breach of the accounting ratio covenant places the firm in default and can lead to bankruptcy.

Breach of a covenant involving accounting ratios, however, does not necessarily lead to bankruptcy. Hence, there is no mechanical association between accounting ratios and bankruptcies because defaults are defined using those ratios. As discussed, the bondholders will not file for bankruptcy if the costs of filing (lawyer and accounting fees and the opportunity costs of using a trustee) outweigh the benefits of eliminating the shareholders' option.

While technical default does not automatically lead to bankruptcy, the use of accounting numbers in covenants to signal default and provide debtholders with the option to force bankruptcy suggests that those numbers and ratios are associated with the value of the firm and the face value of debt.[1] Hence, those numbers are also likely to be measures of the probability of bankruptcy, and it is not surprising that studies use accounting numbers to predict bankruptcy.

There have been two types of bankruptcy prediction studies. The first (e.g., Beaver, 1966) looks at the relation between individual accounting numbers or ratios and bankruptcy (the univariate approach). The other uses several ratios to predict bankruptcy (the multivariate approach). The univariate approach uses one ratio at a time to predict failure. It is likely that different ratios reflect different aspects of the firm's financial position, so better predictions can be obtained by using combinations of ratios instead of one ratio. For this reason, the multivariate approach quickly supplanted the univariate approach. The watershed multivariate article is Altman (1968).

Multivariate Approaches to Predicting Bankruptcy

DISCRIMINANT ANALYSIS

Most multivariate models use linear discriminant analysis. To understand this technique assume that five accounting ratios ($w_1, \ldots, w_5$) are used to predict failure. Let $z = 1$ for nonfailure, 0 for failure. An estimation sample is used to regress z on $w_1, \ldots, w_5$ across all firms in the estimation sample ($i = 1, \ldots, N$),

$$z_i = c_0 + c_1 w_{1,i} + c_2 w_{2,i} + c_3 w_{3,i} + c_4 w_{4,i} + c_5 w_{5,i} + u_i \quad (5.1)$$

where c_j ($j = 1, \ldots, 5$) is a parameter. The estimated parameters are used to obtain a $\hat{z}_i$ for each firm in the estimation sample:

$$\hat{z}_i = \hat{c}_0 + \hat{c}_1 w_{1,i} + \hat{c}_2 w_{2,i} + \hat{c}_3 w_{3,i} + \hat{c}_4 w_{4,i} + \hat{c}_5 w_{5,i} \quad (5.2)$$

Finally, the cutoff level for $\hat{z}$ is chosen to minimize some objective function. The usual objective is to minimize the number of misclassifications (i.e., the number of failed firms incorrectly classified as nonfailed—Type I errors—plus the number of nonfailed firms incorrectly classified as failed—Type II errors).

This basis for determining the cutoff level is not optimal for many purposes. Suppose that a bank is considering a loan. It would weight each type of error by the cost of that type of error and minimize the weighted sum of the errors (i.e., minimize costs). Type I and Type II

---

[1] See Smith and Warner (1979), Fogelson (1978), and Leftwich (1983) for analyses of the role of covenants using accounting numbers in debt agreements.

errors would be weighted differently because classifying a failed firm as nonfailed is more costly than is classifying a nonfailed firm as failed.

After estimating equation (5.1) and calculating the optimal cutoff for the z score, the estimated equation (5.2) is applied to a holdout sample and z scores are calculated. Those firms with z scores above the cutoff are predicted not to fail and those below the cutoff are predicted to fail. In actually applying the multivariate discriminant analysis, many variables (w_j) are tried and only the set of variables that "best" distinguishes between the failed and nonfailed groups is used to estimate z scores.

Altman (1968) uses multiple discriminant analysis to distinguish between bankrupt and nonbankrupt manufacturing firms in the period 1946–1965. Altman adopts a paired sample approach. He matches 33 bankrupt and 33 nonbankrupt firms on industry and asset size. Twenty-two variables, measured in the year before bankruptcy, are considered as candidates for the discriminant function. The combination finally chosen and the estimated discriminant function is

$$z = .012w_1 + .014w_2 + .033w_3 + .006w_4 + .999w_5 \qquad (5.3)$$

where

w_1 = working capital/total assets
w_2 = retained earnings/total assets
w_3 = earnings before interest and taxes/total assets
w_4 = market value of equity/book value of total debt
w_5 = sales/total assets

In Altman's estimation sample, equation (5.3) correctly identifies 31 of the 33 bankrupt firms and 32 of the 33 nonbankrupt firms. To validate the equation, Altman gathers data on a new sample of 25 bankrupt and 66 nonbankrupt firms. The model estimated using the initial 33 pairs (equation (5.3)) is used to classify the firms in the new sample (holdout sample). The model correctly identifies 24 of 25 bankrupt firms and 52 of 66 nonbankrupt firms.

The use of a holdout sample is important methodologically. Knowledge of a firm's ratios and whether it went bankrupt or not is used to determine the discriminant function and the "optimal" z score cutoff for the estimation sample. Essentially, hindsight is used. When the discriminant function and "optimal" cutoff is applied to another sample, the effect of hindsight is not present and the discriminant function will not predict as well. Hence, the use of a holdout sample is necessary to evaluate the discriminant function's predictive ability.

Altman also investigates the predictive ability of the model five years before bankruptcy. Using the original sample of 33 bankrupt firms, he finds that the model is able to predict the bankruptcy of 36 percent of those firms five years before bankruptcy. In a later study, Altman, Haldeman, and Narayanan (1977) report 70 percent of the bankrupt firms correctly classified five years before bankruptcy.[2]

Altman's findings and those of other studies (e.g., Deakin, 1972) suggest that accounting data are useful in predicting bankruptcy. However, they do not provide evidence that accounting-based models outpredict the market. Westerfield (1970) and Aharony, Jones, and Swary (1980) find that the bankrupt firms' stocks begin earning negative abnormal returns five years before bankruptcy. That indicates the market is revising downward its performance expectations for bankrupt firms five years before bankruptcy.

EXTENSIONS

Two recent papers (Altman, Haldeman, and Narayanan, 1977; Ohlson, 1980) add methodological refinements. As noted, most studies estimate models that minimize the *number* of misclassifications. Such an approach assumes that Type I and Type II errors are equally costly. Altman, Haldeman, and Narayanan (1977), using bank data on loan losses and lending rates, estimate the relative cost of the two types of errors. The data suggest making a loan that subsequently defaults (Type I error) is 35 times more costly than rejecting a loan that will not default (Type II error). Using these relative misclassification costs, Altman, Haldeman, and Narayanan (1977) calculate a different "optimum" cutoff.

Ohlson (1980) points out that earlier studies assume (often incorrectly) that the financial statements for the bankruptcy year are disclosed prior to the bankruptcy filing. This erroneous assumption causes the overstatement of the model's forecasting ability. Ohlson uses financial data from firms' 10-K SEC reports because he can determine when those reports are publicly available. Ohlson draws his sample from the period 1970–1976.

---

[2] There is a problem with interpreting these accuracy rates. Altman, Haldeman, and Naryanan (1977) report the probability of bankruptcy, given the firm is predicted to go bankrupt, $P(B|PB)$. But this conditional probability depends on the sample proportions of bankrupt and nonbankrupt firms, $P(B)$ and $P(NB)$. From Bayes's theorem,

$$P(B|PB) = \frac{P(PB|B)P(B)}{P(PB|B)P(B) + P(PB|NB)P(NB)}$$

From this equation, Altman's prediction accuracy, $P(B|PB)$, depends on the sample proportions, $P(B) = P(NB) = .5$. By constructing his sample of equal numbers of bankrupt and nonbankrupt firms, Altman overstates the model's predictive ability because in reality, $P(B) \cong .02$ and $P(NB) \cong .98$. The correct comparison of the model's predictive ability is performed by Ohlson (1980) who estimates the model using a sample that corresponds to the population proportions of bankrupt and nonbankrupt firms. Then he compares the predictive accuracy to a naïve model that predicts all firms will not go bankrupt.

Another important point in Ohlson's study is that assessment of a model's predictive ability requires the sample proportions of bankrupt and nonbankrupt firms be the same as the population proportions. Otherwise the estimate of the model's accuracy is misstated. The bankrupt sample consists of 105 firms while the nonbankrupt sample consists of 2,058 nonfailed firms on the *Compustat* file. Ohlson compares his model to a naïve model that predicts that no firms fail. The naïve model misclassifies 4.85 percent of the firms; 105/(2,208 + 105). Ohlson's model for predicting bankruptcy within one year, using nine accounting ratios and a cutoff point that equally weights Type I and Type II errors, misclassifies 3.88 percent of the firms.[3]

A problem common to all studies is ad hoc selection of independent variables. There isn't an underlying theory of accounting ratios' magnitudes prior to bankruptcy. Hence, the selection of variables depends on the researcher's intuition and, more often than not, the availability of data. The development of such a theory would be a major but difficult extension.

CONCLUSIONS

Numerous studies conclude that accounting ratios can be used to predict bankruptcy. Whether accounting ratios can predict better than stock prices is an open question. However, it appears that models using accounting ratios are useful for predicting the bankruptcy of unlisted firms and therefore useful for predicting those firms' expected cash flows.

ACCOUNTING DATA AND STOCK RISK

β—The Measure of Risk

Chapter 2 discusses the CAPM asset risk measure. That measure is the asset's β:

$$\beta_i = \frac{\text{cov}(r_i, r_m)}{\sigma^2(r_m)} \tag{5.4}$$

The expected rate of return on an asset and the asset's market price depend upon its β.

Typically, the β for an individual security is estimated from the *market model* using the ordinary least squares regression (OLS):

---

[3] Ohlson uses LOGIT analysis, which is a maximum likelihood procedure that overcomes several problems in discriminant analysis including the assumptions that financial ratios are normally distributed and that bankrupt and nonbankrupt firms have the same variance-covariance matrix.

$$r_{i,t} = a_i + b_i\, r_{m,t} + e_{i,t}; \qquad t = 1, \dots, T \tag{2.32}$$

The computed $\hat{b}_i$ is an estimate of β_i. The regression equation and the multiperiod CAPM of Chapter 2 assume that β is stationary over time. But β could in fact vary from period to period.

The β's nonstationarity requires the researcher to make a trade-off. If β is stationary, the longer the estimation period for equation (2.32), the "better" (more efficient, less measurement error) the β estimate. On the other hand, the longer the estimation period, the more likely β changes. Bogue (1972) and Gonedes (1973) investigate this issue, and their conclusion (on empirical grounds) is that for monthly rates of return, 60 months is the optimal period for their sample.

The estimated $\hat{b}_i$ from equation (2.32) is an *unbiased* estimate of β_i. However, $\hat{b}_i$ measures β_i with error, and it is possible that additional information can be used to obtain a "better" estimate of β_i than that obtained from estimating equation (2.32). A better estimate of a security's current β would enable one to make better estimates of its β and expected rate of return in future periods. Such information enables investors better to eliminate risk from their portfolios, to form more efficient portfolios in the sense that the portfolios have the lowest possible rate of return variance for a given expected rate of return.[4]

There are reasons to believe that accounting data can be used to provide estimates of β for unlisted securities. Further, it is possible that better β estimates can be obtained for listed securities by using accounting data in combination with the market model estimate of β.

Accounting Data and β Estimates

In Chapter 2 the rate of return on a firm's stock for a given period is a function of the firm's realized cash flows for that period. Hence, a firm's β can be expressed as a function of the covariance between the firm's cash flows and a market index of cash flows (see Fama and Miller, 1972, p. 296). If accounting earnings are a surrogate for cash flows, an accounting β (the covariance between a firm's earnings and an earnings market index divided by the variance of the earnings market index) could be a surrogate for the firm's β. And it is likely that accounting earnings can be used to obtain β estimates.

Accounting earnings is not the only accounting variable likely to be useful in estimating a security's β. In Chapter 2 we assume that the firm is unlevered (i.e., has no debt in its capital structure) so that the firm's β is its stock's β. However, if a firm has debt, its β differs from

---

[4] Klein and Bawa (1976, 1977) show that the error in estimation of the parameters of rate of return distributions affect the optimal portfolio choice, where optimality is defined in terms of mean-variance efficiency.

its stock's β. In that case the firm's leverage (its debt/equity ratio) affects its stock's β and so is useful in estimating that β. If debt and equity market values are unavailable, the accounting book values can be used as leverage surrogates in estimating β.

Analytically (in the no-tax CAPM world of Chapter 2), the relation among the betas of the stock, $\beta_{S,i}$, debt, $\beta_{B,i}$, and the firm, $\beta_{V,i}$ is:

$$\beta_{V,i} = \frac{B_i}{V_i} \beta_{B,i} + \frac{S_i}{V_i} \beta_{S,i} \qquad (5.5)$$

where B_i, S_i, and V_i are the market values of the debt, stock, and total firm, $V_i \equiv B_i + S_i$ (see Brealey and Myers, 1984, Ch. 17). Equation (5.5) expresses the risk of the firm, $\beta_{V,i}$, as a weighted average of the stock and debt betas where the weights are the relative proportions stock and debt. Rearranging equation (5.5) yields

$$\beta_{S,i} = \beta_{V,i} + \frac{B_i}{S_i} (\beta_{V,i} - \beta_{B,i}) \qquad (5.6)$$

In the no-tax CAPM world, the value of the firm is independent of the firm's capital structure (i.e., the proportion of the firm that is financed with debt; see Modigliani and Miller, 1958; Brealey and Myers, 1984, Ch. 17). This in turn (given the firm's cash flows) implies that $\beta_{V,i}$ is independent of leverage, B_i/S_i, so increasing leverage does not change $\beta_{V,i}$. However, increasing leverage increases the beta of the firm's stock, $\beta_{S,i}$, since $\beta_{V,i} > \beta_{B,i}$ (see equation (5.6)).[5]

It is important to remember, however, that variations in leverage are likely to be associated with variations in the operating characteristics of the firm (e.g., mergers, acquisitions, spinoffs). These variations in operating characteristics in turn can be associated with variations in $\beta_{V,i}$. So, in net, $\beta_{S,i}$ may vary positively or negatively with leverage (see Smith, 1979, p. 90).

The leverage just discussed (e.g., the proportion of debt financing) is **financial leverage**. Finance theory also suggests β varies with **operating leverage**. Hence, operating leverage is also likely to be useful in estimating β. Operating leverage is the ratio of fixed to variable costs. Lev (1974) shows that the higher the operating ratio, the higher the firm's β. His empirical results confirm this. Estimates of fixed and variable costs used to calculate the operating ratio are obtained from accounting data.

---

[5] If the debt is risky, increasing the leverage also increases the beta of the debt, $\beta_{B,i}$. Given that, it is not obvious from equation (5.6) that $\beta_{S,i}$ increases with leverage, but it must. The reason is that as leverage, B_i/V_i, increases in equation (5.5), more weight is put on the β of the debt, which is lower than the β of the equity. To maintain a constant β, the β of the shares must increase.

One caveat should be offered on the operating leverage effect on β. We expect firms' capital structures and operating leverage to be associated (Myers, 1977). Firms with more fixed assets are able to obtain lower-cost, long-term financing and hence will be more highly levered. Lev's (1974) tests of the effect of operating leverage on β do not control for financial leverage. Hence, his measure of operating leverage may proxy for financial leverage.

From this discussion, there are reasons to believe that accounting data are useful in estimating stock βs, not only for unlisted firms but also for listed firms whose stock β can be estimated using the market model. Because accounting numbers are likely to vary with β, they can be used to reduce the measurement error in the market model β estimate and provide a better estimate. Consequently, researchers have investigated the association between accounting data and estimates of β.

The Ball and Brown Study

The earliest published study that examines the association between accounting numbers and market model β estimates is Ball and Brown (1969). An *accounting* beta is estimated from the following regression:

$$\Delta A_{i,t} = g_i + h_i \Delta M_t + \omega_{i,t}; \qquad t = 1, \ldots, T \qquad (5.7)$$

where $\Delta A_{i,t}$ is the accounting earnings change for firm i for year t, ΔM_t is the change in a market index of accounting earnings for year t, $\omega_{i,t}$ is an error term, and g_i and h_i are parameters. h_i is the "accounting beta." Ball and Brown estimate both equations (2.32) (market model) and (5.7) for 261 firms over the period 1946–1966 to obtain estimates of β, $\hat{b}_i$, and the accounting beta, $\hat{h}_i$. The Spearman rank order correlation coefficients between the accounting and market model β estimates for operating income, net income and income available for common are .46, .39 and .41, respectively. From the correlations, it is clear that "accounting betas" are associated with market model β estimates.

The Ball and Brown results are for accounting earnings. The influential Beaver, Kettler, and Scholes (1970) paper extends the Ball and Brown study by calculating the associations between other accounting variables (in addition to accounting betas) and the market model β.

The Beaver, Kettler, and Scholes Study

The variables chosen by Beaver, Kettler, and Scholes are ones that "conventional wisdom" says vary with risk. There are theoretical reasons for believing some of the variables vary with risk, but not for others.

The variables are

1. Dividend payout
2. Asset growth
3. Leverage
4. Liquidity
5. Asset size
6. Earnings variability
7. Accounting beta

Each of these variables is discussed in the paragraphs that follow.

Dividend payout is measured by Beaver, Kettler, and Scholes as the ratio of dividends paid to income available for common stock. It is often asserted that higher-risk firms pay out a smaller fraction of earnings. The usual rationale is that firms are reluctant to cut dividends and that the higher the risk of the firm, the greater the variance of earnings and the lower the payout rate necessary for a low probability of having to cut dividends. This rationale is due to Lintner (1956) and is an empirical assertion.

Nevertheless, the asserted *negative* association between payout rate and β might be expected in light of the empirical evidence. It has been observed that dividend payout rates vary negatively with debt/equity ratios (e.g., Ben-Zion and Shalit, 1975). If higher debt/equity ratios lead to higher β's (see equation (5.6)), a negative association between dividend payout and risk might be expected.

Asset growth is defined as the rate of growth in total assets over the period. It is predicted by Beaver, Kettler, and Scholes to be *positively* associated with β. There is no theoretical basis for this prediction.

Leverage is defined as the average of total senior debt to total assets over the period. From equation (5.6), the greater a firm's leverage, the greater the β on the firm's stock, assuming that leverage itself is not related to the underlying risk of the firm's cash flows (β_V in equation (5.6)), a questionable assumption. Beaver, Kettler, and Scholes predict a *positive* relation between leverage and risk.[6]

Liquidity is defined as the average current ratio over the period. Based on conventional wisdom, Beaver, Kettler, and Scholes predict the greater the liquidity, the lower the risk (i.e., a *negative* relation). There is little theory to support the prediction.

Asset size is estimated as the average of the logarithms of total assets over the period. The conventional wisdom is the larger the firm,

---

[6] Beaver, Kettler, and Scholes and other studies use book value of debt in the leverage measure. Bowman (1980a) finds that the use of market values of debt instead of book value does not alter the conclusions. Also, see Bowman (1980b).

the lower the risk. Portfolio theory predicts larger firms have lower variances on their rates of return, but not necessarily lower β's. As a firm becomes larger, its β will tend to one (the market β), not necessarily to zero. Thus, the prediction of a *negative* association between risk and size is based on conventional wisdom, not theory.[7]

Earnings variability is measured by the standard deviation of the earnings/price ratio over the period. The earnings/price ratio is a crude estimate of the firm's expected rate of return.[8] Hence, the standard deviation of the earnings/price ratio could be positively related to the standard deviation of the rate of return. Since the standard deviation of a stock's rate of return is positively related empirically to β (even though it need not be in theory), earnings variability might be *positively* related to β.

The *accounting beta* of a firm is estimated as the regression coefficient of that firm's accounting earnings on a market index of earnings, as in equation (5.7). However, both firm and market earnings are defined as the earnings/price ratio. Since the earnings/price ratio is a crude measure of the expected rate of return, the estimated accounting beta might be a crude estimate of the market β. Thus, a *positive* relation is expected between the accounting beta and the market beta.

RESULTS—ASSOCIATION BETWEEN ACCOUNTING DATA AND RISK

Beaver, Kettler, and Scholes examine 307 NYSE firms listed on *Compustat* over two periods: 1947–1956 and 1957–1965. In addition to investigating correlations between the accounting variables and the estimated β at the firm level, Beaver, Kettler, and Scholes investigate the correlations at the five-firm portfolio level. Grouping the firms into

---

[7] Watts and Zimmerman (1978), however, posit an alternative hypothesis to explain a negative relation between firm sizes and both variance and β. Large firms are more subject to political pressures (Chapter 10). Large reported profits bring about adverse media attention and political charges that the firms must defend. It is hypothesized that large firms tend to invest in low-β, low-variance projects to avoid the likelihood of embarrassingly high profits. To the extent that low-variance projects also have low betas (an empirical question), then size and betas are negatively related.

[8] If interest rates and firms' expected cash flows are constant in the future, and, if current earnings (A_0) are equal to the expected cash flows, the equation for the value of the firm in the multiperiod CAPM world of Chapter 2 becomes

$$V_0 = \frac{E(C)}{E(r)} = \frac{A_0}{E(r)}$$

Further, dividing the foregoing equation by the number of shares outstanding (n_0), and rearranging yields:

$$\frac{A_0/n_0}{P_0} = E(r)$$

where P_0 is the current market price of the shares and $(A_0/n_0)/P_0$ is the earnings/price ratio. Under these assumptions, the earnings/price ratio is equal to the expected rate of return on the stock.

TABLE 5.1

*Contemporaneous Association Between Market-Determined Measure of Risk and Seven Accounting Risk Measures**

| Variable | Period One (1947–56) | | Period Two (1957–65) | | Predicted Sign |
	Individual Level	Portfolio Level†	Individual Level	Portfolio Level†	
Payout	−.49	−.79	−.29	−.50	−
	(−.50)	(−.77)	(−.24)	(−.45)	
Growth	.27	.56	.01	.02	+
	(.23)	(.51)	(.03)	(.07)	
Leverage	.23	.41	.22	.48	+
	(.23)	(.45)	(.25)	(.56)	
Liquidity	−.13	−.35	.05	.04	−
	(−.13)	(−.44)	(−.01)	(−.01)	
Size	−.06	−.09	−.16	−.30	−
	(−.07)	(−.13)	(−.16)	(−.30)	
Earnings Variability	.66	.90	.45	.82	+
	(.58)	(.77)	(.36)	(.62)	
Accounting beta (β_i)	.44	.68	.23	.46	+
	(.39)	(.67)	(.23)	(.46)	

* Rank correlation coefficients appear in top row; product moment correlations appear in parentheses in bottom row.

† The portfolio correlations are based upon 61 portfolios of five securities each.

Source: W. H. Beaver, P. Kettler, and M. Scholes, "The Association Between Market Determined and Accounting Determined Risk Measures," *Accounting Review* 45 (October 1970), Table 5, p. 669.

portfolios and calculating the portfolio variables reduces the variables' measurement errors and increases the probability of observing associations. They form the portfolios by ranking the firms on an accounting variable and grouping firms of similar rank into portfolios. The five firms with the highest values are grouped into the first portfolio, the firms with the sixth to tenth highest values are grouped into the second portfolio, and so on. This produces 61 portfolios of five firms each.

Table 5.1 presents the Spearman rank correlations and the product moment correlations (in parentheses) between the accounting variable and estimated β at the individual firm level and at the five firm portfolio level for the two periods (1947–1956 and 1957–1965). The only correlations that do not have the predicted sign in Table 5.1 are those for the liquidity variable in the 1957–1965 period.

Four of the seven variables (payout, leverage, earnings variability, and accounting beta) have correlations that are consistently significant at the .01 probability level for both periods at both firm and portfolio level. So there is an association between accounting variables and risk. It is interesting to note that the three variables with insignificant correlations are the three for which there is little theoretical reason to expect a relation.

The Ball and Brown (1969) and Beaver, Kettler, and Scholes findings have been reproduced and extended by other studies (e.g., Bildersee, 1975; Eskew, 1979; Elgers, 1980). The results suggest that accounting variables can be used to estimate β and the market's expected rate of return in circumstances where it is not possible to estimate the market model.

RESULTS—PREDICTION OF RISK USING ACCOUNTING DATA

Besides finding an association between accounting variables and stock market β's, researchers have investigated whether accounting variables can be used to predict next period's market β. Typically, a cross-sectional regression such as the following is estimated for a given period:

$$\hat{b}_i = c_0 + c_1 w_{1,i} + c_2 w_{2,i} + \ldots + c_5 w_{5,i} + u_i \qquad (5.8)$$

where $\hat{b}_i$ is the market model estimate of β for firm i in that period and $w_{j,i}$ is firm i's jth accounting variable in that period.

Then, using the estimated coefficients ($\hat{c}_0$, $\hat{c}_1$, ..., $\hat{c}_5$) and the accounting variables (w_1, ..., w_5) a predicted β, based on the accounting variables, $\hat{b}_i^A$, is calculated for each firm i:

$$\hat{b}_i^A = \hat{c}_0 + \hat{c}_1 w_{1,i} + \hat{c}_2 w_{2,i} + \cdots + \hat{c}_5 w_{5,i} \qquad (5.9)$$

This β predicted on the basis of the accounting variables of a given period is then used to predict the market model β estimate of the *next* period. If the accounting variables are useful in predicting β's, the accounting-based predicted β, $\hat{b}_i^A$, should predict the next period's market model β estimate more accurately than this period's market model β, $\hat{b}_i$, estimate.

Several studies (Beaver, Kettler, and Scholes, 1970; Bildersee, 1975; Rosenberg and Marathe, 1975; Eskew, 1979) find that models based on accounting variables forecast future levels of market risk more accurately than do models relying solely on prior market model estimates of β. However, Elgers (1980) finds that after controlling for measurement errors in estimated OLS β's using Bayesian statistical techniques, accounting variables do not produce more accurate estimates of β.

Conclusions

It is apparent from the evidence that accounting variables are associated with market-based measures of risk and can be used to produce estimates of risk for unlisted securities. In that sense the accounting data are useful. It is not as apparent that accounting data can be used to improve the market model risk estimates for listed securities.

ACCOUNTING DATA AND BOND RISK

Bond Ratings and Risk

Bond ratings issued by rating agencies are widely used by fiduciary trustees and regulators to assess corporate and municipal bond risk (see Wakeman, 1981). Presumably, many investors also use bond ratings for that purpose. The two major rating agencies are Moody's and Standard & Poor's, and some observers think these two agencies' ratings can substantially affect bond prices (see Wakeman, 1981, pp. 28–29). For example, Ross (1976, p. 133) states that

> Moody's and Standard & Poor's may be wrong sometimes, but the ratings they stamp out can make a difference of millions in borrowing costs—or even determine whether you can borrow at all.

Under CAPM, the risk measure of a bond is its β. If bond ratings are measuring risk, ratings should be cross-sectionally correlated with β. Percival (1973) and Rozeff (1976) investigate this cross-sectional relation and conclude that corporate bond β's are systematically negatively related to ratings—the higher the rating, the lower the β. Further, if the CAPM is descriptive and rating agencies do measure risk, ratings should be more highly associated with β than with other measures of risk, such as the variance of the rate of return. Urwitz (1975) finds that the correlation for ratings and β is significantly higher than is the correlation for ratings and variance. The evidence is consistent with the hypothesis that rating agencies measure risk.

Not only do rating agencies appear to measure risk, the evidence suggests that they use accounting data in that measurement. If they do, given that the ratings are correlated with the bonds' β's, it is likely that the accounting data are useful for measuring bond risk.

Evidence That Rating Agencies Use Accounting Data

Wakeman (1981, p. 5) points to three sets of evidence that rating agencies use publicly available corporate accounting data to rate corporate bonds: (1) the explanations given by the agencies, (2) the timing of rating changes, and (3) empirical studies that attempt to explain ratings or rating changes.

Explanations. The first set of evidence consists of the explanations given by the rating agencies for changes in bond ratings. Wakeman reports that an analysis of the reasons Moody's gave for changing bond ratings in the period 1974–1976 showed that accounting-based reasons accounted for more than two-thirds of the changes not involving new financing. According to Sherwood (1976), Standard & Poor's assesses five areas in determining a bond's rating: indenture provision, asset protection, financial resources (liquidity), future earning power, and management. All or part of the analysis of the first four areas is based on published accounting reports.

The timing of ratings changes is not uniform over the year. Wakeman reports the distribution of Moody's ratings changes by month over the period 1950–1976. The ratings changes are most common in May and June, both of which shortly follow the availability of most annual reports (April). The difference in the time distribution of changes is significant. The null hypothesis that the frequency of changes is the same in each month is rejected at the .001 probability level.

Empirical studies employ techniques to predict ratings or rating changes that are similar to the multivariate techniques used to predict bankruptcy. The models typically use only data from published accounting reports and are able to rate correctly up to 80 percent of the bonds in holdout samples.[9] An example of one of these studies is Kaplan and Urwitz (1979). They use a multivariate statistical procedure called N-Probit (similar to Ohlson's LOGIT technique) to find that total assets, long-term debt to total assets, and the stock's beta are statistically associated with the ratings of outstanding bonds and newly seasoned bonds. They are able to classify correctly two-thirds of their holdout sample. Besides replicating the earlier results that accounting numbers are useful in predicting bond ratings, they also find that their more complicated statistical procedure did not improve the results over OLS. They conclude that OLS "seems robust and does not bias the equations" (Kaplan and Urwitz, 1979, p. 260).

Bond Ratings and Market Efficiency

If bond ratings are based solely on publicly available accounting data and if the capital markets are efficient, then, unless the analysts in the bond rating agencies are better able to use the data than others in the market, the bond market should not react to rating changes at the time they are made. Instead, the bond price changes associated

---

[9] See Kaplan and Urwitz (1979) and Altman (1977).

with the risk change reflected by the revised rating should occur prior to the rating change announcement.

Studies by Weinstein (1977) and Wakeman (1981) find no bond price effect at the time of the rating change. The Wakeman study also finds no stock price effect at the announcement of bond rating increases and a slight negative stock price reaction at the announcement of a ratings decrease. This evidence is generally consistent with the bond rating change not conveying information to either the bond or stock markets. Instead, the bond rating agencies use publicly available accounting data to document bond risk changes that have already been reflected in market prices. Given that bond ratings are not a timely information source, Wakeman (1981) advances the hypothesis that ratings still serve a valuable role in monitoring contracts by providing an easily understood and accurate measure of the bond's risk.

These studies show that accounting data are useful in estimating the risk of bonds. However, the risk measures calculated from publicly available accounting data are already reflected in both bond and share prices.

SUMMARY

The evidence summarized in this chapter indicates that accounting data other than accounting earnings are associated with factors affecting securities' values (i.e., expected future cash flows and risk). Accounting data are associated with the bankruptcy probability and, hence, with expected future cash flows. They also are associated with stock and bond βs.

The ability to predict bankruptcies "better" with accounting data than with a naïve model (i.e., the actual frequency of bankruptcies) suggests that accounting data are useful in situations where the market price of a claim cannot be observed. For example, it suggests that accounting data are useful in making loans. The fact that lending decision models based on accounting data are being used by banks confirms the implication. However, if a market exists for the firm's claims, there is no evidence available to suggest accounting data can be used to obtain a "better" prediction of bankruptcy than that implicit in the price of the firm's stocks or bonds. The drop in share price observed five years before bankruptcy (combined with the evidence on bond ratings changes in particular and market efficiency in general) makes it doubtful that such a "better" prediction can be obtained.

The correlation between accounting numbers and estimated βs and bond ratings indicates that accounting numbers are useful in terms of obtaining estimates of the risk of a firm's securities in situations in which market prices or bond ratings of the securities cannot be observed. Given the relevance of risk to the corporate investment decision and the individual investment decision, this is an important result.

CHAPTER SIX

Forecasting Earnings

Over the last 20 years a substantial literature developed on the empirical description of the behavior of accounting earnings over time and on the use of observed patterns to forecast future earnings. One stimulus for the development of the literature on the **time series** of earnings came from researchers trying to use models (such as those discussed in Chapter 2) to value securities.[1] These researchers wanted forecasts of earnings to use as surrogates for future cash flows. Another stimulus for the literature was the demand for "better" earnings expectations models by researchers studying the relation between stock prices and accounting earnings (such as the studies examined in Chapter 3). A third stimulus was an early attempt to explain managers' choices of accounting procedures (Gordon, 1964), a forerunner of the studies examined later in this book (e.g., in Chapter 11).

This chapter begins by explaining the reasons the time series of accounting earnings is important to researchers in the three areas and consequently to accountants and financial analysts. Then the alternative types of time series models are considered and the identification and estimation of time series models are illustrated using Eastman Kodak's

---

[1] A time series is a time-dated sequence of observations that are realizations from a stochastic (probabilistic) process.

earnings. The implications of the alternative models for market valuation, stock price studies, and managers' choices of accounting procedures are investigated. After that, the evidence on earnings time series and its implications for valuation are presented.

THE RELEVANCE OF TIME SERIES FORECASTS OF EARNINGS

In examining a time series, researchers try to *infer* the process generating the numbers by looking only at the numbers' sequence. For example, consider the sequence of winning numbers from a roulette wheel (17, 28, 1, 0, 19, 11, . . .). We examine the time series of winning numbers to determine the process generating the numbers and to formulate a betting strategy. If the numbers are drawn from a uniform distribution (i.e., all numbers are equally likely) that is independent and identical across time (i.e., the past draws do not affect the probability distribution of future draws), one strategy will be as good as another in terms of winning. However, if one number is found to have a higher probability of winning, a betting strategy based on that number should be adopted. Or, if the probability of a number's winning depends on the past sequence of numbers (i.e., there is **serial correlation** in the sequence of numbers), a betting strategy can be developed. The time series of winning numbers from a roulette wheel provides information on the future outcomes and influences our actions.

Similarly, we might investigate the time series of the past earnings of a firm (e.g., Eastman Kodak) to try to determine what it tells us about the firm's future earnings. If we find that earnings increases tend to follow earnings increases and decreases tend to follow decreases (i.e., there is positive serial correlation or **serial dependence** in earnings changes), we can use that knowledge to predict next year's earnings. If this year's change is positive, we would predict larger earnings next year. On the other hand, if we find negative serial dependence (i.e., earnings decreases tend to follow increases), we would predict smaller earnings next year if earnings increase this year. Researchers are interested in the time series of earnings for several reasons.

Use of Forecasts of Earnings in Valuation Models

Most valuation models for corporate securities price the claims in terms of the future cash flows of the firm. Both the Fisher model (equation (2.4)) and the CAPM (equation (2.11)) have this characteristic. Use of those valuation models requires estimates of expected future cash flows, and typically such estimates are not available, so surrogates are used. One of the most popular surrogates is a forecast of future accounting earnings.

Accounting earnings incorporate accounting accruals (e.g., depreciation) and exclude investment outlays (e.g., an outlay for purchase of a plant) and receipts (e.g., a receipt from the sale of a motor vehicle). Consequently, it is only under certain extreme conditions that future accounting earnings equal future cash flows.[2] Rappaport (1983) discusses some of the reasons for the lack of correspondence between earnings and future cash flows. Nevertheless, because they have operating cash flows in common, future accounting earnings and cash flows are correlated. Indeed, some accountants think that the accrual process could cause current earnings to be a better index of future cash flows than current cash flows (see Chapter 3).

The preceding rationale for the use of predicted accounting earnings in valuation models is certainly consistent with traditional financial analysis. For example, the classic investment analysis text, Graham, Dodd, and Cottle (1962, p. 28) states that

> The most important single factor determining a stock's value is now held to be the *indicated average future earning power*, i.e., the estimated average earnings for a future span of years. Intrinsic value would then be found by first forecasting this earning power and then multiplying that prediction by an appropriate "capitalization factor."

One way to predict accounting earnings is to estimate a process that describes the time series behavior of past earnings and use that

---

[2] See Chapter 2. An example provides an illustration of the extreme assumptions required. Assume a static firm. Its assets consist of N assets each with an economic and book life of N years and a cost of $\$I$. Further assume the machines' ages are distributed uniformly from 0 years to $N - 1$ years and the firm will replace each machine at the end of its life at a cost of I. Depreciation is the firm's only accrual, and by replacing the machines infinitely in the future, the firm expects to generate cash flows of C infinitely into the future. The market's expected rate of return for the firm for all periods is constant. Under these assumptions, the firm's expected accounting earnings each year in the future (A) are

$$A = C + I - D$$

where D is the depreciation expense. I is added because C is total cash flows including outlays for investment, I. Hence, $C + I$ is operating cash flows. Since the ages of the firm's machines are always uniformly distributed across N years, the depreciation each year must be equal to the cost of one machine (I) regardless of the depreciation method adopted. Hence, we have

$$A = C$$

for all years in the future. The expected accounting earnings (A) are equal to the expected cash flows (C) forever into the future.

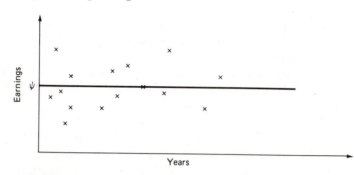

FIGURE 6.1

Plot of earnings assuming they follow a constant process

$$\tilde{A}_t = \psi + \tilde{\omega}_t$$

process to forecast future earnings. For example, earnings ($\tilde{A}_t$) might follow the process

$$\tilde{A}_t = \psi + \tilde{\omega}_t \qquad (6.1)$$

where ψ is a constant and $\tilde{\omega}_t$ is a disturbance term, $E(\tilde{\omega}_t) = 0$, and variance (ω_t) = σ_ω^2 for all t. The tilde (˜) denotes a random (stochastic) variable. Earnings for each future period are predicted to be $\$\psi$ (i.e., $E(\tilde{A}_{t+\tau}) = \psi$ for all $\tau > 0$).

Equation (6.1) is a **constant process**. It has a constant mean and constant variance.[3] Suppose that this very simple process generates annual earnings. Figure 6.1 plots how earnings vary over time if they follow a constant process.

Notice that under a constant process, earnings fluctuate randomly about ψ and the variance of the fluctuation is constant over time. One's best guess of earnings next year, or 10 years from now, is $\$\psi$. Reported earnings do not follow this process, but if they did, an analyst would value the firm using an estimate of $\$\psi$. That estimate could be obtained from an average of the firm's past earnings. Denote the current period as time t. The average earnings over the last 10 years ($\bar{A}$) would be, from equation (6.1),

$$\bar{A} = \psi + \sum_{\tau=t-9}^{t} \frac{\omega_\tau}{10} \qquad (6.2)$$

By the law of large numbers, the average disturbance term— $\sum_{\tau=t-9}^{t} (\omega_\tau/10)$— should be close to its mean (zero). So $\bar{A} \cong \psi$. Since earnings (and cash flows) are expected to be constant forever

---

[3] This process is also called a mean reverting process.

into the future, the value of the firm is the value of a **perpetuity** of ψ.[4] And, for a perpetuity of ψ, equation (2.14) becomes

$$V_0 = \frac{\psi}{E(r)} \tag{6.3}$$

The financial analyst, then, would multiply the estimate of ψ (the average of past earnings) by the capitalization factor $1/E(r)$ to obtain the value of the firm, just as described by Graham, Dodd, and Cottle.

Information other than the past time series of earnings is probably useful in predicting future earnings (e.g., knowledge of new sales contracts). Lev (1980) finds that macroeconomic variables like gross national product (GNP) aid in predicting firms' earnings. However, in the absence of other information, a time series prediction that takes advantage of any observed dependencies in the data will be useful.

Security analysts are not alone in using predictions of future accounting earnings in valuation models. Economists also use accounting earnings as surrogates for cash flows in valuation models (e.g., Modigliani and Miller, 1958). Indeed it was an economist's concern with the time series behavior of accounting earnings as a surrogate for returns that led to two of the earliest studies of the time series behavior of accounting earnings (Little, 1962; Little and Rayner, 1966).

Obtaining "Better" Earnings Expectations Models

In using time series models to forecast earnings for use in valuation models, surrogates are obtained for the market's expectation of future earnings or, more precisely, of future cash flows. As indicated in Chapters 2 and 3, studies of the information content of annual or quarterly earnings, such as Ball and Brown (1968) and Foster (1977), also attempt to obtain surrogates for the market's expectation of accounting earnings. In those studies, it is assumed that if earnings are greater than expected, it is likely that current cash flows are greater than expected and the mean of the probability distribution of future cash flows has increased. Hence, the claim represented by a share is likely to yield larger future cash flows and the price of the claim increases. Thus, unexpected increases (decreases) in earnings lead to increases (decreases) in stock prices.

In Ball and Brown's methodology, the better the approximation of the market's expectation of earnings, the more accurately earnings are separated into unexpected increases and decreases and the more likely the hypothesized increases or decreases in stock price are observed.

---

[4] A perpetuity is just a promise to pay a given sum (in our case, $\$\psi$) every period forever.

To see this point, assume that the researcher's surrogate for the market's earnings expectation is uncorrelated with the market's expectation. Then the researcher's subsample of unexpected increases in earnings will include both increases and decreases and the average stock price effect for the subsample will be zero. As the expectation model more closely approximates the market's, fewer decreases and more increases will be classified as increases and included in the unexpected increase subsample so the average stock price effect will become more positive. The same is true of the negatives. Thus, the likelihood of observing the positive relation (positive stock price effect for unexpected earnings increases) directly depends on the accuracy with which the researcher's expectation model for earnings approximates the market's expectation.

In an efficient market, the stock price will impound information that is available to many investors at low cost. The past time series of a company's annual and quarterly earnings is readily available in financial services such as *Moody's*; hence, the market's expectation of future earnings is likely to impound this information. Thus, in trying to derive a surrogate for the market's expectation of earnings, researchers using Ball and Brown's methodology are interested in the time series behavior of past earnings. This motivation led to the studies by Foster (1977) and Watts (1978) of the time series behavior of quarterly earnings.

Explaining Management Choice of Accounting Techniques

Chapter 1 described the lack of well-developed theory of accounting. In Chapter 4, this lack of a theory creates severe problems for those investigating the stock price effects of changes in accounting procedures. Without a theory as to why procedures are chosen, it is very difficult to control for the cash flow effects of changes in procedures. However, in the mid-1960s Gordon (1964) put forward what amounted to a theory of managerial choice of accounting techniques. In that article, Gordon assumes that

1. The corporate manager maximizes his or her utility.
2. Corporate stock prices are a function of the level, the rate of growth, and the variance of accounting earnings changes.
3. The corporate manager's compensation (and, hence, his or her utility) depends on the corporation's stock price.

In assumption 2, Gordon adopts the mechanistic hypothesis—the stock market could be "fooled" by accounting procedures. Hence, Gordon suggests that managers select accounting procedures to increase re-

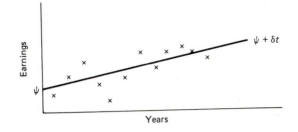

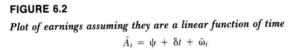

FIGURE 6.2

Plot of earnings assuming they are a linear function of time

$$\tilde{A}_t = \psi + \delta t + \tilde{\omega}_t$$

ported earnings and the growth rate of reported earnings and to decrease the variance of earnings changes.

Gordon, Horwitz, and Meyers (1966) test Gordon's propositions, particularly the proposition that managers try to reduce the variance of earnings changes—to "smooth" reported earnings. The Gordon, Horwitz, and Meyers paper is subject to many methodological problems, so that it is difficult to interpret the results. However, the paper generated a substantial literature on "income smoothing."[5]

The empirical tests of the "income smoothing" hypothesis are typically tests of a joint hypothesis; that is, in the absence of manipulation by management, accounting earnings follow a particular process *and* managers adopt or change accounting procedures to reduce the variance of that process. For example, it is often assumed that earnings before manipulation are generated by the following process,

$$\tilde{A}_t = \psi + \delta t + \tilde{\omega}_t \tag{6.4}$$

where $\tilde{A}_t$ is the earnings of period t, ψ and δ are parameters, and $\tilde{\omega}_t$ is a random disturbance term—$E(\tilde{\omega}_t) = 0$ and σ_ω^2 is constant for all t—and that managers select accounting procedures to reduce σ_ω^2.

Figure 6.2 illustrates how annual earnings behave if they are a linear function of time as in equation (6.4).[6] Notice that the variance about the trend line is constant over time.

The assumptions of the "income smoothing" literature have implications for the time series of reported earnings. For example, in the preceding case, if "true" earnings follow the process described by

[5] For example, see Dopuch and Drake (1966), Copeland (1968), Copeland and LiCastro (1968), Gagnon (1967), Barefield and Comiskey (1972), Barnea, Ronen and Sadan (1975), and Ronen and Sadan (1981).

[6] This process is also called a mean reverting process with a trend.

equation (6.4) *and* managers smooth by reducing the variance of earnings around the line, $\psi + \delta t$, the reported earnings ($\hat{A}_t$) will also follow a linear process. In fact, the process will be

$$\hat{A}_t = \psi + \delta t + \tilde{v}_t \tag{6.5}$$

where $\tilde{v}_t$ is a disturbance term. If managers smooth successfully, $\sigma_v^2 < \sigma_\omega^2$. Hence, the joint hypothesis (smoothing and equation (6.4)) can be tested by observing whether the time series of reported earnings do, in fact, follow a process such as equation (6.5). Such a test by Ball and Watts (1972) is described later in this chapter.

ALTERNATIVE TIME SERIES MODELS

The Lack of Theory

Researchers have used various statistical approaches to explaining the time series behavior of earnings. They examine the properties of reported earnings, derive a statistical model that has those properties and fit it to the data. There have been few attempts to develop a theory that explains why reported earnings follow one particular process or another (Lev, 1983).

Developing a theory is a very difficult task that, for convenience in exposition, can be separated into two basic parts:

1. Explaining the cash flows of firms
2. Explaining the firm's choice of the accounting procedures that process the firm's cash flows to determine reported earnings

As suggested in Chapter 4 and as developed in greater detail in the second half of the book, the two tasks are not independent. The choice of accounting procedures affects cash flows (e.g., because of taxes) and the pattern of cash flows affects the choice of accounting procedures (e.g., the choice of LIFO over FIFO to minimize the present value of income taxes). However, even if that dependence is ignored, the task of developing a theoretical model is still very difficult. Economists have been concerned with explaining the cash flows of firms for a long time, but no theory of the firm has emerged to provide that explanation.

Without theories of the firm's underlying cash flows and the choice of accounting procedures, it is difficult to address the issues that motivate researchers to investigate the time series of earnings. In testing valuation models (e.g., models that predict stock prices as a function of cash flows) and the effect of unexpected earnings on stock prices, two things are being tested simultaneously: the valuation model and the extent to which reported earnings approximate the cash flows. In testing the "smoothing" hypothesis, two things are also being tested simultaneously: the assumed time series of cash flows, before management applied accounting procedures, and smoothing.

Simple Types of Time Series Models

There are two extreme types of time series processes: a process in which the currently observed earnings do *not* cause a revision of expected future earnings and a process in which expected future earnings depend *solely* on the currently observed earnings. The first process in which future earnings are independent of current earnings can be represented by **deterministic models**, whereas the second model where future earnings depend solely on current earnings can be represented by **random walk models**.

Deterministic models forecast future earnings to be deterministic and not to depend on observed earnings. Two simple deterministic models are equations (6.1) and (6.4):

$$\tilde{A}_t = \psi + \tilde{\omega}_t \qquad\qquad (6.1)$$

$$\tilde{A}_t = \psi + \delta t + \tilde{\omega}_t \qquad\qquad (6.4)$$

The earnings *expected* for future period $t + \tau$ under the two models are

$$E(\tilde{A}_{t+\tau}) = \psi; \qquad\qquad \tau = 0, \ldots, \infty \qquad\qquad (6.6)$$

and

$$E(\tilde{A}_{t+\tau}) = \psi + \delta(t+\tau); \qquad \tau = 0, \ldots, \infty \qquad\qquad (6.7)$$

respectively. Neither expectation depends on the most recently observed earnings A_t or the earnings of any period before t.

Random walk models generate expectations of future earnings that depend solely on the most recent earnings observation. These models have been used to describe the time series of stock prices. The simple random walk model is[7]

$$\tilde{A}_t = A_{t-1} + \tilde{\omega}_t \qquad\qquad (6.8)$$

[7] The model derives its name from an important theoretical problem addressed by mathematicians at the turn of the century. The problem concerns the search for a drunk who was left wandering in a random fashion in a field one night (time $t - 1$). Where should we look for him the next morning (time t)? The solution is to look at the spot where he was last observed (i.e., A_{t-1}) since that is the best guess as to where he will be in the morning.

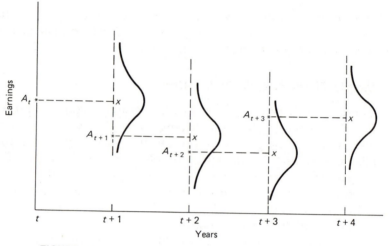

FIGURE 6.3

Time series plot of earnings assuming they follow a random walk

$$\tilde{A}_t = A_{t-1} + \tilde{\omega}_t$$

where $E(\tilde{\omega}_t) = 0$, σ_ω^2 constant for all t, and $\text{cov}(\tilde{\omega}_t, \tilde{\omega}_{t+\tau}) = 0$ for all τ $\neq 0$. Notice that while $\tilde{A}_t$ is a random variable denoted with a "$\tilde{\ }$", A_{t-1} is not, because it has been realized by period t. The expectation of earnings τ periods into the future is

$$E(\tilde{A}_{t+\tau}) = A_{t-1}; \qquad \tau = 0, 1, \ldots, \infty \qquad (6.9)$$

and depends solely on the most recently observed earnings.[8]

Figure 6.3 plots what a firm's earnings might look like if they followed a random walk. The actual earnings are represented in Figure 6.3 by an "*" and are labeled A_t, A_{t+1}, . . . , and so on. The frequency distributions of each year's earnings (given the previous year's earnings) are superimposed on the figure with the expectation represented by an "x." Once year t's earnings are realized (A_t), they become the expected earnings for year $t + 1$'s earnings. Year $t + 1$'s earnings are drawn from a distribution with mean A_t and variance σ_ω^2. The frequency distributions are the same from year to year but shift up or down depending on the last year's realization. For example, earnings in year $t + 1$ are well below the earnings of year t, and hence subsequent earnings are expected to be at this lower level. Notice that the random

---

[8] In Chapter 3 we referred to a martingale model. A martingale model is a model whose expectation can be described by equation (6.9). A simple random walk is a martingale model. It is distinguished from other martingale models by the assumption on the dispersion of ω_t (i.e., ω_t is independent and identically distributed for all t).

walk can wander all over—there is no tendency to return to a given level such as "ψ" in the constant process represented by equation (6.1) or a given trend line such as $\psi + \delta t$ in the linear process represented by equation (6.4).

A random walk model can have a trend (or drift term). For example, the following model is a random walk with a trend,

$$\tilde{A}_{t+\tau} = A_{t-1} + \delta\tau + \tilde{\omega}_t; \qquad \tau = 1, \ldots, \infty \qquad (6.10)$$

where $E(\tilde{\omega}_t) = 0$, σ_ω^2 is constant for all t, and $\text{cov}(\tilde{\omega}_t, \tilde{\omega}_{t+\tau}) = 0$ for all $\tau \neq 0$. The expectation of earnings for period $t + \tau$ then is

$$E(\tilde{A}_{t+\tau}) = A_{t-1} + \delta\tau; \qquad \tau = 1, \ldots, \infty \qquad (6.11)$$

and depends on the most recently observed earnings but *not* on any earnings observed before then.

Deterministic and random walk models are extremes in the sense that in deterministic models, the most recent observation of earnings has no effect on expected future earnings. In the random walk models, the most recent observation determines expected future earnings. There are other time series models of earnings in which the most recent observation causes a change in expected future earnings but does not totally determine expected future earnings. Those more general time series models are described in Nelson (1973).

THE APPLICATION OF TIME SERIES MODELING TO EASTMAN KODAK

The • in Figure 6.4 represents the time series of Kodak's actual annual earnings per share for 1946 to 1983. How would one forecast Kodak's earnings in the future? First, the underlying process is identified. To illustrate the practical problems with identifying the underlying process, the analysis is restricted to two of the extreme cases—a random walk model (equation (6.8)) and a linear deterministic model (equation (6.7)). In reality, there are an infinite number of processes: autoregressive, polynomial, moving average, trigonometric, and so on. Our purpose is not to present a thorough exposition of time series analysis (see Nelson, 1973) but, rather, to acquaint the reader with the basics.

Figure 6.4 portrays a generally increasing time series. Without any underlying theory, is a random walk better than a linear model? Which fits the data better? Answering these questions requires a definition of "better." The data can be fitted perfectly, if enough parameters are used in the model. For example, suppose that a fifth-

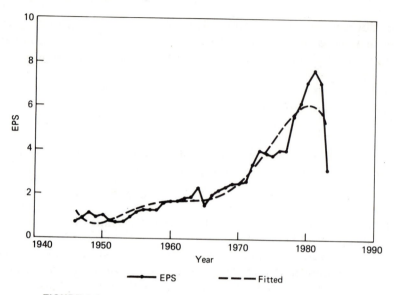

FIGURE 6.4

Eastman Kodak's earnings per share (actual EPS and estimated polynomial equation), 1946–1983

degree polynomial in time is fitted to the data. The resulting estimated regression is

$$\tilde{A}_t = 1.78 - .732t + .145t^2 - .001t^3$$
$$(2.2) \quad (-1.9) \quad (.24) \quad (-2.7)$$
$$(t\text{-statistics})$$
$$+ 3.3 \times 10^{-4}t^4 - -3.7 \times 10^{-6}t^5$$
$$(3.1) \quad (-3.3)$$

$$(6.12)$$

$$R^2 = .89$$

The dotted line in Figure 6.4 plots the fitted regression line. Clearly, by adding higher-order terms to the regression (e.g., t^6, t^7, t^8, ...) every wiggle in the actual time series can be explained ($R^2 \approx 1$). But this would "overfit" the data and produce a model with less predictive power than would a simpler model. The reason is that coefficients would be added to account for wiggles that are realizations of the disturbance term and will not be repeated in future periods. In other words, a model is fitted to wiggles in the data that are specific to the estimation period. One way to solve this problem is to ask how well the model predicts? To answer this question, some of the data must be withheld from the estimation phase and used to test the model's predictive ability.

We will use the "holdback" or "holdout" procedure to test the relative predictive ability of the linear deterministic model and the random walk. There are no parameters in the random walk model, so no holdout sample is required to estimate that model. However, a period is required to estimate the coefficients of the linear model (ψ and δ in equation (6.7)). Equation (6.7) is estimated for the period 1946–1970 and the following estimated equation obtained:[9]

$$A_t = .48 + .076t \qquad t = 1, \ldots, 25$$
$$(5.3) \quad (12.2) \qquad R^2 = .86 \tag{6.13}$$

(*t*-statistics in parentheses)
Mean sum of squared residuals = .05

To predict 1971 earnings, $t = 26$ is substituted into equation (6.13) to obtain $E(\tilde{A}_{26}) = .48 + .076 (26) = \$2.45/share$. Actual earnings per share in 1971 are $2.60. Hence, our model's prediction error is $+\$.15$. The squared prediction error is $(.15)^2 = .0225$ (squaring prediction errors provides a measure of accuracy that abstracts from the sign).

How are 1972 earnings to be predicted? We could substitute 27 into equation (6.14) and get $E(\tilde{A}_{27}) = \$2.53$. But this ignores 1971 actual earnings. If a linear model is used to forecast Kodak's earnings, after 1971 earnings are known, one would want to incorporate those 1971 earnings into the estimation of the model. One way to do this is to reestimate the linear model using the latest 25 observations. Dropping the first observation and adding 1971 earnings yields a revised linear model:[10]

$$\tilde{A}_t = .44 + .078t \qquad t = 2, \ldots, 26$$
$$(4.6) \quad (12.7) \qquad R^2 = .87 \tag{6.14}$$

(*t*-statistics in parentheses)

Notice the slightly higher-slope coefficient, which is due to the higher 1971 earnings. This updated linear model yields a prediction for 1972 earnings of $2.56/share, which is $.03 higher than the number calculated from the old model.

Adding the latest earnings and dropping the earliest earnings (maintaining an estimation period of 25 years) and forecasting one period ahead is one way an analyst might predict Kodak's earnings— one period ahead. How well would those predictions perform over the period 1971–1983? The first five columns of Table 6.1 summarize the results. The average prediction error is $.75, meaning that on average

---

[9] There are some econometric problems with this model. In particular, the residuals are excessively autocorrelated, which suggests that the model is misspecified.
[10] This model still has excessive dependence in the residuals.

TABLE 6.1

Relative Predictive Ability of Linear and Random Walk Models for Eastman Kodak's Earnings, 1971–1983

Year	Actual Earnings	Linear Model			Random Walk		
		Predicted	Prediction Error	Squared Prediction Error	Predicted	Prediction Error	Squared Prediction Error
1971	$2.60	$2.45	$ .15	$ .02	$2.50	$ .10	$ .01
1972	3.39	2.56	.83	.68	2.60	.79	.62
1973	4.05	2.80	1.25	1.56	3.39	.66	.44
1974	3.90	3.13	.77	.59	4.05	−.15	.02
1975	3.80	3.40	.40	.16	3.90	−.10	.01
1976	4.03	3.63	.40	.16	3.80	.23	.05
1977	3.99	3.84	.15	.02	4.03	−.04	.00
1978	5.59	4.01	1.58	2.50	3.99	1.60	2.56
1979	6.20	4.40	1.80	3.24	5.59	.61	.37
1980	7.15	4.87	2.28	5.20	6.20	.95	.90
1981	7.66	5.45	2.21	4.88	7.15	.51	.26
1982	7.12	6.07	1.05	1.10	7.66	−.54	.29
1983	3.41	6.53	−3.12	9.73	7.12	−3.71	13.76
Mean			.75	2.30		.07	1.49

the linear model is below the actual Kodak earnings by $.75/year. The average squared error is $2.30. How does the linear model compare to a random walk?

The last three columns of Table 6.1 summarize how well an analyst would have done using a random walk. The random walk predicts that next year's earnings are the same as the current year's. Thus, the column labeled "Predicted" consists of last year's earnings. The average prediction error is $.07 and the average squared prediction error is $1.49, both well below the errors produced by the linear model. In fact, the random walk model produces smaller absolute errors in 11 of the 13 years. Hence, the random walk model is better.

One might argue that a period of 25 years is too long for estimation of the linear model's regression or that an exponential model is more appropriate. But all these arguments are with the aid of hindsight. Place your hand over the 1971–1983 earnings in Figure 6.4 and ask yourself which is the best model. Or, alternatively, which model do you want to use to forecast 1984 earnings?

Again, refer back to Figure 6.4. Is the time series stationary? That is, is the stochastic process generating earnings the same over time? The "interoccular test" applied to Kodak's earnings suggests that the underlying process has changed. The year-to-year variation in earnings was small up to 1972. The average change in earnings was around $.25/ share per year. Since 1972, the average change in earnings has been around $.50/share per year. The variance in earnings changes has increased dramatically. It appears that there has been a *structural change* in the stochastic process. One source of additional variance is FASB Statement No. 8, which required foreign currency gains and losses to be included in earnings. In fact, many accounting changes induce nonstationarities into the time series. Inflation has probably also caused the earnings series to change structurally.

The structural changes drastically complicate identification and estimation of time series models. Clearly, one might exclude from model estimation those time periods that differ from the present. However, this usually results in dropping all but the last few years of data. Alternatively, one can try to adjust the past data to make them comparable to the new situation. For example, past earnings can be restated into 1983 dollars. But this is ad hoc and probably not very realistic. Kodak would probably not have made the same business decisions it did in 1946 if the inflation rate had been 15 percent instead of 2 percent. In short, there is no good solution for handling structural change other than to be aware of the problem and try to focus on the periods that are most relevant to the forecasting period. Notice that structural change favors a random walk. Since the random walk requires the least amount of data, it is less susceptible to structural changes (i.e., it adjusts faster than other models).

The random walk works better than the time trend model for Kodak, but does it for other firms? Later we discuss the evidence on this issue. Now we examine what the alternative models imply for market valuation and the smoothing hypothesis.

IMPLICATIONS FOR STOCK PRICES AND THE SMOOTHING HYPOTHESIS

Random walk models and deterministic models have very different implications for the relation between earnings and stock prices and for the smoothing hypothesis.

The Relation Between Earnings and Stock Prices

If the process generating accounting earnings is indicative of the process generating cash flows, the earnings generating process has implications for the magnitude of stock price changes associated with unexpected earnings. For example, the annual earnings generating process has implications for the magnitude of cumulative abnormal returns observed for the 12 months up to and including the month of an earnings announcement in studies such as Ball and Brown (1968). In addition, the earnings generating process has implications for the relation between a firm's observed earnings and the probability of that firm's liquidation.

For a given level of unexpected earnings, the stock price change is much greater if earnings follow a random walk than if they follow a deterministic process. The intuition behind this result is straightforward. Suppose *unexpected* earnings are +$2. If earnings follow a deterministic process, the value of the firm before dividends only rises by the $2. But if earnings follow a random walk, the value of the firm (again before dividends) rises by much more than $2 because the entire future expected stream of earnings (and cash flows) has shifted up by $2. If the expected rate of return on the stock is 10 percent, the increase in the value of the firm is $22. Under the deterministic model, future expected earnings (and cash flows) are unaffected by the higher earnings this period.

Similar analysis applies to liquidations. If a firm has very low (or negative) earnings, liquidation is less likely if earnings follow a deterministic process than if they follow a random walk. With a deterministic process, low earnings in this period reveals nothing about earnings in the next period that are expected to return to its trend. Under a random walk, low earnings reveals that expectations of future earnings should be lowered to the current level, and hence, liquidation is more likely.

The "Smoothing" Hypothesis

The nature of the process generating reported earnings has important implications for the "smoothing" hypothesis. Often this hypothesis assumes earnings are generated by equation (6.4) (i.e., the linear model) *and* that managers "smooth." If managers are completely successful in their smoothing, the variance of $\bar{\omega}$ in equation (6.4) would be zero. In other words, reported earnings would be *on* the straight line:

$$A_t = \psi + \delta t \tag{6.15}$$

If managers are able to reduce σ_ω^2, but not to zero, reported earnings would still be described by an equation similar to (6.4). Hence, observing that earnings are generated by equation (6.4) is consistent with the joint hypothesis of the proponents of the "smoothing hypothesis." However, observing that earnings are generated by a random walk is inconsistent with the joint hypothesis.

While a random walk is inconsistent with the joint hypothesis advanced in the smoothing literature, it is not inconsistent with smoothing per se. The original earnings process might be something other than equation (6.4). That is, managers can smooth, but the underlying cash flows and the resulting reported time series are not following a deterministic time trend. However, the reported earnings series (the only numbers observable by researchers) can be a random walk.

To illustrate how managers might smooth, assume that earnings (before manipulation by management) are generated by the process

$$\tilde{A}_t = A_{t-1} + \tilde{\omega}_t - \theta\omega_{t-1} \qquad (6.16)$$

where $E(\tilde{\omega}_t) = 0$ and $0 < \theta < 1$. This process is described in Nelson (1973). For our purposes here, period t earnings are equal to last period's earnings (A_{t-1}), a random error term ($\tilde{\omega}_t$), and less some fraction of last period's error term ($-\theta\omega_{t-1}$). Instead of reporting A_t, the manager reports $\hat{A}_t$, where

$$\hat{A}_t = \tilde{A}_t - \theta\tilde{\omega}_t \qquad (6.17)$$

by changing earnings by $\theta\omega_t$. That is, the manager "smooths" current earnings by $-\theta\tilde{\omega}_t$. Suppose that $\omega_t > 0$. The manager reduces reported earnings by "overaccruing" expenses by $\theta\omega_t$. Next period ($t + 1$) the firm's earnings will be greater by $\theta\omega_t$. Suppose that unexpected earnings are negative in period $t + 1$ (i.e., $\omega_{t+1} < 0$). The manager reports

$$\hat{A}_{t+1} = \tilde{A}_{t+1} - \theta\tilde{\omega}_{t+1} \qquad (6.18)$$

If $-\omega_{t+1} = \omega_t$ the manager does not have to manipulate accruals to produce an income of $\hat{A}_{t+1}$ because the "overaccrual" in the earlier period increases the earnings of period $t + 1$ by $-\theta\omega_{t+1}$. If $-\omega_{t+1} < \omega_t$, the manager "overaccrues" expenses by θ ($\omega_t + \omega_{t+1}$) to produce $\hat{A}_{t+1}$. If $-\omega_{t+1} > \omega_t$, the manager "underaccrues" expenses by θ ($-\omega_{t+1} - \omega_t$) to produce $\hat{A}_{t+1}$. The manager continues on in each year "under-" or "over-" accruing to produce the relation between reported earnings and underlying earnings represented by equations (6.17) and (6.18).

Given the manager adopts the foregoing strategy (by using "under-" and "over-" accruals or other means), what process will reported earnings follow? Substituting equation (6.16) for A_{t+1} into the equation (6.18) yields

$$\hat{A}_{t+1} = A_t + \tilde{\omega}_{t+1} - \theta\omega_t - \theta\omega_{t+1} \qquad (6.19)$$

which from equation (6.17) is

$$\hat{A}_{t+1} = \hat{A}_t + (1 - \theta)\tilde{\omega}_{t+1} \qquad (6.20)$$

The residual variance of reported earnings is now $(1 - \theta)^2 \sigma_\omega^2$, which, since $0 < \theta < 1$, is less than the original residual variance σ_ω^2. Thus, the manager has reduced the variance of unexpected changes in earnings—she has "smoothed" *and the reported series* (equation (6.20)) *is a random walk.*

Note that managers will not put themselves into an impossible position with this manipulation. The "overaccrual" or "underaccrual" will not become very large. Over time the manipulations will average to zero because $E(\tilde{\omega}_t) = 0$.

The important point of this example is that managers can be smoothing earnings *and* the time series process of reported earnings can be a random walk. However, the presmoothed series cannot be a random walk.

THE EVIDENCE ON THE TIME SERIES OF ANNUAL EARNINGS AND ITS IMPLICATIONS

Early Studies

In 1962 Little, and in 1966 Little and Rayner, investigated the growth rates in the accounting earnings of British companies. They found the growth rates to be random and appropriately entitled their papers "Higgledy-Piggledy Growth" and "Higgledy-Piggledy Growth Again," respectively. In 1967, Lintner and Glauber investigated the growth rates for earnings of 309 U.S. corporations and found very little association between the growth rates of successive periods. These results suggest that changes in earnings are random (i.e., annual earnings follow a random walk). However, measuring the earnings changes as growth rates increases the instability of earnings changes and biases the results toward randomness. Growth rate is measured as the ratio of the change in reported earnings over earnings. If earnings are close to zero in one year, the subsequent year's growth rate is very large. Thus, the variance in growth rates becomes large, making it likely that a statistically insignificant association be found.

The preceding results led Ball and Watts in 1968 to investigate the time series of annual earnings of U.S. corporations. They assume all firms have the same earnings generating process. The reason for this assumption is that the single-firm results may be the result of measurement error.

The Ball and Watts Study

Since they do not have a theory to predict the behavior of earnings changes, Ball and Watts subject their sample to a variety of tests for different kinds of statistical dependencies in earnings. The sample is drawn from *Compustat* and covers the period 1947–1966. All firms that have 20 years of data available are included, so that the final sample varies around 700 firms depending on which definition of earnings is used. Four time series are investigated:

1. Net income
2. Earnings per share (adjusted for stock splits and dividends)
3. Net income deflated by total assets
4. Sales

RUNS TEST

The first test Ball and Watts use is a runs test. The test is whether the sequential arrangement of signs of *earnings* changes is random. Earnings changes (i.e., first differences) are examined to see if positive changes follow positive changes and negative follow negative. A run is defined as a succession of earnings changes of the same sign. It ends when an earnings change of the opposite sign is observed. For example, consider the following two series of earnings for firms *X* and *Y*:

t	*Earnings of X*	*Sign of Earnings Change*	*Earnings of Y*	*Sign of Earnings Change*
1	.93		.85	
2	.80	−	.80	−
3	.75	−	.87	+
4	.70	−	.90	+
5	.80	+	.85	−
6	.85	+	.91	+
7	.90	+	.88	−
8	.95	+	.87	−

The earnings of firm *X* has two runs; the earnings of *Y* has five runs. If earnings follow a simple random walk, the sequence of signs of earnings changes is random. However, if earnings follow equation (6.1) (a constant process), then successive earnings changes are negatively correlated.

If the sequence of changes is random, the mean number of runs expected ($\overline{N}_{\text{RUNS}}$) is

$$\overline{N}_{\text{RUNS}} = \frac{2N_1 N_2}{N} + 1 \qquad (6.21)$$

where N_1 is the number of positive earnings changes, N_2 is the number of negative earnings changes, and N is the number of earnings changes. The estimated standard deviation of the number of runs (σ_{RUNS}) is

$$\sigma_{RUNS} = \frac{[2N_1N_2(2N_1N_2 - N)]^{1/2}}{N(N + 1)^{1/2}} \qquad (6.22)$$

If both N_1 and N_2 are "large," the statistic

$$Z = \frac{(N_{RUNS} - \overline{N}_{RUNS})}{\sigma_{RUNS}} \qquad (6.23)$$

(where N_{RUNS} is the number of runs) is normally distributed with the limiting distribution being normal with a zero mean and a standard deviation of 1.

Table 6.2 reports the distribution of Z statistics for net income and earnings per share and the distribution of firms with more or less runs than expected. If there are more runs than expected, it indicates negative dependence in the changes; if there are fewer than expected, it indicates positive dependence. From Table 6.2 the total number of runs for the whole sample is 6,522, almost exactly the same as the expected number 6,524, Also, the median Z statistics for runs in net income and in earnings per share are $-.12$ and $-.13$, respectively, and are far from significant. The Z statistics would have to be greater in absolute value than 2 (approximately) to reject the null hypothesis of randomness at the .05 probability level. Thus, the runs tests indicate that the signs of changes in earnings for the sample as a whole are random. This, in turn, suggests that earnings could be following a random walk but is inconsistent with earnings following a constant process (equation (6.1)).

SERIAL CORRELATION

The second set of tests used by Ball and Watts involves serial correlation coefficients or autocorrelations. The autocorrelation for lag τ, ρ_τ, is computed as follows,

$$\rho_\tau = \frac{\text{cov}(\omega_t, \omega_{t+\tau})}{\sigma_\omega^2} \qquad (6.24)$$

where ω_t is the change in earnings for period t. If earnings follow a random walk, the autocorrelation for any lag τ for earnings changes should be zero.[11]

[11] If earnings follow a different process, ρ_τ is not necessarily zero. For example, if the process is a moving average process in the first differences (equation (6.16)), the first-order autocorrelation is expected to be $-\theta/(1 + \theta^2)$ and the higher-order autocorrelations are zero.

TABLE 6.2

Distribution of Runs in Signs of Earnings Changes—the Ball and Watts Sample

						Decile				
Earnings Variable	*Mean*	*.1*	*.2*	*.3*	*.4*	*.5*	*.6*	*.7*	*.8*	*.9*
Net income Z value	−.03	−1.37	−.94	−.49	−.22	−.12	.34	.50	.74	1.20
EPS Z value	−.04	−1.22	−.04	−.61	−.22	−.13	.25	.39	.72	1.01

	Net Income		EPS	
	Number	*Percent*	*Number*	*Percent*
Firms with more runs than expected under independence	348	48.7%	326%	48.0%
Firms with fewer runs than expected under independence	366	51.3	353	52.0
	714	100.0%	679%	100.0%
Total runs in sample	6,522	100.0	6,338	99.8
Total expected runs, assuming independence	6,524	100.0	6,350	100.0

Source: R. Ball and R. Watts, "Some Time Series Properties of Accounting Income," *Journal of Finance* 27 (June 1972), Table 2, p. 670.

TABLE 6.3

Distribution of Autocorrelation Coefficients: Net Income Changes and EPS Changes—the Ball and Watts Sample

Lag τ	Net Income				EPS			
	Mean	.1 Decile	.5 Decile	.9 Decile	Mean	.1 Decile	.5 Decile	.9 Decile
1	− .030	− .386	− .075	.388	− .200	− .453	− .198	.057
2	− .040	− .368	− .067	.315	− .076	− .375	− .081	.208
3	.006	− .306	.001	.321	− .061	− .331	− .073	.259
4	− .007	− .320	− .013	.313	.023	− .300	− .052	.319
5	.005	− .277	.047	.403	.010	− .346	− .024	.318

Source: R. Ball and R. Watts, "Some Time Series Properties of Accounting Income," *Journal of Finance* 27 (June 1972), Tables 3 and 4.

The distribution of estimated autocorrelations for earnings differences for lags 1–5 obtained by Ball and Watts is reported in Table 6.3. The median autocorrelations for all five lags for both series (changes in net income and the changes in earnings per share) are close to zero and are insignificantly different from zero at any reasonable probability level. The only median autocorrelation that exceeds an absolute value of .1 is the first-order autocorrelation of earnings per share changes (−.198). As seen later, there is some reason to believe that number is not due to chance. However, given the results in Table 6.3, the null hypothesis that earnings changes for the sample as a whole are independent over time is not rejected.

OTHER TESTS

Ball and Watts also calculate mean squared successive differences and estimate exponential smoothing models. The results of these tests are consistent with the previous findings in that they suggest annual earnings for firms in general can be characterized as a random walk.

The results of *all* of Ball and Watts's tests are consistent with earnings being generated by a random walk process (simple or with a trend). The results for net income and EPS have been replicated by many other researchers. However, some contradictory evidence exists on other aspects of the Ball and Watts results.

Further Evidence on Annual Earnings

TREND

The Ball and Watts results are ambiguous about the importance of a trend term. Ball, Lev, and Watts (1976) produce some evidence that a trend existed at least in the 1958–1967 period.

RATE OF RETURN

Although Ball and Watts's results suggest that net income deflated by total assets follows a random walk, Beaver (1970) and Lookabill (1976) provide evidence that the rates of return on assets and on equity do not follow random processes. This issue is unresolved.

Individual firms' processes may differ significantly from a random walk even if firms' earnings in general follow a random walk. The Ball and Watts results are based on the mean and median results for a large sample of firms. That approach assumes that all firms have the same process and that differences across firms are due to sampling error. However, it could well be that the diversity is due to differences in individual firms' processes.

Watts (1970) investigates whether individual firm processes differ from a random walk. He uses the Box–Jenkins methodology[12] to estimate the processes generating "earnings available for common"[13] for 32 firms in three industries over the 1927–1964 period. Watts finds that the number of firms' estimated processes that differed from a random walk is larger than would be expected by chance. He also finds similarities between the processes of firms in the same industry.

However, when Watts compares the predictions of his estimated models to those of random walk and random walk with trend models in years outside the estimation period (1965–1968), he finds that the random walk models predict as well as the estimated models. This suggests that the Box–Jenkins models "overfitted" the data or that the process is not stationary in the estimation period 1927–1964. Watts also finds that the residual variance of the models changed over the 1927–1962 period, casting doubt on the tests that suggested that the estimated models differ from a random walk. The variance change is also consistent with the hypothesis that a structural change occurs in the earnings process during the period. The overall results suggest that individual firms' earnings can be approximated by a random walk. (Note, though, that Watts' sample is only from three industries: railroads, petroleums, and metals.)

Watts and Leftwich (1977) update the Watts (1970) study and also find that individual firms earnings can be described as a random walk. Albrecht, Lookabill, and McKeown (1977) investigate the period 1947–1975 and come to the same conclusion:

> we found little difference in the predictive accuracy of the best random walk model and the fitted Box–Jenkins models. (Albrecht, Lookabill, and McKeown, 1977, p. 242)

[12] For descriptions of the Box–Jenkins methodology, see Box and Jenkins (1970) and Nelson (1973).

[13] Earnings available for common is defined as net income less preferred stock dividends.

Implications and Evidence on Those Implications

The evidence suggests that annual earnings are well described by a random walk process. This finding contradicts the implications of the usual joint smoothing hypothesis, that is, that the underlying process is a deterministic function of time and managers smooth earnings. However, the evidence does not refute the proposition that managers smooth earnings. As seen, a random walk can result from smoothing actions if the underlying process is a first-order moving average process in the first differences of earnings (equation (6.16)).

As described earlier in this chapter and in Chapter 3, annual earnings described by a random walk process implies (if earnings are approximately equal to cash flows) that abnormal rates of return associated with an annual earnings change should be approximately equal to the percentage earnings change. The findings of Beaver, Lambert, and Morse (1980) reported in Chapter 3 are inconsistent with this prediction. In fact, their findings are inconsistent with both a random walk and constant process. These results, they claim, are due to the way in which earnings are aggregated into annual earnings (i.e., annual earnings are the sum of four quarterly earnings). That explanation also suggests that annual earnings will "appear" to be generated by a random walk (see Beaver, Lambert, and Morse, 1980).

THE EVIDENCE ON THE TIME SERIES OF QUARTERLY EARNINGS

Watts (1975, 1978), Griffin (1977), and Foster (1977) investigate the time series properties of quarterly earnings. All three find that quarterly earnings are composed of an adjacent quarter-to-quarter component and a seasonal component.

Foster (1977) chooses the following model as descriptive of the data,

$$\tilde{A}_t = A_{t-4} + \phi(A_{t-1} - A_{t-5}) + \psi + \tilde{\omega}_t \qquad (6.25)$$

where ϕ is an autoregressive parameter. The fourth lag (A_{t-4}) accounts for the seasonal component and the autoregressive parameter for the adjacent component.

Foster (1977) and Benston and Watts (1978) find that equation (6.25) is a good predictor (in terms of both squared and absolute errors) in the period 1962–1968. They also find that unexpected earnings generated by equation (6.25) separate firms into the positive and negative unexpected earnings change samples that produce the highest

CARs from the market model when compared with alternative time series models of earnings. That suggests that equation (6.25) approximates the markets' expectations of quarterly earnings.

The cross-sectional means of the parameters of equation (6.25) obtained by Benston and Watts (1978) estimated over the period January 1950–December 1967 for 83 firms are $\phi = .37$ and $\psi = .03$. If equation (6.25) is the generating process for quarterly earnings, negative autocorrelation in the first differences of annual earnings will be observed (see Watts and Leftwich, 1977, pp. 269–270). In fact, Ball and Watts observe a median negative autocorrrelation coefficient of $-.2$ for earnings per share. However, this dependence cannot be modeled using Box–Jenkins techniques on *annual* earnings. Hence, the best time series predictions of annual earnings is likely to result from using quarterly, not annual earnings. That is, if one wants to predict annual earnings, the best way to do this is to predict the next four quarterly earnings using a quarterly forecasting model and then sum the four quarters.

THE PREDICTIVE ABILITY OF FINANCIAL ANALYSTS

Another question addressed by the earnings time series studies is, Are financial analysts' earnings forecasts better or worse than the forecasts generated by naïve time series models? The simple random walk model is quite robust when applied to annual earnings. Furthermore, it is easy to apply—requiring no estimation. If financial analysts are unable to predict better than a simple random walk, then why are resources being consumed in this endeavor? On the other hand, if the analysts are able to outpredict a random walk, how much better are they? These questions have led to financial analyst forecasts' being evaluated relative to naïve time series models.

Brown and Rozeff (1978) compare the forecasting ability of Value Line's analysts to three time series models. Value Line is an investment advisory service that forecasts quarterly earnings four times a year for 1,600 firms. Brown and Rozeff (1978) draw a random sample of 50 firms which had a complete history of quarterly earnings available from 1951 and a December fiscal year end. The analysts' forecast errors are compared with random walk and Box–Jenkins models' forecast errors. Annual forecast errors are generated by summing the four quarterly forecasts and subtracting actual annual earnings. Table 6.4 summarizes the frequency distribution of errors (expressed as the absolute value of the error divided by the absolute value of actual earnings). Value Line analysts produce more small annual errors and fewer large annual errors than do the three time series models.

TABLE 6.4

Annual Earnings Forecast Errors for Time Series and Value Line Forecasts

Forecasts	Error Distribution, 1972–1975						
	$< .05$	$.05–.10$	$.10–.25$	$.25–.50$	$.50–.75$	$.75–1.00$	> 1.00
Random walk*	17	26	55	60	16	7	19
Seasonal random walk†	37	22	49	38	22	8	24
Box–Jenkins‡	30	23	56	53	13	4	21
Value Line	36	28	63	46	8	3	16

* The random walk, one-quarter-ahead forecast is $E(\tilde{A}_{t+1}) = A_{t-3}$.

† The seasonal random walk, one-quarter-ahead forecast is $E(\tilde{A}_{t+1}) = A_{t-3} + (A_t - A_{t-4})$.

‡ Box–Jenkins refers to a mixed autoregressive, moving average model estimated using past quarterly data from 1951 to 1971.

Source: L. D. Brown and M. S. Rozeff, "The Superiority of Analyst Forecasts as Measures of Expectations: Evidence from Earnings," *Journal of Finance* 33 (March 1978), Table 2, p. 7.

Brown and Rozeff also test the predictive ability of the analysts at forecasting quarterly earnings. They find similar results to those in Table 6.4 and conclude, "In summary, the evidence strongly supports the hypothesis that Value Line consistently makes better predictions than time series models" (1978, p. 11). Brown and Rozeff also replicate their results using analyst forecasts in the Standard & Poor's *Earnings Forecaster* with similar results.

The Brown and Rozeff results are not terribly surprising. Value Line publishes its forecasts for the last quarter and the current quarter some 70–80 days into the current quarter. Given that quarters are about 90 days long, the analysts are able to use a lot of other data appearing in the current quarter (e.g., unit sales, shipments, contracts awarded, union strikes) that have not appeared in earnings yet to revise their forecasts. Fried and Givoly (1982) find that one-year-ahead analyst forecasts have a greater association with abnormal stock returns over the next year than do one-year-ahead time series models of earnings forecasts.

In summary, security analysts are able to outpredict simple time series models that only rely on past values of earnings. But can analysts outpredict econometric models of past earnings *and* current quarter information that are available 70–80 days into the current quarter? That is an unanswered question.[14]

[14] See Brown, Griffin, Hagerman, and Zmijewski (1984) for evidence addressing this issue.

SUMMARY

This chapter investigated the evidence on the time series behavior of accounting earnings. The time series of earnings is of interest because of the use of earnings expectations in valuation models and in event studies such as Ball and Brown (1968) and because it has implications for hypotheses advanced in the smoothing literature. The evidence suggests that *annual* earnings are well described as a random walk. This result casts doubt on the joint hypothesis advanced in the smoothing literature (i.e., that managers smooth annual earnings and that underlying annual earnings follow a linear time trend). The result also suggests that changes in earnings will have a substantial impact on stock price changes.

However, the evidence on the time series of quarterly earnings indicate that they do not follow a random walk. Instead, quarterly earnings contain an adjacent quarter component and a seasonal component. This result, in turn, suggests that annual earnings are better forecast using quarterly earnings instead of a simple random walk model. It also suggests that annual earnings appear to follow a random walk because they are an aggregation of quarterly earnings. This implication is supported by Beaver, Lambert, and Morse (1980). Finally, security analysts appear to produce more accurate forecasts of earnings than time series models, probably because they are able to take advantage of other information disclosed in the current and previous quarters that have not appeared in earnings yet (e.g., strikes and the awarding of a government contract).

CHAPTER SEVEN

Evolution of Disclosure Regulation Rationales: Prelude to a New Theory

Chapters 3 to 6 summarize the evolution of one line of positive accounting theory from the early applications of the efficient markets hypothesis and the capital asset pricing model to the present day. Early researchers took the EMH as given and viewed accounting's role to supply information for valuation purposes. These precedents were followed by later researchers. Earnings were found to supply information to the capital markets (Chapter 3). Other accounting numbers reflected CAPM variables and, hence, could supply information on nontraded securities (Chapter 5). These findings led to further investigation of accounting's information role, for example, Do earnings supply more information than the information in cash flows (Chapter 3)? and Is the stock price change associated with earnings changes consistent with earnings generating processes (Chapter 6)? These topics occupied researchers through the 1970s and continue to be pursued.

Toward the end of the 1970s, a new line of economics-based positive accounting research emerged from this approach. This research emphasizes the explanation of accounting practice variations across firms and industries, not accounting's role in providing valuation information. The impetus for this new research came from two directions. One was the ongoing debate over government disclosure regulation. The other was Chapter 4's accounting change studies. Both the studies and the debate raised questions about the reasons for particular accounting practices and changes in those practices.

The practice-oriented accounting research is the subject of Chapters 8 to 13. This chapter discusses how researchers came to realize information value-oriented theory did not provide satisfactory explanations of accounting practice. It concentrates on one of the catalysts for the new research line, the disclosure regulation debate. The evolution of that debate chronicles how some accounting researchers came to realize that the behavior of politicians and regulators can be modeled using the assumption that they act in their own self-interest. Along with that realization, researchers recognized the existence of nonzero contracting and information costs in the political process. Those costs enable accounting procedures to affect firm cash flows and values and so provide the potential to build a theory of accounting. In discussing the evolution of disclosure regulation rationales, the chapter analyzes those rationales in detail.

Accounting researchers in the positive economics tradition were asked by those involved with the APB, FASB, and SEC to provide analyses of the EMH's implications for disclosure regulation and its traditional supporting arguments. Such analyses were soon forthcoming (e.g., Beaver, 1973, 1976; Beaver and Demski, 1974; Benston, 1969 a and b, 1973). In this chapter, we first discuss the implications of the EMH for those traditional arguments. The EMH reduces those arguments to, at best, unsubstantiated claims about relative costs and benefits. However, positive accounting researchers did not stop there. In response to demands for regulation rationales, they introduced more sophisticated rationales from the economics literature. Second, we present and critically evaluate these rationales in the section that follows. Introduction of these rationales led to their analysis and the consequent realization that they all degenerate to social cost/benefit comparisons of alternative disclosure scenarios. Hence, disclosure rationales are empirical issues. Unfortunately, many costs and benefits are unobservable *opportunity* costs and benefits.

Realization that existing disclosure rationales are empirical arguments caused researchers to ask whether politicians and regulators act accordingly (e.g., are they concerned with estimating the social costs and benefits of alternative regulations?) This question is raised in the third section. It led researchers to question the conventional assumption that individuals in the political arena are motivated by social welfare considerations. And it led to the assumption that politicians and regulators, like individuals in general, act in their own self-interest and that there are nonzero information costs in the political process. That set the stage for the beginning of the regulation theory that is outlined in the second half of this book. That theory enables accounting procedures to affect a firm's cash flows and so can explain why managers change procedures in the presence of regulation.

The last section also asks questions raised by Chapter 4's capital market evidence. Those questions led to the development of a theory as to why, in an efficient market and in the absence of regulations and taxes, managers change accounting procedures. The chapter ends with a summary of the evolution of disclosure rationales and of the questions that evolution, and the empirical evidence in earlier chapters, posed for accounting researchers.

Before proceeding to the disclosure debate, we note that researchers in the positive economics tradition, whether investigating valuation or practice issues, regard the EMH as a **maintained hypothesis** (i.e., they assume it is descriptive). Today, the acceptance of the EMH is such that empirical regularities apparently inconsistent with the hypothesis are called **anomalies** (e.g., Ball, 1978). This acceptance is based on the accumulated empirical evidence in finance and accounting. It is unaffected by the inability to date to discriminate between the no-effects and mechanistic hypotheses (see Chapter 4). The no-effects hypothesis is a joint hypothesis of the EMH, CAPM, and zero transactions and information costs and is not a direct implication of the EMH.

EMH AND EARLY RATIONALES

Many of the early rationales for corporate disclosure regulation have a common theme, that investors, and the stock market in general, cannot distinguish between efficient and less efficient firms. A variety of reasons are given for this inability to distinguish. Leftwich (1980) lists some of the reasons:

1. Monopoly control of information by management
2. Naïve investors
3. Functional fixation
4. Meaningless numbers
5. Diversity of procedures
6. Lack of objectivity

The following analysis of the EMH's implications for these arguments draws heavily on Leftwich's summary article.

Monopoly control of information by management is discussed in Chapter 4. Corporate accounting reports are often claimed to be the only source of information available to investors, and as a consequence, it is argued, managers are able to manipulate stock prices to their own advantage.

In an efficient market, the stock price adjustment to an accounting report is unbiased, so the second part of the claim does not follow, managers cannot *systematically* mislead the stock market.

The evidence on the EMH suggests that the first part of the claim is also incorrect; that is, it suggests that there are alternative sources of information. Further, given the EMH, the evidence presented in Chapter 3 suggests that the market can discriminate between efficient and less efficient firms, at least to some degree.

The criticism could be restated to make it potentially valid in an efficient market. If management has more information than is available via other sources but does not provide the information to the market, it can be argued that the market cannot discriminate between efficient and less efficient firms as accurately as it otherwise might. Hence, governmentally enforced disclosure improves the ability of the capital market to discriminate between firms and to allocate capital appropriately.

This restated criticism has some difficulties. Why don't the alternative sources produce, or why doesn't the management disclose, the additional information? In an efficient market, if the alternative sources do not produce the additional information, it must not pay them to do so. The production costs exceed the revenue derived from sale of the information. The managers also do not disclose the information because the production costs of disclosure (not their forgone profits on insider trading) exceed the market value of the information (discussed shortly). Hence, required governmental disclosure can only be superior *if* the costs of production are less with required disclosure and/or the social value of the information is greater than its market value (see the next section). The issue is an empirical one, and a priori it is not apparent that any managerial monopoly power over information leads to a nonoptimal ability of the market to discriminate between efficient and less efficient firms.

In competitive markets, managers do not earn an abnormal rate of return by withholding and trading on information because the manager's equilibrium compensation is reduced by the amount of profits he is expected to earn from insider trading (see Manne, 1966). In an efficient market, the firm's stock price is such that investors outside the firm (from whom the managers earn their insider trading profits) earn a normal rate of return. Thus, the effect of insider trading is to lower the firm's stock *price* without increasing (on average) the managers' compensation. To the extent that insider trading interferes with the managers' production/investment and financing decisions, it lowers the market value of the firm even farther.

If, by providing additional information, managers can persuade the market that they will engage in less insider trading, they can increase the firm's market value and, given that their compensation depends on the market value, their own welfare. Consequently, managers have incentives to disclose the information and will do so if the costs of disclosure are less than the effect of the disclosure on the value of the firm.

The criticism of *naïve investors* maintains that accounting numbers cannot be interpreted by investors who do not have accounting training. For example, such "naïve" investors cannot compare the reported earnings of firms that use different accounting procedures.

In an efficient market, a firm's stock price incorporates an unbiased assessment of the information in the accounting numbers, so naïve investors cannot (on average) be hurt by their inability to understand accounting (i.e., they are **price protected**). They buy at a price that is "fair" in the sense that *on average* they earn a normal rate of return. If naïve investors systematically lose, a simple trading rule exists to earn abnormal returns (i.e., sell when they buy and buy when they sell).

In an efficient market, tailoring financial statements to naïve investors does not increase their wealth or the firm's value. A better prescription is for naïve investors to diversify their portfolios to reduce the probability that they will lose (make negative abnormal returns).

The term *naïve* investor is misleading, for these investors are not necessarily naïve. Either they have chosen not to invest in acquiring skills in accounting, finance, and economics or they do not have a comparative advantage for that type of analysis. Leftwich uses the example of a purchaser of stereo equipment to illustrate the point. That purchaser can make an informed purchase of stereo equipment even though he has not acquired the skills to understand fully the technical complexities of the equipment. All that he need do is purchase information on the performance of stereo equipment from *Consumer Reports* or stereo magazines. Similarly, naïve investors can purchase information from sophisticated analysts such as Value Line or Standard & Poor's. That information is costly, so investors trade off the expected cost of a mistake against the cost of the information. A choice not to invest in information is not necessarily naïve; it can merely reflect the investor's personal trade-off.

The hypothesis of *functional fixation* maintains that individual investors interpret earnings numbers the same way regardless of the accounting procedures used to calculate them. If all investors acted this way, there would be a mechanical relation between earnings and stock prices, and the stock market would not discriminate between efficient and less efficient firms.[1]

---

[1] The mechanistic hypothesis discussed in Chapter 4 is a hypothesis about *market* relations (i.e., stock prices react mechanistically to earnings changes). Functional fixation is a hypothesis about *individual* investors.

One interpretation of the functional fixation hypothesis is that investors do not discriminate between earnings calculated using different procedures because it is costly to adjust the numbers. However, the effects of changes in accounting procedures are publicly disclosed, and there are numerous "sophisticated" investors in the marketplace who can make the adjustment at low cost. Hence, the stock market prices would behave "as if" all investors discriminated between earnings calculated under different accounting methods. The semi-strong form of the EMH has that implication. Those functionally fixated investors who do not discriminate are essentially naïve investors and do not lose (on average) in an efficient market.

An alternative interpretation of the functional fixation hypothesis is that investors are irrational. That interpretation is inconsistent with the EMH and indeed economics itself because economics assumes rationality. Even if investors behave irrationally in making investment decisions, those who, by chance, choose rational investment rules prosper and those who do not eventually do not have funds to invest.[2] This tendency is reinforced by those who imitate the investment rules of successful investors.

In *meaningless numbers,* some critics charge that, because earnings are calculated using several different methods of valuation (e.g, historical cost, current cost, and market value), the earnings numbers are meaningless *and* stock prices based on those numbers do not discriminate between efficient and less efficient firms. Given the EMH, Chapter 3's evidence is inconsistent with this criticism. Positive stock price changes are associated with positive unexpected earnings and negative stock prices with negative unexpected earnings. Therefore, since the stock price is an unbiased estimate of value, earnings changes are measures of value changes.

The more interesting issue is whether different and more meaningful methods of calculating earnings lead to *better* estimates of value by the market, to market prices that better discriminate efficient firms. This issue raises the same question that accompanied our restatement of the management monopoly of information criticism: since such a better earnings calculation method would provide outside producers of information or managers with an abnormal return, why isn't it currently provided by outside producers or managers? In an efficient market, the lack of provision of these methods indicates that, at the individual level, the system's costs exceed its benefits to managers or producers. Governmentally required use of that better method would only improve welfare if the resultant costs of production are less than in the free

---

[2] See Alchian (1950) for a discussion of economic Darwinism.

market and/or the social benefits are larger than the private benefits. This issue is addressed in the next section.

Diversity of procedures is another reason given for the inability of the capital market to distinguish between efficient and less efficient firms and is often given in conjunction with the naïve investor criticism. As indicated in discussing the other criticisms, in an efficient market, managers cannot use diverse procedures to mislead investors systematically. Investors are price protected. Also, as suggested, managers and outside producers of information have incentives to reduce the confusion due to the diversity of accounting procedures. To argue that government-imposed uniformity increases social welfare requires that either (1) disclosure costs are less with government-imposed uniformity or (2) the benefits of uniformity are greater than those currently being captured by individuals (i.e., social benefits exceed private benefits).

The *lack of objectivity* criticism states that under current practice, different accountants produce different accounting numbers from the same set of facts. The reason is that the accountant has the freedom to choose among a set of accounting procedures and has to make subjective estimates (e.g., depreciation). But objectivity per se is not necessarily valuable. The issue is the number's usefulness and its production cost. Hence, if objective accounting measures are not observed in an efficient market, it is probably because they are not cost effective.

These criticisms do not imply that accounting prevents an efficient capital market from distinguishing between efficient and less efficient firms. Further, the criticisms do not imply that government regulation of accounting improves the market's ability to allocate capital in an efficient manner. This issue is an empirical one, depending on relative costs and benefits of private production of information and governmentally regulated production of information.

RATIONALES FROM THE ECONOMIC LITERATURE

The EMH reduces those early disclosure regulation rationales that survive analysis to claims about relative costs and benefits. However, researchers who adopt the EMH as a maintained hypothesis raised other potential justifications for regulation of accounting reports and financial disclosure (e.g., Gonedes and Dopuch, 1974). These rationales were taken from the economic literature on **market failures**. In turn, these rationales were criticized using arguments existing in the economics literature. The following analysis of the alleged market failures draws heavily on a summary by Leftwich (1980).

The Alleged Market Failures

A market failure exists when the quantity or quality of a good produced in a free market differs from the supposed social optimum. The social optimum is the output that maximizes some social welfare function. The optimum is attained only if the goods' prices equal their social marginal costs. In private markets, individuals maximize their own utility and equate their private marginal benefits and costs. If a good's private costs are less than its social costs, too much of the good is produced in a free market; there is *overproduction* of the good. If a good's private benefits are less than its social benefits, too little of the good is produced; there is *underproduction* of the good. The over- or underproduction is relative to the production level chosen by a benevolent, social welfare maximizing dictator. As described later, the benchmark's definition calls into question many of these conclusions.

The following apple and honey bee example is often used to illustrate a market failure. The beekeeper and an apple grower have adjacent land so that the bees, besides producing honey, pollinate the apples and the apple blossoms, besides making apples, provide the bees with nectar. However, the beekeeper does not capture the benefits of his bees' pollinating actions nor does the apple grower capture the benefits of his blossom's nectar. Both ignore these benefits when making their output decisions and, as a result, underproduce both honey and apples.

Market failures suggest that social welfare can be improved in a Pareto sense by government regulation moving the private output closer to the social optimum. The ability of the government to increase welfare in a Pareto sense means it can induce an output change that makes at least one person better off without making anyone worse off. In the bee and apple example, the social marginal benefits exceed social marginal cost, so the government would increase the output of honey and apples. After compensating those who bear the regulation's costs, additional honey and apples are available.

An accounting market failure is alleged to exist because the output of information in accounting reports in the absence of regulation is nonoptimal in a Pareto sense. Or an accounting market failure exists because the resource allocation resulting from the market for financial information is inequitable, that is, "unfair" to some groups or individuals (e.g., Burton, 1974). This type of market failure has not been pursued by accounting researchers who apply economics because it is impossible to define an optimality criterion of "fairness" that is acceptable to everyone. Each individual would rank the resource allocation in terms of his preferences, and in general there is no reason to believe that those preferences can be aggregated into a consistent social welfare function.[3] Assessments of "fairness" are personal value judgments.

Accounting researchers tended to concentrate on alleged *under-production* of information resulting from the public goods problem.[4] However, an alleged *overproduction* resulting from the signaling problem has also been addressed. Those problems are described next, together with another overproduction case raised in the economics literature, overproduction due to speculation.

THE PUBLIC GOOD PROBLEM

The distinguishing feature of a **public good** is that one person's consumption of it does not reduce the quantity available for others to consume. A traditional example of a public good is national defense. One person's consumption of a private good (apples) does reduce the quantity available for others.

Information in accounting reports is assumed to be a public and not a private good (e.g., Gonedes and Dopuch, 1974). However, accounting information has both public and private good attributes. Consumption (use) of information by one investor reduces the ability of others to use the information and reap the same rewards (prices have adjusted). Also, there is an indirect cost to the disclosing firm if the information has adverse effects on its competitive position (Beaver, 1981, p. 191). The issue is whether models of information as a public good produce implications more consistent with the evidence than models in which information is a private good. Little evidence exists as to which is the better assumption for accounting information. Nevertheless, to pursue the analysis, this chapter assumes information is a public good.

The public good attribute of information does not of itself lead to a market failure per se. The failure comes about if the private producers cannot exclude nonpurchasers of the good from using it or cannot perfectly price discriminate among purchasers. In the case of corporate financial statements, it is claimed that corporate managers cannot exclude nonpurchasers (Gonedes and Dopuch, 1974). Investors who do not hold securities in the firm can obtain the information in the firm's report without paying anything toward the information's production. Because they are not paid for the use of information by nonpurchasers (e.g., nonshareholders), corporate managers do not take the value of the information to those nonpurchasers into account when

---

[3] See Arrow (1963) and Demski (1974).
[4] For example, Gonedes and Dopuch (1974), Gonedes (1976), May and Sundem (1976), and Beaver (1976).

determining the quantity of information to produce (private benefits are less than public benefits). Hence, the managers "underproduce" information in the absence of regulation. There is an alleged market failure.

THE SIGNALING PROBLEM (ALSO CALLED THE "SCREENING" PROBLEM)

The problem arises because one party to a potential transaction has more information than another; that is, there is **information asymmetry.** The problem was developed in the economics literature by Akerlof (1970), Arrow (1973), Spence (1973), and Stiglitz (1975a), among others, and Gonedes, Dopuch, and Penman (1976) and Gonedes (1978) suggest that the problem is applicable to accounting information.

A simple example should make clear the nature of the market failure resulting from the signaling problem. Consider a labor force made up of two types of individuals, one being more productive than the other. While the individual workers know their productivity before contracting in the labor market, their potential employers do not because it is too costly for them to determine. As a result, the suppliers are paid based on average, or expected, productivity. The more productive individuals are paid less than they would if employers could distinguish them; hence, they have an incentive to spend resources to signal they are more productive. One way to do this is to attend college. The more productive workers attend college and signal their productivity, thereby increasing their wage. Only the more productive attend college because it costs them less to signal. The less productive do not attend and implicitly signal that they are less productive.

If college does not increase anyone's productivity, the resources spent on college do not increase output. The wages of the more productive workers are raised at the expense of the less productive workers. In a Pareto sense, the education expenditure is wasteful. The benefits of education to the more productive individual are greater than the benefits to society and there is an overproduction of college education.

The problem is extended to corporate disclosure by noting that corporate managers have more information about the value of the corporation than do outside investors. Those firms whose share prices are undervalued have an incentive to expend additional resources on financial information to signal that fact. The remaining, overvalued firms implicitly signal that fact by not providing additional information, and the value of their shares drops to the average value for the overvalued group. Now, some of those firms' shares are "undervalued," and they expend resources to provide additional information. The process continues until only the very worst performing firms do not signal. We use the term **signaling hypothesis** to refer to the proposition that signaling motivates corporate disclosure.

Clearly the expenditure of resources on information in our corporate example improves the allocation of capital and increases output (i.e., the most efficient firms receive more capital). However, part of the expenditure is related to past performance and may not be related to future performance and hence not yield any social benefits. To that extent, signaling can cause an overproduction of information in accounting reports.

THE SPECULATION PROBLEM

This problem was advanced in the economics literature by Hirshleifer (1971) and Fama and Laffer (1971). It concerns overproduction of information by individuals outside the firm for speculative purposes. Barzel (1977) illustrates the nature of the speculation problem. Suppose that a wheat farmer plants his wheat and expects to harvest a crop of 1,000 bushels in six months. The price of the crop depends on weather conditions in other growing areas and will be 50 cents or $1.50 per bushel with equal probability. Now suppose that it is possible to predict the weather in the other areas with certainty if one expends resources costing $100. Knowledge of that weather does not enable the wheat farmer to change his crop. But individuals have an incentive to invest in the prediction. Without the prediction, a future contract will sell for $(.5)(.50) + (.5)($1.50) = 1.00 per bushel. If the individual speculator investing in the prediction discovers that the price will be 50 cents, he sells a future contract to deliver wheat at $1 per bushel and then later fulfills the contract using wheat costing 50 cents per bushel. If the forecast price is $1.50 per bushel, the speculator buys a futures contract at $1 per bushel and takes delivery of the wheat that he can sell at $1.50 per bushel. In either case, the speculator makes 50 cents per bushel, which on the farmer's crop amounts to $500 or $400 after the expenditure on the prediction.

In this example, the $100 spent on generating the weather prediction does not alter the output of wheat; it merely reallocates wealth. So while the private benefits to the speculator of the investment in the prediction model are positive, the social benefits are zero. The case is analogous to investing resources to develop a scheme for predicting the outcome of a horse race. Presumably, resources are overspent on predicting corporate winners when such predictions do not enable firms to change production decisions.

Fallacies in the Market Failure
Rationales[5]

The three market failures just outlined involve the same fallacies. First, they are generated in very stylized worlds, and it is then assumed that they also occur in practice. That is a very big assumption, as we shall see. The simple worlds ignore important market attributes, attributes that reduce the likelihood of market failure. Second, in claiming that the alleged market failures justify government regulation to achieve the optimal level of information, the proponents of these market failures commit the "grass is always greener fallacy" (see Demsetz, 1969). They assume the governmental alternative achieves the optimal output and fail to examine that alternative's outcome as closely as they examine the market outcome. Leftwich (1980) suggests that those proponents commit another fallacy—they do not show that the supposed optimum, to which they compare the market, can be produced by any feasible set of institutional arrangements. Hence, it is questionable whether it is an optimum.

The individual market failures are now examined to determine what is missing from the simple scenarios. Then the question of how one would determine the existence of a market failure is addressed.

THE PUBLIC GOOD PROBLEM

There is evidence that private producers of public goods have been able to contract to receive payment from some of the users of those goods (Coase, 1974; Cheung, 1973). Further, there is evidence that firms provided accounting reports long before those reports were required by law (Benston, 1969a). If private producers contract for payment from some of those who receive benefits from the public good, why don't they contract with those who "free ride"? One answer, of course, is the cost of contracting with those individuals. Presumably, the payment (benefit) the private producer would receive from contracting with those individuals exceeds the cost of contracting with them. By definition, this is why these consumers are "free riders."

Once contracting costs are admitted, it is no longer apparent that the public good problem results in a market failure. The costs of contracting are just as real as any other production costs. If private contracting costs are greater than the private benefits to be captured, there is only a market failure if government's contracting costs are lower than the private costs. No evidence has been presented to support that condition.

[5] The interested reader is encouraged to see Verrecchia (1982) for further analysis of these issues.

THE SIGNALING PROBLEM

This problem also ignores contracting costs (Barzel, 1977). Suppose that contracting costs are zero (as is usually assumed by market failure proponents). Then, in our college education example, a contract can be constructed that is Pareto superior to signaling via a college education.

A college education takes 4 years, so let an employer be able to determine perfectly and at zero cost whether an employee is more or less productive after 10 years. Then the employer can offer a contract that everyone will prefer. For the first 10 years, the employer pays every employee slightly more than the value of the product of a less productive individual. When productivity is resolved after 10 years, no adjustment is made for the less productive individuals. However, the more productive individuals receive a bonus equal to the value of their extra output during the first 10 years minus slightly less than the cost of a college education. All parties are better off with this contract than with signaling by college education. The less productive individuals earn a higher income, the more productive individuals have higher wealth (the bonus is reduced by an amount less than the cost of college), and the employer has to pay less. College would not be used to signal.

To be optimal, the signaling problem has to assume high contracting costs. However, as we have argued, if those costs are the same for the individuals and the government, there is no market failure.

THE SPECULATION PROBLEM

Barzel (1977) points out that the speculation scenario (Hirshleifer, 1971) assumes zero transactions costs. In that world, is there an alternative contract that is superior for the farmer and the consumer? The expected price for the farmer dealing exclusively with the informed speculator is $(.5)(1.00) + (.5)(.50) = 75$ cents a bushel. Remember, in our example that half the time he buys (from the farmer) a future contract for delivery at $1 per bushel and half the time the speculator buys wheat at 50 cents per bushel. The expected price for the consumer dealing exclusively with speculators is $(.5)(1.50) + (.5)(1.00) = \$1.25$ per bushel. When the speculator buys a future contract at $1 per bushel, he sells to consumers at $1.50 per bushel, and when he buys wheat at 50 cents a bushel, it is in fulfilling a futures contract (sold to consumers) at $1 per bushel. In this world the farmer and the consumers can avoid the speculator by writing long-term contracts at $1 per bushel and not dealing with the speculator. Both the farmer and the consumer are better off. The farmer would receive $1.00 per bushel instead of 75 cents, and the consumer would pay $1 per bushel instead of $1.25. Since the speculator contributes nothing, the farmer and the consumer would not trade with him. Resources would not be wasted, and the market failure would not exist.

Resources would only be spent on the wasteful prediction if the contracts between farmers and consumers were more costly. However, in that case since the forecasting speculator is the cheapest way to arrange the contract, it is not very meaningful to describe it as inefficient; there is not a market failure.

The three alleged market failures ignore the private costs of contracting. But private contracting costs are required in these theories to explain why nonpurchasers are not excluded, why signaling behavior is engaged in, or why resources are spent on speculative prediction. In other words, the analysis is incomplete, and there is not any necessary market failure. While private contracting costs are assumed high, the government's costs of remedying the market failure are often assumed to be zero (or at least lower than private contracting costs). Otherwise, it would not be obvious that the government could achieve a better output level.

The existence of a market failure in the production of information in accounting reports depends on the costs of private contracting and production of information relative to the costs of government achieving the private level of output. If the government's costs are substantial, it is not apparent that there is any market failure in the private production of information in corporate accounting reports. To illustrate this point, the costs of government regulation of accounting disclosure are briefly considered.

The Cost of Regulation

The cost of regulating corporate financial disclosure is not solely the direct cost of resources consumed by regulatory bodies in making and enforcing rules and regulations and by firms in meeting those rules and regulations. The regulations also affect the investment, production, and financing decisions of firms and not necessarily in a way that improves welfare in a Pareto sense. Those indirect costs also have to be considered and are probably much larger than the direct costs.

THE DIRECT COSTS

The SEC was established by the Securities Exchange Act of 1934. Its role is to administer the Securities Act of 1933 and the Securities Exchange Act of 1934. The SEC was given the power to specify the form and content of corporate financial statements—including accounting procedures. Since 1937 the commission has published a series of accounting releases that, while dealing primarily with what firms must and must not disclose (disclosure matters), have also dealt with accounting standards. The commission's effect on disclosure has varied. For example, firms must disclose quarterly sales, but until recently, they were not allowed to disclose upward revaluations of assets. The number of the SEC's releases has increased dramatically since 1972. Clearly, the SEC consumes resources in developing these releases and in monitoring and enforcing compliance.

While the SEC issues accounting series releases, it has nominally delegated its power to set standards to other bodies. In 1938, in response to SEC prodding, the AICPA established a committee to determine accounting standards. The SEC required financial statements filed with the commission to use those standards. The AICPA Committee on Accounting Procedures (CAP) determined standards from 1939 to 1959. In 1959 the AICPA replaced the CAP with another committee, the APB. The APB determined standards from 1959 to 1973. In 1973, due to criticism of its performance, the APB was replaced by the FASB, which continues to issue accounting standards.

In 1936 the total appropriations for the SEC were $3 million. Twenty-five years later, in 1961, total appropriations had increased by 314 percent to $9.5 million. In the next 10 years (to 1971), they increased by 248 percent to $23.6 million, and finally in the last 9 years (to 1980), they increased by 307 percent to $72.3 million. The increasing rate of growth in resources consumed (even allowing for inflation) is apparent. The Consumer Price Index has tripled over the period 1936 to 1976, while the SEC's appropriations have increased 15-fold.

The regulation of accounting standards per se probably represents only a very small part of the SEC's total appropriations. But in addition to the SEC's resources, there are also the resources consumed by the FASB. A rough index of that number can be obtained from the contributions to operate that body. In 1975, those contributions were $4.13 million.

In addition to the direct costs of the SEC and FASB, there are the costs incurred by the accounting firms and corporations complying with the standards as well as the costs of lobbying on proposed accounting standards. Accounting firms, corporate managers, and industry representatives frequently make submissions before the FASB and SEC on proposed standards.

An example of the corporations' direct costs for *one* rule can be found in Bastable (1977). He surveys 18 corporations as to the incremental cost of complying with Accounting Series Release (ASR) 190— the requirement that firms publish replacement cost data. The average incremental direct cost of meeting ASR 190 in its first required year for the 13 firms that answered Bastable's survey was approximately $12,400. Multiply this by the number of corporations required to meet the requirement (1,000), and the total annual incremental direct cost of corporations meeting ASR 190 in 1976 is $12 million. And this is the cost of only one (but one of the most costly) of the disclosure requirements promulgated in 1976.

In an unusual study for the SEC, the Advisory Committee to the SEC on Corporate Disclosure estimated some of the costs of meeting the SEC's regulations. Using those numbers, Phillips and Zecher (1981, Ch. 3, p. 28) estimate the variable costs to firms of filing 10-K, 10-Q, and 8-K forms with the SEC in 1975 at $213 million. Those costs do not incorporate the SEC's own costs, and they have certain biases that cause an underestimation (see Phillips and Zecher, 1981, Ch. 3, pp. 28–30).

The costs of monitoring, compliance, and lobbying are not the only direct costs of regulations that are imposed on corporations or public accounting firms. For example, there is also the expected increase in losses from lawsuits against accountants and corporations as a consequence of rules that increase disclosure.[6] In addition, many contracts (e.g., management compensation contracts, lending agreements) use accounting numbers. When standards change, the accounting numbers can change and the terms of these contracts may have to be renegotiated—a costly process.

THE INDIRECT COSTS OF REGULATION

Some accounting standards appear to cause corporate managers to change their financing, investment and/or production decisions in a fashion that imposes costs on firms. A few isolated examples illustrate this point. The Monumental Corporation argued that it would invest more in bonds and less in stocks if unrealized gains and losses on securities were to be included in income.[7]

Another claimed example of firms changing economic decisions as a consequence of an accounting standard is the reaction by some firms to FASB Statement No. 8, "Accounting for the Translation of Foreign Currency Transactions and Foreign Currency Financial Statements." After imposition of that standard, some firms engaged in (costly) hedging operations to reduce the effects of FASB 8 on the variance of their reported earnings. Further, some banks developed and apparently successfully marketed models that told firms how to manage their overseas assets to reduce exposure to the effects of FASB

---

[6] It is possible that accounting regulation on net reduces legal liability and, hence, expected litigation costs by giving accountants and their clients the defense that they were following standard disclosure rules.

[7] See Foster (1977, p. 536). Note that in Monumental's case, it issued a statement. We do not know whether, in fact, it would have changed investment policy.

8—again a costly exercise.[8] Given that managers had these options available to them before FASB 8, if the managers are maximizing the market value of the firm, these hedging and asset rearrangements represent costs to the firms and to society unless society receives some benefit that the firm does not.

Note that systematic resource consuming actions such as those in response to FASB 8 suggest (in an efficient market) that accounting procedures affect the firm's future cash flows. Otherwise, managers would not systematically undertake costly actions to offset the accounting consequences. These actions suggest that Chapter 4's assumption (i.e., accounting procedures do not affect cash flows) is not warranted.

The costs of disclosure regulation are borne by society via higher taxes to pay for the promulgation and enforcement of the disclosures and in lower returns on corporate equity. Who bears these costs is unknown, but they include the shareholders, managers, and consumers of the corporation's products.

It appears from the preceding that the costs of regulating disclosure, in particular of regulating accounting procedures, are substantial. Without evidence on (1) the magnitude of those costs relative to private costs of contracting and producing information and (2) the benefits of regulation, it is not apparent that government regulation of financial disclosure improves social welfare.

The Stock Price Effects of Regulation

Researchers have attempted to assess the stock price effects of regulation of disclosure. Presumably, those stock price effects provide evidence on some of the costs and benefits of regulation.

Benston (1973) represents one of the earliest of these studies and certainly one of the most ambitious. He attempts to test whether the securities acts met one of their stated objectives and increased the information available to investors. If those acts did increase information, Benston argues, investors should alter their assessments of firms' risk and expected rates of return, and, hence, the firms' stock prices should change. He investigates changes in firms' estimated risk ($\hat{b}$), average monthly abnormal rates of return ($\bar{e}$), and the variance of monthly abnormal rates of return (σ_e^2) around the time of the securities acts.

The only item of additional information that firms supplied after, but not before, the securities acts was sales. And *some* firms even supplied sales before the securities acts. Benston separates his sample into firms that did and did not publish sales before the securities acts and compares the changes in $\hat{b}$, $\bar{e}$, and σ_e^2 at the time of the acts for

---

[8] For reports of the responses by management, see *Business Week,* January 26, 1976 and February 14, 1977.

those samples. Benston finds no differences in the changes. In essence, Benston finds no evidence of costs or benefits of the securities acts.

Benston's methodology has been criticized (Gonedes and Dopuch, 1974, pp. 93–96). For example, there is no theoretical reason for σ_e^2 to be affected. Also, it seems reasonable to hypothesize that if the acts were beneficial, they would increase the attractiveness of investing in listed stocks *in general* instead of increasing the attractiveness of some stocks relative to others (as measured by $\hat{e}$).

While Benston finds no evidence of costs or benefits of regulation, a number of other studies (discussed in later chapters) suggest that accounting regulation imposes costs on firms. For example, Chow (1983) finds that the 1933 Securities Act reduced the wealth of shareholders of firms that were affected by the act relative to those firms not affected by the act (OTC stocks). Hence, there is evidence that regulation imposes private (e.g., the stock price effects) and social costs (e.g., the resources spent by the SEC) and little evidence of benefits.

The evidence on costs, and more important, the tendency of regulation rationales to ignore relative cost issues that bias the assessment toward government regulation, led researchers to question whether the objective of regulation and regulators is to remedy market failures. Asking that question represented a breakthrough in accounting research. It meant that the assumption that regulation is a response to market failure would no longer be automatic. And it provided the opening for models of the political process and its participants' behavior. Development of a theory of the political process is important to a theory of accounting practice via practice affected by government regulation.

The application of the EMH to accounting was responsible for accountants' questioning regulation's objective. It led to the first steps in the evolution of the regulatory debate. However, the EMH led to another question that also opened the door for developing a theory of accounting practice. That question came from Chapter 4's evidence that managers engaged in costly accounting procedure changes. If an accounting change that does not affect taxes is costly and has no other effect on firm value, why do managers make those changes? Why do they care about accounting procedures?

TWO IMPORTANT QUESTIONS

What Is the Objective of Disclosure Regulation?

There has not been a thorough investigation of the costs and benefits of disclosure from the time the securities acts were passed until the present. Identifying *possible* market failures does not imply government action unless there *is* a market failure. Nor does the SEC seem concerned with assessing whether government regulation improves welfare.

ASR 190 serves to illustrate the SEC's apparent lack of concern with evaluating the social costs and benefits of regulation. ASR 190 required (issued March, 1976) that all large corporations disclose the current replacement cost of inventories, plant, and equipment. The SEC justified ASR 190 on the grounds that investors would find such data useful:

> [T]he Commission recognizes that the cost of implementing this rule will be significant, particularly in the first year of preparing the necessary data.
> The Commission has carefully considered the cost of implementation and weighed it against the need of investors for replacement cost information. It has concluded that in the case of companies of large size which generally have the largest public investor interest, the data are of such importance that *the benefits of disclosure clearly outweigh the costs* of data preparation. (emphasis added; SEC, ASR 190, March 23, 1976)

Although the SEC states that the benefits clearly outweigh the costs, no evidence is offered by the SEC to support this assertion.

These data not being produced privately by the firms prior to ASR 190 suggest that the private costs of production exceeded the private benefits. Part of the private costs of production include the costs of disseminating the information, billing the users, and collecting these bills. Given those costs, some of the users of this information would be free riders (i.e., nonpayers), and there could be a market failure.

For government regulation to be efficient (i.e., for ASR 190 to increase welfare),

1. The costs of the SEC monitoring this disclosure and the costs of corporations complying must be less than the costs corporations would have incurred providing this information voluntarily, *and*
2. The total amount all users would be *willing* to pay exceeds all the costs incurred in providing the information.

Using security prices, a number of researchers are *unable* to find a stock price reaction *when* firms disclosed ASR 190 data.[9] Thus, there is no evidence that shareholders found the SEC mandated data useful in valuing their firms. These research studies provide evidence that does *not* support the assertion that the private benefits exceed the private costs.

[9] See Gheyara and Boatsman (1980), Beaver, Christie, and Griffin (1980), and Ro (1980).

However, these studies do not assess all the private and social costs and benefits. For example, the replacement costs of firm X *may* be of use to the investors in firm Y (a private and social benefit) or *may* induce large social costs to be incurred (the SEC *may* have to hire personnel to file the disclosures, monitor and enforce the disclosures, etc.). Without evidence on the costs and benefits, almost any government regulation can be justified if all possible benefits are included.

ASR 190 is not an isolated example; the SEC spends virtually none of its budget in systematically assessing the costs and benefits of regulation. Most of the budget is spent in making, monitoring, and enforcing rules and regulations. Little serious concern is given to making rules that further or even consider economic efficiency.

A former assistant solicitor of the SEC, Homer Kripke (1979, pp. 58–59) supports this impression:

> In the current world of tax revolt and demands for deregulation, discussions by and about regulators in the language of weighing costs and benefits have become fashionable. The Commission has used this rhetoric several times (as in ASR 190), but has never persuaded this reader that such analysis contributed to the Commission's conclusion. On the contrary, I infer that this language is tossed off as a makeweight explanation of a conclusion for which the real reasons lie in the Commission's obsessive approach that more disclosure is per se better.

A former chief economist of the SEC and one of his staff (Phillips and Zecher, 1981, Ch. 6, p. 3) are just as blunt:

> Nonetheless, the generalizations remain valid that the SEC, like most regulatory agencies, has rarely attempted to measure the success of its programs in attaining various goals, nor has it devoted significant resources to answering the much easier question of how much the programs cost society, who pays, and how the resources are reallocated.

Just as the accountants' and managers' statements that the market is inefficient do not mean the market is inefficient (see Chapter 4), these statements by former SEC officials do not necessarily imply that the SEC does not maximize social welfare. However, the lack of concern with that objective and the comments do suggest that the descriptive ability of the social welfare maximization objective should be investigated.

Fortunately for accounting researchers concerned with apparent inconsistencies between the SEC's objectives and actions, economists and political scientists had encountered similar regulatory inconsistencies. Until recently, economists too had assumed regulation was intended to increase social welfare.[10] However, the apparent inconsistencies between regulators' actions and the "public interest" hypothesis caused economists to investigate the extent to which that assumption provides an empirical explanation for the regulators' behavior. The empirical inconsistencies of the "public interest" hypothesis revealed by such investigations led some economists and political scientists to assume that politicians and regulators are no different from anyone else; that is, they act in their own self-interest.[11] Further, those economists and political scientists argue that information and contracting costs in the political process explain the inconsistencies between politicians' and regulators' actions and the public interest hypothesis.

In attempting to build a theory of disclosure regulation, positive accounting researchers borrowed heavily from the economists. The rudimentary theory outlined in the following chapters not only assumes that politicians and regulators maximize their self-interest, but it uses the economists' theories based on that assumption.

The economists' theories include an assumption of nonzero information costs in the political process. That assumption has important implications for accounting theory. It enables the firm's accounting procedures to affect the political process's outcomes and hence the firm's cash flows. For example, it means that accounting procedures can affect the rates allowed by utility commissions. Given those cash flow effects, firm managers are no longer indifferent among tax-neutral accounting procedures (as assumed in Chapter 4) and accounting choices can affect firm value. Hence, there is the potential to develop a theory explaining the managers' choice of accounting procedures.

Why Do Managers Care About Accounting Procedures?

Chapter 4 reviews attempts to discriminate between EMH and the mechanistic hypothesis using changes in accounting procedures. Those studies assume that the only cash flow effects of accounting changes are any accompanying tax effects. This assumption was influenced by finance theory of the time (e.g., Modigliani and Miller, 1963). However, the studies produced evidence that many firms in an industry change nontax accounting procedures at the same time (e.g., the steel industry switched back to straight-line depreciation method in 1968). This cross-sectional dependence made researchers suspect that the no-effects

[10] For a summary of the literature based on this assumption, see Posner (1974) and McCraw (1975).

[11] See Downs (1957a and b), Niskanen (1971), Stigler (1971), and Peltzman (1976).

assumption is not descriptive. Why would firms influenced by similar economic variables switch at the same time?

One explanation is the one just given—that accounting procedures affect the outcome of the political process. However, many of the systematic changes cannot be explained by regulation or the political process effect. Thus the question could be rephrased. Why in the absence of political process effects would firms influenced by similar economic variables switch procedures at the same time?

An explanation consistent with the no-effects hypothesis is that because accounting procedures do not affect value, managers develop arbitrary ways to select accounting procedures. One such rule is to imitate a given firm in the industry. In economic Darwinism such changes are *neutral mutations* (see Miller, 1977). This argument, however, is only viable if such changes are costless. If the changes are costly (as they are) and recurring over time, they cannot be neutral mutations; they must have offsetting benefits.

The tendency of whole industries simultaneously to change procedures reminded researchers that firms in the same industries tend to use the same accounting methods. For example, profit recognition is usually at sale in manufacturing and retail industries, but it is often at production in mining. Positive accounting researchers asked themselves whether such systematic variation is due to neutral mutation or to variation in procedures' costs and benefits across industries.

Fortunately for positive accounting research, finance faced a very similar question at the same time. The Modigliani and Miller analysis suggested that all firms, regardless of industry, should have the highest debt/equity ratios the Internal Revenue Service would allow because of the tax deductibility of interest payments. Yet debt/equity ratios varied systematically across industries, and the industry difference continued over long time periods (see Schwartz and Aronson, 1967). Finance theorists sought an offsetting cost of debt to explain these capital structure differences. One solution was to drop the assumption of zero transaction, information, and contracting costs. Bankruptcy and contracting costs were assumed to vary with the debt/equity ratio.

The dropping of the zero contracting costs assumption also provided the opportunity for accounting procedures to affect the value of the firm. The contracting explanation for capital structure variations introduced into finance (Jensen and Meckling, 1976) included a role for accounting procedures. A firm's contracting costs could depend on the procedures it used. So it is not surprising that attempts to build an accounting theory to explain accounting procedure variations across firms used finance's contracting theory. The following chapters describe those attempts.

SUMMARY

Requests from standard setters for guidance led positive accounting researchers to analyze the implications of the EMH for the traditional rationales for disclosure regulation. Those analyses tended to discredit the traditional rationales. However, positive researchers introduced new rationales from the economics literature, rationales based on market failures. In their time, these new rationales (the public good problem, the signaling problem, and the speculation problem) were analyzed, and the conclusion is that a priori there is no clear justification for corporate disclosure regulation. It is an empirical question of relative costs and benefits.

The conclusion that the value of regulation is an empirical question conflicted with an apparent lack of concern by regulatory authorities with assessing the costs and benefits of regulation. This, in turn, led to questioning the assumption that regulation is motivated by the "public interest." That opened the door to modeling the behavior of participants in the political process as being motivated, like those in the market process, by self-interest. And it suggested the existence of nonzero information costs in the political process. Those nonzero information costs provided a reason for managers to care about the choice among tax-neutral accounting procedures. That reason serves as one basis for the rudimentary theory of accounting practice outlined in the following chapters.

The EMH led to another question and another basis for the theory of accounting practice. In the attempts to discriminate between the no-effects hypothesis and the mechanistic hypothesis, researchers noted systematic changes in accounting procedures that could not be explained by regulation or the political process. Firms in the same industries tended to change procedures at the same time, just as at any given time firms in the same industry tend to use the same procedures. This systematic behavior caused researchers to question the no-effects hypothesis.

At the same time finance researchers were questioning the hypothesis that, apart from tax effects, capital structure had no effect on firm value. The hypothesis could not explain systematic industry variation in capital structure. Finance theorists attempted to remedy the lack of explanation by assuming nonzero contracting costs. The same assumption provided a potential firm value effect for accounting procedures and therefore a potential explanation for cross-sectional and time series variations in accounting procedures.

CHAPTER EIGHT

The Contracting Process

Positive accounting researchers developed theories of accounting practice by applying economic theories that assume nonzero contracting and information costs. This cost assumption allows accounting procedures to affect the firm's or firm manager's cash flows and so provides the opportunity to explain variations in procedures across firms and time. Accounting is no longer mere form as in Chapters 3 to 6.

Contracting and information costs are assumed to be nonzero in both the firm's contracting process and in the political process that determines government regulation of the firm's activities. Accounting procedures affect those costs in both processes and, hence, the firm's or firm manager's cash flows. Consequently, the choice among procedures depends on both contracting and political process cash flow effects. However, for analytical purposes, it is useful to separate the two processes' effects. This chapter and Chapter 9 address cash flow effects in the contracting process and their implications for accounting procedure choice. The cash flow effects in the political process are left to Chapter 10. Between them, Chapters 8, 9, and 10 represent a rudimentary theory of accounting and auditing practice.

This chapter explains the economic theory of the firm that accounting researchers use to generate cash flow effects for accounting procedures. Then the chapter explains accounting's role in the theory and contrasts it to the role assumed for accounting in the positive accounting research summarized in Chapters 3–6. Chapter 9 concentrates on accounting's role under the theory in two specific contracts (management compensation plans and debt agreements) and develops hypotheses that are tested in Chapters 11 and 12.

The literature encompassing the economic theory covered in this chapter is often called the "property rights" literature because of its emphasis on rights established by contract (e.g., Coase, 1937, 1960; Alchian and Demsetz, 1972; Jensen and Meckling, 1976; and Fama and Jensen, 1983a, 1983b). In that theory, accounting is an integral part of the contracts that define the firm. These contracts include formal contracts, such as debt contracts between the firm's managers and debtholders, and informal contracts, such as unwritten working arrangements between managers. Those contracts also include the firm's organization chart and its evaluation and compensation schemes. The firm's contracting costs are as important to its profitability and survival as its production costs. The magnitude and cross-sectional variation of contracting costs are as important in explaining a firm's organization or accounting practices as are the magnitude and cross-sectional variation of production costs in explaining the firm's pricing decisions and industry structure.

The chapter develops the demand for contracts among the firm's parties by analyzing the demand for contracts in two simple situations: (1) a firm whose only parties are an owner-manager and outside nonvoting shareholders and (2) a firm whose only parties are an owner-manager and fixed debt claimants. These analyses show that the shareholders' and debtholders' *price protection* (see Chapter 7) leads the manager to demand management and debt contracts that restrict the actions he or she can take as manager. This demand, in turn, produces a demand for accounting and auditing. Following these simple cases, the analysis is extended to large firms with professional managers and both outside shareholders and debtholders and to the theory of the firm in general. The contracting role of accounting and its relation to the role assumed in Chapters 3–6 are then outlined, and the chapter concludes with a summary of the economic theory of contracting and accounting's role in that theory.

THE DEMAND FOR CONTRACTS BETWEEN OWNER-MANAGERS AND OUTSIDE SHAREHOLDERS

Jensen and Meckling (1976) model the contract between the shareholders of a firm and an owner-manager. For convenience, they assume that there are no other contractual parties to the firm. Jensen and Meckling call the contract between the owner-manager and shareholders an **agency relationship**. They define an agency relationship as "a contract under which one or more (principals) engage another person (the agent) to perform some service on their behalf which involves delegating some decision-making authority to the agent" (Jensen and Meckling, 1976, p. 308). In the manager-shareholder contract, the owner-manager is viewed as the agent and the shareholder as the principal.

The simplest Jensen and Meckling scenario involves an individual who owns 100 percent of the firm selling some nonvoting shares to outsiders while still managing the firm. This individual derives utility from money (pecuniary benefits) and nonpecuniary benefits such as on-the-job leisure (shirking), attractiveness of the workplace, and so on. The analysis compares the owner-manager's behavior before and after shares are sold. In particular, it investigates changes in the owner-manager's consumption of nonpecuniary benefits.

The analysis involves several simplifying assumptions (Jensen and Meckling, 1976, p. 314). However, the essential results can be obtained even if some of the assumptions are relaxed. Two particularly important assumptions are that the owner-manager's money wage is fixed and that no monitoring or bonding activities are possible. The second assumption is dropped later in this section and the first is dropped later in the chapter.

Jensen and Meckling define **bonding** activities to be the expenditure of resources by owner-managers to guarantee that they will limit their activities in accordance with a contract. For example, the owner-manager can deposit $100,000 with a third party who will idemnify the owners if the owner-manager defrauds them. **Monitoring** activities involve the expenditure of resources by the outside shareholders to guarantee that owner-managers limit their activities in accordance with a contract. In this book, monitoring is defined to include both monitoring and bonding.

The amount an owner-manager spends on nonpecuniary benefits depends on the fraction of the firm owned by the owner-manager. First, consider the owner-manager's expenditures on nonpecuniary benefits when all the firm's shares are owned by the manager.

Owner-Manager with No Outside Shareholders

The analysis depends on whether the nonpecuniary benefits are, or are not, *job specific*. If the manager prefers the business purchasing the benefits and consuming them at work to being paid the cost of the benefits and purchasing and consuming them privately, the benefits are job specific. If the manager is indifferent, the benefits are not job specific. If the nonpecuniary benefits are *not* job specific and markets are competitive, the owner-manager maximizes the present value of the firm's cash flows (also the value of the shares' cash flows since there is no debt) (see Brealey and Myers, 1984, Ch. 2). Spending on nonpecuniary benefits continues until an extra dollar spent on benefits increases the market value of the firm's cash flows by a dollar (i.e., until the net effect on the cash flows' present value is zero). Let the value of the firm's cash flows at that point be $\overline{V}$.

Now assume job-specific benefits so the owner-manager values consuming them at work (i.e., prefers consumption at work to private consumption). Then nonpecuniary benefits consumption is increased from the $\overline{V}$ level. At $\overline{V}$ the owner-manager values the marginal one dollar spent on nonpecuniary benefits at its one dollar present value effect *plus* the extra utility received from the nonpecuniary benefit. Hence, more is spent on nonpecuniary benefits even though the present value of cash flows from the extra nonpecuniary benefits is less than their cost (i.e., their net present value is negative). Spending continues until the marginal utility of an extra dollar spent on nonpecuniary benefits is equal to the marginal utility of the reduction in the present value of the firm's cash flows. Call the present value of the firm's cash flows at this point V^* ($V^* < \overline{V}$) and the cost of the increased nonpecuniary benefits $F^* \equiv \overline{V} - V^*$.

As an example of this effect, consider an owner-manager who is planning the number of business trips to take. If *no* utility is derived from business traveling other than the pecuniary returns to traveling, the owner-manager selects the level of travel that maximizes the value of the firm. However, if the owner-manager also enjoys business travel (i.e., derives nonpecuniary benefits in addition to the pecuniary rewards), additional travel is undertaken. The cost of that increased travel (the perquisites or "perks") is the resultant decrease in the present value of the firm's cash flows.

The Owner-Manager with Outside Shareholders

Assume that the owner-manager sells a fraction of the firm $(1 - \alpha)$ (where $0 < \alpha < 1$) in the form of nonvoting shares and retains a fraction (α). How does this change the owner-manager's decision on the quantity of perquisites? If perks are job specific and it is costless to force the owner-manager to consume the same level of perks, the fraction $(1 - \alpha)$ of the shares could be sold for $(1 - \alpha)V^*$. That is, if the outsiders were sure that the owner-manager would still consume

F^* dollars of perquisites, the value of the whole firm would be V^* and they would pay $(1 - \alpha)V^*$ for the shares purchased.

Suppose that the owner-manager can sell the fraction $(1 - \alpha)$ of equity for $(1 - \alpha)V^*$, but cannot be forced to take the same actions as if the manager owned 100 percent of the firm. Will the owner-manager consume the same level of perquisites (i.e., F^*)? The answer is no. Now increasing consumption of perks by one dollar costs the owner-manager only $\$\alpha(\alpha < 1)$. The outside shareholders bear $\$(1 - \alpha)$ of the cost. The marginal cost of the extra dollar of perks has dropped, and the owner-manager consumes more perks. Consumption of perks continues until the owner-manager values additional perks that reduce the firm's value by one dollar at $\$\alpha$. Call that level of perk expenditure F'.

As the owner-manager increases the amount spent on perks, the value of the firm falls. At the new equilibrium, when the owner-manager is purchasing perks costing F', the value of the firm is $V' = \overline{V} - F'$ and is less than its value before the outside shares were sold: $V^* = \overline{V} - F^*, F^* < F'$. If the outside shareholders paid $(1 - \alpha)V^*$ for their shares, they lose when the owner-manager consumes additional perks.

The preceding points can be illustrated by our travel example. Suppose three trips per year maximize the value of the firm at $100,000. If the owner-manager owns all the firm, the utility maximizing amount of travel is four trips. The net present value of the fourth trip is $-\$10,000$, so the value of the firm is $90,000. If the owner-manager is able to sell 30 percent of the firm to outsiders for 30 percent of $90,000 or $27,000, will the manager continue to take four business trips? Probably not. Suppose that the net present value of a fifth trip was also $-\$10,000$. Before selling 30 percent of the firm, that extra business trip would cost the owner-manager $10,000 (ignoring taxes). But now, the cost of the additional trip to the owner-manager is only $7,000, because the outside owners pay 30 percent of the cost, or $3,000. With that drop in cost, it is possible that the marginal utility of the fifth trip to the owner-manager exceeds its cost to the manager ($7,000) and that an additional trip each year is chosen. If so, the value of the firm drops to $80,000 and the outside shareholders lose 30 percent of the $10,000 drop ($3,000).

An important point in the Jensen and Meckling article is that if the capital market is characterized by **rational expectations** (i.e., if the market's expectations of future events are unbiased) as it is under the EMH, the outside shareholders do not, on average, lose from the owner-manager's changed behavior. Those shareholders are price protected (see Chapter 7). They buy at a price that incorporates the owner-manager's changed behavior. The market expects owner-managers to equate their marginal rates of substitution between wealth and nonpecuniary benefits and prices the shares appropriately. Consequently, the outside shareholders pay only $(1 - \alpha)V'$ for the outside shares.

Because of price protection, the owner-manager bears the full cost of the changed behavior, the reduction in the value of the firm from V^* to V'. After the sale of outside shares the owner-manager's wealth drops by $V^* - V'$. The reduction in the owner-manager's utility is the **agency cost** (the cost of the agency relationship between the owner-manager and the outside shareholders). Agency costs cause owner-managers to write contracts with shareholders to restrict their actions, thereby reducing agency costs.

Given the agency cost, why do we observe anything other than single proprietorships? The obvious reason is that the Jensen and Meckling analysis is partial. There are offsetting benefits to the costs of agency that the analysis omits (see the later discussion).

The Owner-Manager with Outside Shareholders and Monitoring Expenditures

The preceding analysis does not allow owner-managers to contract to restrict their perk consumption (including shirking). By such contracting and incurring expenditures for monitoring contracts owner-managers can convince the capital market that they will abide by the contracts. Suppose that by writing contracts and arranging for their monitoring and enforcement at a cost, owner-managers convince the market to expect less (but not zero) perk consumption. Assume the reduction in the cost of perks is greater than the monitoring cost. Then the outside shares sell for more and the owner-manager's wealth including monitoring costs is greater than the precontracting wealth. Hence, if owner-managers value this increase in wealth more than the reduction in perks, they contract to restrict their actions and arrange for monitoring of the contract.

This result provides the prime insight in the Jensen and Meckling analysis: the agent, not the principal, has the incentive to contract for the monitoring. The outside shareholders do not care if monitoring (often involving accounting and auditing) is conducted. Competition in the capital markets leads to price protection and ensures that outside investors earn a normal return. Owner-managers (the agents) have the incentive to offer guarantees to limit their consumption of perks, for owner-managers receive all the gains. If owner-managers can spend $.10 on contracting and monitoring (hiring an auditor) to reduce their perquisites by $1.20, they will do so if the utility of the $1.10 of additional cash is greater than the utility of the forgone $1.20 in perquisites. Because of price protection, it does not matter whether the firm or the owner-manager pays the monitoring expenses. Either way, on average the shareholders receive a normal rate of return.

Nonpecuniary benefits are called "perks" in our discussion, and business trip examples are used. However, nonpecuniary benefits also include on-the-job leisure (shirking). Theft is also encompassed by the Jensen and Meckling analysis. Stealing by the owner-manager is analogous to the owner-manager's overconsumption of perks.

The preceding analysis shows that with competition and rational expectations, owner-managers who have incentives to take value reducing actions (**opportunistic actions**) such as overconsuming perks, shirking, or stealing when they sell outside shares bear the costs of those dysfunctional actions. Hence, they have incentives to contract to limit those actions and to have their actions monitored. This incentive is reduced (but not eliminated) by price protection in managerial labor markets. The foregoing analysis abstracts from that effect by assuming that the owner-manager's wage is fixed. That assumption is relaxed shortly.

The Agency Literature

There is another economics literature, complementary to the property rights literature, that investigates the implications of the agency relationship, for example, Berhold (1971), Ross (1973, 1974), Wilson (1968), Spence and Zeckhauser (1971), Mirrlees (1974, 1976), Stiglitz (1974, 1975b), Holmstrom (1979), and Antle (1982 and 1984). This literature is concerned with the problem of the agent or manager shirking and is therefore related to the property rights literature.

Typically, in the agency literature, there is a (risk-neutral) principal who supplies capital (as do the outside shareholders) and an agent, averse to risk and labor (like the owner-manager), who supplies labor. The principal's problem is characterized as trying to induce the agent to take the action (i.e., expend the effort) that the principal would take. *If* the principal can observe the amount of effort the agent expends, then the optimal contract is to pay the agent a fixed wage if the client takes the right action and impose a penalty if the agent shirks. In this way the principal bears all the risk. The problem arises when the principal *cannot* observe the agent's action. In that case, the optimal contract is to have the agent share in the outcome of his actions to provide him with an incentive to expend the optimal amount of effort.

A problem with the agency literature's characterization of the agency problem is that it ignores the role of markets. In markets with rational expectations the problem becomes the agent's or manager's *not* the principal's.[1] The manager has incentives to find ways of convincing

[1] Even though it is the agent's problem, the principal may have a comparative advantage in solving it (e.g., lenders not borrowers, write debt agreements).

the principal or outside shareholders that the manager will take the optimal actions. Because the manager bears the costs, these incentives lead to the development of institutional arrangements such as the use of accounting numbers in contracts and auditing to reduce the agency problem. Nevertheless, the literature's implication that the owner/manager agency relationship leads to a contract in which the manager shares in the outcome is consistent with many management compensation contracts (see later).

The owner-manager/outside shareholder relationship is not the only contract that induces a demand for monitoring. Debt contracts also produce such a demand.

THE DEMAND FOR CONTRACTS BETWEEN OWNER-MANAGERS AND DEBTHOLDERS

The owner-manager's incentive to overconsume perks or to steal arises because some of the equity is held by outsiders. Hence, it is tempting to suggest that agency costs can be reduced by issuing claims of fixed face value (debt) instead of equity. Then, with no outside equity holders, it appears that the owner-manager bears the full costs of perks and has an incentive to take the correct actions. However, debt provides the owner-manager with incentives to take other actions that reduce firm value. An owner-manager owning 100 percent of the firm and issuing fixed claims on the firm, still has incentives to take investment and financing decisions that reduce firm value.[2]

As in the equity case, in markets characterized by rational expectations, the owner-manager bears the costs of value reducing decisions induced by the presence of debt. And, as before, this provides the owner-manager with incentives to offer contracts and monitoring that restrict his actions.

Investment Decisions

For convenience in exposition, ignore the owner-manager's incentive to take perks and assume that if the owner-manager owns 100 percent of the firm, the market value (net present value) of the firm, V, is maximized. To meet that objective, the owner-manager takes all investment projects with positive net present values, because they increase the owner-manager's wealth. However, by selling debt claims

---

[2] This point is orginally made in Fama and Miller (1972). The analysis in this section relies heavily on Smith (1979) and an unpublished manuscript by Wakeman and Watts (1978). We are grateful to Lee Wakeman for his permission to use the analysis in Wakeman and Watts.

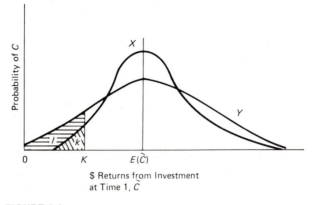

FIGURE 8.1

Probability distributions of returns on two mutually exclusive projects X and Y

to finance the investments, the owner-manager has incentives to take some projects that reduce firm value (have negative net present values) and forgo other projects that increase firm value (have positive net present values).

The owner-manager's incentives to take value-reducing actions arise when debt exists because investment decisions affect not only the value of the firm, but also the owner-manager's share of the value of the firm. In other words, in addition to the project's effect on the *size* of the pie, there is the project's effect on the owner-manager's *relative share* of the pie.

How can the investment decision influence the owner-manager's relative share of firm value? One way is via the investment's effect on the dispersion of the firm's cash flows; another is via its effect on promised debt repayments.

The dispersion effect can be illustrated by a simple example. Assume a one-period world. The owner-manager invests at time 0 and the investment returns an uncertain $\tilde{C}$ at time 1. Any debt (principal and interest) is paid off at time 1 and the firm liquidated. The owner-manager has two mutually exclusive investment projects (X and Y) available, both involving the investment of $\$I$. Further, while the projects' risks, βs, and expected returns, $E(\tilde{C})$, are the same, the standard deviation of returns is lower for project X: $\sigma(\tilde{C}_X) < \sigma(\tilde{C}_Y)$. The probability distributions of both projects' returns are shown in Figure 8.1.

With no outside equity holders and no debt, the owner-manager is indifferent between projects X and Y, as long as the firm represents a small fraction of his portfolio. Since the βs are equal, the market's expected rate of return is the same for both projects, $E(r)$. Thus, since both have the same expected cash flows, $E(\tilde{C})$, the projects' market values are the same at time 0. From equation (2.13)

$$V_{X,0} = \frac{E(\tilde{C})}{1 + E(r)} = V_{Y,0} \tag{8.1}$$

Now assume that the owner-manager issues debt with a promised repayment at time 1 (both principal and interest) of K. Does the debt's value vary with the alternative projects? If the cash flows from the investment ($\tilde{C}$) exceed K, the debtholders receive K; if the cash flows are less than K, the firm is insolvent and the debtholders receive whatever cash flows result (i.e., $\tilde{C}$). With investment X, the probability that the debtholders receive less than K is the area denoted by "k" under the curve X in Figure 8.1 and the probability that they receive K is $1 - k$. With investment Y, the probability that debtholders receive less than K is the sum of area k and area l in Figure 8.1, $k + l$, and the probability they receive K is $1 - (k + l)$. Hence, project Y entails a higher probability of debt default than does X and a lower probability the debtholders receive their promised payment K. This causes the debt's market value at time 0 to be greater if the owner-manager takes project $X(B_{X,0})$ than if the manager takes project $Y(B_{Y,0})$, $B_{X,0} > B_{Y,0}$.

As noted, the value of the firm (V_0) is the same whether the owner-manager takes project X or Y. Also, the value of the firm is the sum of the value of debt (B_0) and equity (S_0):

$$V_0 \equiv S_0 + B_0 \tag{8.2}$$

So, if the value of debt varies with the two projects, the value of the owner-manager's share in the firm must also vary with the projects: $B_{X,0} > B_{Y,0}$ and $V_{X,0} = V_{Y,0}$, so $S_{X,0} < S_{Y,0}$. Since the owner-manager's wealth is greater under project Y, he takes that project. He is no longer indifferent between the two projects as he was in the absence of debt.

If debtholders were shortsighted, the owner-manager could transfer wealth from the debtholders by stating that project X would be taken when the debt is sold so that debtholders paid $B_{X,0}$. Then project Y is taken, reducing the debt's value to $B_{Y,0}$ and increasing the owner-manager's wealth by $S_{Y,0} - S_{X,0} = B_{X,0} - B_{Y,0}$. However, a market with rational expectations expects the owner-manager to take project Y and prices the debt at the lower value, $B_{Y,0}$.[3]

The example illustrates how the owner-manager's investment decision is affected by the existence of debt. In the example, the owner-manager takes investment Y instead of being indifferent between X and Y. While the dispersion effect, by construction in the example, does

---

[3] Fama and Miller (1972, pp. 179–180) present a numerical example that illustrates this point.

not cause the owner-manager to take an investment that reduces the firm's value (or manager's wealth), it can in other cases. For example, the expected return on Y could be less than that on X—$E(C_Y) < E(C_X)$ but not by a sufficient amount to offset the effect of Y's dispersion on the owner-manager's share of the firm's cash flows. Then, the owner-manager would take a value-reducing investment decision, investing in Y instead of X. However, the owner-manager bears the costs, because the debt market expects the action and prices the debt at $B_{Y,0}$ (i.e., the debtholders are price protected).

The foregoing case has a converse. If a new project *decreases* the variance of the firm's cash flows, the owner-manager may not take it even if it has a positive net present value. The reason is the resultant transfer of wealth from the owner-manager to the bondholders may exceed the owner-manager's share of the increased net present value.

As indicated, the effect of the owner-manager's use of investment policy to achieve wealth transfers is expected by the market, and bondholders price the debt ex ante in anticipation of the ex post wealth transfer. Hence, on average, there is no wealth transfer, and the reduction in firm value caused by the owner-manager taking negative net present value projects and rejecting positive net present value projects is borne by the owner-manager. This provides the owner-manager with incentives to contract to restrict his actions.

The repayments effect occurs when the owner-manager is considering a project whose cash flows will be used to pay off an existing debt. In such a situation it can be in the owner-manager's interest not to take the project even if it has a positive net present value (i.e., would increase the value of the firm).

The owner-manager's incentive to forgo the project occurs when an alternative to the project is payment of what amounts to a liquidating dividend now, with the expectation that the firm will go bankrupt in the future when there are insufficient cash flows to repay the debt. Under these circumstances, making the investment involves forgoing a wealth transfer from the debtholders of the face value of the debt. Hence, the owner-manager would only make the investment if its net present value exceeded the debt's face value, not if it exceeded zero.

The debtholders are price protected against the owner-manager's forgoing positive net present value investments because of the repayments effect, so the expected cost of rejecting those investments is borne by the owner-manager.

Financing Decisions

Debt can induce the owner-manager to undertake wealth transfers by two types of financing activities: (1) dividends and (2) reordering of debt claims.

DIVIDENDS

Owner-managers have incentives to forgo positive net present value projects and pay themselves dividends when debt claims exist (i.e., the repayment effect in the preceding subsection). The costs of the resultant actions include the net present values of forgone investments. In addition to future investments, the firm has assets in existing investments. The existence of debt claims provides owner-managers with incentives to sell existing assets and pay the proceeds to themselves either by paying cash dividends or by repurchasing shares. In the extreme, the owner-manager would sell off all the firm's assets, pay liquidating dividends, and walk away, leaving the debtholders with the "shell" of the company.

As with the other value-reducing actions, owner-managers bear the cost if debt markets price debt rationally (i.e., taking account of the likelihood of being left with a shell). Owner-managers bear any reduction in firm values (the size of the pie). Consequently, they have an incentive to offer contracts that restrict dividend payments to try to convince bondholders that funds will be kept within their firms to take positive net present value projects.

REORDERING OF FINANCIAL CLAIMS

In the previous examples of the agency costs of debt, it is assumed that there is only one class of debtholders. Actually, the owner-manager can issue other debt instruments after the original debt is issued. Issuance of additional debt transfers wealth from the original debtholders to the manager and in the process creates costs that reduce the value of the firm. *First*, assume that the owner-manager issues additional debt of priority equal to or higher than that of the original debt. Equal or higher priority means *in theory* that in bankruptcy the new debt gets paid off at the same time or before the old debt.[4] In this situation, the original debtholders are worse off if the money received from the sale of the new debt is paid out to the owner-manager as a dividend.

Second, assume that the new debt is junior to the old debt (i.e., is always paid off in bankruptcy after the old debt). Then the value of the old debt can still fall. If some of the proceeds of the new debt are paid out in dividends, the probability of bankruptcy increases. Bankruptcy leads to cash outflows for trustee fees, court fees, and nonoptimal decisions by trustees, all of which reduce firm value and the value of all the debt. Even if the proceeds from the sale of the new debt are invested in positive present value projects and the probability of

---

[4] The words "in theory" are underlined because the courts do not always enforce the priorities listed in the debt agreements (see Warner, 1977, pp. 242–243).

bankruptcy doesn't increase, the additional debt may lead to more positive net present projects' being rejected.

As with the other value-reducing actions, the possible reordering of financial claims is impounded into the original debt issue price, so on average it is the owner-manager who bears the agency costs. In sum, all these costs provide incentives for the owner-manager to contract to restrict value reducing actions on investment and financial policy and to have those contracts monitored.

THE DEMAND FOR CONTRACTS BETWEEN PROFESSIONAL MANAGERS AND OUTSIDE CAPITAL SUPPLIERS

The preceding analyses of agency costs consider the owner of a firm selling shares or debt to outsiders and staying on as owner-manager. In that situation the owner-manager who is expected to take firm value-reducing actions bears the costs of those actions via the reduction in price paid for the outside shares or debt. However, large corporations have professional managers who own a small percentage of the shares. Hence, at first glance, the manager would appear to bear only a small part of any reduction in the market value of new shares or debt. If so, what are professional managers' incentives to contract to restrict their actions?

Existing Contracts

First, actions of large corporations' managers are already constrained by existing contracts. Every large traded corporation had an initial sale of shares and/or debt to the public. At that point its shares were owned by an individual, a family, a promoter, or the like. Hence, those individuals bore a reduction in share and debt prices for agency costs, even if they did not stay on as manager. This provided them with incentives to write contracts, including corporate bylaws, that are binding on future managers and reduce the managers' incentives to take firm value-reducing actions.

Competition in the Labor Market

A second constraint on professional corporate managers owning a small share percentage is competition in the managerial labor market both within the corporation and without. That competition causes managers to bear costs of value-reducing actions not covered by existing contracts and encourages them to write new contracts restricting their actions (e.g., at the time of new debt or equity issues).

INTERNAL COMPETITION

Within a large corporation, there is competition for promotion. Vice-presidents compete for promotion to president, divisional managers compete for promotion to vice-president, and so forth. Incentives exist for subordinate managers to monitor their superiors mutually (Zimmerman, 1979, pp. 509–510; Fama, 1980, p. 293). Typically, there are several management members in addition to the president or chief executive officer (CEO) on the board of directors. The fact that managers on the board can only be fired with the board's knowledge reduces the president or CEO's control on information flowing to directors who are not part of the full-time management (**outside directors**) (see Fama and Jensen, 1983a). The outside directors, like auditors, have incentives to monitor the manager for possible opportunistic behavior (behavior that increases his wealth but reduces firm value). Likewise, the executive vice-president has incentives to inform the directors of CEO opportunism if this enhances the likelihood of becoming CEO.

EXTERNAL COMPETITION

Boards of directors occasionally hire a president or vice-president from outside the firm. The outside directors who are typically a majority of the board and play an important role in hiring top managers usually are themselves top managers of other corporations. Their breadth of knowledge of alternative managers combined with their knowledge of current compensation levels puts the outside directors in a position to determine the competitive compensation for top managers.

Competition in the managerial labor market means that on average managers receive only the competitive compensation for their position. If managers are expected to overconsume perks or gain from insider trading (or even steal), their compensation is reduced to the point that in total they earn only the competitive wage. Hence, managers of large corporations bear the agency costs arising from their actions and, like owner-managers, have incentives to contract to restrict value-reducing actions and to have those contracts monitored.

The Effect on the Manager's Reputation

Fama (1980) suggests that information on managers' opportunistic value-reducing behavior eventually becomes known and affects their reputation. As a consequence, if managers consume a large quantity of perks (e.g., shirks), it eventually becomes known and they acquire a reputation. Such managers are expected to overconsume perks in the future, and their future compensation is reduced. Hence, even if managers' compensation is not adjusted in the period in which they overconsume, they still bear a cost for that overconsumption—the present value of the reductions in their future compensation. This effect is mitigated if the manager is close to retirement and does not have any deferred compensation (i.e., compensation paid after retirement).

In essence, the shareholders and bondholders are price protected against value-reducing actions of professional managers by the managerial labor market. If managers do not use the most efficient existing means of convincing the labor market that they will consume no more than the average perquisites, they bear the cost in a lower pecuniary compensation.

The importance of the earlier assumption of fixed wage for the owner-manager should now be apparent. The suppliers of outside capital are price protected through both the capital and labor markets. We also assumed earlier that the labor market does not discipline the owner-manager but that the capital market does. In this section the professional manager doesn't own the firm and is not completely disciplined by the capital market. However, extra discipline is applied via the labor market.

The property rights literature incorporates much more than an analysis of the demand for contracts between firm managers and suppliers of outside capital. It includes explanations for the existence of firms and useful concepts of the nature of firms, among other things. Empirical studies in the literature proceed on the assumption that contracting arrangements that persist over time are likely to be efficient in reducing agency costs.

THEORY OF THE FIRM

Why Do Firms Exist?

While price protection in the capital and labor markets causes managers to contract to restrict value-reducing actions and reduce agency costs, as long as such contracting is costly there is still some agency cost; not all value-reducing actions are eliminated. Given that cost, why do *firms* exist? Why isn't all business conducted by sole proprietorships? The answer is that firms have offsetting benefits. Those benefits include economies of scale, diversification, and specialization.

ECONOMIES OF SCALE

Individuals have limited wealth. Hence any one individual may not be able to supply sufficient capital to take advantage of economies of scale. In that case, agency costs have to be traded off against increased economies of scale.

DIVERSIFICATION

Even if an individual has sufficient wealth to finance a firm at its optimal size, that person may not want to because of the effect on the risk of his or her investment portfolio. Based on portfolio theory, the relevant risk measure for an individual is the variance of the rate of return on that person's investment portfolio. However, the only part of that variance for which the market compensates the individual in terms of expected rate of return on his or her portfolio is the part which is due to the variance of the rate of return on the market portfolio (see Fama and Miller, 1972).

If individuals have to invest all their wealth in a firm to take advantage of economies of scale, they incur risk, which reduces their utility. Individuals will accept some agency costs to reduce these risks. That is, they may be prepared to sell a portion of the firm so that they can reduce their portfolio risk.

SPECIALIZATION

Those with the wealth may not be the best managers. Consider an owner-manager who is an efficient manager but whose only heir, while intelligent, is an incompetent manager. The owner-manager dies and leaves the business to the heir. If the heir manages the business, the value of the firm drops because of his lack of managerial skill. If the professional manager is hired, the value of the firm drops because of agency costs. A wealth-maximizing heir hires the professional manager if the agency costs of the manager are less than the decline in firm value due to the heir's lack of skill.

Nature of the Firm

The law views the corporation as a separate entity able to act as an individual. Under the property rights or contracting view, the firm has no separate existence; it is a "nexus of contracts" and not an individual. As a result, the firm does not have an objective, such as maximizing profits. Instead, the firm is composed of individuals who have contracted with the legal entity, the corporation, for certain property rights, and it is these individuals who have objectives—maximize their utility.[5]

Under the property rights approach, the firm is viewed as a team of self-interested individuals who recognize that their own welfare depends on the firm's success in competition with other firms. Each of the individuals comprising the firm contributes some input to the firm's production process (labor, managerial skills, capital, raw materials, technology, etc.). Individuals supply inputs in expectation of earning a return on their investment. Further, each individual recognizes that the other individuals will take actions to maximize *their* utility not *his* or *her* utility. Individuals recognize that conflicts of interest will arise and, to reduce these conflicts, write contracts that specify each individual's specific rights in the firm's outputs under various contingencies (i.e., each individual's *property rights*). Debtholders, preferred stockholders, common shareholders, lessors, managers, labor, and trade creditors—all have contracts that specify how the cash flows arising from the firm (even in the event of bankruptcy) will be distributed. These contracts include corporate charters and bylaws. In addition, many laws, such as bankruptcy laws, define the property rights in the various assets of the firm.

Survivorship Principle

Price protection encourages the parties to the firm to use the most efficient available contracting procedures (i.e., most efficient in the sense that they lead to the highest firm value). Further, the parties to the firm have an incentive to innovate, to find new procedures that further restrict value-reducing actions. The consequent increase in firm value can be shared among the parties. Hence, the set of contracts that survive over time are efficient in terms of reducing the costs of conflicts of interests or equivalently maximizing the firm's value (Fama and Jensen, 1983a, 1983b).

The important assumption underlying this analysis is the **survivorship principle** or economic Darwinism (Alchian, 1950). Competition among firms implies that operating procedures and contracting techniques that are used systematically by *surviving* organizations are efficient. If this were not the case, then contracting parties could adopt the other procedures and earn above-normal (competitive) returns. The survivorship principle allows researchers to analyze the costs and benefits of the contracts and their concomitant accounting procedures

---

[5] The assumption that individuals within the firm act in their own self-interest can be traced to Adam Smith (1776) and more recently Berle and Means (1932). It has also been used by Simon (1959) and Williamson (1964) among other economists.

that survive under the assumption that *on average* the benefits of those contracts and procedures exceed their costs.

THE CONTRACTING ROLE OF ACCOUNTING

Contracts will not reduce the costs of conflicts (agency costs) unless the parties can determine whether the contract has been breached. Hence, in the "nexus of contracts" view of the firm, there is a demand for monitoring contracts. The "property rights" or contracting literature suggests the hypothesis that accounting plays an important role both in contract terms and in monitoring those terms. Accounting numbers are frequently used in contracts (debt contracts, management compensation plans, corporate charters, and bylaws). These contracts often include restrictions on parties' actions conditional on certain accounting numbers. Hence, there is a demand for the calculation and reporting of those numbers (i.e., a demand for accounting).

There are abundant examples of the systematic use of accounting in the firms' contracts. Lending agreements between firms' managers and their banks often require the firms to maintain interest coverage ratios (earnings before interest and taxes to interest) above a certain level. This generates a demand for accounting earnings to determine whether the interest coverage covenant is met. Bonus plans are a frequent component of executive incentive compensation plans. The plans' formulas are based on accounting earnings and so require the calculation of those earnings. Also, accounting earnings are used to assess the firms' profit center managers and accounting costs to assess cost center managers.

Auditing also plays a role in contract monitoring. The firm's external auditors contract with debtholders to report any observed breaches of restrictive covenants (such as the interest coverage ratio covenant). Also, audited earnings numbers are used in bonus plans.

If accounting is an important part of the firm's contracting process and agency costs (and, hence, firm value and/or managers' compensation) vary with different contracts, accounting procedures have the potential to affect firm value and/or the manager's compensation. If surviving types of contracts are more efficient in reducing agency costs than others, the procedures used to calculate accounting numbers used in those contracts are more efficient than are alternative procedures. Using alternative procedures increases agency costs and reduces firm value or manager compensation. This is an important cash flow and value linkage introduced by accounting's contracting role. It provides an explanation for managers' choice of accounting procedures.

The hypothesis that accounting fulfills a role in contracts and monitoring of contracts is not new to the accounting literature, at least with respect to the manager/shareholder relationship. The hypothesis that accounting reports are demanded to monitor that relationship is called the **stewardship concept** and was popular in the literature in the late nineteenth and early twentieth centuries. It is also popular with accounting historians as an explanation for the existence of accounting. Yamey (1962, p. 15) writes,

> The origins of accounting and indeed of written records are probably to be found in the need of an "accounting" officer to render a statement of money and other assets received in his charge on behalf of his employer or disbursed on his behalf. There was a need for a check on the honesty and reliability of subordinates.

The notion that the demand for accounting in monitoring managers' or employees' actions is not new to the accounting student either. Managerial accounting texts usually discuss the use of accounting reports to report on individual manager performance, and auditing texts describe the use of internal control and accounting to restrict managers' or employees' ability to steal.

There is a long history of voluntarily supplied audited corporate accounting reports. Managers presented accounting reports to investors long before they were required to do so by law. Well before the securities acts, many U.S. corporations published reports.[6] Watts and Zimmerman (1983) trace the provision of audited reports to shareholders back to the earliest English joint stock companies (late sixteenth century) and to the predecessors of those companies (regulated companies to merchant guilds).

The hypothesis that accounting and auditing arose as a monitoring device for the firm's contracts contrasts with the common hypothesis that investors demand accounting reports as a source of information for investment and valuation decisions. The information hypothesis, which emerged after the securities acts and implicitly underlies much of the research in Chapters 3–6, asserts that investors demand information on current and future cash flows and the market value of assets and liabilities (to calculate the value of the firm in orderly liquidation). An example of this hypothesis is in the AICPA Trueblood Committee Report (1973, p. 20):

---

[6] Among the U.S. corporations that published accounting reports in 1899 were American Tobacco Company, General Electric Company, Continental Tobacco Company, American Hide and Leather Company, National Biscuit Company, and Federal Steel Company (see Hawkins, 1968, p. 25).

An objective of financial statements is to provide information useful to investors and creditors for predicting, comparing, and evaluating potential cash flows to them in terms of amount, timing and related uncertainty.

The two hypotheses are not mutually exclusive. Both the contract and information roles could exist at the same time. Information that enables individuals to determine certain contractual requirements have been met is often useful in valuing the firm's securities (e.g., the earnings used in the interest coverage debt covenant provides share value information; see Chapter 3).

If the two hypotheses are not mutually exclusive, why concentrate on the contracting hypothesis? Why not use both hypotheses to explain accounting? The reason is utilitarian. Researchers have been able to generate links between accounting procedures and the firms' or manager's cash flows under the contracting hypothesis, links that are consistent with the EMH. Based on these links, they can generate predictions about the accounting procedures used by firms. Under the information hypothesis researchers have not been able to generate links consistent with the EMH.[7]

In analyzing the contracting demand for accounting, researchers have concentrated on two of the many types of contracts that comprise the firm. They are management compensation agreements and lending or debt agreements. The next chapter investigates the use of accounting in those two contracts and generates hypotheses about the managers' choice of accounting procedures and the stock price effects of procedure changes.

SUMMARY

Positive accounting researchers attempting to develop theories to explain accounting have adopted the "property rights" theory of the firm. In that theory, the firm is a nexus of contracts between self-interested individuals. Each individual recognizes that his or her own welfare depends on the firm's survival but at the same time has incentives to take actions that reduce the firm's value and chance of survival.

The value-reducing actions (agency costs) are motivated by attempts to transfer wealth from other parties associated with the firm. Price protection causes the individual taking value-reducing actions to bear their cost and encourages contracting to restrict those actions. Corporate managers in particular have incentives to contract to restrict their overconsumption of perquisites, including their shirking.

---

[7] Gordon (1964) hypothesizes that the manager's selection of accounting procedures is driven by the procedures' effects on share prices. However, the linkage between procedures and share prices assumes an inefficient capital market (see Chapter 6).

Accounting numbers are used in the firm's contracts that are designed to reduce agency costs. Ratios such as debt/equity ratios are used in debt contracts to restrict managers' actions that transfer wealth from debtholders. Accounting earnings are used in bonus plans, presumably to reduce manager shirking. Such use of accounting numbers requires their calculation and their monitoring for breach of contract. It is hypothesized that auditing fulfils the monitoring role.

The contracting role of accounting allows accounting procedures to have a cash flow and valuation effect. If a contract's effect on agency costs varies with the procedures to calculate the accounting numbers used in the contract's covenants, the firm's and/or manager's cash flows vary with the accounting procedures. This cash flow linkage provides a potential explanation for tax-neutral cross-sectional variations in firms' accounting procedures and for systematic accounting procedure changes observed in Chapter 4. The next chapter develops the cash flow linkage for two particular firm contracts and generates hypotheses about the manager's choice of accounting procedures and the stock price effect of procedure changes.

CHAPTER NINE

Compensation Plans, Debt Contracts, and Accounting Procedures

Researchers have used management compensation plans and debt contracts to generate hypotheses about accounting procedure variations across firms and industries and about procedure changes and their stock price effects. The reason is that data are available on those contracts (e.g., management compensation plan details are available in proxy statements). Data are not readily available for many other formal and informal firm contracts.

This chapter explains how the hypotheses are generated from the compensation plans and debt contracts. In the process, we investigate accounting's role in those contracts in greater detail than in Chapter 8. Also, we explain further the link between the accounting procedures used in the contracts and the firm's cash flows.

We begin with a discussion of accounting's role in management compensation plans and proceed to the effects of the plans on firms' accounting procedures. Then we cover accounting's role in debt contracts and debt contracts' effects on firms' accounting procedures. Hypotheses about variation in procedures across firms and industries are also generated. Hypotheses about the stock price effect of procedure changes are then discussed. We conclude with a summary of the chapter.

ACCOUNTING'S ROLE
IN COMPENSATION PLANS

Early corporations' audited accounts appear aimed at controlling managers' expenditures and malfeasance rather than their shirking. However, by the end of the nineteenth century, English audited accounting reports had come to serve as a basis for management compensation, presumably to reduce shirking. At that time, some English corporate articles or bylaws tied the manager's compensation to reported earnings (Watts, 1977, p. 57; Matheson, 1893, pp. vii–viii; Pixley, 1881, p. 114). Also by the early twentieth century, earnings-based management incentive compensation was the norm in Europe (see Taussig and Barker, 1925). While development of formal earnings-based management compensation plans occurred later in the United States (see Taussig and Barker, 1925), by the 1950s many U.S. corporate executive compensation schemes included incentive plans that formally tied the manager's compensation to the earnings numbers in the firm's annual audited report.

The growth and survival of earnings-based compensation plans suggest that they are efficient contracts (i.e., maximize firm value). However, the analysis in Chapter 8 suggests that an efficient management contract motivates the manager to maximize firm value. Hence, compensation plans that directly tie managers' compensation to their impact on the firm's market value would seem more efficient than an earnings-based plan. Why then are accounting earnings-based plans used?

Reasons for Using Accounting
Earnings-Based Plans

There is no theory that explains the composition of management compensation schemes. However, the literature does include hypotheses about the role of those schemes and the incentive effects of their components (see Smith and Watts, 1982). Further, besides the hypothesis that the plans are designed to provide managers with an incentive to maximize firm value (incentive hypothesis), the literature includes the nonmutually exclusive hypothesis that the plans are designed to reduce the present value of corporate and manager taxes (tax hypothesis, see Miller and Scholes, 1980).[1]

There are two basic types of compensation plans that reward management performance as measured by accounting numbers (usually

---

[1] Two other hypotheses are that the plans are adopted to signal good performance and are used to screen managers. The screening occurs because only particular types of managers (e.g., less risk averse) will seek such employment under such plans (see Raviv 1985).

earnings): bonus plans and performance plans (performance share and performance unit plans). From the literature, we suggest three possible factors motivating accounting earnings-based compensation plans: (1) inability to observe firm market value, (2) disaggregation of performances, and (3) taxes.

NONOBSERVABILITY OF FIRM MARKET VALUE

This problem arises because much corporate debt is not traded, and hence, the change in the total value of the firm (stock plus debt) is not observed. In that event, the firm's earnings (i.e., accounting earnings with interest expense added back) could be the most cost beneficial index of changes in firm value. We expect the firm's value to vary with its earnings like share values vary with earnings (see Chapter 3). Approximately one-third of the bonus plans investigated by Healy (1985) add interest back to earnings in their bonus formulas.

DISAGGREGATION OF PERFORMANCE

Even if total firm value is observable, only the top managers (e.g., the president) are responsible for the whole firm. The market values of the firm's subunits (e.g., divisions) for which other managers are responsible cannot be observed. Consequently, those other managers' effects on the firm's market value cannot be directly observed.

Accounting earnings can be calculated for various subunits of the firm and are indices of market value (see Chapter 3). Hence, it is not surprising that bonus plans use accounting earnings and that most of those plans consider subunit performance as well as firm performance in determining bonus awards for subunit managers (see Conference Board, 1979).

TAXES

Performance plans typically last five years (see Smith and Watts, 1982). They defer management compensation for five years and, if corporate tax rates are less than management tax rates, reduce the present value of total taxes paid by the corporation and its managers (see Miller and Scholes, 1980). Given limitations on the use of other incentive compensation for tax purposes, the existence of performance plans could be explained by the tax hypothesis (see Miller and Scholes, 1980).

Bonus plans typically defer compensation for less than a year. Hence, their tax benefits are likely to be small. Set against this benefit is the increased management compensation necessary to offset the bonus plans' effect on the manager's risk. The present value of the manager's compensation typically forms a large part of the manager's portfolio. Tying that compensation to the firm's earnings (versus paying salary) increases the variance of the returns on the manager's portfolio. Given that top managers are risk averse and not well diversified, they require (and are apparently paid) greater compensation on average when their firm has a bonus plan.[2] This increased cost accompanying the small tax benefits suggests that additional benefits are necessary to explain the existence of bonus plans (e.g., incentive benefits).

The fact that division managers' bonuses depend on division earnings reinforces the foregoing conclusion. The variance of the division managers' portfolio returns increases less if the bonus is tied to the firm's earnings than if it is tied to the division's earnings (diversification reduces risk). Hence, if tax benefits are the sole reason for bonus plans, we would not expect division managers' bonuses to be tied to their divisions' performances. However, under the incentive hypothesis, we expect division managers' compensations to depend on their divisions' performances.

Which Firms Use Accounting Earnings-Based Plans?

Research explaining why some firms use earnings-based plans and others do not is sparse. We know from Conference Board studies (e.g., Conference Board, 1979) that the frequency of use of such plans varies by industry. For example, a greater proportion of manufacturing firms than retail firms use bonus plans. However, we do not have a theory to explain why manufacturing firms are more likely to use a bonus plan than retail firms. Nevertheless, we can think of intuitively plausible hypotheses about which firms use earnings-based plans. One such hypothesis is suggested by the analysis in the preceding section and Chapter 8.

For bonus plans to provide the manager with an incentive to maximize firm value, the performance index in the bonus calculation (earnings) must be correlated with the effect of the manager's actions on the value of the firm. Ceteris paribus, the greater the correlation between earnings and the effect of a given manager's actions on the value of the firm, the more likely an earnings-based bonus plan will be used to reward the manager. For example, one would not expect a high correlation between the accounting earnings of a research and development firm and the manager's effect on its market value. So we would expect bonus plans to be less frequently used by such firms (see Smith and Watts, 1984).

---

[2] See Conference Board (1979) for evidence that managers of firms with bonus plans are paid more. An alternative hypothesis is that managers' marginal products are higher in industries that have bonus plans.

Accounting numbers are used in earnings-based compensation plans for purposes other than measuring performance. They are used to measure the plan's parameters. For example, in bonus plans accounting numbers (equity or total assets) are used to set the earnings level required for a bonus award. Many of those parameter uses can be rationalized in terms of reducing agency costs (see Smith and Watts, 1982). However, accounting researchers have typically taken the parameters of the compensation plans as given and on that basis investigated the effect of the plans on accounting procedures. We follow the same course.

COMPENSATION PLANS' EFFECTS ON ACCOUNTING

We noted earlier that in England, managers' compensation was tied formally to reported earnings as early as the nineteenth century, before the accounting procedures used to calculate reported earnings numbers were regulated. It is likely that informal ties between managers' compensation and earnings existed even before that time in England and in the United States. If this connection between reported earnings numbers and management compensation was widespread (due to formal plans or to salary adjustments based on reported profits), the connection probably influenced the procedures used to calculate reported earnings in England and the United States. What implications can we draw for accounting procedures?

If managers controlled the calculation of earnings to the extent that they could report any number they wished, earnings-based bonus plans would not exist for incentive purposes. The market expects managers to manipulate the numbers to their own advantage, reporting arbitrarily high earnings rather than taking actions that increase earnings because they increase firm value. As a result, neither the managers' compensation nor the value of the firm would be increased by earnings-based bonus plans and they would not be used. If earnings-based plans are used to reward managers for incentive reasons, there must be some restriction of the methods managers use to calculate earnings. And the restrictions must be monitored or audited. Further, the restrictions must result in earnings numbers that reflect the effect of managers' actions on the firm's market value.

It is unlikely that the manager's choice of accounting procedures will be totally restricted. Managers are likely to know best which accounting procedures are optimal for motivating their subordinates. Likewise, the costs of government regulations can vary with accounting procedures (see Chapter 10), and the manager is likely to know best which procedures minimize those costs. Hence, in restricting the set of accounting procedures available to managers, the benefit of reduced managerial opportunistic actions resulting from the restrictions has to be traded off against the cost of forgoing procedures that are optimal for other purposes (e.g., reducing regulatory costs).

As long as contracting and monitoring is costly, not all managerial accounting manipulation will be eliminated. It may be too costly for the board of directors' compensation committee to eliminate all manipulation. Remember also that in labor and capital markets characterized by rational expectations, managers will not, on average, gain from such manipulation; their average compensation incorporates the average effect of manipulation (see Chapter 8).

In summary, given an earnings-based compensation plan, we expect the manager's choice of accounting procedures to be restricted, but not totally restricted. However, we can say more. The motivation for restricting accounting procedures provides explanations for the type of accounting procedures from which the manager can choose (i.e., the **accepted procedures**) and how they vary across firms and industries. Most of these explanations are essentially ex post rationalizations, but they are intuitively appealing. When we consider the manager's choice among accepted methods, we can do more than ex post rationalize. If we take the set of accepted procedures as given (as researchers do), we can make testable predictions about the choice.

Accepted Procedures

Examination of early accounting and auditing texts indicates that the manager's choice of accounting methods was restricted before regulation and provides evidence on the type of restriction. These texts indicate that the compensation plan role was important at that time. They discuss the reluctance of managers to charge depreciation when the manager's compensation is tied to earnings:

> Auditors, and especially those who have to deal with joint-stock or other concerns where the remuneration of the management is made wholly or partly dependent on declared Profits, know in what varied forms resistance to an adequate charge against profits for Depreciation is presented. (Matheson, 1893, pp. vii–viii).

The quotation suggests a potentially testable proposition: companies with earnings-based compensation plans were more likely to be audited before auditing was legally required.

Conservatism was emphasized in the texts. Conservatism means that the accountant should report the lowest value among possible alternative values for assets and the highest alternative value for liabilities. Revenues should be recognized later rather than sooner and expenses sooner than later. Conservatism is exemplified by managers in most industries having to calculate earnings using the lower of cost or market inventory valuation rule. A stated function of the accountant's conservatism (see Hendricksen, 1982, p. 82) was to offset the manager's optimism (presumably encouraged by earnings-based compensation plans).

The use of lower of cost or market and conservatism in general suggest a potential explanation of why accounting earnings are calculated under a mixture of historical cost and market value bases and are not calculated according to the market valuation theories presented in Chapter 2. Such calculation requires estimates of the assets' market values and future cash flows. In many cases, managers are better able to estimate market values of assets, for example, than auditors. This provides managers with ability to influence the earnings number in their favor. If managers use this influence to their own advantage, the association between earnings numbers and managers' effects on firm values is likely to be reduced, reducing the effectiveness of the incentive compensation.

The manager's ability to affect the earnings calculation under a particular earnings definition has to be traded off against the extent to which earnings, calculated according to that definition, are correlated with the manager's effect on firm value. This explains the accountant's concern with **objectivity**, the concern that the numbers can be verified (e.g., Paton and Littleton, 1940, pp. 18–21).

Variations in accepted accounting procedures across industries can also be explained by earnings-based compensation plans. For example, while the recognition of profit at sale and the valuation of inventories at the lower of cost or market is common in most industries, they are not always used in the construction and mining industries. In those industries, profit is often recognized at the point of production rather than sale and inventories carried at net realizable value. This exception to the general rule probably also existed in the late nineteenth century.

Consider using the recognition of profit at production in a manufacturing firm with an earnings-based compensation plan. The procedure gives the manager an incentive to produce as much as possible (since whatever is produced is valued at selling price and increases earnings) and not worry about sales. Most of the production ends up in inventory, and eventually the firm is in financial trouble. Adopting the recognition at production method would be disastrous and, hence, is not accepted in most industries.[3] Why then does it survive in construction and mining?

The reason is that many firms in construction and mining have contracts for the sale of their production. For example, a mining firm audited by one of us recognized profit at production. The firm had long-term contracts for the sale of all the production of its major product (rutile or titanium dioxide) to Dupont at the prevailing world price. Hence, there was no difficulty in selling as much as could be produced. The management-controlled variables that determined profitability were production and the cost of production. Consequently, the firm had an incentive scheme based on profits recognized on a production basis. We expect that most mining firms that recognize profits at production have long-term contracts for the sale of their product. In the construction industry, the percentage-of-completion method of recognizing profit is used when the firm has a contract for the sale of the construction project.

Empirical researchers have not investigated the effect of management compensation plans on accepted accounting methods. Instead, the concentration has been on management's choice among accepted methods (e.g., the choice between straight-line and accelerated depreciation). We now turn to an analysis of the implications of compensation plans for that choice. In investigating that choice, researchers take both the bonus plans and the accepted methods as given.

Choice Among Accepted Procedures

Even prior to regulation of disclosure, it is likely that the auditor would have reported departures from accepted procedures of the time to the directors and if necessary to the shareholders (see Pixley, 1881, pp. 157–159). That report would signal the nonmanagement directors, who determine the manager's compensation (the compensation committee), to adjust the earnings used in calculating the manager's compensation.

While there were regularities and accepted practices in accounting prior to regulation, there was also a large area of practice over which managers could exercise their discretion and not draw an auditor's special report. For example, a manager would not have been reported for switching from accelerated to straight-line depreciation. Even without the report, it is possible that the compensation committee adjusted compensation for the higher earnings resulting from the manager's

---

[3] Notice that full absorption cost accounting produces the same dysfunctional incentives. By increasing production, the average cost per unit is lower and profits are higher. However, these incentives are reduced by the lower of cost or market rule.

changed accounting procedures. However, it seems highly unlikely that adjustments were made for all the methods over which management exercised its discretion. Given the costs of monitoring, many adjustments by the compensation committee would not pay. If the compensation committee could costlessly adjust management compensation, accounting-based incentive plans would not exist. So the existence of the plans suggests positive monitoring costs and the ability of managers to choose methods and change methods to try to increase their compensation. Of course, with rational expectations, as seen in Chapter 8, on average such attempts would not pay because the equilibrium compensation reflects the effects of the manipulations.

Today, changes in accounting practices draw an audit qualification, and their effects in the year of the change are reported. However, managers still have the ability to influence earnings via accounting methods without drawing an audit qualification. For example, estimating the future costs of restoring land after strip mining involves sufficient uncertainty to give management substantial latitude in determining the cost to be charged off in any given year.

Most empirical research has investigated the effect of bonus plans rather than performance plans on the manager's choice of accounting procedures. The parameters of bonus plans are set such that bonuses are awarded in most years (see Smith and Watts, 1982), and, if a bonus can be awarded, the maximum amount is a positive linear function of reported earnings. This has led most researchers to assume that the manager's compensation under a bonus plan increases as reported earnings increase. Under that assumption, an increase in the present value of a firm's reported earnings increases the present value of the manager's compensation. This result produces an hypothesis that has been tested in several studies:

> **Bonus plan hypothesis**. Ceteris paribus, managers of firms with bonus plans are more likely to choose accounting procedures that shift reported earnings from future periods to the current period.

This hypothesis is given a name because it is tested relatively frequently. Other frequently tested hypotheses about the manager's procedure choice will also be labeled for future reference.

The bonus plan hypothesis is derived from a simple model of bonus plans and is reasonable for an early study of the impact of bonus plans on accounting procedures. But the particular details of bonus plans provide much richer implications than the bonus plan hypothesis and more powerful tests of the proposition that the manager's choice of accounting procedures is influenced by bonus plans. So we'd expect later researchers to develop and use these richer implications and more powerful tests. Healy (1985) does just that.

As an example of the richer implications available from plan details, consider the manager's incentives to manipulate reported earnings under a typical bonus plan. In some years the manager has an incentive to *reduce* earnings, contrary to the bonus plan hypothesis.

Typically, bonus plans provide a maximum amount that can be transferred to the "bonus pool" from which bonuses are paid. The maximum transfer is commonly some proportion of earnings over a "target earnings" number. The "target" is usually a percentage of shareholder equity or total assets. If earnings are less than the target, no bonuses can be awarded. Some plans also have an upper limit placed on the transfer.

If the compensation committee uses the formula for setting the bonus and does not adjust the bonus for changes in accounting procedures, the bonus gives the manager an incentive to use procedure changes to increase earnings in some years and decrease them in others. The incentive depends on whether the earnings are below the target, between the target and the upper bound, or above the upper bound. If the earnings are above the upper bound, the manager has incentives to reduce reported earnings by deferring earnings. The bonus is lost forever on any excess of earnings over the upper bound. Deferring the excess earnings increases expected future bonuses. If current earnings are between the target and the upper bound, the manager has incentives to shift sufficient earnings to make current earnings equal to the upper bound. The increase in a bonus is received now rather than later and so has a higher present value. If earnings are below the target, the manager has an incentive to take what is commonly known as a "big bath."

According to the financial press, if a firm has a loss, managers increase the loss by including all possible future losses that they can write off—take a "big bath"—so that future periods' earnings are higher (Healy, 1985). The big bath phenomenon is consistent with the bonus formula. If earnings are below the target, any attempt to increase earnings above the target by shifting earnings forward in time involves the permanent loss of some of the bonus. Of course, this will tend to be offset by the fact that whatever bonus is earned, it is earned now rather than later. However, if earnings are far below the target, the permanent loss of bonus will predominate. Then, the manager has incentives to use accounting methods to reduce reported earnings further so that expected future earnings (and bonuses) are increased.

The foregoing implications suggest that managers would not just adopt the set of procedures that increase the present value of reported earnings but would also try to adjust procedures from year to year. It would not be very likely that managers would switch back and forth between accounting methods such as straight-line and accelerated depreciation since those changes are readily apparent to the compensation committee (the effect would have to be reflected in notes to the financial statements, and the auditor would give a consistency qualification). Instead, accruals such as the recognition of losses and future costs (such as strip mining restoration expense) are more likely candidates.

It is interesting to compare the implications of bonus plans to the income smoothing hypothesis (see Chapter 6). If the lower bound on the bonus transfer did not exist but an upper bound did, managers would try to smooth income to the upper bound. If the upper bound is a percentage of a return on shareholders' equity, managers have an incentive to report earnings equal to that return each year. However, the lower bound does exist, and its presence means that managers do not always attempt to reduce the rate-of-return variance. These implications are testable. Chapter 11 reports evidence on the extent to which net accruals vary with the relation between reported earnings and the upper and lower bounds on bonus plans.

ACCOUNTING'S ROLE IN DEBT CONTRACTS

While there is little direct evidence that audited financial statements were used to monitor debt contracts prior to the nineteenth century, there is ample evidence that audited financial statements currently fulfill that purpose (see Smith and Warner, 1979; Leftwich, 1980). Contracts for both public debt (i.e., publicly traded debt) and private debt include covenants that use numbers from the published audited financial statements to restrict managements' actions. Any breach of those covenants is considered a default, providing the lender with the right to take the actions normally associated with a default (e.g., seizure of collateral). Managers of the borrowing firm are required to provide an annual Certificate of Compliance certifying that they have reviewed the financial statements and have no knowledge of a breach. Similarly, the debt contract normally requires the auditor to certify annually that he or she has no knowledge of any default.

Covenants That Use Accounting Numbers

The covenants that use accounting numbers in debt contracts appear to be designed to restrict the types of value-reducing investment and financing decisions discussed in Chapter 8. They are described in the paragraphs that follow. The description is taken from Leftwich

(1980) and Smith and Warner (1979). Those papers base their observations on the American Bar Association's *Commentaries on Indentures*, which is a "cookbook" of typical covenants found in lending agreements and a sample of lending agreements.

DIVIDEND AND SHARE PURCHASE RESTRICTIONS

These are common in debt contracts. They serve the purpose of preventing the manager from paying liquidating dividends. The dividend constraint normally defines an inventory of funds available for dividends (**inventory of payable funds**) over the life of the debt. Dividends are only payable out of that inventory. The typical definition of the inventory for quarter t (IPF_t) is (Kalay, 1982):

$$\text{IPF}_t = k \left(\sum_{\tau=0}^{t} A_\tau \right) + \left(\sum_{\tau=0}^{t} \text{SS}_\tau \right) + \text{DIP} - \left(\sum_{\tau=0}^{t-1} \text{DIV}_\tau \right) \quad (9.1)$$

A_τ is the *reported* earnings for quarter τ, SS_τ is the proceeds from the sale of common stock net of transactions costs, DIP is a fixed number known as the "dip," k is a constant ($0 \le k \le 1$), and DIV_τ is cash or asset dividends and share repurchases in quarter τ. The inventory depends on the accumulated earnings since the debt issue ($\tau = 0$), the amount of new shares issued since $\tau = 0$, and the total dividends since $\tau = 0$. Repurchases of shares and other distributions of cash or assets are treated the same as dividends for the purpose of the dividend covenant (see Kalay, 1982).

Dividend restrictions are effectively minimum investment restrictions on the shareholders. They force managers to invest and make them less likely to forgo positive net present value projects. If the inventory is zero or negative, the firm is not in default, but it cannot pay dividends.

MAINTENANCE OF WORKING CAPITAL

Some contracts require the firm to maintain working capital above a certain minimum level. This covenant uses accounting numbers (i.e., current assets and current liabilities) and helps prevent the payment of a liquidating dividend. It is like the dividend constraint, a minimum investment constraint.

RESTRICTIONS ON MERGER ACTIVITY

One way the manager can increase the firm's risk after a debt issue is to merge with a riskier firm. Sometimes mergers are prohibited by the debt contracts. Other contracts allow mergers, provided that the net tangible assets of the firm after the merger meet a minimum level (or be within a fixed fraction) of long-term debt. These restrictions reduce the manager's ability to use mergers to increase the firm's risk and thereby reduce the existing debt's value (see Chapter 8).

RESTRICTIONS ON INVESTMENTS IN OTHER FIRMS

The manager can also change the firm's risk by investing in other firms' securities. Some agreements prohibit such investments. Others permit them if net tangible assets meet a certain minimum. Still others allow investments if in aggregate they are below a given level or are below a given percentage of the total of equity and long-term debt.

RESTRICTIONS ON THE DISPOSITION OF ASSETS

These restrictions also reduce the manager's ability to change the firm's risk. Such dispositions are often prohibited. If permitted they are restricted to a given dollar value, or the proceeds are required to be used to purchase new fixed assets or to retire debt. In addition to restricting the management's ability to change the firm's risk, these restrictions reduce its ability to pay liquidating dividends.

RESTRICTIONS ON ADDITIONAL DEBT

Chapter 8 pointed out that an issue of debt of higher priority can reduce the value of existing debt if the proceeds of the new issue are paid out as dividends. Covenants either prohibit the issuance of new debt with higher priority or require that if new debt is issued with higher priority, the existing debt's priority must be upgraded to be equal to that of the new debt.

Issuance of new debt of equal or lower priority (when accompanied by dividend payments) can reduce the value of existing debt. In addition to prohibiting the issuance of higher-priority debt, covenants prohibit the issuance of *any* debt or only allow the issue if certain conditions are met. These conditions include aggregate dollar restrictions, minimum net tangible assets to long-term debt ratios, minimum ratios of long-term debt and equity to long-term debt, and minimum ratios of reported earnings to interest charges.

There are many more covenants restricting managers' actions in debt agreements, but the preceding are the principal types that use numbers in the audited financial statements. Public debt contracts typically use reported numbers and require them to be consistent with **generally accepted accounting principles (GAAP)**. In contrast, private debt contracts occasionally adjust the reported numbers to "undo" some GAAP procedures. For example, some of Prudential Insurance Company's contracts require the use of the cost method of reporting unconsolidated subsidiaries in situations where GAAP requires the equity method.

GAAP are accounting principles that have "substantial authoritative support" in the opinion of the SEC. This is distinct from our term "accepted procedures," which is the set of accounting procedures used in contracts.

The Use of GAAP in Debt Contracts

Even if some GAAP procedures are undone, debt agreements basically use reported GAAP accounting numbers. The variations take the form of bottom-line adjustments rather than complete recalculation of accounting numbers. For example, the income from subsidiaries under the equity method is deducted from GAAP earnings and the cost method income added. The specification and preparation of an additional set of accounting statements solely for a debt contract is costly. Given that cost, it is probably cheaper for the shareholders to use GAAP and bear any additional cost of "creative accounting" via the debtholders' *price protecting* themselves when the debt is initially sold.

The reason GAAP variations are more common in private debt contracts than in public debt contracts is probably the difference in renegotiation costs for the two types of debt. Private debt is usually placed with a few insurance companies or banks. These private lenders are well informed and are usually ready to renegotiate contracts if a technical breach occurs in situations where the value of the firm is not below the face value of the debt. This type of breach occurs if a change in GAAP causes the debt/equity ratio to change, for example. Such technical defaults are probably more expensive to renegotiate in the case of public debt. The trustee for the debt usually has to obtain approval of the holders of two-thirds of the outstanding debt to change the contract. And buying some of the debt will not help the firm renegotiate, since it is not allowed to vote the debt it holds. The more costly it is to renegotiate technical breaches of covenants, the less restrictive covenants we expect to observe.

A change in GAAP can cause a technical default on a firm's existing debt contracts because the accounting numbers in the contract's covenants are calculated using GAAP at the time of the calculation, not at the date of the issue of the debt. As a result the covenants and contracts are affected as GAAP changes.

DEBT CONTRACTS' EFFECTS ON ACCOUNTING

Like accounting-based compensation plans, accounting-based debt covenants will be effective only if some restrictions are placed on managers' abilities to control the calculation of the numbers (i.e., if their choice of accounting procedures is restricted). Consequently, if accounting procedures used to calculate reported numbers were not regulated, a set of accounting procedures that restrict the manager's choice and are acceptable to each party would emerge either as common practice or as explicit specification in debt contracts.

The nature of current debt contracts' variations from GAAP provides evidence as to the nature of accepted procedures that would evolve. If debt contracts influenced accounting practice prior to the regulation of disclosure, the variations would also give insights as to why accounting practice took the form it did in the United States prior to the 1932 and 1933 securities acts.

Accepted Procedures

Debt contracts' variations from GAAP typically do not allow certain increases in earnings and asset values permitted by GAAP and require certain decreases in income and asset values or increases in liabilities not necessary under GAAP. The *excluded* increases in earnings tend to be noncash revenues or credits. For example, the equity method of recording a subsidiary's earnings brings into the parent's income the parent's share of the subsidiary's earnings for that period. This method is specified by GAAP, but some debt agreements substitute the cost method whereby only the dividends received by the parent are recorded as income. Assets allowed by GAAP but excluded in debt contracts consist primarily of intangible assets. For example, goodwill from consolidation is often excluded by the covenants.

One example of a liability that bond covenants have required, but GAAP has not, is the lease liability. Many lease liabilities were not, until recently, recognized by GAAP. However, some debt agreements required them to be included in calculating the debt/equity and other ratios used by the contracts along with an offsetting asset—the leased asset. The net effect is to increase the debt/equity ratio and the debt/total assets ratio.

All the variations from GAAP are consistent with conservatism. They delay recognition of revenue (cost method for unconsolidated subsidiaries) and choose lower values for assets (exclude intangible assets). In the one case where an additional asset is included (leasing), the net effect is conservative because the accompanying liability ensures an increase in the firm's debt/equity ratio. The variations appear designed to offset the manager's tendency to overstate earnings and assets, to reduce the manager's ability to use accounting manipulation to cause debt covenants to be ineffective. The exclusion of intangible assets prevents the manager from inflating those assets to avoid debt/equity or debt/total assets constraints. The undoing of the equity method eliminates from earnings funds that may not be legally available to meet the parent's interest obligations. Hence, it prevents overstating the parent's times charges earned ratio.

The variations from GAAP in debt contracts are attempts to undo GAAP standards and so suggest that in the absence of regulation and GAAP, the conservatism and objectivity principles would be observed. Debt contract usage of reported accounting numbers reinforces the bonus plan's effects on accepted procedures.

The previous discussion is basically an intuitively pleasing rationalization of accepted accounting practice prior to regulation. It is difficult to develop the implications for accepted procedures formally and to formally test them. However, if we take the set of accepted procedures and the terms of debt contracts as given, we can make formal testable predictions about the manager's choice of procedures from among accepted procedures.

Choice Among Accepted Procedures

GAAP leaves managers with considerable discretion in the choice of accounting procedures. For example, the manager can choose straight-line or accelerated depreciation, FIFO or LIFO valuation methods for inventories, and the deferred or flowthrough method of accounting for investment tax credit. A default on a debt contract is costly,[4] so contracts that define a breach in terms of accounting numbers provide managers with incentives to choose accounting procedures that reduce the probability of a breach. Ceteris paribus, they would like to choose procedures that increase assets, reduce liabilities, increase revenue, and decrease expense (i.e., are nonconservative). Further, if a breach is going to occur under one accounting method, one would expect managers to switch procedures to avoid the breach.

The preceding analysis provides testable propositions about the variation in accounting procedures across firms and about the nature of firms that change accounting techniques. For example, firms with debt contracts are more likely to use earnings and asset increasing accounting procedures (e.g., straight-line depreciation in most cases) than are firms with no debt. Also, among firms with debt, the closer a firm is to its restrictive covenant on the ratio of interest to earnings,

---

[4] If the default is technical, the debtholders may be prepared to renegotiate the debt rather than have it paid off, particularly if the debt is private. Public debt can be more difficult to renegotiate (see earlier in the chapter). Private lenders, such as insurance companies, are prepared to renegotiate, because that flexibility affects their future business. However, the renegotiation is still not costless. For example, if interest rates have changed substantially since the debt issue, the lender may require a new interest rate between the old rate and current market rate (see Chapter 12).

the more likely the firm will use straight-line depreciation, assuming that straight-line increases earnings.

The preceding hypothesis on variation in accounting procedures among firms with debt depends on the details of debt covenants. Just as early researchers chose to investigate the bonus hypothesis rather than hypotheses based on the details of bonus plans, they also chose to investigate a simple debt contract hypothesis rather than hypotheses based on the details of debt covenants. Bonus plan and debt covenant details are costly to gather, and simple hypotheses such as the bonus plan hypothesis are one way to see whether incurring that cost is likely to pay off.

We call the simple hypothesis early researchers chose to investigate the debt/equity hypothesis:

> **Debt/equity hypothesis**. Ceteris paribus, the larger a firm's debt/equity ratio, the more likely the firm's manager is to select accounting procedures that shift reported earnings from future periods to the current period.

The debt/equity hypothesis can be derived from the hypothesis (based on debt covenants) that the closer a firm is to a particular restrictive accounting-based covenant the more likely the manager is to use procedures that increase current earnings.

To see the connection between the debt/equity hypothesis and the covenant-based hypothesis, consider the inventory of payable funds covenant (equation (9.1)). From the shareholders' perspective, there is an equilibrium level of payable funds inventory that is the result of a trade-off between two costs (Kalay, 1979). One is the cost of the forgone wealth transfers from debt, and it increases as the inventory increases. The other is the expected cost of negative net present value projects that have to be taken if the inventory of payable funds is zero and no dividends can be paid. This latter cost increases as the inventory of payable funds decreases. Ceteris paribus, the wealth transfers forgone are larger, the larger the debt/equity ratio, so firms with higher debt/equity ratios have lower equilibrium inventories of payable funds. Hence, firms with higher debt/equity ratios are closer to their inventory of payable funds constraint and are more likely to adopt procedures that shift reported earnings from future periods to the current period.

Additional assumptions are required to derive the debt/equity hypothesis from the inventory of payable funds effect on accounting procedure choice and so it is a less direct and less powerful test of the theory. Hence, as the literature develops, we expect more researchers to concentrate on testing hypotheses that use the details of covenants rather than the debt/equity hypothesis. As we shall see in Chapter 11, such a change has occurred (e.g., Holthausen, 1981).

There are some problems with hypotheses based on covenant details. One is the difficulty of observing how close the firm is to its covenants. Consider the inventory of payable funds. The effective inventory is not necessarily the inventory of payable funds calculated according to equation (9.1). If a firm is using accelerated depreciation, it can usually increase its earnings and inventory of payable funds by switching to straight-line depreciation. Hence, the effective inventory of payable funds depends on both the inventory of payable funds calculated under existing accounting methods and the "hidden" inventory (i.e., increases in the inventory due to changes in accounting methods). Managers may prefer to let the reported inventory of funds run down first before changing methods to increase earnings and retained earnings. Switching to an earnings increasing method increases other costs (see Chapter 10); it may also reduce future discretion since future debt contracts will set the inventory based on earnings using the new method. Offsetting this is the incentive to adopt earnings increasing methods for compensation purposes.

STOCK PRICE EFFECTS OF PROCEDURE CHANGES

Accounting's role in debt and compensation contracts provides the opportunity for changes in tax-neutral accounting procedures to affect stock prices. Changes in accounting procedures affect agency costs and can transfer wealth between parties to the firm. The studies reviewed in Chapter 4 did not have a theory to tell them where to look for stock price changes accompanying tax-neutral procedure changes and so could not design powerful tests of the hypothesis that tax-neutral procedure changes have stock price effects. What are the predictions of the contracting theory for the stock price tests and can we generate powerful tests of those predictions?

The analysis of the stock price effects of procedure changes depends on whether the changes are made voluntarily by the manager or are mandated by a FASB statement or SEC release.

Voluntary Changes

A manager voluntarily changes accounting procedures because the firm's accepted set of accounting procedures has changed or because the manager's optimal choice from among the accepted set has changed. The firm's accepted set of procedures can change for at least two reasons: (1) the firm changes industries and the new industry has a different set of accepted procedures, or (2) there has been an accounting innovation such that a new set of procedures is optimal for the firm's industry (i.e., maximizes industry market value). The manager's optimal choice from among accepted procedures can change because the firm's fortunes have changed. For example, the firm has had losses such that it is close to a debt covenant ratio and a change is necessary to prevent technical default.

CHANGES IN THE SET OF ACCEPTED PROCEDURES

At the present stage of development of the contracting theory, there are no predictions about the stock price effects of changes in accepted procedures. For example, if a firm changes industries, the stock market will expect the firm to adopt the accepted accounting procedures of its new industry. Those procedures presumably maximize firm values in that industry. Hence, the stock market impounds the expected agency costs under the expected new procedures at the time it learns of the firm's industry change. Expected agency costs borne by shareholders may increase or decrease but in any event will be hidden in the stock price change due to the changed investment. Further, it isn't apparent what share of any change in agency costs is borne by the shareholders, much of it might be borne by the manager.

CHANGES IN THE CHOICE AMONG ACCEPTED PROCEDURES

The stock price effects of these changes depend on whether they are induced by bonus plans or debt contracts. An earnings increasing change to increase the manager's bonus presumably transfers wealth from the shareholders to the manager and causes stock prices to decrease to the extent it is unexpected. However, the relative price decrease for each share is likely to be trivial and unobservable. An earnings increasing change to prevent an impending technical default increases stock prices to the extent it is unexpected. Since the costs of technical default are limited by the costs of renegotiating the debt or repaying it (the manager will take the least cost alternative), the stock price increase is likely to be very small and difficult to observe.

The difficulty of observing stock price effects of voluntary changes between accepted accounting procedures is increased by the fact that the market is likely to expect the change. If a firm is in danger of violating a debt/equity constraint because of recent losses, the market will expect the change with high probability (and impound its effect in the stock price). There will be little surprise (and hence little stock price effect) when the firm actually changes procedures.

Investigating only the largest stock price effects will not produce more powerful tests. There isn't likely to be any predictable variation in surprise (and stock price effect on announcement) across firms. The market will assess the firm's change as more likely, the higher a technical default's cost (e.g., the higher the renegotiation cost). Hence, the firms with the highest cost will have the lowest change in probability (to one) on announcement. This will offset their higher cost so their stock price change on announcement may not be higher than those of other firms.

The conclusion is that it is not possible to predict the stock price effect of voluntary changes in accounting procedures resulting from changes in the set of accepted procedures and very difficult to design powerful tests for the stock price effects of voluntary changes among accepted procedures.

Mandated Changes

A change in accounting standards (via an FASB statement or an SEC release) affects existing contracts and future contracts. Existing contracts are affected because they use accounting numbers calculated according to current GAAP rather than GAAP in force at the time the contract was written (as discussed earlier). A change in accounting standards changes GAAP and changes existing contracts. This can lead to a wealth transfer to shareholders (a stock price increase) or away from shareholders (a stock price decrease). Future contracts are affected because a change in GAAP makes some accounting procedures more or less costly and changes the optimal contracting technology. For example, FASB 19's ban on the full-cost method of accounting for oil and gas firms increases the cost of some firms' using a method that may have been optimal for contracting purposes (i.e., full-cost method). Part of this increased cost is borne by shareholders in the form of a decrease in share prices.

The stock price effect of a change in accounting standards depends on whether the change expands or restricts the set of available accounting procedures.

A restriction of the accounting procedure set occurs when an existing procedure is eliminated by a standard. If the eliminated procedure is part of a firm's optimal contracting technology (i.e., would be an accepted accounting procedure in the absence of regulation), the firm's stock price falls. The firm's stock price drops also if the procedure could be used to reduce the probability of default on existing debt. This latter effect is reduced by the manager's inability to use the method to increase his or her bonus.

An expansion of the set of accounting procedures occurs when a standard allows a previously disallowed accounting procedure. If the newly allowed procedure becomes part of the firm's optimal contracting technology, the firm's stock price rises. That rise is reinforced if the new procedure allows the manager to reduce the probability of default on existing debt contracts. Again, that latter increase in price is partially offset by any increased ability on the manager's part to increase his or her bonus.

Under either a restriction or an expansion of the set of accounting procedures, the stock price effect via existing debt contracts is bounded by the cost of renegotiating the debt contract or repaying the debt. The stock price effect via existing bonus plans is bounded by the management compensation committee's cost of adjusting for the change. These bounds reduce the magnitude of the expected stock price effect and make its observation more difficult.

Nevertheless, the stock price effects of mandated changes are likely to be more observable than those of voluntary changes. Standards may be less predictable than managers' actions (i.e., their voluntary accounting changes), and even if they are not, their stock price effects can vary across firms in a predictable fashion. In voluntary changes, the larger a voluntary change's benefit, the greater probability the market attaches to the change. This greater probability reduces the announcement stock price effect and offsets the larger benefits. Accounting standards typically apply to many firms, so the probability of change on announcement of an accounting standard is the same for many firms.[5] If that is the case, the announcement's stock price effect will vary across firms as the standard's costs and benefits vary. If the cross-sectional variation in costs and benefits is predictable, the cross-sectional variation in stock price announcement effects is predictable.

SUMMARY

Researchers use formal management compensation plans and debt contracts to generate hypotheses from contracting theory about the manager's choice of accounting procedures and the stock price effects of accounting procedure changes. They use those contracts because data are available on their existence and their details. They assume that the contracts' function is to reduce agency costs.

Compensation plans and debt contracts use accounting numbers. If the accounting-based provisions are to be effective in restricting the managers' firm value-reducing actions, there must be some restrictions placed on the managers' methods of calculating the accounting numbers. The costs of writing and monitoring such calculation method restrictions means that the manager's discretion in choosing accounting procedures

---

[5] The probability of the standard's adoption differs for some marginal firms if there is uncertainty as to whether the standard would apply to them or not. For example, ASR 190 only applied to firms above a particular size, and this size threshold changed as the proposed standard moved through the political process.

is not totally eliminated. Hence, we expect a set of accepted procedures to evolve and the manager to have discretion in choosing from among that set.

We can learn something about the nature of the accepted set of procedures from accounting and auditing texts prior to procedure regulation and from the GAAP variations that are explicitly incorporated in debt contracts. Both suggest that accepted procedures are conservative and emphasize objectivity to offset the managers' incentive under both contracts to overstate earnings and assets.

Researchers generate predictions about the manager's choice among accepted procedures by assuming that the compensation plans, debt contracts, and accepted accounting procedures are given. Two commonly tested hypotheses (bonus and debt/equity hypotheses) use simplified versions of compensation plans and debt contracts. The bonus hypothesis predicts that managers of firms with bonus plans choose procedures to increase current earnings. The debt/equity hypothesis predicts the higher the debt/equity ratio, the more likely a manager is to choose earnings increasing procedures. Later studies tend to generate more powerful tests of the theory using the details of the contracts.

The contracting theory implies that changes in accounting procedures can have stock price effects. We are unable to predict the direction of the stock price effect of voluntary changes in accounting procedures that occur because of changes in the accepted set of procedures. The direction is predictable for voluntary changes in accounting procedures that occur to increase bonuses or reduce the probability of default. However, the magnitude of those changes is limited, and they are likely to be associated with other events and so are expected by the market. Consequently, the stock price effects will be difficult to observe. The stock price effects of accounting procedure changes that are due to changes in standards (mandated changes) depend on whether the set of available accounting procedures is expanded or restricted. Expansions tend to increase stock prices and reductions to decrease them.

Accounting procedures can affect the firm's cash flows via the political process as well as via the contracting process. The next chapter (Chapter 10) develops the political process's link between accounting procedures and cash flows and generates additional hypotheses about the manager's procedure choice and the stock price effects of procedure changes. Chapter 11 reviews empirical tests of the accounting procedure choice hypotheses generated in this chapter and in Chapter 10. Chapter 12 reviews empirical tests of the stock price effect hypotheses.

CHAPTER TEN

Accounting and the Political Process

Chapters 8 and 9 describe the development of a theory of accounting practice resulting from assuming nonzero contracting and information costs. That accounting theory parallels the development of finance capital structure theory that occurred when finance theorists assumed nonzero contracting costs. In a similar fashion, this chapter develops hypotheses about the political process's effects on accounting practice based on the assumption of nonzero information, lobbying, and coalition costs. This analysis likewise parallels, and borrows from, developments in the economic theory of regulation that assume nonzero information, lobbying, and coalition costs.

These economic theories of the political process adopt the self-interest view that assumes politicians maximize their utility. Under this assumption, the political process is a competition for wealth transfers. Taxes and regulations transfer wealth to individuals via government services (highways, education, parks), subsidies, protective tariffs, and government-created monopolies (professional entry barriers). Participation in the competition involves nonzero information, lobbying, and coalition costs. Individuals must incur costs of coalescing into voting/lobbying groups and becoming informed about how prospective government actions (e.g., proposed legislation) will affect them. The magnitudes of these costs and their distribution across groups determine the outcome of the political process.

The political process theories suggest hypotheses about the use of accounting numbers in the political process. For example, politicians are hypothesized to use large reported earnings as "evidence" of a monopoly. These large earnings can be caused by numerous factors including (1) low earnings in the previous period that are being used as the benchmark, (2) changes in accounting procedures, (3) fluctuations in foreign currency exchange rates, (4) inventory profits due to inflation, and (5) monopoly. Since it is costly to assess the real reason for the large earnings and benefits from investigation are small, many voters rationally choose to remain ignorant. Politicians and bureaucrats seeking to make themselves better off propose solutions to the "crisis" causing the high profits, thereby gaining media exposure and improving their reelection chances.

Accounting numbers also are used in setting "voluntary" price guidelines to "control" inflation. Accounting numbers are used in regulated industries to set rates (public utilities) and regulate the quantity and type of services offered (banking). Finally, tax policy is influenced by financial accounting standards (e.g., inflation accounting).

To the extent that a given firm is subject to potential wealth transfers in the political process, its manager is hypothesized to adopt accounting procedures that reduce the transfer. In particular, managers of firms that are blamed for a "crisis" (e.g., big oil companies) are more likely to use accounting procedures that reduce expected earnings and the variance of earnings than are managers of firms that are not subject to these political pressures. Managers of regulated firms also take account of how their regulators use the reported numbers (Prakash and Rappaport, 1977).

In this chapter the nature of the political process and information's role in that process are described first; then the effects on accounting are detailed. Based on the economic analysis of the political process and its impact on accounting, the incentives of managers of large firms to choose income reducing accounting procedures are discussed next, followed by a critical evaluation of the analysis. Hypotheses about accounting procedure changes' stock price effects via the political process are then discussed. The chapter concludes with a summary.

THE NATURE OF THE POLITICAL PROCESS

Chapter 7 discussed the view that the political process is a way of remedying perceived market failures (e.g., not "enough" corporate disclosure). An alternative view is based on the assumption that individuals in the political process, like individuals in the market, act in their own self-interest (e.g., Olson, 1971; Stigler, 1971; Peltzman, 1976). Under this alternative theory, the political process is a *competition among individuals for wealth transfers*. There is evidence consistent with this alternative theory (Posner, 1974; McCraw, 1975).

The economic theories of the political process focus on the incentives of individuals to coalesce into groups to lobby for wealth transfers (Stigler, 1971; Peltzman, 1976). A few examples illustrate group lobbying. The Cattlemen's Association lobbied with Congress for quotas on imported beef, presumably to reduce competition and increase their wealth at the expense of beef consumers. The railroads supported the first Interstate Commerce Act, which reduced competition among railroads and transferred wealth to their managers and shareholders at the expense of the consumer. Unions lobby for minimum wage laws. Such laws reduce competition and increase union members' wealth at the expense of consumers and individuals whose equilibrium wage is below the minimum wage (e.g., the young).

Under the economic theories, the existing set of laws and regulations are the equilibrium result of two opposing forces—those who receive the benefits and those who provide the benefits. In equilibrium, those receiving the benefits are incurring costs at the margin just equal to their expected marginal benefits and those providing the wealth transfer are incurring costs at the margin just equal to the expected marginal reduction in the wealth transfer. The factors hypothesized to affect the equilibrium are discussed next.

Factors Affecting Success in the Political Process

INFORMATION COSTS

Downs (1957a, 1957b) points out that the probability that one individual's vote affects the outcome of an election is usually very small. The expected benefit of being informed depends on the likelihood that the voter's actions (e.g., voting) will affect the outcome. Hence, the expected value of a single person's vote is trivial, and ceteris paribus, the individual has little incentive to gather information relevant to voting. At any one time, there are a large number of bills in Congress and state and local governments, and the costs of being informed *and* determining those bills' effect on one's own welfare are substantial. There are services that keep track of representatives' votes, thereby reducing information costs. But, in many circumstances, information costs are likely to be substantially greater than the benefits of being informed.

Information costs explain the existence of interest groups in the political process. There are economies of scale in information generation. The Sierra Club gathers information on the effect of political actions on wilderness areas and national parks and the positions of politicians on issues relevant to members. For labor unions, the marginal cost of informing their members of their political representatives' voting record is low.

HETEROGENEITY OF INTERESTS

The economies of scale in information production suggest that large groups tend to be successful in the political process. However, there are factors that limit interest group size. One is the heterogeneity of group members' interests.

If the interests of the group differ, group action will not be in a particular member's interest. Except for differences of seniority, the interests of members of a union are usually homogeneous on employment matters. Hence, the per member expected benefit of the union's taking an active role in the political process on issues affecting the members' employment is relatively high. On the other hand, the American Accounting Association or American Economic Association represents a heterogeneous group—academics, government bureaucrats, corporate managers, and so on—and the expected per member value of political action is low. Consequently, those two associations do not lobby in the political process as frequently as do unions.

ORGANIZATION COSTS

These costs also limit the size of interest groups in the political process. Not only must the interest group bear the information costs to assess the impact of particular issues, but it must organize to translate its interests into effective support for politicians who will act in those interests. The group must mobilize its own vote, raise resources to support politicians' campaigns, and prevent "free riders" (i.e., individuals who have the same interests and hence benefit from any actions but who do not contribute to the cost of those actions). Unions are better organized to collect from their members and to prevent "free riders" via "closed shop" rules than, for example, the Sierra Club.

There is likely to be a limit to the economies of scale in organization costs. First, as the size of the interest group seeking wealth transfers increases, the number of individuals who supply the wealth to be transferred decreases. This increases the taxed group's incentive to oppose the wealth transfer. At some point, those who are being taxed will organize to oppose the political actions. Second, as the size of the group seeking wealth transfers increases, there is a greater incentive for group members to free ride, thereby increasing the monitoring costs to the group to reduce free riding (Olson, 1971).

The preceding analysis suggests the existence of an optimal size for interest groups. It is likely to be well below a simple majority of voters, certainly at the national and state levels. This, combined with the lack of incentive to be informed at the individual level, suggests that policies that transfer small amounts of wealth from a majority of voters are likely to succeed.

The preceding factors affect the relative success of various interests in the competition for wealth redistribution. The analysis does not imply that the ability of any one group to transfer wealth to its members is unrestricted. As noted, success will generate opposition. Further, the amount of wealth available for transfer is limited, and this generates competition among interest groups. The equilibrium outcome and the ability of groups to obtain and oppose wealth transfers varies over time. For example, Peltzman (1976, p. 227) argues that in depressions regulation tends to be more heavily weighted toward "producer protection" and toward "consumer protection" in expansions.

Politicians and Bureaucrats in the Political Process

Politicians and bureaucrats, like everyone else, are hypothesized to have incentives to seek wealth transfers via the political process. They are not purely brokers between competing interest groups. They are interest groups themselves.[1] Politicians and government bureaucrats of all political parties have incentives to increase the resources controlled by the government, since that increases their ability to grant favors (Meckling, 1976a).

Costly information in the political process provides opportunities for politicians and bureaucrats to generate laws and regulations that transfer control of resources to the government and wealth to themselves. For example, consider the rationale for the securities acts that poor disclosure contributed to the 1929 stock market crash. Based on the evidence, that rationale is questionable. Why then does it exist, and why did the securities acts pass?

One hypothesis is that the Great Crash provided politicians with a chance to transfer resources to themselves. Individual voters felt the effects of the Great Crash and of the depression. They preferred to avoid future crashes and depressions, and they demanded action to achieve that end. However, it is costly for individuals to learn the causes

---

[1] Economists have argued that politicians and bureaucrats are not passive but actually create issues; politicians are entrepreneurs (Jensen, 1976a; Meckling, 1976a; Jensen and Meckling, 1976).

of stock market crashes and depressions, and individuals have little incentive to incur the costs. Hence, under this hypothesis, the crash created an opportunity for politicians to earn votes by appearing to be preventing future stock market crashes and at the same time to transfer resources to their own control. The securities acts provide politicians with control over resources, and they provide an appearance of solving the problem. They enable politicians to grant favors to several interest groups (e.g., lawyers and accountants). Notice that this securities acts explanation also applies to the oil and gas regulation acts and federal drug laws, mine safety laws, and federal aviation acts.

Competition among interest groups could lead Congress into taking actions that prevent future crashes and depressions by, for example, specifying a better money supply policy, if money contraction was the real cause of the depression. But this appears unlikely. The group from whom wealth is transferred by the securities acts is very large (i.e., taxpayers for whom future taxes and product prices are increased) and, therefore, difficult to organize. The average per capita amount of wealth transferred is small. Hence, while the costs of being informed are substantial, the benefits are small.

The ability of politicians and bureaucrats to take advantage of crises such as the Great Crash depends on the number of special interest groups opposed to the regulations. As noted, it is often too costly for diffuse voters who pay for the regulation to organize into effective political coalitions.

Under this economic theory of the political process, no one is being "fooled." Voters expect that most legislation will *not* make them better off. Voters' expectations are rational (i.e., are on average fulfilled). The costs of becoming informed and of lobbying are more than the expected benefits (e.g., the wealth transfers eliminated). Furthermore, the party proposing the legislation or program can further increase the opposition's costs by developing elaborate justifications or public interest theories as to why their proposals make everyone better off. These theories or justifications must then be answered (or refuted) by the opposition, thereby raising their costs.

Comparison of the Market and Political Processes

Information plays an important role in both the market and political processes. Whether "more" information is generated and used under one or the other process is an empirical question. However, the analyses of Downs (1957a and 1957b), Stigler (1971), Peltzman (1976), and Alchian (1975) suggest that there is less incentive for information to be produced and used in the political process than in the market process. The reason is that in the political process individuals have less ability to capture the information's benefits.

In the market process, individual investors own a very small fraction of the firm and, therefore, have little incentive to discover information about the firm. They can "free ride" on others. But other individuals such as brokers or entrepreneurs specialize in information production. By concentrating their ownership, or by the use of stock options, these specialists can capture the gains from their information production. If that information suggests, for example, that the firm's securities should be valued less, that individual can short sell those securities or buy puts and capture the gains. Further, if the reduction in value is due to managerial inefficiency, there are incentives for individuals to take over the firm, change the firm's policies, and capture capital gains from the changed policies.

If there are gains from a change in a government policy, only land values directly capitalize the future consequences of the policy change. There are no security markets that directly capitalize the future stream into a present amount. Thus, it is more difficult to capitalize on a government policy change because of the higher transaction costs of trading land (Alchian, 1975; Zimmerman, 1977).

For example, consider a local government that is levying annual property taxes of $1 million to fund a service the taxpayers (and consumers) value at $750,000. Managerial opportunism or inefficiency is consuming the remainder. To capture all the benefits of eliminating the service, an individual would have to buy all the taxable land in the locality and convince voters that the service and taxes should be eliminated. One way this might be done is to pay the voters some amount (less than the total gain of $250,000) to forgo the inefficient service. Then the individual would gain the remainder of the $250,000. That is, the individual would gain from the increase in land values due to the difference between the decreased present value of taxes and the cost of the eliminated service.

However, consider the costs of this strategy. It is costly to monitor voting. Individually, voters have little incentive to vote as they promise since their vote cannot be observed and they place a positive value on the eliminated service. Further, purchasing votes is illegal, and there are incentives for politicians to reveal bribery, so vote purchasing is costly.

The transactions costs of trading land are substantially higher than trading securities. Title insurance, brokerage fees, attorney fees, and closing costs can amount to 5 to 10 percent on land compared to one-half of 1 percent for listed securities. Because of the higher transaction costs of trading land than corporate securities, voters have less incentive to acquire information about government operations than corporate operations.

In both the market and political processes, individual shareholders owning a small fraction of the firm have little incentive to monitor the firm's managers just as individual voters have little incentive to monitor government officials. Both behave as free riders. But the two processes are hypothesized to differ in terms of the costs to concentrate the benefits of increased monitoring. The costs of concentrating the benefits of reduced managerial opportunism are hypothesized to be lower in the market process than in the political process.

Notice that the difference between the market and political processes results from assumed differences in the costs of transacting/concentrating property rights of improved monitoring. If the costs in the two processes are zero, we return to the no-effects hypothesis discussed in Chapters 3 to 6. If the costs in the two processes are equal and positive, individuals have similar incentives in both processes to acquire information. The accounting research to date has assumed the transaction costs in the political process are substantially larger than in the market process. And, therefore, individual voters have less incentive to acquire information.

THE POLITICAL PROCESS'S EFFECT ON ACCOUNTING PROCEDURES

This section applies and extends the economic theories of the political process to accounting. In particular, if accounting numbers (e.g., earnings) are used in the political process to either advocate government regulation (e.g., windfall profits tax) or in administering existing regulation (e.g., public utility rate setting), what incentives are created for managers when choosing accounting procedures? This section outlines some of these incentives created by the political process.

Asymmetric Loss Function

Economists argue that the incentives to produce information in the political process and the cost of that information induce a bias in the regulations issued by bureaucrats. Peltzman (1974, p. 83) argues that officials of the Federal Drug Administration are more likely to be blamed for "crises" when the effects are readily apparent. For example, the cost to the bureaucrat of approving a drug that causes observable side effects (e.g., the drug thalidomide and the consequent birth defects) is relatively greater than the cost of not issuing a drug (e.g., lives lost that might have been saved by a new drug). This induces a bias in the bureaucrats' decisions—they will be unduly reluctant to approve new drugs.

The SEC's effective outlawing of asset revaluations from the 1930s until recently is analogous to the drug case. Failures of large corporations (bankruptcies) are potential political crises that direct attention to the SEC (e.g., the Penn Central Railroad). If it turns out ex post that the failed corporation's assets were "overvalued," the SEC is likely to be blamed. Investors' losses are apparent (even if they are not due to accounting). On the other hand, it is difficult to make a crisis out of a corporation's success. Little sympathy is garnered by potential investors claiming that a profit was forgone because the firm's assets were undervalued. Given this asymmetry in losses, the SEC bureaucrat has incentives to eliminate potential sources of overstatement of assets (i.e., revaluations) and not eliminate sources of understatement.

This asymmetric loss function is the result of information costs. Government actions, or inactions, that result in realized accounting losses to individuals are less costly to document than are those that impose economic losses but do not result in realized accounting losses.

Effects of Potential Crises

Numbers in accounting reports are used by politicians in creating or resolving "crises." Reported earnings receive particular attention. For example, oil firms' profits attract politicians' attention in periods of rapidly increasing oil prices and/or governmentally induced "shortages" of oil. This occurred in 1971 with price controls, in 1974 with the Arab oil embargo, and again in 1979 with large increases in third quarter reported profits.

In 1974 the oil companies' profits fueled politicians' attempts to break up those companies. The 1979 third quarter profits were labeled by politicians as "obscene" and "pornographic." The U.S. House of Representatives had decontrolled the price of gas at the pumps one week before the earnings announcements; after the earnings announcements, they immediately reversed themselves and voted to reimpose controls. This occurred even though part of the increase in profits was due to FASB Statement No. 31 (see "Profits Windfall," in *Barron's*, October 29, 1979), and most of the rest was due to overseas operations and inventory holding gains. These two examples suggest that "reported" profits influence the actions of Congress. Exactly when Congress chooses to look at reported profits is not well documented, but it appears to be related to the rate of increase in an industry's prices. For example, the steel industry came under attack in the 1960s after it posted price increases in excess of the government's guidelines. Also, bills to break up oil companies and the oil windfall profits tax follow rapid oil price increases.

It is probable that reported profits also affect the actions of regulatory agencies. Both the Antitrust Division and the Federal Trade Commission (FTC) tend to institute actions against corporations whose shares have earned abnormal rates of return (see Ellert, 1976). It is likely that those firms have also had abnormally large increases in reported earnings.

The use of reported profits by politicians and regulators is hypothesized to provide corporate managers with an incentive to adopt accounting procedures that reduce reported earnings (e.g., accelerated depreciation). Lower reported profits reduce the likelihood of adverse government actions against, and increase the likelihood of government subsidies to the firm, if the politicians, regulators, and those opposing the actions that benefit the firm do not adjust the reported profits to undo management's earnings reducing accounting choices. As long as it is costly for outsiders to undo the accounting choices, management has an incentive to choose accounting procedures that report lower earnings in the current year.

High inflation is another example of a "crisis" that creates incentives for managers to choose earnings reducing accounting procedures. Politicians attempt to solve inflation by a variety of programs and legislation (e.g., wage and price controls and guidelines, gasoline price controls, import restrictions, and monetary and fiscal policy). Some of these government programs use accounting numbers. For example, on November 1, 1978, President Carter issued Executive Order 12092, "Prohibition Against Inflationary Procurement Practices." This order's purpose was to reduce inflation by monitoring the prices of government contractors. However, companies were excused from complying with the order if their reported profits had not increased. All companies selling goods or services to the government had to comply with this standard. The profitability exclusion provision is another example of how the political process creates incentives for managers to choose accounting procedures that reduce reported profits.

Rate Regulation

Many corporations have their prices or rates set by government regulatory agencies (e.g., utilities, banks, insurance companies, oil firms). In many cases, the rates or prices are set on the basis of formulas that use accounting-determined costs. For example, most public utility commissions set revenues (and prices) according to the following equation:

$$\text{Revenues} = \frac{\text{operating}}{\text{expenses}} + \text{depreciation} + \text{taxes} + r_A \times \frac{\text{asset}}{\text{base}} \quad (10.1)$$

where r_A is the allowed rate of return on capital. For example, if a utility has \$250 million (book value) of capital invested in utility assets and the commission sets $r_A = 8$ percent, rates are set to recover operating expenses, depreciation, taxes, and a \$20 million return (\$250 × .08). In determining which accounting procedures to use in rate-making equations such as equation (10.1), the courts and regulatory bodies use the opinions, statements, and standards of accounting standard setting bodies (i.e., the CAP, APB, and FASB) as precedents. This creates an incentive for corporate managers whose rates are regulated to lobby with regulatory agencies and standard setting bodies for accounting procedures that yield the most favorable rates.

Many accounting standards result from accounting disputes that originate in the utility rate-making process. For example, the business combination issue arose in the utility area (i.e., purchase versus pooling, see Moonitz, 1974b, pp. 44–47). Utilities are allowed to earn a normal rate of return on their asset base (see equation (10.1)) and are not supposed to earn monopoly rents. When one utility acquires another, the price presumably includes a payment for any monopoly rents. This "goodwill" is capitalized separately and is not included in the rate base. However, in the early part of this century when utilities merged, they used the purchase method of accounting that revalues the firm's assets. The purchase price (including the payment for the franchise—the monopoly rents) was allocated across the tangible assets and incorporated in those assets' stated value (see Jarrell, 1979). That way, rents are incorporated in the asset base and continue to be earned via equation (10.1). The first mention in the literature of the pooling method that pools merging firms' assets at book value was in 1943. It was introduced in *Niagara Falls Power Company* v. *Federal Power Commission*, presumably to prevent the practice of incorporating monopoly rents into the asset base.

Another issue where utilities played an important role was the investment tax credit debate. When the investment tax credit was introduced in 1962, Arthur Andersen and its utility clients wanted amortization of the investment tax credit over the life of the asset. This would avoid large increases in reported earnings in years of large capital expansion and presumably avoid rate hearings.

Utilities lobbying before the APB and FASB for a particular accounting procedure affect the set of accounting procedures chosen by their public utility commissions and therefore utility rates. The reason for this linkage between financial reporting standards and statutory accounting procedures of utility commissions is due to the use of APB opinions and FASB standards as precedents by the courts and commissions. Lobbying before the APB or FASB affects not only the procedures chosen by utility commissions but also the financial accounting procedures of unregulated firms.

Taxes

Currently, if a firm uses LIFO for tax purposes, it must use LIFO for financial reporting. This linkage is a result of interest group competition. Before 1930, the nonferrous and petroleum products industries used the base stock method of inventory valuation for tax purposes. However, in 1930 the Supreme Court disallowed that method. In 1934 the American Petroleum Institute (an organization of oil firms) recommended LIFO as a replacement, and in 1936 that recommendation was endorsed by the AICPA. The Treasury Department lobbied against LIFO. The outcome was that Congress allowed LIFO, but in a compromise to the Treasury, Congress specified that LIFO was available only if the taxpayer used it for financial reporting (Moonitz, 1974b, p. 33).

Because an inventory method affects income taxes, corporate managers consider those tax effects when making that choice (Morse and Richardson, 1983). Undoubtedly, part of the popularity of LIFO for reporting purposes is due to tax effects. Since risk is likely to change with changes in inventory methods, that decision is a risk/return decision (see Chapter 4). This may explain why some firms do not switch to LIFO when the inflation rate rises. LIFO could increase the variability (and covariability) of the firm's cash flows.[2]

Other reporting methods are not tied to income tax methods. However, lobbying for an accounting method for tax purposes is enhanced if the same procedure is adopted for reporting purposes. Consequently, potential tax effects can influence the selection of accounting procedures. For example, much of the interest in FASB 33 ("Inflation Accounting") was likely due to the potential tax relief firms would receive if taxes were tied to inflation-adjusted depreciation and cost of goods sold. One way to rationalize modifying the tax system to adjust for inflation is to adopt such adjustments for financial reporting.

Franchise taxes are imposed on businesses by some states on the basis of book values of assets. This provides managers with incentives to adopt accounting procedures that reduce assets' book values. Finally, to reduce duplicate record-keeping costs, managers have incentives to use the same accounting procedures for both tax and financial reporting.

---

[2] Switching to LIFO may not be a positive net present value project when the future tax savings are discounted at the higher, risk-adjusted opportunity cost of capital.

Variance Effects of Procedures

The foregoing influences of the political process create incentives for politically sensitive firms to choose accounting methods that defer the reporting of earnings. However, it is also likely that the political process creates incentives to reduce the variance of reported earnings changes. The variance is important because political and regulatory sanctions are likely to be imposed on corporations for "large profits" in a single period and give little recognition to other periods in which earnings are lower. This asymmetry is consistent with information costs. The media often calculates percentage increases in earnings over the same period last year. Use of the earnings number in this fashion provides managers with an incentive to reduce the variance of reported earnings.

To illustrate, consider the following example. A firm is currently using a particular set of accounting procedures that produces the following quarterly earnings series denoted as A.

	19X0					19X1				
	Q1	*Q2*	*Q3*	*Q4*	*Total*	*Q1*	*Q2*	*Q3*	*Q4*	*Total*
A	$1.00	$1.05	$1.03	$1.10	$4.18	$1.15	$1.10	$1.20	$1.05	$4.50
	Percentage change from same quarter in previous year:					15%	5%	17%	−5%	
B	$1.10	$1.13	$ .90	$1.05	$4.18	$1.20	$ .95	$1.40	$ .95	$4.50
	Percentage change from same quarter in previous year:					9%	−16%	56%	−10%	

A new accounting standard is adopted that increases the variance of the quarterly earnings but does not alter annual earnings. This new standard produces the quarterly earnings series denoted as B. The greater variance in reported earnings increases the likelihood of large positive and negative percentage earnings changes. It is the large positive increases that attract attention since they are used to support a "crisis" of big business or charges of monopolization. The large percentage increases can come from an unusually good current quarter or an unusually bad quarter last year.

THE SIZE HYPOTHESIS

The previous section presented several examples of the incentives created by the political process regarding choice of accounting procedures. These examples and their underlying analyses have suggested a general hypothesis about the effect of the political process on accounting procedures.

Accounting researchers, relying on economists' conjectures, assume that large firms are more politically sensitive than small firms[3] and, therefore, face differential incentives in their choice of accounting procedures (Gagnon, 1967; Watts and Zimmerman, 1978). A 200 percent increase in Exxon's profits is hypothesized to attract much more attention in the press and Washington than is a 200 percent increase in Sybron's profits. (Sybron is a small NYSE-listed firm.) Size of a corporation is explicitly used in regulations that impose costs on corporations (e.g., the SEC's ASR 190 required firms with assets in excess of $100 million to disclose replacement cost data). If firms' political sensitivity varies with size, larger firms are more likely to adopt accounting procedures that defer reported earnings.

Accounting researchers have used firm size to proxy for a firm's political sensitivity and thus the incentive of managers to choose earnings reducing accounting procedures. We call this the size hypothesis.

> **Size Hypothesis.** Ceteris paribus, the larger the firm, the more likely the manager is to choose accounting procedures that defer reported earnings from current to future periods.

Tests of this hypothesis are generally consistent with the hypothesis (see Chapter 11).

The size hypothesis is based on the assumption that large firms are more politically sensitive and have relatively larger wealth transfers imposed on them (**political costs**) than smaller firms. Zimmerman (1983) tests this assumption. The most direct way to transfer corporate assets is via the tax system, and therefore, income taxes are *one* component of political costs borne by firms. Zimmerman (1983) examines the empirical relationship between corporate tax rates and firm size. Larger firms incurring higher taxation rates than smaller firms is consistent with the proposition that they bear higher political costs, assuming that the nontax components of political costs do not vary in an opposite and offsetting fashion. That is, large firms might have higher tax rates, but they may also be receiving more political benefits (profitable government contracts, import restrictions, etc.) that offset the higher tax rates. Zimmerman's (1983) tests do not control for these nontax political cost components. He finds some evidence that large firms have higher tax rates than smaller firms. But this relationship varies over time and across industries, suggesting that firm size is a

---

[3] Alchian and Kessel (1962, p. 162) suggest that large firms, especially if their profits are large, fear greater government action. Also, see Jensen and Meckling (1978).

noisy proxy for political costs (assuming that the nontax political cost components are not offsetting the tax component).

Zimmerman analyzes both financial statement data (from *Compustat*) and aggregate tax return data (from the Internal Revenue Service). The two are used to help ensure that any observed associations are not due to peculiarities of the accounting system. Just the results from the financial statements are described here because the IRS results are similar. Using data from published financial statements, an *effective* tax rate is calculated for each company in each year 1947–1981 for which data are available. "Effective tax rates" are defined as the ratio of worldwide corporate taxes (income tax expense less the change in deferred taxes) divided by either operating cash flows or pretax income. The choice of denominators does not alter the inferences. Using data from the *Compustat* industrial files produces 43,515 usable observations.

The next step classifies firms into either a "large" or "other" portfolio. The roughly 50 largest firms based on sales are classified as "large," and all other firms are classified as "other." The choice of 50 firms is based on several accounting studies (reviewed in Chapter 11) that find that only the largest firms in the economy face differential political costs. The mean tax rates in each of these two portfolios are calculated in every year. The means are not different until the 1970s. Tax rates have been declining since the Korean emergency for both portfolios except in the 1970s when the "large" portfolio's mean tax rate increased.

Table 10.1 presents the *t*-statistics of the difference in means. A positive *t*-statistic indicates that the mean tax rate in the "large" portfolio exceeds the mean tax rate in the "other" portfolio. The column labeled "All Industries" presents the *t*-statistics for the entire sample. While 1968 is marginally significant, 1971 and all years following indicate that the "large" firms have statistically significant higher tax rates than do "other" firms. The remaining columns in Table 10.1 assign the "large" and "other" firms to one-digit SIC code industries and conduct separate *t*-tests within each industry.

As seen in Table 10.1, the results are to a large extent caused by the oil industry. In 1969 and 1974, the oil depletion allowance was reduced. Since the "large" firms tend to be oil companies,[4] their effective tax rates were raised relative to non-oil companies. These results are important because they suggest that the oil industry has incurred the largest political costs. In later chapters, we will see that the oil companies again dominate the results in many studies.

---

[4] In 1975 oil firms comprised roughly 30 percent of the "large" portfolio while nondurable manufacturers comprised 20 percent and durable manufacturers, 30 percent. Communications, shipping, airlines, and trade accounted for the remaining 20 percent.

TABLE 10.1

t-statistics of Difference in Tax Rates (Income Taxes/Operating Cash Flow) of the Largest Firms and All Other Firms on Compustat, 1947–1981 (size = sales)

One-Digit SIC code:	All Industries	Mining, Petroleum, Construction 1	Manufacturing Nondurables 2	Manufacturing Durables 3	Communications, Shipping, Airlines 4	Trade 5
1947	− 1.33	− 1.02	− .01	.21		− .75
1948	− .71	− 1.09	− .56	1.23		− 1.03
1949	− .52	− 1.54	.33	1.20		− 1.05
1950	.17	− 1.69	− .14	3.29		− 1.35
1951	.53	− 1.29	.77	2.28		− 1.39
1952	− .71	− 1.53	− .44	.94		− 1.04
1953	.43	− 2.07	1.31	1.68		− 1.61
1954	− 1.21	− 1.42	.25	.65		− 1.64
1955	.38	− .67	.05	1.94		− 1.54
1956	− .52	− 1.12	− .16	.39		− 1.52
1957	− .57	− 2.02	.58	.86		− 1.63
1958	− 1.26	− 1.75	.44	.83		− 1.89
1959	− 1.10	− 1.53	.52	.45	.08	− 1.66
1960	− .50	− .61	.48	1.03	.28	− 1.52
1961	− .04	− 1.16	.39	2.05	1.02	− 1.13
1962	− .43	− .91	.88	1.12	1.21	− 1.41
1963	− .48	− 1.03	.67	1.31	1.63	− 1.97
1964	.56	− 1.50	1.40	1.62	1.67	− .49
1965	1.17	− 1.10	.13	3.27	1.54	− .20
1966	.23	− .56	.35	1.33	1.29	− .77
1967	− .19	− .01	.67	.01	.59	− 1.26
1968	1.62	− .10	1.57	2.28	1.05	.19
1969	− .16	.23	.69	.58	1.26	− .64
1970	.47	1.84	1.39	− .49	.61	− .52
1971	2.01	2.71	1.76	.11	− .10	− 1.01
1972	1.91	3.42	2.34	.29	− .26	− .94
1973	3.50	4.34	3.75	.55	− .76	− 1.01
1974	4.40	5.77	2.03	.49	− .70	− .74
1975	2.87	4.38	.15	.16	− 1.14	− .61
1976	2.59	4.47	.86	.55	− .78	− 1.08
1977	3.48	4.54	3.85	.54	− .61	− 1.11
1978	3.22	3.49	3.63	.42	.34	− .92
1979	2.20	2.52	2.72	− 1.23	− .39	− 1.04
1980	3.58	4.23	2.36	− .19	− .37	− .81
1981	2.54	4.11	2.28	− .88	− .75	− 2.07

Source: J. L. Zimmerman, "Taxes and Firm Size," *Journal of Financial Accounting and Economics* 5 (August 1983), Table 2.

The larger firms in the two manufacturing industries (SIC codes 2 and 3) have higher tax rates than other firms in those industries in most years. These differences are statistically significant at the .10 level in 8 of the last 10 years for nondurables (chemicals, paper, drugs, etc.) and in 8 of the last 35 years for the durables (autos, steel, machinery, etc.).

The results for the last two industries in Table 10.1 (SIC codes 4 and 5) are inconsistent with the size hypothesis. These industries contain relatively few large firms. Industry 4 is regulated, and this may reduce the incentives to use the tax system to transfer wealth from these firms. The trade industry is anomalous. Thirty-four of the 35 years show the large trade firms having *lower* tax rates than other trade firms. These results are inconsistent with the proposition that large firms bear higher political costs. The accounting studies reviewed in Chapter 11 also find that large trade firms do not choose accounting procedures that reduce reported earnings.

Subject to the caveat that only the income tax component of political costs is being measured, the following conclusions are drawn. (1) The relation between firm size and tax rates is not uniform over time or across all industries. For example, the increased political sensitivity of the large oil firms is a 1970s phenomenon. Large nondurable manufacturers have only recently been taxed at a higher rate, and large durable manufacturers were taxed at higher rates in the 1950s and 1960s but not in the 1970s. Therefore, firm size (measured by sales) is not a perfect proxy for political sensitivity as measured by effective tax rates. (2) The oil industry and changes in tax codes in this industry are the primary reasons the large firms have higher effective tax rates.

These findings suggest that there are problems with the size hypothesis. The next section explores some of these problems and those associated with the economic theory of the political process.

CRITIQUE OF THE ANALYSIS

The economic theory of the political process is not fully formulated. While this literature has made some progress in developing testable propositions, there are still many unanswered questions and unexplored areas. For example, the economic theory is unable to explain the form the wealth transfer takes. The transfer can be a direct cash subsidy, government protectionism, tax credits/deductions, or government contracts. For example, why do dairy farmers receive their wealth transfer in the form of a price support system instead of via a direct cash subsidy?

Much of the economic literature of the political process is ex post rationalization of existing regulation. Given the relative youth of this literature, these case studies are to be expected and they provide the "raw data" required to formulate a more general (powerful) theory. But, at the same time, one should be very careful about the inferences drawn from these findings.

Similar cautions extend to the role of corporations and accounting in the political process (Holthausen and Leftwich, 1983, p. 108). The size hypothesis relies on the assumption tested by Zimmerman (1983) that large corporations are more politically sensitive than smaller corporations. There are several weaknesses in this assumption. First, large firms, while they might be prime targets, are also powerful adversaries in the political process. Large firms are observed receiving large wealth transfers (e.g., the loan guarantees to Lockheed and Chrysler, trigger price import protection for U.S. steel makers, and the "voluntary" import quotas by Japanese automakers). Large corporations seem to receive wealth transfers when they are in financial distress. This suggests that a better proxy for the negative/positive corporate wealth transfers is a firm's accounting earnings instead of firm size (total sales or assets). While earnings and size are highly correlated, size does not differentiate firms that are receiving from those providing wealth transfers. And the sign on the wealth transfer might affect a manager's incentive to choose income-reducing accounting procedures.

Besides the firm's size, its industry probably also affects its political vulnerability. Firm size proxies for industry because firms within an industry have simiiar sizes (Ball and Foster, 1982, p. 183). Therefore, industry membership is a confounding factor. Finding a statistical association between firm size and choice of accounting procedures might be due to firm size proxying for industry membership.

Zimmerman's (1983) results also suggest that firm size as a proxy for political sensitivity varies over time. Peltzman (1976) argues that government regulation will tend to vary over the business cycle. During contractions, regulation is pro-producer and during expansions it is pro-consumer. Thus, firm size is likely not a stationary measure of political costs borne by firms. Besides, other omitted factors are likely affecting firms' political exposure (e.g., recent price increases, the extent of unionization, and consumer versus producer oriented products).

The preceding problems suggest caution in interpreting the empirical tests of the size hypothesis is warranted. But early progress in developing theories requires the use of "crude" or "unsophisticated" proxy variables. Highly aggregated proxy variables (like firm size) are used because the theory is not sufficiently developed to produce more specific, refined hypotheses or proxy variables. The highly aggregate proxy variables still provide information that allow richer theories to be produced, which in turn lead to more refined proxies (Zimmerman, 1982).

STOCK PRICE EFFECTS OF PROCEDURE CHANGES

Just as costly contracting provides the opportunity for tax-neutral changes in accounting procedures to affect stock prices, so does a political process that involves costly contracting and information. Accounting procedure changes affect political costs and the political process's wealth transfers. What testable predictions can we draw for the stock price effects of procedure changes? As for contracting effects, the analysis of the changes' stock price effects via the political process depends on whether the change is voluntary or mandated.

Voluntary Changes

It is difficult to design powerful tests of the stock price effects of voluntary changes induced by the political process, just as it is difficult to design powerful tests of the stock price effects of voluntary changes induced by the contracting process. The change is the result of other changes affecting the firm's value, and its stock price effect is difficult to separate from the stock price effect of those other changes. Also, voluntary changes will be expected by the market, and the market will attach a higher change probability to the firms that benefit more from the change.

If a manager changes an accounting procedure to reduce reported earnings and political costs, it is because political costs have changed. For example, the firm, or its industry as a whole, has become more profitable and attracted the attention of regulators (e.g., the oil industry in 1974). The marginal stock price effect of an accounting change designed to reduce political costs is a stock price increase. However, if the change is induced by increased industry political costs, it is difficult to disentangle the change's positive effect from the increased industry political costs' negative effect.

The preceding example also illustrates the expectation problem. The increased political costs would cause the market to expect the change. The greater the increase, the more likely the firm is to change procedures to reduce political costs.

Mandated Changes

The stock price effects of mandated accounting changes via the political process depend on whether the change restricts or expands the set of available procedures.

A restriction of the accounting procedures set increases stock prices if it eliminates an accounting procedure that reports higher earnings and assets than alternative procedures. The reason is that the set of available procedures affects the firms' opponents' ability to claim that the firms' earnings are understated. For example, managers of utilities might want the elimination of the investment tax credit flowthrough method. That elimination makes it more difficult for the utilities' opponents to argue that large reported earnings increases resulting from the flow-through method in years of heavy capital expenditures are grounds for rate hearings (discussed earlier).

A restriction of the procedure set reduces stock prices if it eliminates an accounting procedure that reports lower earnings than alternative procedures. That elimination prevents managers from re-ducing political costs by adopting the eliminated procedure.

The variance of earnings can also affect political costs. If there are two procedures that on average produce the same earnings level, but one produces a higher earnings variance, the manager will prefer the lower earnings variance procedure. The reason is that opponents in the political process only seize on "high profits" and ignore "large losses." The higher earnings variance procedure is more likely to produce "high profits." A restriction that eliminates a high earnings variance procedure increases share prices (ceteris paribus), and a restriction that eliminates a low earnings variance procedure reduces shares prices (ceteris paribus).

An expansion of the procedure set increases share prices via the political process if it adds a procedure that reduces the level or variance of profits (ceteris paribus) and decreases share prices if it adds a procedure that increases the level or variance of reported earnings. The reasoning is the obverse of that for a restriction.

Stock price effects of mandated changes via the political process are bounded by the costs of alternative ways of reducing political costs. And the announcement stock price effect is reduced to the extent that the standard is expected. These effects make powerful tests of stock price effects difficult. However, like mandated changes' announcement stock price effects via the contracting process (see Chapter 9), the announcement effects via the political process can vary across firms in a predictable fashion. Standards apply to many firms, so the change in probability of the standard on announcement is the same for many firms, allowing larger announcement stock price effects for firms whose political costs are most affected by the standard.[5] This possibility and the possibility that standards are less easily forecasted by the market

[5] The probability change can differ if some firms have the possibility of being excluded from the standard (see Chapter 9, footnote 6).

than voluntary changes suggest to us that more powerful stock price tests are possible for mandated changes than for voluntary changes.

SUMMARY

This chapter examines the political process's effect on management's choice of accounting practice. The reason the political process affects accounting practice (beyond taxes) is because information, lobbying, and coalition costs are assumed to be positive. Assuming that these costs are nonzero is analogous to the nonzero contracting costs assumed in Chapters 8 and 9 to derive the contracting hypotheses.

Economists view the political process as a competition for wealth transfers. Because information, lobbying, and coalescing to affect the political process is costly, some individuals decide to remain ignorant, just as some shareholders remain ignorant of the firms they own and free ride on others' monitoring. But if the magnitude of monitoring costs to reduce managerial opportunism and wealth transfers is substantially larger in the political process than in the market process, the political process will exhibit more opportunistic behavior than the market process. One hypothesized way in which political wealth transfers are accomplished is by government officials' "solving" perceived or actual crises. Accounting numbers are often used in the political process as examples of a perceived crisis. They are also used in the regulations solving perceived crises. For example, large increases in oil company profits in the 1970s were cited as evidence of an oil monopoly, and these profits were the target of the 1980 windfall profits tax.

Given this particular view of the political process, managers of politically sensitive firms are expected to choose accounting procedures that defer reported profits to later periods and reduce the variability of reported profits. Managers of regulated firms take account of the particular regulations affecting them in choosing accounting procedures.

Information costs in the political process allow changes in accounting procedures to have stock price effects. Changes that increase earnings reduce stock prices and changes that decrease earnings increase stock prices. The stock price effects via the political process of announcements of voluntary procedure changes undertaken to reduce political costs should be positive. However, those effects are difficult to observe because they are entangled with the stock price effects of changed political costs or other factors that induce the manager to change procedures. Observation is also difficult because the market expects the change. The stock price effects via the political process of announcements of mandated procedure changes are more likely to be observable because they vary with the changes' effect on the firms' political costs.

Both regulated and politically sensitive firms still have the agency problems discussed in the last chapter and still use accounting numbers to reduce agency costs in bond covenants and management compensation plans. But, with the introduction of nonzero costs in the political process, the accounting numbers affect the firm's future cash flows in additional ways. The manager must consider these additional factors in selecting accounting procedures.

The incentives provided by the political process (to reduce earnings) are in direct opposition to the incentives provided by management compensation contracts (to increase earnings) with respect to the level of reported earnings. On the other hand, both sets of incentives suggest a reduction in the variance of reported earnings (except for the "big bath" phenomena as discussed in Chapter 9).

Managers trade off the costs and benefits of alternative accounting procedures. The procedure that is optimal, ceteris paribus, for political or regulatory reasons may not be optimal, ceteris paribus, for management compensation or debt contract purposes. Little is known about the relative magnitude of political, regulatory, and contracting costs. Hence, the parameters of managements' decisions and how they vary across firms cannot, a priori, be specified. However, empirical evidence indicates that the selection of accounting procedures varies with variables that are likely to be related to political costs and contracting costs. Thus, some statements and predictions can be made as to the trade-off of political costs and contracting costs. The evidence on those predictions is provided in Chapter 11.

Just as the political and contracting processes provide the manager with opposing incentives in the choice of accounting procedures, they suggest opposing predictions as to the stock price effect of changes in accounting procedures. A change that increases earnings increases stock prices because it reduces the probability of a debt agreement technical default and decreases stock prices because it increases political costs. In investigating the stock price effects of changes, variables likely to be related to contracting and political costs are used to estimate the opposing stock price effects. Chapter 12 summarizes the evidence on those effects.

CHAPTER ELEVEN

Empirical Tests of Accounting Choices

Chapter 1 describes a successful accounting theory as one that explains accounting phenomena. The previous three chapters provide the outline of a theory that might meet that criterion. This chapter assesses the theory's ability to explain two important sets of accounting phenomena, the accounting procedures used by large U.S. corporations and the positions taken by the managers of those corporations on proposed accounting standards. The theory's ability to explain stock price changes associated with mandatory and voluntary changes in accounting procedures is addressed in Chapter 12.

In Chapters 9 and 10 we describe the three hypotheses about managers' procedure choices that have been tested most frequently by accounting researchers: the bonus plan hypothesis, the debt/equity hypothesis, and the size hypothesis. All three hypotheses are generated from simplistic assumptions: the bonus plan hypothesis assumes a simplified bonus plan (see Chapter 9); the debt/equity hypothesis assumes that the higher a firm's debt/equity ratio, the closer the firm is to its debt covenants (see Chapter 9); and the size hypothesis assumes political costs vary directly with firm size (see Chapter 10).

Concentration on a few simple hypotheses is to be expected in early empirical tests of a new theory. As argued in Chapter 1, simplicity is a desirable attribute of a theory, and if simple aggregate predictions are borne out, the theory is more likely to win acceptance. Once some general tendencies are observed, empirical research typically progresses to testing the detailed implications.

Overall, the evidence discussed in this chapter is consistent with the debt/equity hypothesis and the size hypothesis (at least in the oil and gas industry). The higher a firm's debt/equity, the more likely it is to use procedures that increase current earnings, and the larger the firm, the more likely it is to use procedures that reduce current earnings. These empirical relations between accounting procedure choice and firms' leverage and size were not widely recognized (at least in the academic literature) before the development of the theory in Chapters 8–10. The directions the theory gave on where to fish for empirical regularities (see Chapter 1, p. 10) have paid off.

Of course, the empirical regularities could be due to causes other than those elaborated in Chapters 9 and 10. Researchers may have caught something other than the fish they sought to catch. More powerful tests of the theory, using details of the debt contracts and compensation plans, will provide evidence on that issue. But even if a better explanation is found for the debt/equity and size regularities, the research has been worthwhile; it produced regularities to explain.

The evidence on the bonus hypothesis is mixed. However, like tests of the debt/equity and size hypotheses, tests of the bonus plan hypothesis are weak tests of the theory. They ignore important aspects of the plans (e.g., existence of bounds). More powerful tests of the effect of bonus plans on accounting procedures recognize those aspects. Healy (1985) conducts such a test and finds evidence consistent with the proposition that the manager's choice of accounting procedures is affected by a bonus plan.

While tests of the three simple hypotheses have uncovered empirical regularities in accounting procedure choice, the hypotheses explain relatively little of the cross-sectional variation in accounting procedures. They cannot predict firms' combinations of procedures significantly better than the naïve prediction that all firms use the most common combination. This result does not deny the observed regularities, and, given the equivalent predictive ability, the theory and the three simple hypotheses are preferred to the naïve prediction because they offer a much richer *explanation* for procedure choice.

Nevertheless, the result suggests the theory be developed further to increase its predictive and explanatory power. Using the contract details, as in Healy (1985), is one way to proceed. Another is to develop more sophisticated political hypotheses than the size hypothesis. A third way to proceed is to derive hypotheses not just from debt contracts and bonus plans, but also from the firms' other contracts.

According to the bonus plan and debt/equity hypotheses, the manager has incentives to use accounting procedures to increase current reported earnings, while according to the size hypothesis the manager has incentives to reduce current reported earnings. How does the manager trade off these incentives? We begin the chapter by addressing that question. In the process, we explain why one report is generally used for all three (debt contract, compensation plan, and political cost) purposes. We also explain why, in general, managers are more concerned with the combination of procedures (portfolio of procedures) used by the firm than with the individual procedures.

Then we review a study that uses the three commonly tested hypotheses to explain firms' portfolios of accounting procedures (Zmijewski and Hagerman, 1981). Most other studies concentrate on explaining one single procedure choice and for that reason are less powerful tests of the hypotheses. These single procedure choice studies are reviewed in the third section.

Some of the single procedure choice studies in that section test hypotheses based on detailed debt covenants as well as the three commonly tested hypotheses. However, Healy (1985) presents a more powerful test of the theory using contract detail-based hypotheses rather than the three simple hypotheses and is reviewed in more depth next.

A review of a study of the effect of utility regulation on asset valuation and a study of the manager's choice of reporting frequency (i.e., quarterly or annual reporting) follows. Neither study tests the three simple hypotheses or uses contract details. The chapter ends with a summary of the chapter.

THE MANAGER'S ACCOUNTING PROCEDURE CHOICE

Choice Among Accepted Procedures

The bonus plan, debt/equity, and size hypotheses are all about the manager's choice among the set of accepted procedures. They reflect empirical researchers' concentration on explaining that choice rather than on explaining the nature of the set of accepted procedures, the set of procedures existing prior to disclosure regulation and currently used in contracts. All of the studies discussed in this chapter are studies of the choice *among* accepted procedures.

As explained in Chapter 9, the reason for the concentration on the manager's choice among accepted procedures is the cost of generating hypotheses. Taking the contracts and accepted procedures as given, researchers can readily generate hypotheses about the manager's choice. The political process is treated as another variable impacting that choice. Explaining the choice of accounting procedures to use in contracts (the choice *of* accepted procedures) requires a theory explaining the detailed structure of contracts. Contracting theory is not yet developed to that point.

Use of One Set of Reports

As noted, the contracting and political processes provide the manager with opposing incentives to choose among accounting procedures. For example, consider the choice between the deferral and flowthrough methods of accounting for the investment tax credit by the manager of a large, profitable, but politically sensitive, corporation that has a bonus plan. To avoid congressional and regulatory agency attention with its consequent costs (and reduction in management compensation), the manager prefers the deferral method since it *usually* reduces the level and variance of reported earnings. However, if the deferral method reduces current reported earnings, it also reduces the present value of reported earnings-based compensation, providing the manager with incentives to prefer the flowthrough method.

Producing different sets of accounting reports for different purposes would appear to solve the manager's problem. However, the fact that the one set of published reports tends to be used for all these methods suggests that there are reasons the different reports strategy is not optimal.

The different reports approach is used for debt contracts to the extent that private debt agreements sometimes specify non-GAAP (generally accepted accounting principles) procedures (e.g., the cost method of accounting for unconsolidated subsidiaries). However, those differences are due to differences between GAAP and accepted contracting procedures and are intended to make debt covenants more effective, not to allow the manager to avoid debt covenants. Debt contracts probably use the published reports as the basis for their numbers because this use reduces manager manipulation and agency costs. Those numbers are audited, and the political costs provide the manager with an incentive not to inflate earnings. Likewise, the use of published reports for compensation plan purposes probably occurs because it restricts the manager's ability to manipulate earnings and reduces agency costs.

Use of different reports can also be costly in the political process. If the alternative reports were publicly available, those seeking wealth transfers from the firm would use whichever of the reports furthers their ends (i.e., the one reporting the highest earnings). Keeping reports with higher earnings private and publicly reporting lower earnings would be more damaging in the political process if the private reports later became publicly known. These costs reinforce the contracting incentives to use one set of published reports.

Choice of a Procedure Portfolio

In the three commonly tested hypotheses, it is the earnings number that is important to the manager. This number is the result of a portfolio of accounting procedures. Given the firm's cash flows, numerous combinations of procedures available give a manager a range of reported earnings.

In some cases, the manager may choose an extreme portfolio of procedures (i.e., all the procedures in the portfolio increase current earnings or all the procedures decrease current earnings). For example, if the firm is not politically sensitive but has a bonus plan without an upper bond (see Chapter 9), the manager would choose a portfolio that maximized the present value of reported earnings. Or, if the firm has high political costs and no bonus plan or debt, the manager would choose a portfolio of procedures that minimized the present value of earnings. In many cases, however, there may be trade-offs between the political costs and contract effects of earnings so the manager will not choose to maximize or minimize the present value of earnings. The optimal earnings lie somewhere in between. There may be several different portfolios of accounting procedures that produce the optimal current earnings number.

If managers choose accounting procedures on a portfolio basis, investigations of individual procedure choices are not powerful tests of the three commonly tested hypotheses. A firm with high political costs may use a procedure portfolio that produces relatively low current earnings, as predicted, but use a current earnings increasing procedure for the particular procedure investigated. A more powerful test (one that has a lower chance of rejecting a correct hypothesis) would try to explain firms' portfolio procedures. The first such large-scale study using the bonus plan, debt/equity, and size hypotheses was Zmijewski and Hagerman (1981).

A STUDY OF PROCEDURE PORTFOLIO CHOICE (ZMIJEWSKI AND HAGERMAN)

The Portfolio of Accounting Procedures

Zmijewski and Hagerman (1981) investigate firms' portfolios of four accounting procedures. The procedure choices investigated are:

1. Inventory procedures

2. Depreciation procedures
3. Investment tax credit procedures
4. The amortization period for past service pension costs

Zmijewski and Hagerman assume that FIFO, straight-line depreciation, flowthrough treatment of the investment credit, and amortization periods of more than 30 years for past pension costs increase earnings. LIFO, accelerated depreciation, the deferred method for the investment tax credit, and amortization periods less than or equal to 30 years are assumed to decrease earnings. These definitions undoubtedly introduce some errors; for example, LIFO could increase the present value of earnings for electronics firms whose inventory prices are falling. However, for the majority of firms, the classifications are likely to be correct.

Given two choices for each of the four procedures, there are 16 portfolios that firms can use. To test the effects of political costs and contracting costs on the choice of a portfolio, the effects of the 16 portfolios on the present values of earnings must be determined. Zmijewski and Hagerman assume that the relative effect on earnings of a given portfolio is the same for all firms. Further, they make three different assumptions about the relative effect of each of the four particular procedures to assess the earnings effects of different portfolios.

1. All four procedures have the *same* impact on reported earnings (i.e., the earnings increasing procedure for depreciation has the same effect on reported earnings as the earnings increasing procedure for the investment tax credit). This assumption reduces the 16 portfolios to five different effects on reported earnings. In Table 11.1, the column labeled "Classification of Strategies, 5" groups the 16 portfolios into 5. The extreme earnings decreasing and increasing portfolios (1 and 16) are coded as "1" and "5." All portfolios with one earnings increasing procedure are coded as strategy "2." Portfolios with two earnings increasing procedures are coded as "3" and so forth.

2. The effects of pension and investment tax credit procedures on earnings are assumed to be half the effects of the depreciation and inventory procedures. Among the 16 portfolios, this assumption produces seven different effects on earnings (see Table 11.1). For example, strategies labeled as "2" under the column "7" have either a pension or investment credit earnings increasing procedure. If a firm has earnings increasing procedures for both pension and investment credit or an earnings increasing procedure for either depreciation or inventory, they are coded as strategy "3" and so forth.

3. The effects of pension and tax credit procedures on earnings are less than one-half the effects of the depreciation and inventory methods. Among the 16 portfolios, this assumption produces nine different earnings effects (see Table 11.1).

TABLE 11.1

Alternative Combinations of Accounting Policies and Income Strategies for Watts–Zimmerman (W–Z) and Hagerman–Zmijewski (H–Z) Samples

Combination	Possible Policy Alternatives				W–Z Sample		H–Z Sample		Classification of Strategies		
	Depreciation	Inventory	Pension Costs	Investment Tax Credit	No.	%	No.	%	5	7	9
Most decreasing 1	0	0	0	0	4	11.77%	10	3.33%	1	1	1
2	0	0	1	0	2	5.88	0	0.00	2	2	2
3	0	0	0	1	0	0.00	9	3.00	2	2	2
4	0	0	1	1	0	0.00	1	0.33	3	3	3
5	1	0	0	0	0	0.00	29	9.67	2	3	4
6	0	1	0	0	4	11.77	11	3.67	2	3	4
7	1	0	1	0	2	5.88	8	2.67	3	4	5
8	0	1	1	0	4	11.77	1	0.33	3	4	5
9	1	0	0	1	0	0.00	68	22.67	3	4	5
10	1	1	0	1	6	17.64	12	4.00	4	5	5
11	0	0	1	1	0	0.00	24	8.00	4	5	6
12	1	1	0	1	1	2.94	1	0.33	3	5	6
13	1	1	1	1	1	2.94	17	5.67	4	5	7
14	1	1	0	0	2	5.88	7	2.33	4	6	8
15	1	1	1	0			75	25.00	4	6	8
Most increasing 16	1	1	1	1	8	23.53	27	9.00	5	7	9
					34	100.00%	300	100.00%			

where

Policy	Income Decreasing Policy 0	Income Increasing Policy 1
Depreciation	Accelerated method	Straight-line method
Inventory	LIFO	FIFO
Amortization of past costs	Less than 30 years	30 years or more
Investment tax credit	Deferral method	Flowthrough method

Source: M. Zmijewski and R. Hagerman, "An Income Strategy Approach to the Positive Theory of Accounting Standard Setting/Choice," *Journal of Accounting and Economics* 3 (August 1981), Table 1, p. 135.

Zmijewski and Hagerman rank the 16 portfolios by their earnings effects under the three different assumptions. They explain which earnings effect is chosen using the relative political and contracting costs of the particular firm. For example, they hypothesize that the higher the political costs of a given firm, the less likely the firm is to choose a portfolio of accounting procedures that increases reported earnings.

Measures of Political and Contracting Costs

Ideally, we would estimate the manager's contracting and political process benefits from particular procedure portfolios (or from a single procedure) and predict the manager's choice on the basis of those benefits. However, a priori we cannot specify the relative magnitude of these benefits. Consequently, studies explaining accounting procedure variations use separate independent variables as surrogates for the offsetting incentives and test the direction of the variables' choice effects.

Four variables are used to proxy for political costs:

SIZE

Following Jensen and Meckling (1976) and Watts and Zimmerman (1978), Zmijewski and Hagerman hypothesize that because political costs increase with corporate size, managers of larger corporations are more likely to choose an earnings decreasing portfolio of accounting procedures. This is the size hypothesis.

RISK

Zmijewski and Hagerman also hypothesize that political costs vary with the firm's risk and that high-risk firms are likely to choose an earnings decreasing portfolio of procedures. Their reasoning follows two lines. First, high-risk firms also have high variances of earnings changes and hence are more likely to report "large profits." Second, because of information costs, voters, politicians, and bureaucrats may not adjust for risk when considering the level of reported earnings.

Studies investigating political and contracting costs' ability to explain accounting procedure variation take the firm's cash flows and investment policy as given. Zmijewski and Hagerman implicitly make this assumption in addressing the hypothesis that risk is cross sectionally related to attempts to decrease earnings. However, arguments in the economics literature suggest that investment policy is not independent of political costs, and as a consequence Zmijewski and Hagerman's hypothesis may not hold. Managers of firms more subject to political costs are, according to Peltzman (1976), likely to undertake less risky investments for the very reasons Zmijewski and Hagerman suggest that they reduce the probability of larger earnings. Hence, those firms' risk is likely to be below average even though they try to reduce reported earnings. The net result could be a negative (not positive) relation between risk and attempts to decrease reported earnings.

CAPITAL INTENSITY

Zmijewski and Hagerman suggest that because of information costs, voters, politicians, and bureaucrats do not adjust reported earnings for the opportunity cost of capital. Hence, they hypothesize that capital-intensive firms are subject to relatively more political costs and are more likely to reduce reported earnings.

CONCENTRATION

The Anti-trust Division and the FTC use a measure called a concentration ratio to determine the degree of competition in an industry. Therefore, an industry's concentration ratio will indicate the likelihood of antitrust action against firms in the industry. The concentration ratio is defined as the percentage of total industry sales made by some specified number of the largest firms in the industry (usually eight). The higher the concentration ratio, the more likely the manager is to use earnings decreasing procedures.

Two variables from the bonus and debt/equity hypotheses are used to proxy for contracting benefits:

EARNINGS-BASED COMPENSATION PLAN

The presence or absence of an earnings-based compensation plan is used to proxy for the effect of a compensation plan on the firm's portfolio of procedures. Managers of firms with a compensation plan are more likely to use earnings increasing procedures. Since most earnings-based compensation plans are bonus plans, this is a test of the bonus hypothesis.

DEBT/TOTAL ASSETS

The debt/total assets ratio is used to represent the manager's incentive to increase earnings under debt contracts. The higher the debt/total assets ratio, the more likely the manager is to use earnings increasing procedures. Since the debt/total assets ratio is a positive function of the debt/equity ratio, this is a restatement of the debt/equity hypothesis.

The Variables' Effect on Managers' Choice

The variables' effect on the managers' choice of a procedure portfolio is estimated using N-Probit analysis. Probit analysis is a statistical procedure, similar to regression analysis, to estimate the linear relation between the independent and dependent variables when the dependent variable takes the values of 0 and 1. N-Probit allows the dependent variable to take multiple (N) discrete values.

The equation estimated by Zmijewski and Hagerman is

$$\text{STRATEGY}_i = c_0 + c_1\text{PLAN}_i + c_2\text{RATIO}_i + c_3\text{BETA}_i$$

Predicted signs $\qquad$ $(+)$ $\qquad$ $(-)$ $\qquad$ $(-)$

$$+ c_4\text{SIZE}_i + c_5\text{INTENSITY}_i + c_6\text{DEBT}_i \qquad (11.1)$$

$\qquad\qquad$ $(-)$ $\qquad\qquad$ $(-)$ $\qquad\qquad$ $(+)$

$$i = 1, \ldots, 300 \text{ firms}$$

where

PLAN_i = 1 if firm i has an earnings-based compensation plan in 1975; 0 if firm i does not have an earnings-based compensation plan in 1975

RATIO_i = eight-firm concentration ratio for firm i's industry for 1975

BETA_i = beta of firm i's stock, estimated using CRSP data

SIZE_i = total assets of firm i in 1975

INTENSITY_i = capital intensity of firm i (gross fixed assets/sales)

DEBT_i = total debt/total assets of firm i in 1975

The predicted sign of each coefficient is noted below each coefficient of equation (11.1).

Under the first assumption about the earnings effect of the four procedures (all procedures have an equal effect on earnings), the dependent variable, STRATEGY_i, takes the value 1 to 5 depending on the relative earnings effect of the particular portfolio. Five is the value for the portfolio that yields the maximum earnings. Under the other assumptions, STRATEGY_i takes values between 1 and 7 and 1 and 9.

Sample and Data

Zmijewski and Hagerman draw a random sample of 300 CRSP firms for which the 1975 annual reports and SEC 10-K filings are available and which disclosed their choice of accounting procedures. The 300 firms are of average riskiness since their mean beta is .963.

The frequency with which the 300 firms chose the various accounting procedures is given in Table 11.2. It is interesting that, for

TABLE 11.2

*Accounting Procedures Used by the Zmijewski and Hagerman Sample
of 300 Firms in 1975*

	Depreciation	Inventory	Pension Costs	Investment Credit
Income increasing policy	255	151	69	217
Income decreasing policy	$\frac{45}{300}$	$\frac{149}{300}$	$\frac{231}{300}$	$\frac{83}{300}$

Source: R. Hagerman and M. Zmijewski, "Some Economic Determinants of Accounting Policy Choice," *Journal of Accounting and Economics* 1 (August 1979), Table 2, p. 148.

depreciation and the treatment of the investment credit, most managers chose income increasing policies, while for the only procedure that affects taxes directly, the inventory method, managers are about evenly split between LIFO and FIFO. The high proportion choosing income decreasing methods for past pension service costs is misleading. The income decreasing choice was defined as amortization over the median time period used, 30 years, or less. Since 30 years was the most popular choice, it inflates the income decreasing number. In fact, the choice was from 10 to 40 years, so 30 years is income increasing relative to the middle of the amortization range (25 years).

Zmijewski and Hagerman also use a sample of 34 unregulated firms that Watts and Zimmerman found lobbied on a 1974 FASB Discussion Memorandum on General Price Level Adjustment (GPLA). They compare this sample's distribution of procedure portfolios to their random sample of 300 firms.

The distributions of accounting procedure portfolios for the two samples are presented in Table 11.1. An important point to note in comparing the two distributions is that the 34 GPLA lobbying firms have a greater relative frequency of extreme portfolios than does Zmijewski and Hagerman's random sample of 300. Extreme strategies comprise 35 percent of the GPLA firms and only 12 percent of the random sample. The difference between the two relative frequencies is significant at the .05 level. This indicates that managers are more likely to lobby if they have extreme portfolios because they have less ability to adjust for changes in standards than mixed portfolio firms.

If a proposed standard increases reported earnings beyond the optimum, the mixed portfolio firm can change another procedure and offset the effect of the standard. However, if a standard increases the reported earnings of a firm with an extreme earnings reducing portfolio, the firm has to resort to other more costly ways to offset the effect (e.g., lobbying to have the standard overturned).

TABLE 11.3

Probit Analysis of Accounting Strategies

	Dependent Variable		
Independent Variables and Statistics	*Five-Strategy Case*	*Seven-Strategy Case*	*Nine-Strategy Case*
Constant	3.10356†	3.03981	3.03283
	(7.515)	(7.598)	(7.592)
Management compensation (+)*	.31259	.26812	.26055
	(2.409)	(2.112)	(2.055)
Concentration ratio (−)	−.63437	−.61523	−.61678
	(−2.214)	(−2.193)	(−2.200)
Systematic risk-beta (−)	−.13656	−.09032	−.08168
	(−.765)	(−.518)	(−.469)
Size-log of net sales (−)	−0.32095	−0.32406	−.32351
	(−2.638)	(−2.720)	(−2.717)
Capital intensity (−)	−.12651	−.12218	−.12091
	(−.959)	(−.945)	(−.935)
Total debt to total assets (+)	.35747	.40935	.40930
	(1.718)	(2.005)	(2.005)
Estimated R^2	.09030	.09066	.08983
Probit analysis χ^2 (d.f. = 6)	26.3675	26.5813	26.3490
% correctly classified	40.00%	33.00%	33.00%
Sample size	300	300	300

* Expected sign of coefficient.
† Coefficient (asymptotic *t*-statistic).
Source: M. Zmijewski and R. Hagerman, "An Income Strategy Approach to the Positive Theory of Accounting Standard Setting/Choice," *Journal of Accounting and Economics* 3 (August 1981), Table 2, p. 141.

RESULTS

Table 11.3 reports the results from estimating equation (11.1) on the 300 firm sample under the three different assumptions as to the magnitude of earnings effects. The results are essentially the same regardless of the assumption used.

The χ^2 tests reported in Table 11.3 are for the null hypothesis that the model is no better than a naïve prediction that assumes an equal probability of each strategy. The χ^2 statistic indicates that the null hypothesis can be rejected at the .001 level under all three assumptions. However, when the model is compared with a naïve strategy of predicting that firms adopt the most common strategy in the sample, the null hypothesis can be rejected only at the .25 level.

While the estimated models do not perform very well against the second naïve forecast, Table 11.3 presents strong evidence that management's choice of a portfolio of accounting procedures varies with the variables used to represent political and contracting costs. All estimated coefficients have their predicted signs. Further, the coefficient of the size variable is significant at the .01 level under all three assumptions, consistent with the size hypothesis. The coefficients of the concentration ratio and the management compensation dummy are significant at the .05 level under all three assumptions. The latter result is consistent with the bonus hypothesis. The coefficient of the debt/assets ratio is significant at the .10 level for the first assumption and at the .05 level for the other two assumptions. These results are consistent with the debt/equity hypothesis. The coefficients of the other variables (risk and capital intensity) are not significant.

Zmijewski and Hagerman investigate the size effect further. In an additional analysis, they find the size effect is driven by large firms (i.e., among smaller firms there is no association between portfolio choice and size). This result is consistent with Zimmerman's tax results (1983) and Watts and Zimmerman's findings (1978) that GPLA only affects the lobbying positions of very large firms. It is likely that these size results of Zmijewski and Hagerman, like those of Zimmerman (1983) and Watts and Zimmerman (1978), are driven by oil and gas firms (see the later discussion).

The failure of the cross-sectional model (equation (11.1)) to predict significantly better (by conventional standards) than the most common portfolio strategy and the model's low R^2 indicate plenty of room for improvement in the model. This is particularly true given that the prediction is compared on the estimation sample not on a holdout sample (see Chapter 5). Incorporating the details of compensation plans and debt contracts (discussed earlier) would improve the results. Another potential source of improvement is use of a political costs measure that is more refined than size.

More powerful tests of the theory using contract details and more sophisticated political cost measures can do more than increase the theory's predictive ability. They can also increase our confidence that the size effect is attributable to political costs and the debt/equity effect is due to contracting costs. Those variables can proxy for factors other than political and contracting costs (see Ball and Foster, 1982, and the evaluation of Watts and Zimmerman, 1978, in Appendix 11).

In summary, Zmijewski and Hagerman's results provide strong evidence that the manager's choice of a portfolio of accounting procedures varies with the presence of an earnings-based compensation plan, the firm's debt/equity ratio, the firm's size, and the concentration ratio in its industry. The three simple hypotheses *are* consistent with the evidence. The low predictive power doesn't deny the result and the naïve benchmark is a poor alternative theory because it provides an explanation for the cross-sectional variation in accounting procedures that is not very rich and not very intuitively pleasing (i.e., firms use the most commonly used procedure). However, the low predictive power of the contracting and political theory suggests that researchers should derive more powerful hypotheses from it.

STUDIES OF SINGLE PROCEDURE CHOICE

Unlike Zmijewski and Hagerman, most studies testing the bonus, debt/equity, and size hypotheses have investigated managers' choices of a single procedure (e.g., the use of accelerated or straight-line depreciation) rather than their choices of a portfolio of procedures. As has been argued, this reduces the power of those tests. Nevertheless, the studies have produced evidence generally consistent with the debt/equity and size hypotheses. The results for the bonus plan hypothesis are less consistent.

This section reviews the single procedure studies' evidence on the three commonly tested hypotheses. Table 11.4 summarizes each study and denotes whether the evidence is consistent or inconsistent with each of the three hypotheses. The studies are organized by accounting procedure investigated (column 1). Appendix 11 contains details of each study.

Debt/Equity Hypothesis

The results of the single procedure tests of the debt/equity hypothesis are summarized in column 4 of Table 11.4. All six tests of the debt/equity hypothesis (in six different studies) lead to rejection of the null hypothesis that leverage and accounting procedure choice are unrelated. Those studies are not independent (for example, the Deakin, 1979, and Dhaliwal, 1980, studies of oil and gas accounting use samples of oil firms in 1976), but overall it appears that the larger the debt/equity ratio, the more likely the firm is to use a procedure (or portfolio of procedures) that increases current period reported earnings. Those results reinforce those of Zmijewski and Hagerman.

Size Hypothesis

The single procedure choice studies are also generally consistent with Zmijewski and Hagerman's results for the size hypothesis. Out of the 10 tests of the size hypothesis (column 5), 6 result in rejection of the null hypothesis at least at the .10 level and 2 at the .15 level. While all these tests are not independent (e.g., the oil and gas studies), the preponderance of tests confirming the size hypothesis suggests that large firms choose accounting procedures that reduce current period reported earnings.

TABLE 11.4

Summary of the Results of Empirical Studies of the Use of and Lobbying for Single Accounting Procedures

Accounting Procedure (1)	Study (2)	Consistency with Commonly Tested Hypotheses			Other Results (6)	Comments (7)
		Bonus Plan Hypothesis: Bonus plans increase the likelihood of procedures that increase current period earnings. (3)	Debt/Equity Hypothesis: High debt/equity ratios increase the likelihood of procedures that increase current period earnings. (4)	Size Hypothesis: Large firm size increases the probability of procedures that reduce current period earnings. (5)		
1. General price-level adjustments (GPLA)	Watts and Zimmerman (1978)	Inconsistent*		Consistent		* The test is weak because the price level adjustments did not affect earnings currently used in bonus plans.
2. Oil and gas accounting Full cost versus successful efforts	Deakin (1979)		Consistent	Consistent		
	Dhaliwal (1980)		Consistent			
	Lilien and Pastena (1982)		Consistent	Consistent	Consistent with firms using procedures to reduce the variance of earnings. That proposition could be developed from political costs or contracts.	
3. Interest capitalization Whether interest is capitalized or not	Bowen, Noreen, and Lacey (1981)	Inconsistent*	Consistent	Inconsistent†	*Consistent* with the proposition that firms with small inventories of payable funds are more likely to capitalize. *Consistent* with the proposition that the smaller the interest coverage ratio the more likely the firm is to capitalize.	* The test is weak because interest is added back to earnings by many bonus plans. † *Consistent* for the oil industry.
4. Research and Development Whether research and development	Daley and Vigeland (1983)		Consistent*	Consistent†	*Consistent* with the proposition that the lower the inventory of payable funds the more likely the firm is to capitalize. *Inconsistent* with	* No significant difference between the effects of public and private debt on capitalization.

	expenditures are capitalized or not			the proposition that the smaller the interest coverage ratio, the more likely the firm is to capitalize.	† The size effect is driven by the smaller firms.
5.	Depreciation Accelerated versus straight line	Hagerman and Zmijewski (1979)	Consistent	Consistent	*Consistent* with risk producing political costs and affecting choice. *Inconsistent* with concentration ratios and capital intensity producing political costs and affecting choice.	
		Dhaliwal, Salamon, and Smith (1982)	Consistent*	Consistent		*If manager controlled firms are more likely to have bonus plans. † At .15 probability level.
		Holthausen (1981)			*Inconsistent* with hypothesis that firms with relatively smaller inventory of payable funds are more likely to change to straight line.	
6.	Inventory LIFO versus FIFO	Hagerman and Zmijewski (1979)	Inconsistent	Consistent*	*Consistent* with capital intensity and concentration ratios measuring political costs and affecting choice. *Inconsistent* with risk measuring political costs and affecting choice.	* At .15 probability level.
7.	Investment tax credit Deferral versus flowthrough	Hagerman and Zmijewski (1979)	Consistent*	Consistent	*Consistent* with concentration ratios measuring political costs and affecting choice. *Inconsistent* with risk measuring political costs and affecting choice.	* Power of test reduced by fact that taxes are added back to earnings in many bonus plans.
8.	Amortization of past service costs Amortization period ≤ 30 yr versus > 30 yr	Hagerman and Zmijewski (1979)	Consistent	Inconsistent	*Inconsistent* with risk and capital intensity measuring political costs and affecting choice. *Consistent* with concentration ratios measuring political costs and affecting choice only that the .15 level.	

Zmijewski and Hagerman (1981) found that their size result is due to large firms; the size hypothesis does not hold for smaller firms. This result is consistent with the result in Zimmerman (1983) that it is only the largest firms that have effective tax rates (and presumably political costs) higher than other firms. It is also possible that Zmijewski and Hagerman's result is due not to the largest firms in general but to the largest firms in the two industries in which Zimmerman finds the largest firms have higher effective tax rates (oil and gas and manufacturing). The individual procedure choice studies shed some light on this possibility.

One of the two single procedure tests that yield insignificant results for the size hypothesis across industries (Bowen, Noreen, and Lacey, 1981) does find a significant association between size and accounting procedure choice for the petroleum industry. The direction of the association is consistent with the size hypothesis and supports the proposition that Zmijewski and Hagerman's size result is industry specific. Also consistent are the results in the Watts and Zimmerman (1978) study of manager lobbying on GPLA and the two oil and gas accounting procedure choice studies (Deakin, 1979; Lilien and Pastena, 1982). The significant size result in Watts and Zimmerman (1978) is driven by large oil firms.

Despite the studies just cited, it is premature to conclude that the size result is driven by the large firms in the oil and gas industry. It is not obvious that the oil and gas industry drives the association between size and procedure choice in Dhaliwal, Salamon, and Smith (1982) that rejects the null hypothesis at the .15 level. Further, Daley and Vigeland (1983) find that their significant association between size and choice of research and development procedures only holds for their subsample of smaller firms. It does not hold for the subsample of larger firms.

The possibility that the size result is industry specific is reinforced by results for the retail industry. Zimmerman (1983) reports that large retail firms have *lower* effective tax rates than do small retail firms. Watts and Zimmerman (1978) report that two of their four misclassified firms are the only two retail firms lobbying on GPLA. And Bowen, Noreen, and Lacey (1981) report that large retail firms are less likely to choose income inflating accounting procedures (i.e., capitalize interest).

Bonus Plan Hypothesis

The results of single procedure tests of the bonus plan hypothesis are less consistent than are tests of the debt/equity and size hypotheses. Four of the seven tests of the bonus hypothesis are conducted by Hagerman and Zmijewski (1979). The only inconsistent result in those four tests is on the choice of LIFO or FIFO. The fact that the LIFO/ FIFO model is misspecified, perhaps because of tax effects (see the appendix to this chapter), tends to discount that exception. On the other hand, in the three cases where Hagerman and Zmijewski (1979) find results consistent with the bonus plan hypothesis, they do not control for debt contracts. The existence of debt contracts is associated with the existence of bonus plans. This defect is remedied in the portfolio study (Zmijewski and Hagerman, 1981), and the bonus hypothesis is still confirmed. Hence, overall the Hagerman and Zmijewski tests are consistent with the bonus plan hypothesis.

Of the three tests conducted by others, Dhaliwal, Salamon, and Smith (1982) obtain results consistent with the bonus plan hypothesis *if* firms with dispersed ownership are more likely to have a bonus plan (see the appendix). The other two studies (Watts and Zimmerman, 1978; Bowen, Noreen, and Lacey, 1981) fail to reject the null hypothesis. However, both tests are weak: Watts and Zimmerman's because GPLA does not directly affect the earnings used in bonus plans and Bowen, Noreen, and Lacey's because interest is added back to earnings in many bonus plans. In essence, Watts and Zimmerman and Bowen, Noreen, and Lacey ignore important details of the bonus plan. The result in Healy (1985) that net accruals are significantly associated with the level of earnings vis-à-vis the parameters of the particular bonus plans (see next section) not only emphasizes the problem of ignoring plan details in testing the bonus plan hypothesis, it also supports the Hagerman and Zmijewski finding that bonus plans influence accounting procedure choice.

Other Hypotheses

The single procedure studies test hypotheses in addition to the three commonly tested. The results on those other hypotheses are mixed.

POLITICAL COSTS

The results of the single procedure studies in Hagerman and Zmijewski (1979) are consistent with the results of the procedure portfolio study of Zmijewski and Hagerman (1981) on the association between concentration ratios and procedure choice. Both suggest an association between industry concentration ratios and choice of accounting procedures consistent with concentration ratios measuring political costs. The null hypothesis is rejected at the .10 level for two of the four individual procedures. It is also rejected at the .15 level for one other procedure.

The Hagerman and Zmijewski papers provide little support for an association between risk and capital intensity and the choice of accounting procedures. Hagerman and Zmijewski hypothesized the existence of such associations based on political cost consideration (see the previous section).

DEBT CONTRACT VARIABLES

Bowen, Noreen, and Lacey (1981) and Daley and Vigeland (1983) provide evidence that the *inventory of payable funds* is associated with the decisions to capitalize interest and research and development expenditures. On the other hand, the time series evidence of Holthausen (1981) indicates no relation between the inventory of payable funds and changes in depreciation. The *interest coverage ratio* is found to be significantly associated with the capitalization of interest (Bowen, Noreen, and Lacey, 1981) but not with the capitalization of research and development expenditures (Daley and Vigeland, 1983).

The mixed results of debt contract variable based tests could be due to the single procedure tests' lack of power. A more powerful test of the contracting theory would investigate the relation between contract details and the portfolio choice. Healy (1985) conducts such a test using bonus plans.

A TEST USING BONUS PLAN DETAILS
(HEALY)

The Effect of Bonus Plan Details

Zmijewski and Hagerman (1981) and studies reviewed in the previous section test the bonus plan hypothesis when investigating the effect of earnings-based compensation plans on accounting procedure choice. However, as recognized in Chapter 9, bonus plans do not provide the manager with incentives to *always* adopt accounting procedures that increase current period reported earnings. If current earnings are below the target earnings set by the plan (lower bound), the manager has an incentive to reduce reported earnings for the current year and to transfer earnings to future years. Also, if the bonus plan has an upper bound on the maximum transfer to the bonus pool and actual earnings are above this bound, the manager has an incentive to reduce current reported earnings.

Healy (1985) investigates whether firms' annual net accruals (the difference between annual earnings as defined in the bonus plan and cash flows from operations) are affected by the bounds in the firms' bonus plans. Since the manager has incentives to reduce reported earnings if earnings are below the target or above the upper bound (if it exists), net accruals are more likely to be negative in those two cases. If earnings are between the lower bound (target) and the upper bound, the manager has an incentive to increase earnings, and net accruals are more likely to be positive.

Power of the Test

Net accruals reflect the effects of all accounting procedures on net earnings. Hence, they capture the effect of the firms' portfolio of procedures of the type investigated in the previous two sections (e.g., depreciation methods). Because of this, the power of a net accruals–based test is greater than a single procedure–based test. The accrual-based test's power is also greater because accruals capture many other, difficult to observe, accounting choices. For example, a manager whose oil firm's earnings are above its bonus plan's upper bound can defer earnings by keeping a tanker at sea until after the fiscal year end. If a sale is recognized when the tanker reaches port, delaying the tanker transfers earnings from one year to the next.

A difficulty with Healy's use of net accruals that reduces the test's power is lack of a theory to predict what the accruals should be in the absence of the manager's manipulation. In plans with a lower bound and no upper bound, we expect manipulation to induce larger net accruals when earnings are above the lower bound than when earnings are below the lower bound. However, that relation could exist in the absence of manipulation. Because earnings are based on cash flows and accruals, higher earnings probably have higher accruals. This situation is alleviated by the presence of the upper bound. It seems unlikely that in the absence of manipulation, accruals first increase as earnings increase (as we go from below the lower bound to above it) and then decrease (as we go from below the upper bound to above it).

Another problem reducing the test's power is the assumption that compensation committees mechanically follow the bonus formula in awarding bonuses. The formula is for the *maximum* bonus the committee can award. To the extent that the committee does not actually award bonuses in accordance with the formula, the power of Healy's test is reduced; the hypotheses are less likely to be confirmed.

Sample and Results

Healy uses 94 firms in the *Fortune* 250 that have data available. Those 94 firms yield 1,527 usable observations over the period 1930–1980. Of those 1,527 observations, 1,080 are plans with a lower bound but no upper bound and 447 are plans with both bounds.

TABLE 11.5

The Association Between Accruals and Bonus Plan Parameters

	Number of Observations with Accrual Signed			Mean Standard Accrual	t-Test for Difference in Means
	Positive	*Negative*	*Total*		
Cases where upper bound is binding	14	130	144	−.0536	
Cases where lower bound and upper bound (if it exists) are not binding	489	798	1,287	−0.117	7.46
Cases where lower bound is binding	30	66	96	−.0437	4.32
	533	994	1,527		

Source: P. Healy, "The Impact of Bonus Schemes on the Selection of Accounting Principles," *Journal of Accounting and Economics* 7 (April 1985), Table 2.

Table 11.5 gives the sign of each firm/year's net accrual according to whether the earnings are above the upper bound (if one exists), above the lower bound and not above the upper bound (if it exists), or below the lower bound. As expected, the frequency of negative net accruals is greater for the observations where earnings are above and below the upper and lower bounds, respectively. The χ^2 statistic for testing the null hypothesis that the sign of the net accrual is unrelated to the position of earnings vis-à-vis the bounds is significant at the .05 level.

Each accrual is divided by the mean of the absolute accruals (across years) for the particular firm. The mean of these standardized accruals is reported by category of earnings in Table 11.5. The relative magnitudes of the means of each category are consistent with the theory (i.e., the means for the two categories where earnings are outside the bounds are significantly lower than the mean for earnings within the bounds).

Healy's results suggest that the details of bonus plan parameters are important in determining whether bonus plans influence choice of accounting procedures. Healy's evidence on the calculation of earnings in bonus plans also suggests that the failure of some of the studies to reject the null hypothesis for the bonus plan hypothesis results from not using the plans' earnings definitions. As we noted, Bowen, Noreen, and Lacey (1981) ignore the fact that some plans add interest back to earnings in investigating the capitalization of interest (33.5 percent of Healy's 1,527 observations), and Watts and Zimmerman (1978) ignore the fact that GPLA was to be supplemental. Also, Healy (1985) finds that 52.7 percent of the sample add tax expense back to earnings for bonus purposes. This suggests the Hagerman and Zmijewski (1979) test of the effect of the bonus plans on the method of treating the investment tax credit is not very powerful.

OTHER STUDIES OF ACCOUNTING CHOICE

This section reports on two studies that try to explain accounting practice using the contracting and/or political processes described in Chapters 8–10 but do not test the bonus plan, debt/equity, and size hypotheses and do not use contract details to explain procedure choice. One is a study of the effect of utility regulation on asset valuation. The other is a study of reporting frequency (i.e., why firms report quarterly or annually).

Utility Asset Valuation (Jarrell)

Jarrell (1979) investigates whether state regulation of electric utilities in the period 1912–1917 led utility managers to inflate the value of assets and hence the rate base (see Chapter 10 for utility rate-setting formulas). Inflating the asset base reduces the calculated rate of return and allows arguments for utility rate increases. In essence the hypothesis is that the regulatory process affected the manager's choice of accounting procedure.

Prior to 1907, electric utilities were regulated by the municipality in which they operated instead of being regulated, as they are today, by state commissions. Often two or more utilities competed in the same municipality with parallel transmission lines. In 1907, New York and Wisconsin enacted state public utility laws with the official objective of reducing "ruinous competition." Jarrell (1978) hypothesizes that the objective was in fact to enable the utilities to monopolize their industry by limiting entry and establishing exclusive franchises. Jarrell reports that after the establishment of state commissions, electricity prices increased 25 percent on average and profits increased 35 percent.

Jarrell (1979) hypothesizes that the utilities regulated by state commissions earned monopoly profits by incorporating the capitalized value of the rents in their asset bases. This enables them to earn monopoly profits even though they are regulated. For example, assume that two identical competitive utilities exist in a given city. Each has physical assets with a cost and market value of $100 and no liabilities. Assume that the allowed rate of return and the market rate of return are 10 percent. Suppose that the market value of the two firms operating as a monopoly is $300 and that the two firms merge, with each firm valuing its assets at $150 (the market value of their shares). The asset base for the new firm is now $300 and consumers now pay 10% ×

$300 = $30 to compensate the providers of capital instead of 10% × $200 = $20. The $10 difference is the monopoly profit (see Wyatt, 1963, pp. 22–23).

If Jarrell's hypothesis is correct, a given asset is expected to have a higher value on the books of a utility regulated by a state commission than on the books of a utility subject to municipal regulation. Jarrell estimates cross-sectional equations to explain the ratio of total reported assets to electricity produced and the ratio of total reported assets to dynamo capacity in 1912, 1917, and 1922. Independent variables are included to account for different operating characteristics, and a dummy variable is included to represent state regulation or municipal regulation. Overall, the results indicate that state commission–regulated utilities had significantly higher reported asset values in 1912, 1917, and 1922.

Reporting Frequency

Leftwich, Watts, and Zimmerman (1981) investigate cross-sectional variation in the frequency of public financial reporting by 83 NYSE and 82 ASE firms in 1948 when interim reporting was not required. At that time, some firms reported only annually, while others reported semiannually or quarterly. Leftwich, Watts, and Zimmerman also investigate the changes in frequency of reporting by their sample between 1937 and 1948.

The variables Leftwich, Watts, and Zimmerman use to explain the cross-sectional variation of frequency of reporting are meant to surrogate for the benefit of increased reporting in terms of reduced agency costs of debt and equity and for the cost of the increased reporting. The variables are the ratio of fixed assets to firm value, the ratio of debt to firm value, the ratio of preferred stock to firm value, the presence of a representative of a bank or insurance company on the board of directors, and the stock exchange on which the firm is listed.

Overall, Leftwich, Watts, and Zimmerman have little success in explaining the cross-sectional variation in reporting frequency using contracting process variables. Their lack of results suggests that explaining reporting frequency is more difficult than explaining the particular procedures used to calculate numbers in reports.

SUMMARY

Researchers test the ability of the theory outlined in Chapters 8–10 to explain the accounting procedures used by firms and the positions firms' managers take on proposed standards. Tests using the firm's portfolio of procedures have more power than do tests using a single procedure. The reason is that most firms do not choose an extreme earnings increasing or decreasing portfolio, so a single procedure may not be representative of the firm's procedure choice.

A large-scale study of firms' portfolios of procedures (Zmijewski and Hagerman, 1981) finds evidence consistent with three simple hypotheses that have been relatively widely tested: the bonus plan, debt/equity, and size hypotheses. If a firm has an earnings-based compensation plan or the larger a firm's debt/equity ratio, the more likely it is to choose current earnings increasing procedures. The larger the firm the more likely it is to choose current earnings decreasing procedures.

Studies of single procedure choices, though less powerful than portfolio studies, also find evidence consistent with the debt/equity and size hypotheses. Their evidence on the bonus plan hypothesis is mixed.

There are indications in some of the single procedure studies that the size hypothesis results could be driven by large oil firms and hence be industry specific. Those indications are consistent with Zimmerman's (1983) findings that effective tax rates are higher for large oil firms. However, one study (Daley and Vigeland, 1983) finds the size result exists only among the smaller firms in its sample. More research into the size effect and its variation across industries is required. Such research can provide more powerful tests of whether the size result is due to political costs. For example, studies can investigate whether industries in which the size effect is observed are subject to more government action.

The success of the two simple contracting hypotheses (bonus plan and debt/equity hypotheses) in explaining procedure choice variation led to more powerful tests of the theory using details of contracts and plans. Healy (1985) investigates the implications of firms' bonus plan parameters for the firms' annual net accruals. His results are consistent with the hypothesis that the manager manipulates net accruals to influence bonus awards. Investigations of debt contract details' implications are less supportive of the theory. Two studies find an association, and one study does not find an association, between the inventory of payable funds and procedure choice. One study finds an association between the interest coverage ratio and procedure choice.

A study by Jarrell (1979) finds that state utility regulation had an impact on utility asset valuation consistent with the political process theory outlined in Chapter 10. On the other hand, a study by Leftwich, Watts, and Zimmerman (1981) is unable to explain cross-sectional variations in reporting frequency using contracting variables.

Overall, the tests have discovered empirical regularities. Bonus plans, debt/equity ratios, and firm size are related to firms' procedure choice. However, those variables can predict only a very small amount of the cross-sectional variation in accounting procedures. Healy's results suggest attempts to develop more powerful tests of the contracting theory using details of debt and compensation plans increase that predictive power. Attempts to develop more powerful tests of the effects of the political process could also increase the theory's predictive power. At the same time, more powerful tests will shed light on whether the compensation plan, debt/equity, and size effects are in fact consistent with the theory outlined in Chapters 8–10.

Studies of Single Procedure Choice

This appendix reviews studies of the choice of a single procedure. The papers are organized by accounting topics and are in the order presented in Table 11.4, except that Hagerman and Zmijewski (1979) is discussed first.

DEPRECIATION, INVENTORY, INVESTMENT TAX CREDIT AND PAST SERVICE COSTS (HAGERMAN AND ZMIJEWSKI)

Prior to their portfolio study (Zmijewski and Hagerman, 1981), Hagerman and Zmijewski (1979) investigated the ability of political cost and contracting variables to explain the cross-sectional variation in each of the four procedures (used in the portfolio study) separately. They use the same explanatory variables as they use in the portfolio study except that they omit the debt/total asset variable and add an effective tax rate variable (TAX_i) when investigating the inventory choice. They also use the same 300 firms they use in the portfolio study (Zmijewski and Hagerman, 1981). The findings suggest that the theory is able to

269

explain some of the managers' choices of accounting methods. The χ^2 test rejects the null hypothesis that the model cannot predict the choice of methods better than randomly assigning firms to each method (in the proportion of the relative frequency of that method) at the .01 level for depreciation, the .05 level for inventory, and the .10 level for the investment tax credit and past service amortization methods. Further, 14 out of the 15 estimated coefficients for the three methods that do not have direct tax consequences have the predicted sign.

While the same variables are not significant in every model, the Hagerman and Zmijewski results tend to support the theory laid out in Chapters 8–10. Hagerman and Zmijewski find that larger firms tend to use accounting procedures that reduce reported earnings. Thus, this study supports the size hypothesis. While size is significant at the .05 level only for depreciation and investment tax credit, its significance levels for pension costs and inventory (.17 and .14, respectively) cannot be dismissed, particularly given the results for depreciation and the investment tax credit.

The results for the management compensation dummy (significantly positive in three of the four choices) suggest that the presence of an earnings-based compensation plan makes managers more likely to prefer earnings increasing procedures. To that extent, the results support the bonus plan hypothesis. However, one important problem with the Hagerman and Zmijewski analysis is the lack of inclusion of any variables directly representing debt contracts. The existence of bonus plans and the existence of debt contracts are highly correlated cross sectionally. Hence, the compensation dummy could be capturing debt contract effects and representing the manager's incentive to increase earnings for debt contract reasons.

Another estimated coefficient that is consistent is the coefficient of the concentration ratio. The sign is negative in all four models, and the significance levels are .18, .05, .03, and .14. Together, these results suggest (under the model) that concentration ratios proxy for political costs.

As in Zmijewski and Hagerman (1981) the models do not predict significantly better than does a strategy of predicting that all firms follow the most common method. For example, consider the depreciation method where 255 out of the 300 firms (85 percent) use straight-line depreciation. If all firms were predicted to use straight line, 85.00 percent of the firms would be correctly classified. Hagerman and Zmijewski's model is correct 85.33 percent of the time. This is a valid criticism of the model's explanatory power, but it does not negate the result that size, management compensation, and concentration ratios are statistically associated with the accounting procedures used by firms.

GENERAL PRICE-LEVEL ADJUSTMENTS

Watts and Zimmerman (1978) investigate the positions taken by corporate managers on the FASB's 1974 Discussion Memorandum on GPLA. GPLA would restate firms' accounts as though past transactions occurred at current price levels using the Consumer Price Index.

The major effects of GPLA on a firm's reported earnings arise through depreciation and the gain or loss on net monetary assets (see Davidson, Stickney, and Weil, 1976). In periods of inflation, asset costs rise and price-level–adjusted depreciation is larger than is historical cost depreciation, reducing earnings. Net monetary assets are the difference between the firm's monetary assets (i.e., assets whose nominal values are fixed and do not increase with inflation, e.g., a fixed loan) and its liabilities. If net monetary assets are positive (the firm has more monetary assets than liabilities), under GPLA the firm reports a loss on net monetary assets in an inflationary period. With inflation and negative net monetary assets, the firm reports a gain on net monetary assets.

Watts and Zimmerman (1978) recognize the potential effect of debt contracts (see Watts, 1977) but hypothesize that GPLA would have little direct effect on debt contracts because price-level adjustments were to be supplemental. Further, management compensation contracts are assumed not affected by the price-level adjustments. Hence, the political process effects are assumed to play a dominant role in the effects of GPLA on managers' wealth and their positions on the Discussion Memorandum.

To model the effect of price-level adjustments via the political process, Watts and Zimmerman assume the size hypothesis (i.e., the larger a firm, the more likely the manager chooses accounting procedures that reduce current period earnings). The present value of any potential tax relief as a consequence of GPLA is assumed to vary with firm size. Likewise, the market values of GPLA's effects on costs of threatened political action by Congress or on rate regulation are expected to vary with firm size.

Watts and Zimmerman also consider GPLA's bookkeeping cost. The Discussion Memorandum requires firms to prepare an additional set of statements. This cost is assumed to consist of a fixed component and a component that varies with firm size. The cost is common to all firms and does not depend on the effect of GPLA on the present value of earnings.

Based on the preceding assumptions, a model is constructed that predicts which firms lobby on GPLA and the positions they take. Managers lobby only if they expect the benefits of lobbying to exceed the costs. The lobbying costs are the time and expense to prepare the position for the FASB. The benefit of lobbying is the probability that the position affects the FASB's decision times the present value of the effect of GPLA on the manager's wealth. GPLA's primary benefit is the assumed reduction in the firm's political costs if GPLA decreases earnings. Thus, managers of large firms (that are assumed politically sensitive) lobby in favor of GPLA if GPLA reduces their firm's earnings. Managers of large firms oppose GPLA if their earnings increase (i.e., political costs are higher). All other firms oppose GPLA because they incur additional bookkeeping costs that exceed any benefits. These predictions result from the assumption that the management compensation and debt contracts effects are zero.

The managers of 53, mostly NYSE, corporations filed written comments on the GPLA Discussion Memorandum. The position of the managers of one firm (Transunion) could not be determined. Of the others, 18 were classified as supporting, and 34 were classified as opposing, GPLA. The financial data necessary for the calculation of the independent variables were obtained from the 1973 *Compustat* tapes. The existence of a management compensation plan dependent on earnings was determined from responses to questionnaires mailed to the chief financial officers of each firm, proxy statements, and annual reports.

The tests require an estimate of the direction of the effect of GPLA on reported earnings. A technique for estimating the effect of GPLA on reported earnings was developed by Davidson and Weil (1975a, 1975b) and Davidson, Stickney, and Weil (1976). Using the numbers reported in those studies or using their technique, estimates were obtained of the effect of GPLA on the submitting firms' earnings for 1973. Firm size for the first set of tests is based on the firm's *Fortune* 500 rank on assets. Rank on sales also was used and yielded the same results.

For the model, regulated firms were excluded from consideration because it was not known how utility commissions would treat gains and losses on net monetary assets in assessing GPLA's effects on rates. The position of the unregulated firms who submitted on GPLA, their size, and the effect on their earnings are analyzed. Seven of the 8 firms whose earnings increase as a result of GPLA opposed the standard. On the other hand, of the 26 firms *whose earnings decreased*, 8 favored the proposal. However, the 8 favorable votes came from the larger firms.

Watts and Zimmerman test the prediction that the positions of the managers of firms whose earnings decreased are related to firm size. They cannot predict a priori the asset size at which managers' positions change. Hence, they test whether the eight firms that supported GPLA are drawn from the same population with respect to size as the 18 firms that opposed GPLA. Using a Manne–Whitney U test, they can reject the null hypothesis at the .001 level. Other tests are conducted that show a significant difference in the median rank on asset size for firms supporting and opposing GPLA.

If political costs, given firm size, do not vary across industries, the asset size at which managers' positions change is estimated by minimizing the number of prediction errors. An asset size between the eighteenth and twenty-second largest firms in the *Fortune* 500 in 1973 minimizes the number of misclassifications at 4. Given Watts and Zimmerman's assumptions, this suggests political costs are important only for very large firms. This finding is consistent with Zimmerman's (1983) finding that effective corporate tax rates are higher for roughly the largest 50 firms. And both studies are dominated by the large oil companies.

One problem with these tests is that size could proxy for many variables other than political costs. Ball and Foster (1982, pp. 24–25) point out that size is a surrogate for industry membership and many of the submitting firms are members of the oil industry (also, see Watts and Zimmerman, 1978, fn. 27). For lack of data, the submission predictions were made assuming that political costs varied with size in the same fashion across all industries. Clearly, political costs could vary with industry, *and* it is likely that in 1974 the oil industry was more sensitive to congressional action than were many other industries. Future tests of political costs should incorporate industry variables into the model.

The political sensitivity of industries is not the only factor for which size could proxy, as Ball and Foster (1982, pp. 33–34) point out. The alternatives that Ball and Foster suggest are the competitive disadvantages of disclosure, information production costs, and management ability and advice. However, only one of these three costs has been developed to the point of testability and that is information production cost, which is included in the model. As discussed in Chapter 1, because there are an infinite number of alternative hypotheses, researchers are usually held responsible only for testing those competing hypotheses that have been brought to the point of testability. To advance theory development, the alternative factors for which size surrogates should be specified so that they can be used as further tests of the model.

The Watts and Zimmerman result that size, in conjunction with the direction of GPLA's effect on earnings, is associated with managers' positions on GPLA is, as we have seen, obviously driven by the oil firms. This is consistent with Zimmerman's (1983) results that the large oil companies have substantially higher effective tax rates. Four of the eight large firms whose GPLA earnings decreased and who supported the proposal are oil firms. And, as noted, 1974 was a period of intense pressure on the oil firms. Hence, even if the underlying model is relatively descriptive, it is not apparent that the particular specifications used by Watts and Zimmerman would yield results for other periods and/or standards involving non-oil firms. Further, size might proxy for something other than political costs, so predictions based on that assumption may not be confirmed in other circumstances. See McKee, et al. (1984) for a critique of the Watts and Zimmerman tests.

OIL AND GAS ACCOUNTING: FULL-COST
AND SUCCESSFUL-EFFECTS METHODS

This choice has been studied in several papers. The two methods are used by oil and gas producing firms and differ in their treatment of the costs of wells that do not produce commercially exploitable reserves (dry wells). The full-cost method capitalizes the cost of all wells (wet and dry) and amortizes that cost against the income produced from the wet wells. The successful-efforts method expenses the cost of dry wells and capitalizes only the cost of wet wells.

In December 1977 FASB Statement No. 19 required the use of a successful-efforts method. The SEC reversed FASB 19 in ASR 253 in August 1978 and allowed particular versions of successful efforts and full cost. The stock price effects of these and other rulings are investigated in Chapter 12.

For an expanding firm, the full-cost method typically increases the level and reduces the variability of reported earnings and increases asset values and shareholders' equity vis-à-vis successful efforts (see Sunder, 1976, and Lys, 1982). Hence, the bonus plan hypothesis predicts that ceteris paribus managers of firms with bonus plans prefer the full-cost method. The reduction in variability of bonuses awarded would reinforce this prediction. Further, the debt/equity hypothesis suggests that the larger a firm's debt/equity ratio, the more likely is the firm's manager to increase current income by selecting full cost. On the other hand, the size hypothesis suggests that the larger the firm, the more likely is the manager to use successful efforts because it reduces reported profits and hence political costs. One might expect that larger firms would prefer full cost because it reduces the variability of reported earnings. However, the reduction in earnings variability due to full cost is relatively lower, the larger the firm (see Lys, 1982, pp. 168–169), and this reduces the incentive of larger firms to select full cost.

Deakin (1979) is an early study of the choice between full cost and successful efforts. The study is not designed to test the theory outlined above. Nevertheless, it does provide evidence on the theory.

Deakin discriminates between firms using full cost and firms using successful efforts on the basis of aggressiveness in exploration, the demand for capital, size, and age. He chooses seven variables to represent these four factors: the average depth of exploratory wells, the number of exploratory wells divided by revenues, the ratio of development wells to total wells, the ratio of debt to revenue, the ratio of capital expenditures to revenue, revenue, and the age of the firm. Development wells are drilled in fields with proven reserves while exploratory wells are drilled in fields with no proven reserves. Some of the variables used are related to the debt/equity and size hypotheses.

Deakin excludes from his sample the 24 largest oil and gas producers (because they are less affected by the choice), public utilities and pipeline companies (which are regulated), and diversified industrial companies that explore for oil and gas. Out of the remaining oil and gas producers, Deakin is able to obtain the necessary data for 1976 on 53 firms, of which 28 use successful efforts and 25 use full cost.

Using multiple discriminant analysis to explain the choice of full cost and successful efforts on the sample, Deakin finds that a model including only the debt/revenue and capital expenditures/revenue variables classifies the firms as well as a model including all seven variables. The χ^2 statistic for the model with the two variables in significant at the .002 level. Consistent with the debt/equity hypothesis, Deakin finds that the higher the debt/revenue ratio, the more likely the firm is to use the full-cost method.[1] The correlation of the capital expenditure/revenue variable with the debt/equity ratio is .53, so it is possible that this variable is also representing the debt/equity ratio. When Deakin performs a dichotomous classification test (based on the test in Beaver, 1966; see Chapter 5), using each of the seven variables separately, he finds that the debt/revenue ratio classifies the firms the best. In fact using that ratio *alone*, 73.6 percent of the firms are correctly classified. Both the discriminant analysis using the two variables and the analysis using all variables classify only 71.7 percent of the firms correctly.

Deakin does not report any significant relation between size (as measured by revenues) and the choice of full cost or successful efforts. However, the mean revenues of full-cost firms are smaller as predicted by the size hypothesis and size does discriminate between full cost and successful efforts at the .18 level. One reason for this weak support for the size hypothesis is that Deakin excludes the largest 24 oil and gas producers. The vast majority of those firms are successful-efforts firms and including them makes the size factor highly significant (see Deakin, 1979, p. 727, fn. 4). Taking these into account provides evidence supporting the size hypothesis (i.e., larger firms select accounting procedures to reduce reported earnings).

---

[1] Using the debt/equity ratio, Dhaliwal (1980) reports results consistent with Deakin and the debt hypothesis.

Lilien and Pastena (1982) provide further evidence to support the position that size and debt/equity are associated with the manager's choice of full cost and successful efforts. Firms typically do not follow extreme successful-efforts or full-cost methods. Variations in effects on reported earnings within either the full-cost or the successful-efforts methods can be achieved by varying the definition of a field. Lilien and Pastena point out that there are also other variables within each method that management could use to affect earnings prior to ASR 253 (which overturned FASB 19 and specified a particular version of successful efforts) and ASR 258 (which specified a particular method of full cost). Using these variables, the manager's choice was not between earnings series generated by full cost or successful efforts, but between a whole spectrum of earnings series. Lilien and Pastena explain not only management's choice of full cost or successful efforts (the intermethod choice) but also the management's choice within each method (the intramethod choice).

Lilien and Pastena obtain measures of the extent to which managers maximized or minimized reported earnings prior to ASR 253 and ASR 258 from the adjustments made to retained earnings when firms complied with ASR 253 or 258. Firms were required to adjust their retained earnings retroactively to reflect what those earnings would have been had they always followed the methods set by ASR 253 or 258. Hence, the retroactive adjustment indicates whether the full-cost method followed by the firm generated more or less earnings than the full-cost method set by ASR 258. Likewise, the adjustment for successful-efforts firms indicates whether they used a successful-efforts method that generated more or less earnings than the method set by ASR 253.

Lilien and Pastena use four variables to explain the extent to which managers maximize reported earnings. Size (revenues) is used to reflect the effect of political costs and to test the size hypothesis. The debt/equity ratio is used to test the debt/equity hypothesis. The other variables are the ratio of dry wells/total wells and the age of the firm.

The dry wells/total wells ratio is used to measure the effect of the variance of reported earnings on method choice. Lys (1982, p. 169) reports that if successful efforts increases the variability of reported earnings, the increase is greater the larger the probability of not finding oil in the firm's exploratory activities. Hence, if the dry wells/total wells ratio is a surrogate for the probability of not finding oil, the larger that ratio, the larger the variability of earnings induced by successful efforts. The effect of the probability of dry wells on the variability of the bonus and on political costs suggests that the greater the ratio (the larger the variability under successful efforts), the more likely the manager will choose full cost. Lilien and Pastena generate the same prediction by noting that the greater the probability of not finding oil, the greater the probability of a violation of a debt covenant.

Age is expected to affect the method choice because full cost was not available before the 1950s. Given the costs of changing methods, older firms are more likely to be using successful efforts.

Lilien and Pastena obtain the adjustment to 1978 retained earnings due to ASR 253 or ASR 258 for their sample of 102 firms from the firms' 1978 or 1979 10-K forms filed with SEC. They first use Probit to explain the choice of full cost or successful efforts. The model classifies firms better than the naïve most frequent type benchmark and the naïve benchmark that assigns firms to each type randomly with the relative frequency of each type at the .001 level. Further, the coefficients of all four variables have the predicted sign. Larger and older firms are more likely to use successful efforts and higher exploratory risk, and more levered firms are more likely to use full cost. The age, exploratory risk, and size variables are all significant at the .06 level. The leverage variable is significant at the .18 level.

Another test of the theory is undertaken when Lilien and Pastena use Probit to discriminate between firms that choose extreme methods (i.e., the 50 firms using full-cost methods to report higher earnings than the SEC's full-cost method and the 18 firms that use successful-efforts methods that produce lower earnings than the SEC's full-cost method). If the model is appropriate, the four variables should be more significant for this extreme sample. The results are consistent with the model. The model is significant at the .001 level, and all coefficients have the predicted signs and are significant at the .04 level. Hence, in addition to size and leverage, age and exploratory risk are associated with not only the choice between full cost and successful efforts, but the choice between alternative full-cost methods and alternative successful-efforts methods.

The three studies of the choice of methods in oil and gas accounting are not independent. For example, some of the same firms and their methods appear in all three studies. Nevertheless, the consistency of their results, particularly the association of size and leverage with the choice in the predicted direction, adds weight to the results of the two Hagerman and Zmijewski papers and Watts and Zimmerman (1978). The oil and gas studies add more evidence consistent with the debt/equity and size hypotheses. In addition, the Lilien and Pastena study presents new evidence on exploratory risk that is consistent with the debt and political cost incentives to reduce the variance of reported earnings. The one variable all these oil and gas studies overlook is the effect of management compensation plans on the choice of methods and hence reported earnings (the bonus plan hypothesis).

INTEREST CAPITALIZATION

Bowen, Noreen, and Lacey (1981) investigate the manager's choice between capitalizing and not capitalizing interest costs associated with capital projects. Before 1974, managers could choose either method of accounting for such interest costs. In 1974 the SEC imposed a moratorium on firms adopting interest capitalization, and the FASB put the topic on its agenda. In 1979 the FASB issued Statement No. 34 that required interest capitalization for certain assets and the SEC rescinded the moratorium.

Bowen, Noreen, and Lacey consider the effect of management compensation plans, debt contracts, and political costs on the choice of accounting methods. Interest capitalization increases current period reported earnings, so following the bonus plan hypothesis, they hypothesize that managers of firms with bonus plans are more likely to choose interest capitalization.

In assessing the effects of debt contracts, Bowen, Noreen, and Lacey, unlike previous papers, use variables suggested by details of debt contracts. They hypothesize that (1) firms with higher debt/equity ratios are more likely to use interest capitalization (the debt/equity hypothesis) and (2) the lower the inventory of payable funds and the lower the ratio of earnings to interest expense (the coverage ratio), the more likely the firm is to use interest capitalization.

Bowen, Noreen, and Lacey test two hypotheses on political costs. One is that larger firms in *all* industries are less likely to capitalize interest (because it increases current period reported earnings and thus political costs). The other follows from the observations that oil firms drive the results of Watts and Zimmerman (1978) and that the oil industry was under considerable political pressure in the years Bowen, Noreen, and Lacey investigate (1973 and 1974). The second hypothesis is that the largest firms in the oil industry are less likely to capitalize interest.

The sample consists of 91 matched pairs of firms that did and did not capitalize interest in 1974, before the SEC moratorium. The firms were matched on the basis of their four-digit Standard Industry Classification (SIC). The matched-pair design was chosen because industry membership is highly associated with capitalization and non-capitalization. Using a χ_2 test, Bowen, Noreen, and Lacey reject the null hypothesis that industry membership and accounting methods are independent at the .001 level. If industry membership is not controlled, an independent variable that does not explain the choice of methods, but is associated with industry, can be found to be associated with the choice of methods. On the other hand, controlling for industry reduces the expected association between choice of method and variables that influence the choice but which are associated with industry and hence reduces the power of the tests. Bowen, Noreen, and Lacey deliberately choose to reduce the power of the test.

Applying univariate tests Bowen, Noreen, and Lacey find no association between the presence of a bonus plan and the method chosen for interest costs. Hence, they fail to confirm the bonus plan hypothesis. However, this test of management compensation lacks power. Many bonus plans add back interest expense to define earnings (see Smith and Watts, 1982; Healy, 1985). Capitalizing interest for those firms merely increases the minimum return for a bonus (by increasing total assets or equity) and makes a bonus more difficult to earn. This would lead one to predict that the presence of a bonus plan that adds interest expense back would make the manager less, not more, likely to capitalize.

The univariate tests on the three debt variables are all significant. There are 70 pairs of firms without binding dividend constraints in 1974. In 43 pairs the dividend constraint was relatively more binding for the interest capitalizer, in 23 it was more binding for the noncapitalizer, and in 4 there was no difference. Hence, the lower the inventory of payable funds, the more likely the firm is to capitalize. Using a sign test, the probability of obtaining these results by chance is about .02.

For the other two debt variables the interest capitalizing firms have smaller interest coverage ratios (the .06 level) and lower tangible assets to long-term debt ratios (significant at the .001 level).

To test the hypothesis that the largest firms in the oil industry are less likely to capitalize interest, Bowen, Noreen, and Lacey investigate 38 petroleum refining firms on the *Compustat* Annual Industrial File. Of those 38, 26 do not capitalize interest and 10 capitalize interest. Two firms could not be classified. Consistent with the hypothesis, the mean average sales for 1973 and 1974 is larger for the noncapitalizers ($4.9 billion versus $1.2 billion). Using a *t*-test the difference is significant at the .01 level. While the distribution of the two methods across ranks on sales is not significant using a Mann–Whitney test, Bowen, Noreen, and Lacey find a threshold effect similar to that found by Zimmerman (1983), Watts and Zimmerman (1978), and Zmijewski and Hagerman (1981). The 10 largest oil firms are all interest expensers. A simulation shows that the probability of an outcome as favorable as this occurring by chance is .07. Thus, the results confirm the hypothesis that larger oil firms are less likely to capitalize (consistent with the size hypothesis).

The size effect for firms outside the oil industry is contrary to that predicted. The mean sales for capitalizers is $1.0 billion, which is larger than the sales for noncapitalizers, $.6 billion. Using a *t*-test, the difference between the means is significant (in the wrong direction) at the .10 level, and using a two-tail sign test, the difference is significant at the .05 level.

In addition to the univariate tests, Bowen, Noreen, and Lacey use their five variables—the presence of a bonus plan, the ratio of dividends to inventory of payable funds, the interest coverage ratio, the tangible assets to funded debt ratio, and sales—in a Probit analysis to explain the choice of capitalizing or not capitalizing interest. The results confirm the univariate tests.

In summary the Bowen, Noreen, and Lacey results confirm the association between procedure choice and debt contract variables, particularly leverage. They also confirm the association between size and procedure choice for the oil industry. However, for the whole sample, the association between size and choice is the opposite of that predicted. Finally, no relation is found between the presence of a management compensation plan and interest capitalization, but that result could be induced by a failure to investigate the details of individual compensation plans.

RESEARCH AND DEVELOPMENT EXPENDITURES

Daley and Vigeland (1983) find that the manager's choice between capitalizing and not capitalizing research and development expenditures is associated with contracting variables and firm size. In 1974 FASB Statement No. 2 required firms to expense, not capitalize, research and development expenditures. Before then, managers could expense or capitalize those expenditures. Capitalizing increases current reported earnings and retained earnings.

Daley and Vigeland investigate accounting procedures used for research and development expenditures in 1972 before FASB 2. They test hypotheses that firms are more likely to capitalize research and development expenditures (1) the higher the firm's debt/equity ratio (the debt/equity hypothesis), (2) the lower the firm's interest coverage ratio, (3) the higher the firm's ratio of dividends to inventory of payable funds, and (4) the more public debt in the firm's capital structure. Daley and Vigeland test one political cost hypothesis, the size hypothesis; large firms tend to expense research and development expenditures.

Daley and Vigeland's sample consists of 178 expensing firms and 135 capitalizing firms. The capitalizing firms are identified from firms that are reported to have changed their methods in the *Disclosure Journal Index* after expensing was required. The expensing firms are randomly chosen from other firms on *Compustat* that report 1972 research and development expense.

In their multivariate tests, Daley and Vigeland regress the research and development accounting procedure choice (one for capitalizing firms, zero for expensing firms) on nonpublic debt/total tangible assets, public debt/total tangible assets, interest coverage ratio, sales, and dividends/inventory of payable funds. All coefficients have the predicted sign, and all but the coefficient of the dividends to inventory of payable funds are significant at the .05 level.

Daley and Vigeland also estimate their model on a sample of matched pairs. They match the capitalizing firms with control (expensing) firms in the same four-digit SIC industry. This reduces their sample to 111 pairs of firms. The objective is to control for cross-sectional variation in the optimal leverage (debt/equity ratio), which is expected to vary with industry. All estimated coefficients in the model estimated on the matched pairs have the predicted signs, but only the public and private debt/asset coefficients are significant. Those debt/asset coefficients are more significant than in the previous estimation. The industry control appears to increase the tests' power for the debt/equity hypothesis, but reduce the power for the other hypotheses.

To test whether the size effect exists only for large firms, Daley and Vigeland break their sample of 313 firms into a large firm subsample (156 firms) and a small firm subsample (157 firms). They estimate their OLS model on each subsample separately. The two debt/asset coefficients are significant at the .05 level in both estimations, but the size (sales) coefficient is significant only for the small firms subsample. Contrary to the results of Zimmerman (1983) and Zmijewski and Hagerman (1981), the size effect is not driven by the large firms.

Overall, Daley and Vigeland provide evidence consistent with the debt/equity and size hypotheses. They also provide some evidence that the choice between capitalization and expensing research and development expenditures is associated with the level of the interest coverage ratio. However, contrary to previous results, the size effect is not restricted to large firms; in fact, it is only significant among smaller firms.

DEPRECIATION METHODS

Dhaliwal, Salamon, and Smith (1982) investigate whether owner-controlled and manager-controlled firms use different depreciation methods for reporting purposes. Owner-controlled firms are defined as having one party owning 10 percent or more of the voting stock and being represented on the board of directors or in which one party owns 20 percent or more of the voting stock. Manager-controlled firms are firms in which no one party controls more than 5 percent of the voting stock.

Dhaliwal, Salamon, and Smith expect manager controlled firms to be more likely to use depreciation procedures that shift reported earnings from later periods to the current period (i.e., straight-line depreciation) for two reasons. One reason is the argument of Hindley (1970, pp. 199–200) and Williamson (1967, p. 13) that managers of manager-controlled firms try to report the operations of the firm in the most favorable fashion to reduce the probability of a takeover. The second reason is that manager-controlled firms are more likely to use accounting-based incentive schemes. If this is correct, the bonus plan hypothesis leads to the prediction that manager-controlled firms are more likely to use straight-line depreciation to increase their compensation.

The study examines the depreciation methods used for reporting in 1962 by 42 manager-controlled and 41 owner-controlled firms that used accelerated depreciation for tax purposes. Dhaliwal, Salamon, and Smith also perform a Probit analysis with the dependent variable being 1 if the firm used straight-line for reporting and 0 if it used accelerated. The independent variables are total assets, debt/equity, and a variable that takes the value 0 if the firm is owner controlled and 1 if it is manager controlled. Using a χ^2 statistic, the null hypothesis that the model predicts no better than a naïve model based on the relative frequencies can be rejected at the .01 level. The coefficients of all three variables have the predicted signs. The coefficient of debt/equity is significant at the .01 level, the coefficient of the control variable is significant at the .03 level, and the coefficient of size is significant at the .15 level. These results are consistent with the debt/equity hypothesis (higher debt/equity firms are more likely to use earnings increasing procedures) and the size hypothesis. They are consistent with the bonus plan hypothesis if manager-controlled firms are more likely to have incentive schemes.

Holthausen (1981) investigates the time series of inventory of payable funds for 41 firms that switched back from accelerated depreciation methods to the straight-line method for reporting purposes in the period 1955–1978. The firms remained on accelerated methods for tax purposes. If the debt covenant that restricts dividend payments (i.e., the inventory of payable funds) caused the switchback, the inventory is likely to be closer to zero in the years immediately preceding and in the year of the switchback than in other years.

The time series of the average (across firms) ratios of inventory to dividends, inventory to earnings, and inventory to size, from seven years prior to the switchback to three years after the switchback, are calculated by Holthausen. These time series show no indication of the dividend constraint becoming more restrictive around the switchback year.

Further evidence suggesting that the inventory of payable funds is not instrumental in the switchback comes from comparing the switchback firms to a random sample of firms investigated by Kalay (1979). Only 5 (12 percent) of Holthausen's switchback firms had (or would have had without the switchback) binding dividend constraints over the 11-year period around the switchback (2 occurred before the switchback and 3 afterward). This compares to 14 percent of Kalay's 100 firms that had binding constraints over the 21-year period 1957–1975.

Overall, the Holthausen evidence suggests very strongly that the inventory of payable funds is not motivating the change in depreciation methods. Data constraints prevented Holthausen from investigating the deviations from the leverage constraints.

CHAPTER TWELVE

Stock Price Tests
of the Theory

This chapter assesses the ability of the theory outlined in Chapters 8–10 to explain stock price changes associated with announcements of accounting procedure changes. We analyze four studies of stock price changes and their cross-sectional variations: three studies of price changes accompanying *mandated* accounting changes and one of price changes accompanying a *voluntary* accounting change.[1] The mandated change studies find stock price effects associated with change announcements, the voluntary change study does not.

In Chapters 9 and 10, we note the difficulties of developing powerful tests of *voluntary* changes' stock price effects. These difficulties result from (1) the market expecting the announcement and (2) the greater the benefits of changing, the more the market expects the change, thereby reducing any cross-sectional variations in stock price effects. Market expectations do not eliminate systematic cross-sectional variations in *mandated* changes' stock price effects, and so those stock price effects are more observable. The studies' overall results are consistent with that proposition.

All the *mandated* change studies find average stock price effects of

---

[1] Holthausen and Leftwich (1983) also summarize these studies.

accounting change announcements. They also find that the cross-sectional stock price effect variation is related to some contracting and political cost variables. However, not all variables are significant, or even of the predicted sign, in each study, and different variables are significant across the studies. These inconsistencies could be due to the variables being imperfect proxies for contracting and political costs, to multicollinearity between the variables, to the contracting and political cost functions not being fully specified, and to other methodological problems. A nonmutually exclusive hypothesis is that other explanatory variables are omitted in the studies.

Despite the inconsistencies in results across studies, the *mandated* change studies' results are encouraging for the theory outlined in Chapters 8–10. We have found accounting standard stock price effects that are not obviously due to tax effects. Those effects vary cross sectionally with variables suggested by the theory; some variation is explained. However, the results are only a beginning; we must now explain why different variables are significant across studies and try to develop better proxies for contracting and political costs.

The results of the studies analyzed in this chapter contrast to the results of studies analyzed in Chapter 4. The earlier chapter's studies attempted to discriminate between the mechanistic and no-effects hypotheses. They assume that in an efficient market tax-neutral changes do not affect firms' cash flows and so do not affect stock prices. They do not find stock price effects of tax-neutral changes because they do not look in the right places, they cannot specify which firm's stock prices are most affected by procedure changes. This chapter's studies have a theory to guide their search for effects. One consequence is that Chapter 4's studies tend to concentrate on voluntary changes where we think price effects are less likely to be observed. This chapter's studies concentrate on mandated changes.

We begin this chapter by specifying the type of accounting changes the studies investigate and the stock price effect predictions for those changes. (Stock price effect predictions are given in Chapters 9 and 10). Then we explain the variables used to proxy for the changes' contracting and political costs and review the mandated changes first, since in our opinion they are the most powerful tests. Next we review a study (Leftwich, 1981) of the stock price effects of accounting changes mandated by APB Opinions 16 and 17 (accounting for business combinations), and then we look at the other two mandated change studies (Collins, Rozeff, and Dhaliwal, 1981; Lys, 1984) that examine the stock price effects of FASB Statement No. 19 (oil and gas accounting). Finally, we consider a voluntary change study (Holthausen, 1981) that examines depreciation switchbacks. The chapter concludes with a summary.

STOCK PRICE EFFECTS OF ACCOUNTING CHANGES

This section describes the predicted stock price effects of first the *mandated* then the *voluntary* accounting changes.

Mandated Changes

The two sets of standards (APB Opinions 16 and 17 and FASB Statement No. 19) investigated by the mandated change studies *restrict* the set of available procedures. Both eliminate or increase the cost of procedures that tend to increase reported earnings.

OPTIMAL CONTRACTING

In Chapter 9 we argue that a standard that restricts the set of accounting procedures restricts the contracting technology available to the contracting parties. The eliminated or restricted procedures reviewed in this chapter (e.g., the pooling method and the full cost method) are used for contracting purposes, and so there is a restriction on contracting technology. This causes a fall in the stock prices of all firms that could potentially use the restricted procedures.[2]

WEALTH TRANSFERS VIA DEBT CONTRACTS

By eliminating earnings increasing alternatives, the mandated changes restrict the manager's ability to transfer wealth from the debtholders to shareholders (e.g., by increasing the firm's debt/equity ratio). This effect reduces share prices of all firms that use or could potentially use the restricted methods to make debt covenants less binding. The change increases the probability that debt covenants (e.g., a required times charges earned ratio) will be violated. Hence, the expected cost of a technical default increases, causing a stock price decrease.

WEALTH TRANSFERS VIA COMPENSATION CONTRACTS

If the firm has an earnings-based compensation plan, the restriction in the mandated change reduces the manager's ability to increase his or her compensation by accounting methods. This could cause a very small stock price increase, but we would expect the effect to be limited because the managers' future ex ante compensation must equal his or her competitive wage.

---

[2] We assume that firms can achieve the optimal contracting technology without government regulation of disclosure.

POLITICAL COSTS

APB Opinions 16 and 17 and FASB 19 restrict procedures that report higher earnings. This increases stock prices via a reduction in political costs. The political cost reduction occurs for all firms that could use the procedure, not just those actually using the eliminated procedure (it prevents political opponents' use of the procedure).[3]

Voluntary Change

The voluntary change investigated is the switchback to straight-line depreciation from accelerated depreciation. Holthausen (1981) assumes that it is an opportunistic change, not a change in accepted procedures. The change tends to increase reported earnings and assets.

WEALTH TRANSFERS VIA DEBT CONTRACTS

The change increases the manager's ability to transfer wealth from the debtholders and reduces the probability of costly default. Both effects increase stock prices.

WEALTH TRANSFERS VIA COMPENSATION CONTRACTS

The change tends to increase the manager's bonus and so reduces stock prices.

POLITICAL COSTS

Because the switchback increases reported earnings and assets, political costs increase and stock prices fall.

The foregoing discussion predicts the sign of an accounting change's stock price effect via a particular factor (e.g., via wealth transfers from debtholders). The sign of a change's net stock price effect depends on the relative magnitude of each factor's effect. So does the stock price effect's variation across firms (which the studies want to predict). Hence, the studies use variables to proxy for each factor's stock price effect. They use proxies for the change's effect on optimal contracting costs borne by shareholders, wealth transfers to and from shareholders via debt contracts and via bonus plans, and political costs borne by shareholders.

Typically, the stock price change associated with a change announcement is regressed on the proxy variables. The success of the test depends on the extent to which the proxy variables capture the changes'

---

[3] Restriction of the pooling method restricts a procedure that reduces assets. This tends to increase political costs and reduce stock prices. However, we expect the assets' effect on political costs to be outweighed by the earnings' effect.

effect on the various costs and wealth transfers. It also depends on the extent to which the overall cost is a linear function of the cost effects represented by the proxy variables.

VARIABLES USED TO EXPLAIN STOCK PRICE EFFECTS

All four studies rely heavily on the debt contracts' wealth transfer effect to explain changes' stock price effects. The variables used by the studies and the rationales for their use are explained in the paragraphs that follow. The sign of the relation between each variable and the stock price effects of the mandated changes and the voluntary changes are summarized in Table 12.1.

TABLE 12.1

Predicted Signs of Relation Between the Variable and Stock Price Effect

		Sign of Relation	
		Mandated Changes (APB 16 and 17; FASB 19)	Voluntary Change (Depreciation Switchback)
a.	Optimal contracting costs Zero/one dummy for existence of debt contract and/or compensation plan	−	Not applicable
b.	Wealth transfers via debt contracts Change in tightness of covenants		
	i. Effect on reported earnings, retained earnings and equity	+	+
	ii. Debt/equity ratio	−	+
	iii. Cash flow variance	−	+
	iv. Inventory of payable funds	+	−
	Default cost		
	v. Proportion of public to private debt	−	+
	vi. Debt value difference	+	−
	vii. Term to maturity	−	+
	viii. Debt callability	+	−
	ix. Debt convertibility	+	−
c.	Wealth transfers via compensation plans Zero/one dummy for existence of accounting-based compensation plan	+	−
d.	Political costs Size, firm value	+	−

Optimal Contracting

Collins, Rozeff, and Dhaliwal (1981) include a "zero/one" dummy variable that takes the value of 1 if the firm has a debt contract with restrictive covenants or if the firm has an accounting-based compensation plan. This variable is intended to capture the effects of FASB 19's restrictions on optimal contracting technology. Hence, its coefficient is expected to be negative (i.e., firms with accounting-based contracts tend to have stock price decreases as a result of FASB 19).

The variable also picks up some debt and compensation plan wealth transfers. Because the standard eliminates an earnings increasing procedure, the debt wealth transfer stock price effect is negative, reinforcing the optimal contracting effect. The compensation plan wealth transfer stock price effect is positive (see previous section), but it is likely to be outweighed by the other effects.

The optimal contracting effect only arises with mandated changes since voluntary changes do not affect the set of available procedures.

Wealth Transfers via Debt Contracts

Variables are used to proxy for two factors determining the wealth transfer a change induces via debt contracts. One factor is the effect of the change on the extent to which accounting-based covenants are binding (change in covenant's "tightness"). The other factor is the cost of technical default.

CHANGE IN TIGHTNESS

Consider a firm where debt covenants limit its ratio of fixed charges to earnings. The mandated changes reduce earnings and move the firm closer to the maximum ratio. Hence, a mandated standard's earnings effect can proxy for the extent to which covenants are made more binding ("tighter").

The effect on covenants' tightness is important because the manager's investment and financing decisions vary with the tightness of the covenant. For example, debt agreements often allow takeovers only if a specific debt/equity ratio exists after the takeover. The closer the firm is to that specific ratio, the less likely the ratio will be met after a takeover *and* the more likely the manager is to be forced to forgo positive net present value projects.

The procedure changes' effect on covenants' tightness is also important because it measures the change in the probability of technical default. Technical default is costly in that it leads to concessions to debtholders (e.g., higher interest rates). The more the new accounting procedure tightens covenants, the higher the change in default probabilities, the higher the expected costs of default, and the larger the drop in stock price due to the standard.

DEFAULT COSTS

The other factor (apart from the procedure changes' effect of covenants' tightness) that determines the debt contracts' wealth transfer induced by a procedure change is the cost of technical default. That cost varies across firms. For example, the larger the difference between the current market rate of interest and the debt's nominal interest rate, the more debtholders might charge in renegotiating the defaulted debt.

Variables representing the two factors (change in tightness and default costs) are discussed next.

Change in Tightness Variables

CHANGE'S EFFECT ON REPORTED EARNINGS, RETAINED EARNINGS, AND EQUITY

Ceteris paribus, the greater the earnings decrease caused by the mandated change, the greater the increase in the probability of default under covenants such as the times charges earned covenant. In turn, this means a greater wealth transfer from the shareholders to the bondholders and a greater stock price decline. The greater the decrease in retained earnings and equity, the greater the likelihood of default under debt/equity–type covenants and the greater the stock price drop. Finally, the larger the decrease in retained earnings, the more binding the inventory of payable funds, the smaller the manager's ability to pay dividends and transfer wealth from the bondholders, and the larger the stock price decrease associated with the change.

The preceding arguments imply a *positive* relation between the mandated change's effect on earnings, retained earnings or equity, and the change's stock price effect. The change *decreases* earnings and, hence, *decreases* stock prices. The relation among the voluntary change's effect on earnings, retained earnings or equity, and the change's stock price effect is also positive. The switchback *increases* earnings and, hence, *increases* stock prices.

While the sign of the relation between the earnings effect variable and the stock price effect is the same for both the mandated changes and the voluntary change, the sign of the relation between other debt variables and the stock price effect for the voluntary change is the opposite of that for the mandated changes. The reason is that the earnings effect variable incorporates the earnings effect's direction and the other variables do not. For example, the larger a default cost measure, the larger the cost of a mandated change (since it increases the default probability), and so the larger the stock price *drop*. However, the larger the default cost, the larger the benefits of the voluntary change (since it reduces the default probability), and the larger the stock price *increase*.

The following discussion of the stock price effect of the remaining debt wealth transfer variables addresses the *mandated* accounting changes. The reader should remember that the *voluntary* change leads to a stock price effect of the opposite sign.

DEBT/EQUITY RATIO

A given decrease in reported earnings or equity resulting from the mandated changes increases the probability of default on debt/ equity and times charges earned covenants more, the larger the debt/ equity ratio ceteris paribus. In addition, the larger the debt/equity ratio, the larger the costs per share of technical default. Both these factors combine to produce the prediction that the wealth transfer from shareholders to bondholders (and the stock price drop) is larger the higher the debt/equity ratio. In other words, there is a negative relation between the debt/equity ratio and the stock price effect.

To see why the increase in probability of default is positively associated with the debt/equity ratio, consider two firms with identical investment policies but different financial policies. The distribution of earnings before interest for next period is the same for both firms. The times charges earned constraint for both firms is one.

Figure 12.1 portrays the probability distributions for the firm's earnings next period with and without an accounting change. The distribution with expected value $E(A')$ is the distribution without an accounting change (distribution Y). The distribution with expected value $E(A)$ is the distribution if an accounting change is made that

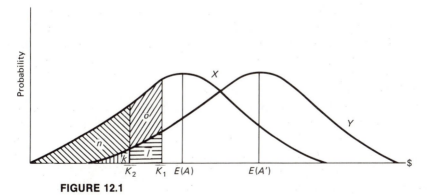

FIGURE 12.1

The effect of the debt/equity ratio on the change in probability of default resulting from a mandated accounting change

decreases reported earnings (distribution X). K_2 is interest expense of the firm with the lower debt/equity ratio, and K_1 is the interest expense of the firm with the higher debt/equity ratio.

Before the mandated accounting change, the default probability for the firm with the lower debt/equity ratio is the shaded area marked k under distribution Y. For the firm with the higher debt/equity ratio, the default probability is $k + l$. The default probability is higher for the firm with the higher leverage. After the accounting change, the probability of default for the firm with the lower debt/equity ratio is the shaded area under distribution X marked $k + n$. For the other firm, it is the area $k + l + n + o$. The increase in the probability of default due to the accounting change is n for the low debt/equity firm and $n + o$ for the high debt/equity firm. The firm with the larger debt/equity ratio has the larger increase in probability of default.[4]

The preceding example can be reproduced for debt/equity constraints. All that is necessary is that K_1 and K_2 represent debt levels and that $E(A)$, $E(A')$, and the distributions represent levels of equity. The same results will hold.

The change in default probability varies with the change in the tightness of the debt/equity constraint, so the debt/equity ratio also measures the change in the tightness of the debt/equity constraint. Since the mandated changes reduce equity, the firm's manager is less likely to be able to take any investment and financing decisions that under the debt agreement are contingent on the firm's debt/equity ratio. Hence, the larger the debt/equity ratio, the larger the stock price decrease.

CASH FLOW VARIANCE

Ceteris paribus, the greater the firms' cash flow variance, the greater the default probability. If the mandated change (by reducing earnings) increases the default probability from zero (because the firm has very little debt), the increase in default probability and the resultant stock price drop is larger, the larger the cash flow variance. This result does not hold in general if the debt is risky before the change (i.e., the probability of default is nonzero). Nevertheless, one mandated change study, Lys (1984), on the basis of the foregoing argument, hypothesizes and tests a negative association between the variance of the firm's cash flows and stock price changes.

---

[4] This result holds as long as K_1 and K_2 are less than the expected earnings $E(A)$. This condition would probably be met in practice, because if it were not, given the evidence that annual earnings follow a random walk, the firm would already be in default (current earnings would be below K and the times charges earned constraint would be violated).

The use of the cash flow variance can also be rationalized on the grounds that the debt/equity ratio arguments (earlier) assume ceteris paribus and, in particular, a constant cash flow variance across firms. Inclusion of the cash flow variance is a way of controlling for cross-sectional fluctuations in the variance. Note that firms' debt/equity ratios are likely to vary with their cash flow variances (see Myers, 1977).

INVENTORY OF PAYABLE FUNDS

The mandated changes decrease earnings and therefore the inventory payable funds. Hence, the probability of the inventory being zero is negatively related to the inventory of payable funds. This prediction is derived in the same manner as the debt/equity ratio prediction (earlier). In turn it leads to the prediction that, ceteris paribus, the smaller the inventory of payable funds, the larger the wealth transfer and stock price decrease resulting from the mandated changes (i.e., a positive relation between the inventory of payable funds and the changes' stock price effect).

Default Cost Variation Variables

PROPORTION OF PUBLIC TO PRIVATE DEBT

When a firm issues debt to the public, a public trustee for the debtholders is appointed (Leftwich, 1981, p. 8). To modify the debt agreement subsequently, the trustee has to obtain the agreement of a substantial majority of the outstanding debtholders (usually two-thirds). This requirement makes it difficult for the manager to renegotiate a debt contract if there is a technical default. Individual debtholders have incentives to hold out for greater payoffs. In the case of private debt, the manager often has to renegotiate with only one debtholder, and if the relationship is an ongoing one, the debtholder is likely not to take as much advantage of technical defaults. Consequently, ceteris paribus, the prediction is the greater the proportion of public to private debt, the greater the wealth transfer and the stock price decrease due to the accounting change (i.e., a negative relation between the public debt proportion and the change's stock price effect).

DIFFERENCE BETWEEN THE MARKET AND NOMINAL VALUE
OF THE FIRM'S DEBT

The more interest rates have risen since the firm issued its debt, the lower the market value of that debt relative to its nominal value. If the firm has to call the debt (typically at a price greater than nominal value) to avoid default or has to repay the debt as a consequence of default, the difference between the debt's nominal and market value is a cost of default. Since the mandated changes increase the default probability, the increase in the expected shareholder cost (and expected bondholder benefit) and the stock price decrease is larger, the larger the difference between the debt's nominal and market value. In other words, there is a negative relation between the value difference and the change's stock price effect. In the one study using this variable (Lys, 1984), the difference is reversed and is calculated as the market value minus the nominal value. Thus a positive relation is predicted in Table 12.1.

TERM TO MATURITY

The longer the term to maturity of debt, the longer the debt restrictions apply and the larger the effect of differences between the debt's nominal rate of interest and the market's rate; hence, the greater the effect of that difference on default costs. Thus, the greater the term to maturity, the greater the stock price decrease accompanying the mandated changes (i.e., a negative relation between the term to maturity and the changes' stock price effect).

DEBT CALLABILITY

If the debt is callable, the call price limits the default costs since the firm has the option of calling the debt to avoid default. Hence, it is predicted that the call feature reduces the stock price effect of an accounting change. The stock price decrease accompanying the mandated changes is less if the firm's debt is callable (i.e., a positive relation between debt callability and the change's stock price effect).

DEBT CONVERTIBILITY

The debt's conversion privilege is an option on the stock price. Hence, any wealth transfer from bondholder to shareholder induced by an accounting change will be reduced if the conversion feature is present. The stock price decrease accompanying the mandated change is less if the debt is convertible (i.e., there is a positive relation between debt convertibility and the change's stock price effect).

Unfortunately, wealth transfers via debt variables are not independent of each other, partially because they are all part of the firm's capital structure decision. For example, Kalay (1979) finds that the higher the firm's debt/equity ratio, the closer it is to its dividend constraint (i.e., the smaller the inventory of payable funds). Likewise, the lower the firm's cash flow variance or the more assets in place, the higher the debt/equity ratio. Because the variables are collinear, trying to disentangle the effect of any one variable is difficult. Consequently, while each of these variables may not be significant in tests of the stock price reaction to accounting changes, as a group they may be significant.

Further, it would appear that some of the variables may not enter the regression equation linearly. For example, the change in default probability variables might be multiplied by the default cost variables. Such specification problems reduce the likelihood of significant explanatory power and suggest that we concentrate on the significance of the groups of variables rather than individual variables' significance.

Wealth Transfers via Compensation Contracts

Holthausen (1981) includes a zero/one dummy variable for the presence of an earnings-based compensation plan. The dummy is expected to be negatively related to the depreciation switchback's stock price effect because the switch increases earnings and bonuses and transfers wealth from the shareholders to the manager (assuming that the compensation committee does not adjust for the change). The mandated change studies do not use this variable. If they did, its coefficient's sign is predicted to be positive.

Political Costs

The only variable the studies use as a proxy for an accounting change's political cost effect is firm size (Leftwich, 1981; Collins, Rozeff, and Dhaliwal, 1981; Holthausen, 1981). The measure is, in all three cases, a function of the book value of the firm's debt plus the market value of its equity. This variable is predicted to be positively associated with political costs. The mandated changes decrease earnings, so larger firms are expected to have larger decreases in political costs and hence more positive stock price effects. The mandated change studies only investigate the stock price effect of firms forced to change accounting procedures.

The depreciation switchback increases earnings and political costs. Hence, the relation between size and stock price effects is expected to be negative for that change.

A STUDY OF MANDATED RESTRICTIONS ON "POOLING OF INTERESTS" (LEFTWICH)

Leftwich (1981) investigates the stock price changes associated with APB Opinions 16, "Accounting for Business Combinations," and 17, "Accounting for Intangible Assets." Those opinions restrict the circumstances under which the "pooling-of-interests" method can be used to account for a business combination. If pooling cannot be used, the purchase method must be used. The opinions require that under the purchase method, any difference between the purchase price and the net asset value be allocated to specific assets if identifiable and, if not, to goodwill, which is to be amortized over a period not exceeding 40 years. The purchase method's effect is to reduce an acquiring firm's after combination earnings relative to pooling and to make debt constraints more binding. Leftwich investigates how restrictions in accounting for business combinations affect the stock prices of firms actively engaging in merger takeovers.

Proxy Variables Used

Leftwich relies primarily on debt wealth transfer variables to explain stock price effects of APB Opinions 16 and 17. He uses variables for debt/equity—debt wealth transfer variable b(ii) in the foregoing section and Table 12.1—the proportion of public to private debt—variable b(v)—debt callability—variable b(viii)—and debt convertibility—variable b(ix). The only other variable used is firm size—variable d, measured as the log of the sum of the market value of equity and the book value of debt.

Modeling Expectations

Leftwich handles the expectations problem by explicitly recognizing that the market expects the standard's provisions prior to the standard's announcement. He assumes that investors have homogeneous expectations regarding the probabilities of various versions of the standard being adopted. If information comes to the market that causes investors to revise their expectations about the various versions' probabilities, the shares' market value changes.

If the share price changes, it can be concluded that investors have revised the version's probabilities. If the price does not change, it *cannot* be concluded that the event did not change the probabilities, given Leftwich's assumptions, because the changes may be offsetting across the firms.

Leftwich uses a sample of firms described by Rayburn (1975) to obtain a sample of 338 NYSE-listed firms that engaged in 1,139 mergers from November 1968 through December 1972. Most of the mergers (90 percent) were treated as poolings, and virtually every firm used pooling at least once. These firms would be expected to be affected by Opinions 16 and 17.

Given his model, Leftwich chooses events where there is evidence that the event conveyed information to the market and the market revised the probabilities attached to versions of the proposed business combinations standard. Using previously published chronologies, he identifies 21 events that could have influenced the market's expectations about a standard restricting pooling. The first event is an article by Briloff in *Barron's* on July 15, 1968, before the APB began deliberations on business combinations accounting (June 1969). The last event is a *WSJ* report that both the NYSE and the ASE required listing applications for shares used in pooling transactions to be accompanied by an auditor's opinion that detailed compliance with the APB criteria for pooling. This event was after Opinions 16 and 17 were issued (August 1970).

Leftwich calculates the abnormal rates of return for his sample of firms affected by the opinions for the period from five days before the event to five days after the event. He finds that the abnormal returns for 9 of the 21 events are significantly different from zero at the 10 percent level (two-tail test). Eight of the events have significantly negative average abnormal returns and 1 has positive average abnormal returns (suggesting less costly versions of the standard became likely with that event). The average abnormal returns surrounding issuance of the final opinions are not significant, suggesting (but not necessarily implying) that the market had anticipated the opinions.

Leftwich expects Opinions 16 and 17 to reduce share values because they make debt covenants more binding. Across all 21 events the average daily abnormal rate of return is $-.55$ percent, which is significant at the 1 percent level.

The only events whose stock prices Leftwich seeks to explain are the 9 events where there is evidence that the market revised its expectations of the standard. He posits that a firm's abnormal return is a linear function of various firm-specific characteristics that proxy for the costs imposed by a particular accounting rule change—variables b(ii) debt/equity, b(v) public debt, b(viii) debt callability, b(ix) debt convertibility, and d size. Then the predicted signs on the coefficients depend on whether the probability of adoption of the standard increases or decreases at the particular event date. For the eight events with stock price decreases, the coefficients' predicted signs are as listed in Table 12.1 for mandated changes. For the one event which has abnormal positive returns, the coefficients are predicted to have the opposite sign to those given in Table 12.1 for mandated changes.

Results

Leftwich estimates the following cross-sectional regression for each event (s):

$$e_i^s = c_0^s + c_1^s \frac{PUB_i}{S_i} + c_2^s \frac{PRI_i}{S_i} + c_3^s \frac{CALL_i}{S_i} + c_4^s \frac{CONV_i}{S_i} + c_5^s LSIZE_i + u_i^s$$

Predicted sign $\quad(-)\qquad\quad(-)\qquad(+)\qquad\quad(+)\qquad\quad(+)$

$$s = 1, \ldots, 9 \quad (12.1)$$

where

e_i^s = the daily abnormal rate of return of the ith firm for the period from five days before event s to five days afterward

PUB$_i$ = book value of public debt, variables b(ii) and b(v)

PRI$_i$ = book value of private debt, variables b(ii) and b(v)

CALL$_i$ = book value of callable debt, variable b(viii)

CONV$_i$ = book value of convertible debt, variable b(ix)

S_i = market value of equity

LSIZE$_i$ = natural log of market value of equity plus book value of debt, variable d

The signs predicted for each coefficient (if the event decreases share prices) are shown under the coefficient. Those signs are the same as shown in Table 12.1. The coefficients should have the opposite signs for the one event that has positive abnormal returns. The coefficients of the public and private debt/equity ratios are expected to be negative, consistent with the debt/equity prediction in Table 12.1. The proportion of public to private debt prediction is tested by comparing the magnitude of the public and private debt/equity coefficients. The coefficient of public debt/equity is expected to be more negative.

Equation (12.1) is estimated separately for each event, allowing the coefficients to vary from event to event. However, Leftwich also pools the events by averaging the abnormal returns (e_i^s) across all 9 events (the positive return event is included after being multiplied by -1) and regressing the resulting average on the same independent variables. This procedure assumes that the coefficients' absolute values are the same across all 9 events.

Leftwich finds some support for the hypotheses listed in Table 12.1 when he estimates the regression averaged across all 9 events. The coefficients of private debt leverage (PRI/S) and the callability feature (CALL/S) have the predicted signs (negative and positive, respectively) and are significant at the .05 level (one-tail test). However, the other debt coefficients are insignificantly different from zero and there is no significant difference between the public and private debt coefficients. In fact the difference is in the wrong direction—the coefficient of private leverage is more negative than the coefficient of public leverage. The size variable's coefficient is positive and significant at the 1 percent level for a one-tail test. The F statistic for the regression is significant at the .01 level.

When equation (12.1) is estimated separately for each event, the regression's explanatory power is reduced. However, 6 of the 9 F statistics are significant at the .05 level. Some coefficient signs are contrary to prediction, but none of these is significant. The coefficients of public leverage, private leverage, and the call feature are significantly different from zero in the predicted direction in several of the separate regressions. The public debt leverage coefficient is significantly more negative (as predicted) than the private debt leverage coefficient in only 1 of the 9 regressions. The convertible debt variable's coefficient is never significant. The coefficient of size is significantly positive (at the .05 level) for 5 of the 8 events where the abnormal rate of return for the event is positive. It is insignificant for the other (negative return) event.

Leftwich also estimates the regressions including variables for the debt's term to maturity (variable b(vii) in Table 12.1), the rating of the firm's debt, and the inventory of payable funds (variable b(iv)). None of those variables is significant.

To ensure that the results obtained in the cross-sectional regressions are not spurious, Leftwich estimates 21 abnormal returns for random dates outside the event period.[5] Only 4 of the 21 "events" have significant returns. When the cross-sectional regressions are estimated separately on the significant and insignificant simulated "events," the frequency of significant coefficients and regressions is much lower than for the 9 actual events' regressions. Also, Leftwich tests whether there is cross-sectional correlation between the firms' abnormal rates of return for each of the 8 "bad" and for the "good" events and finds significant negative correlation.

Conclusions

Overall, Leftwich's results provide partial support for the proposition that accounting standard changes affect firms' share values via their debt contracts. The drop in market value associated with the standard is larger, the larger the debt/equity ratio, and is smaller if the debt is callable. However, the prediction based on public debt being more costly than private debt is not confirmed; neither is the prediction that convertibility reduces the standard's stock price effect. The evidence is generally consistent with the proposition that APB Opinions 16 and 17 reduce political costs and hence increase firms' stock prices (if size reflects political costs).

Leftwich's study is subject to the problems discussed earlier. It isn't clear if the linear specification for equation (12.1) is appropriate; the independent variables are collinear and often measure the same costs. And it isn't apparent how well the various variables proxy for changes in default probability, default costs, or political costs. However, the fact that some of the variables, and the regression equation itself,

---

[5] Jain (1982) suggests that the significance of the coefficients of debt/equity and size variables in cross-sectional regressions of abnormal returns on those variables, when the abnormal rate of return of the overall sample is significant, is a statistical artifact.

are significant holds promise for the hypothesis that the standard's stock price effects are driven by debt contracting.

The Leftwich study also provides insights into the importance of expectations in observing accounting standards' stock price effects. If Leftwich had chosen only the announcement days of APB Opinions 16 and 17 as the event dates, he would not have found any stock price effect. The evidence suggests the final standard was anticipated by the market.

STUDIES OF MANDATED ELIMINATION OF THE FULL-COST METHOD

Collins, Rozeff, and Dhaliwal

Collins, Rozeff, and Dhaliwal (1981) investigate the stock price changes associated with the issuance of the FASB's Exposure Draft of Statement No. 19.[6] That Exposure Draft proposed the elimination of the full-cost method of accounting for oil and gas firms in favor of a particular version of the successful-efforts method. A brief description of the two methods is given in the appendix to Chapter 11. The change from the full-cost method to successful-efforts typically decreases the level of firms' reported earnings, retained earnings, stockholders' equity, and asset values. It also increases their reported earnings' variability (see Sunder, 1976; Lys, 1982). The preceding changes make debt covenants more binding and increase the probability of default.

PROXY VARIABLES USED

Collins, Rozeff, and Dhaliwal recognize the effect of the proposed standard on wealth transfers via debt contracts, but they also recognize the restrictions that the Exposure Draft would place on contracting technology and future contracts and include a dummy variable for those effects. Collins, Rozeff, and Dhaliwal use the following explanatory variables from Table 12.1: contracting dummy (variable a), standard's effect on stockholder equity (variable b(i)), debt/equity ratio (variable b(ii)), and firm size (variable d). They also include a zero/one dummy variable for the existence of public debt (one if public debt exists). The

---

[6] There have been numerous studies of the stock price effects of the release on the Exposure Draft of FASB Statement 19. Those studies include Collins and Dent (1979), Dyckman and Smith (1979), Lev (1979), and Haworth, Matthews, and Tuck (1978). Also, Collins, Rozeff, and Salatka (1982) and Smith (1981a, 1981b) investigate the stock price effects of ASR 253. However, these studies do not attempt to explain the cross-sectional variation in any stock price effects using contracting and political cost variables.

expected sign of the public debt dummy's coefficient is negative consistent with the prediction in Table 12.1.

The final variable included is the proportion of the firm's revenues devoted to exploration. Sunder (1976) shows that the earnings variance increase caused by a change from full-cost to successful-efforts increases with the proportion of the firm's activities devoted to exploration. As a result, the increase in the default probability is greater, the greater that proportion, and so is the predicted stock price drop when the Exposure Draft is announced.

RESULTS

Collins, Rozeff, and Dhaliwal's sample is 57 firms: 47 full-cost firms and 10 successful-efforts firms. The successful-efforts firms were also affected by the Exposure Draft. Their earnings and shareholders' equity are reduced (although not as severely as for full-cost firms) by the particular version of successful efforts imposed. The median effect on earnings of the final version of FASB 19 on the 1977 earnings is −27 percent for the 47 full-cost firms and −13 percent for the 10 successful-efforts firms. The median effect on the 1977 total stockholders' equity is −30 percent for the full-cost firms and −4 percent for the successful-efforts firms.

The Exposure Draft is dated Friday, July 15, 1977, but the *WSJ* did not report its contents until Wednesday, July 20. Collins, Rozeff, and Dhaliwal estimate abnormal rates of return for their firms for the week ending July 15, 1977, and the two weeks ending July 22, 1977, and attempt to explain both abnormal rates of return with cross-sectional regressions. Lev (1979) finds the full-cost firms' shares largest price decline occurs in the period Monday, July 18, to Wednesday, July 20. Using the market model to estimate abnormal rates of return, Collins, Rozeff, and Dhaliwal find a much larger abnormal rate of return for the two-week period than for their one-week rate of return consistent with Lev's results. Lys (1984) reports that the only significant difference in abnormal rates of return of successful-efforts and full-cost firms in the 15 days surrounding July 20, 1977, occurs on July 19, 1977, the day the exposure draft is announced (it appears in the *WSJ* the next day). Based on the foregoing evidence that the information in the exposure draft is conveyed to the market in the second week, we report Collins, Rozeff, and Dhaliwal's two-week abnormal rate of return (calculated using the market model) results.[7]

[7] Collins, Rozeff, and Dhaliwal also use a two-factor model incorporating an industry index in addition to the market index to calculate abnormal returns. The results using the abnormal returns from that two-factor model are essentially the same as using the abnormal returns from the market model.

The cross-sectional regression estimated by Collins, Rozeff, and Dhaliwal is

$$e_i = c_0 + c_1\text{CONTRCS}_i + c_2\text{STCKEQ}_i + c_3\text{DEBT}_i + c_4\text{PUBD}_i$$

Predicted sign $(-)$ $(+)$ $(-)$ $(-)$

$$+ \; c_5\text{SIZE}_i + c_6\text{EXPLOR}_i + u_i \qquad (12.2)$$

       $(+)$ $(-)$

where

e_i = abnormal rate of return for firm i for the two-week period ending July 22, 1977

CONTRCS_i = zero/one dummy variable for the presence of a debt contract and/or a compensation plan based on accounting numbers, variable a

STCKEQ_i = the effect of FASB 19 on the firm's total stockholder equity as reported in the 1977 annual report, variable b(i)

DEBT_i = debt/equity ratio—ratio of the book value of long-term debt and preferred stock to the market value of equity, variable b(ii)

PUBD_i = zero/one dummy variable for the presence of public debt in the firm's capital structure, variable b(v)

SIZE_i = market value of equity plus the book value of long-term debt and preferred stock, variable d

EXPLOR_i = exploration expenditures as a percentage of total revenues as measured by the average of total expected expenditures to total revenues over the period 1974 to 1977

The coefficients' predicted signs are listed below the coefficients. Those predictions are taken from Table 12.1.

Collins, Rozeff, and Dhaliwal's results provide some support for the theory. As in many of these cross-sectional regressions, there is considerable correlation among the independent variables. As a consequence, they estimate equation (12.2) deleting various variables. The results are basically the same under the different specifications. Only three coefficients attain significance, and those coefficients consistently have the same sign and remain more or less significant across all specifications in which their variables are included. The signs of the two that are contracting variables are consistent with the hypotheses listed in Table 12.1. In the full model (equation (12.2)), the coefficient of STCKEQ has the predicted positive sign and is significant at the .01 level (one-tail test), and the coefficient of CONTRCS has the correct negative sign and is significant at the .02 level (one-tail test).

The coefficient of the size variable is consistently negative and is significant at between the .10 and .20 level (two-tail test). This negative sign is inconsistent with the political cost effect of the reductions in earnings and stockholder equity.

The other variables (exploration, public debt, and debt/equity) are insignificant in all specifications of equation (12.2). The debt/equity variable frequently has the incorrect sign (i.e., firms with larger debt/equity ratios have smaller price declines).[8]

The full model (equation (12.2)) has an adjusted R^2 of 23 percent and is significant at the .01 level. This indicates that taken together the variables are able to explain the stock price changes that occurred on the announcement of the Exposure Draft of FASB 19 better than chance.

CONCLUSIONS

Overall, the results of Collins, Rozeff, and Dhaliwal, like those of Leftwich, provide some support for the proposition that changes in accounting standards affect share values via the contracting process. However, the insignificance of the debt/equity ratio and the public debt dummy variables raises questions about the theory and indicates that, at the least, it is not well specified at present. There is some theoretical support for the independent variables included in the cross-sectional models; there is little support for the equation's specified functional form. The next study discussed (Lys, 1984) highlights the problems with the cross-sectional regressions by suggesting that the previous studies have omitted an important variable, the variance of the firms' cash flows.

Lys

Lys (1984) reexamines the stock price effect of the elimination of the full-cost method. While Collins, Rozeff, and Dhaliwal investigate the cross-sectional price effects only at the time of the announcement of the Exposure Draft of FASB 19 (July 19, 1977), Lys identifies three other events that may have caused revisions in the market's expectations about the probabilities of the contents of the final full-cost/successful-efforts methods standard. Those events are (1) the issuance of SEC Release 33-5861 (dated August 31, 1977), which endorsed the FASB Exposure Draft; (2) the issuance of FASB 19 (ratified December 5,

---

[8] Collins, Rozeff, and Dhaliwal estimate equation (12.2) replacing the effect on total stockholders' equity with the effect of FASB 19 on earnings per share. The coefficient of the earnings per share effect is insignificant at any reasonable level. Collins, Rozeff, and Dhaliwal interpret that result as being inconsistent with the mechanistic hypothesis (see Chapter 4) and as suggesting that the contracting hypothesis is applicable. They consider the change in total shareholders' equity to be more important in debt contracts.

1977), which was essentially the same as the exposure draft; and (3) the SEC's issuance of ASR 253 (reported in the *WSJ* on August 30, 1978), which overruled FASB 19. Lys investigates the stock price effects of the Exposure Draft, FASB 19, and ASR 253. He could not identify the date of announcement of SEC Release 33-5861 (it was not reported in the *WSJ*).

Lys employs a two-step procedure like that used by Leftwich (1981). He investigates the abnormal rates of return for a portfolio of full-cost firms, a portfolio of successful-efforts firms, and a portfolio of long positions in successful-efforts firms and short positions in full-cost firms on days surrounding each of the three events of interest. The returns on this last portfolio measure the return differences for full-cost and successful-efforts firms. Then Lys employs a cross-sectional model to explain stock price effects.

The portfolio of full-cost firms earns significant abnormal rates of return (at the .10 level) only on two days: July 19, 1977 and July 20, 1977 (the report of the exposure draft appeared in the *WSJ* on July 20, 1977). But the abnormal rates of return of full-cost and successful-efforts firms differ only on July 19, 1977.

PROXY VARIABLES USED

The arguments that the default probability varies with the firm's debt/equity ratio assume ceteris paribus. Lys points out that these conditions are unlikely to hold. In particular, firms with lower variances of cash flows have higher debt/equity ratios. Further, the higher the cash flow variance, the closer firms are likely to be to their constraints because the debt is more risky and actions such as payment of dividends transfer more wealth from bondholders to shareholders. These two observations imply that the debt/equity ratio is a poor proxy for the tightness of debt constraints. Lys suggests that this is the reason Collins, Rozeff, and Dhaliwal do not obtain significant coefficients for the debt/equity ratio. He attempts to resolve the problem by including in his cross-sectional regression an estimate of the variance of the firm's cash flows (variable b(iii) in Table 12.1) in addition to the debt/equity ratio (variable b(ii)).

Other variables used by Lys include the debt's term to maturity (variable b(vii)) and the proportion of public debt to private debt (variable b(v)). Instead of using the inventory of payable funds as an explanatory variable (variable b(iv)), Lys uses the standard's effect on the inventory of payable funds. He also uses the standard's effect on the firm's proximity to the statutory dividend-paying restrictions. Another variable used is the proportion of revenues derived from oil and gas operations. This proportion is intended to proxy for the impact of the standard on the firm's accounting data (variable b(i)). Finally, Lys includes a debt refinancing cost variable that is estimated as the difference between the debt's market and nominal values (variable b(vi)).

RESULTS

Lys uses a sample of 89 full-cost firms (64 industrial firms and 25 utilities) and 40 successful-efforts firms. As indicated, the only significant abnormal returns for the 89 full-cost firms and the only significant difference between full-cost and successful-efforts firms' returns occur on the issuance of the Exposure Draft. Nevertheless, using 34 industrial full-cost firms that have the necessary data, Lys estimates the regression using abnormal returns on days around all three events' announcements (the Exposure Draft, FASB 19, and ASR 253).

Only one cross-sectional regression achieves significance at the .10 level and that is the regression for the only day on which the returns of the full-cost and successful-efforts firms differ (July 19, 1977). This coordination between the event study and cross-sectional regression results is consistent with the similar coordination in Leftwich's results. Given the theory, it suggests the market revised the likelihood of FASB 19's adoption on that day and that the cross-sectional price effects are related to debt contract wealth transfers.

The F statistic for the full regression rejects (at the .05 level) the null hypothesis of no relation between the debt variables and the abnormal rate of return on July 19, 1977. The model explains 52 percent of the cross-sectional abnormal return variations. However, only two of the nine coefficients are significant at the .05 level, the coefficients of the daily returns standard deviation and the debt/equity ratio. Both have their expected negative signs and remain significant as other variables are dropped from the estimation. This result is consistent with Lys's contention that the omission of the standard deviation of returns (which is assumed correlated with leverage) induces the insignificance of the debt/equity ratio in the Collins, Rozeff, and Dhaliwal study.

The other coefficients are insignificant at the .10 level in the full estimation, but as the variables with the least explanatory power are dropped, the coefficient of the proportion of oil and gas revenues to total revenues becomes significant at the .05 level with the predicted sign. This suggests that the relative revenue variable is serving as a proxy for the effect of the standard on the full-cost firm's accounting numbers.

Like Leftwich, Lys estimates his cross-sectional model on days outside the event period. He calculates abnormal rates of return for the portfolio of 34 firms on 531 days. For each of the 46 days on which portfolio returns are significant at the .10 level, Lys estimates equation (12.3). In contrast to the regression for July 19, 1977, these regressions' average F statistics are not significant at any reasonable probability level, indicating that Lys's results are not a statistical artifact.

CONCLUSIONS

Lys's results, like those of the other two mandated change studies, produce evidence of a stock price effect and of a cross-sectional relation between that stock price effect and two debt variables (the debt/equity ratio and the cash flow variance). However, most variables are not significant.

Table 12.2 presents a summary of the results of the mandated change studies. One problem, apparent in that table, is that there are few common variables used across all three studies. In fact, most variables are used in only one study. Of the two variables used in all three studies, the debt/equity ratio has the most significant results. Leftwich's results for the public and private debt/equity ratios suggests the debt/equity ratio would be significant and have the predicted sign if it were the only debt/equity ratio used in his model. The debt/equity ratio has the correct sign and is significant in Lys's model at the .01 level. It is insignificant in Collins, Rozeff, and Dhaliwal (1981). The significance of debt/equity variables in the mandated change's stock price effect studies is reminiscent of the significance of the debt/equity ratio in the accounting choice studies reported in Chapter 11. It suggests that wealth transfers under debt contracts are important in both accounting choice and standards' stock price effects.

The inconsistent results for given variables across different studies could be due to the failure to use the same combination of variables across the various studies or problems with the proxy measures, misspecified equations, and multicollinearity. They could also be due to other econometric problems in the studies. For example, Salatka (1983) notes that all the studies test hypotheses using OLS regressions of abnormal stock returns on various proxy variables for contracting and political costs. If the variances of these abnormal returns (the dependent variables) differ, then it is more difficult to reject the null hypothesis that the model's coefficients are zero. Weighted least squares (or generalized least squares) is one way to increase the power of the cross-sectional tests.

Collins and Dent (1984), Schipper and Thompson (1983), and Hughes and Ricks (1984) investigate the potential problems caused by cross-sectional heteroscedasticity and contemporaneous cross-correlations of abnormal returns. The mandated change studies' dependent variable is abnormal returns, and all the firms' abnormal returns are for the same calendar day(s). Since stock prices of firms in the same industry move together, their abnormal returns are correlated cross sectionally. Schipper and Thompson (1983) and Hughes and Ricks (1984) use an econometric technique called *seemingly unrelated regressions* to increase the power of the cross-sectional regressions by explicitly controlling for the abnormal returns' dependence. Applications of such techniques to tests of cross-sectional variation in mandated changes' stock price effects might increase the tests' power and provide more evidence on whether the mandated change's stock price effects are due to wealth transfers via debt contracts.

A STUDY OF VOLUNTARY CHANGES FROM ACCELERATED TO STRAIGHT-LINE DEPRECIATION (HOLTHAUSEN)

We have the advantage of hindsight when we argue in Chapters 9 and 10 that it is difficult to design powerful tests of *voluntary* accounting changes' stock price effects. Holthausen's study (1981) provided us with reasons to investigate the power of voluntary change tests.

Holthausen investigates stock price changes associated with the announcement that a firm is switching back to straight-line depreciation for reporting purposes. As noted in Chapter 4, many firms adopted accelerated depreciation methods for both tax and reporting purposes, following the 1954 change in the tax code that allowed accelerated depreciation. In the 1960s and 1970s, many of these firms switched back to the straight-line method for reporting but continued using accelerated methods for income taxes.

Proxy Variables Used

Like the mandated change studies Holthausen relies on debt/wealth transfer variables to explain many switchback stock price effects. He uses variables for the earnings effect of the change (variable b(i) in Tables 12.1 and 12.2), debt/equity (variable b(ii)), the proportion of public to private debt (variable b(v)), the existence of an earnings-based compensation plan (variable c), and size (variable d).

Fifty-four percent of Holthausen's sample of firms switching back announced the switchback simultaneously with an earnings announcement. To control for the effect of the earnings announcement, Holthausen includes "unexpected earnings" as an explanatory variable for the stock price change at the time of announcement of the switchback. "Unexpected earnings" are calculated as the difference between actual

TABLE 12.2

Summary of Results of Cross-Sectional Studies of Stock Price Changes Accompanying Mandated Accounting Changes

	APB 16 and 17	FASB 19	
		Mandated Changes	
Variables	*Leftwich (1981) Pooled Regression*	*Collins, Rozeff, and Dhaliwal (1981) Full Model*	*Lys (1984) Full Model*
a. Optimal contracting costs Zero/one dummy for existence of debt contract and/or compensation plan	Not tested	Significant at .02 level	Not tested
b. Wealth transfers via debt contracts i. Effect on earnings, retained earnings and equity	Not tested	Equity effect significant at .01 level, retained earnings effect not significant	Oil and gas revenues/total revenues significant at .10 level.
ii. Debt/equity ratio	Private debt/equity ratio significant at .01 level. Public debt/equity ratio significant at .12 level.	Not significant	Significant at .01 level
iii. Cash flow variance	Not tested	Not tested	Significant at .01 level
iv. Inventory of payable funds	Not significant	Not tested	Not significant
v. Proportion of public to private debt	No significant difference between private debt/equity	Zero/one dummy for presence of public debt not significant	Not significant

transfer, or political cost variables. The only result is the expected relation between unexpected earnings and abnormal returns.

SUMMARY

The theory outlined in Chapters 8–10 suggests that mandated changes in accounting procedures affect stock prices through their effects on optimal contracting technology, on wealth transfers involving debt contracts and compensation plans, and on political costs. Researchers have investigated mandated changes' stock price effects and their cross-sectional variation. They have used mostly variables representing the wealth transfers under debt contracts to explain cross-sectional stock price variations.

The studies have found significant stock price changes associated with the announcement of mandated changes (accounting standards). However, while the studies have produced significant associations between the cross-sectional variation in stock price effects and some debt variables (notably the debt/equity ratio), the associations are inconsistent across studies. Those inconsistencies could be the result of serious econometric problems that plague the studies. Substantive improvements in the models' specification and the econometric methods employed are necessary to produce powerful tests of the theory. An alternative explanation is the stock price effect's cross-sectional variation is not systematic or is too small to observe.

In Chapters 9 and 10, we argued that market expectations make it unlikely that voluntary change announcements have stock price effects. The results of Holthausen (1981) are consistent with that argument.

CHAPTER THIRTEEN

The Theory's Application to Auditing

The roles of accounting and auditing are closely related in the theory outlined in the preceding chapters. The demand for accounting arises from its use in contracts that reduce the firm's agency costs. However, those contracts are of little use in reducing agency costs unless their provisions are monitored and enforced. Auditing is one of the ways in which the contracts are monitored. The auditor checks that the numbers used in contractual provisions have been calculated using accepted procedures and whether the contractual provisions have been breached (see Chapter 9).[1]

As noted in Chapter 8, auditing and accounting have been companions in the history of the corporate firm for over 600 years. That companionship can be explained by contracting theory.

If contracting theory can explain the existence of auditing and accounting and contributes to the explanation of accounting procedure

---

[1] The auditor checks the calculation of the accounting numbers because the manager whose actions are restricted by the contract is responsible for their preparation. The arrangement survived presumably because it was the most cost effective (see Jensen and Meckling, 1976). At lower levels in the firm, the manager whose performance is evaluated by accounting numbers is not responsible for their calculation. This separation of managerial responsibility from performance measurement at the lower levels of the firm reduces the demand for both internal and external auditing of these levels.

choice (see Chapter 11), it should help to explain auditing practice. Accounting researchers have applied the theory to auditing and have developed intuitive explanations for auditing practice. For example, explanations have been developed for the emphasis on auditor independence and for the existence of professional societies and large audit firms. In addition, researchers have used the theory to predict which firms hire professional auditors when such an audit is not required by law.

In this chapter we review the applications of contracting theory to auditing. The explanations are discussed first, followed by the analysis of a study predicting audits. The explanations are intuitively appealing, and the empirical study has some success in predicting audits.

The political process also has a role to play in explaining modern auditing practice just as it plays a role in explaining modern accounting practice. Regulation affects the audit's nature. It modifies auditing's contract monitoring role and, as a consequence, may reduce the contracting demand for audits. However, regulation provides auditors with additional roles, roles that increase their clients' market values (e.g., an interpreter of the effect of disclosure rules). It also provides auditors with the opportunity to transfer wealth from their clients (e.g., via "make-work" rules). The political process's implications for auditing are also examined and the empirical studies testing the political process's implications for auditor behavior are reviewed. The chapter concludes with a summary.

CONTRACTING EXPLANATIONS
FOR AUDITING PRACTICE

In this section we use contracting theory to derive explanations for audit firms' preoccupation with their reputations, for professional auditor societies, and for audit firms' organizational form, size, and industry specialization. Since the concepts of auditor competence and independence are central to the explanations, we begin with them.

Auditor Competence
and Independence

The auditor's monitoring is not valuable to the parties (or potential parties) to the firm unless those parties consider the probability that he or she will report a contract breach, should one occur, is nonzero. For example, a given auditor's name on the prospectus will not lead to higher prices for a new share issue unless the stock market expects the auditor to reduce agency costs. That requires the market to believe that contract breaches will be reported. The very existence of a demand for the auditor's service depends on assessment of a nonzero probability of reporting a breach. The amount a firm will pay for the auditor's services depends on that probability's level. The higher the probability, the more effective the contracts, the lower the agency costs, and the higher the new issue price.

The probability an auditor reports a breach, conditional on a breach occurring, depends on

1. The probability that the auditor *discovers* a given breach
2. The probability that the auditor *reports* the discovered breach (see Watts and Zimmerman, 1982)

The first probability (discovery) depends on the auditor's **competence** and the quantity of inputs devoted to the audit. The second probability (reporting) refers to the auditor's **independence** from the client. If the client pressures the auditor to *not* disclose a discovered breach, will the auditor withstand the client's pressure?

To create a demand for audit services, auditors have to convince the market that they have some competence (i.e., there is a nonzero probability the auditor will discover a breach) and that they will have some independence from the client (i.e., there is a nonzero probability that the auditor will report a discovered breach). The market will only be convinced of the latter if auditors stand to lose something by never reporting breaches. If auditors have nothing to lose by succumbing to managerial pressures not to report a breach and if managers can impose costs on them, auditors will succumb.

Managers can impose costs on auditors if the auditors do not give in to their pressure. DeAngelo (1981a, 1981b) suggests one way managers impose costs is by changing auditors. This change denies the existing auditor a stream of **quasi-rents**. She suggests that these quasi-rents arise through the practice of **low-balling**.

To understand the nature of quasi-rents and low-balling, consider a simple example. Assume that there are substantial start-up costs on first-time audits. The initial costs could be due to many factors, including costs of initial asset verification and familiarization with the clients' operations. Let the auditor's costs for the initial year of an audit be $150 and for each subsequent year be $100. This cost pattern affects the auditor's fees on subsequent audits. In particular, the auditor charges a fee in excess of the $100 audit costs. If the client changes auditors, the new auditor incurs the higher initial audit cost ($150), some of which will be passed through to the client in a higher fee (now or later). Suppose that the auditor can charge the client $102 for subsequent audits without triggering an auditor change. The $2 difference (\$102 − \$100) between fees and costs represents the future quasi-rent that the auditor is able to capture because the \$50 start-up costs have already been incurred. Notice, this \$2 difference is specific to this client.

Given competition in the auditor market, the future quasi-rent (\$2) is bid away at the time of the initial audit. For example, assume that the present value of the expected quasi-rent stream is \$10.[2] When bidding for the initial audit, a potential auditor's minimum bid for the first year is \$140 (\$150 − \$10). Competition among auditors ensures that at the initial bid no auditor earns a return in excess of total costs. However, subsequent to the initial audit contracting, the incumbent auditor has a cost advantage (having already incurred the start-up costs) that allows the auditor to earn client-specific quasi-rents. But remember, the incumbent auditor "bought" these quasi-rents by bidding a fee *below* the first-year audit costs (\$140 fee versus \$150 cost). Hence this *lowballing* on the initial bid does not enable the auditor to earn an above-market rate of return.

By changing auditors, a manager can impose costs on the incumbent auditor. The auditor loses the client-specific quasi-rents' present value (\$10 in the foregoing example). The manager can threaten to impose such costs if the auditor reports a discovered breach (is independent). Unless the market believes that the auditor will bear costs if he yields to such pressures, it will expect the auditor to yield on every occasion and will not value the services being rendered. And firms will not demand the auditor's services.

Since voluntary corporate auditing has survived for over 600 years (see Chapter 8), institutions and contractual arrangements must exist that provide the auditor with incentives to be independent, to resist the manager's pressures.[3] Those institutions and arrangements include the auditor's reputation, professional societies, the audit firm's organizational form, and large-scale audit firms. Further, the institutions and contractual arrangements have evolved over time as the capital market's structure has changed.

Auditor's Reputation

Reputation gives auditors incentives to be independent (Benston, 1975b). It is costly to establish a track record and reputation for discovering and reporting contract breaches, but once established,

---

[2] The present value is based on an unbiased expectation as to the auditor's length of tenure in the position. As such, it incorporates an expectation of the manager's changing auditors if the auditor reports a contract breach.

[3] Note that we do not expect auditors to be totally independent (i.e., report discovered breaches with probability 1). The auditor trades off the cost of reporting and not reporting a discovered breach, and there is no reason to believe that an extreme policy is adopted.

reputation increases the demand for the auditor's services and fees (since the market attaches a higher probability to reporting a breach). If found to have been less independent than expected, the auditor's reputation is damaged and the present value of the auditor's services is reduced. He bears costs. Thus, the auditor's reputation (a valuable asset) serves as a collateral bond for independence. The auditor's reputation appears to have served this role from the early merchant guild audits until the present day (see Watts and Zimmerman, 1983).

The effect of reputation on the auditor's business causes them to guard their reputation carefully. An example of the auditor's preoccupation with reputation comes from the early days of U.S. professional auditing. In the late nineteenth century, Price, Waterhouse and Company (already prominent in England) sent two (nonpartner) representatives (Jones and Caesar) to establish offices in the United States. However, it did not allow Jones and Caesar to use the firm's name explicitly for fear of damage to Price, Waterhouse's reputation (De-Mond, 1951).

Professional Societies

In large capital markets, it can be very costly for an individual auditor to establish a reputation for independence and competence. An alternative mechanism for reducing the costs of providing investors with information about an auditor's independence and competence is a professional auditors' society that accredits auditors. Such societies (e.g., the Institute of Chartered Accountants in England and Wales) appeared in England in the second half of the nineteenth century, at the time of the replacement of the shareholders' audit committee by professional audit firms (see Stacey, 1954; Watts and Zimmerman, 1983).

The professional societies developed brand names. They gave their members designations (e.g., "Chartered Accountant") that were meant to denote a minimum level of audit competence and independence. To maintain their brand name, the societies encouraged competence by requiring exams and a period of training with a member ("articles") before admission to the society. And they maintained ethics committees that withdrew the accreditation of auditors whose revealed performance was below the society's standards. Membership in the society served as a collateral bond, just like the auditor's reputation. Loss of membership led to loss of audit fees.

Audit Firm's Organizational Form

Professional audit firms evolved as unlimited partnerships. This organizational form makes at least two contributions to the auditor's incentives to be competent and independent and, therefore, increases the market's assessment of the auditor's competence and independence (see Fama and Jensen, 1983b). One contribution is via unlimited liability. If auditors incorporate with limited liability, they reduce the amount of assets available as a bond on their actions. The market will appropriately reduce its assessed probability of their independence. Ceteris paribus, unlimited partnerships provide a greater bond on the auditors' independence.

The other contribution is mutual monitoring by the partners. Because each partner is liable for the other partners' actions, each has incentives to monitor each other's actions. This mutual monitoring increases competence and reduces the probability of a given auditor's yielding to a manager's pressure.

It is interesting that before the development of the professional audit firm the audit was conducted by a *committee* of shareholders. The committee form makes it more difficult for the manager to bribe the auditor, particularly with mutual monitoring by the committee members.

Audit Firm Size

Economies of scale in establishing a brand name is one explanation for the formation of auditors' professional societies in England in the second half of the nineteenth century when the capital market multiplied many times in size. Another is that the societies were formed to accredit accountants who acted as trustees in bankruptcy (see Watts and Zimmerman, 1983). Given the fixed costs of establishing a society and a brand name had been borne for bankruptcy work, the marginal cost of accrediting auditors was relatively small. Perhaps because accountants did not perform bankruptcy work in the United States, the formation of professional societies and the growth of the auditing profession lagged that in England.

Brand-name economies of scale can also encourage the formation of large audit firms. And large audit firms have a couple of advantages over the professional society in providing an audit brand name. One is the size of the bond of the large firm and the other is mutual monitoring.

A large audit firm provides a much larger bond for its audit services than does a single auditor accredited by a professional society. The bond consists of not merely the assets of the partnership and the individual partners' assets but also all the partners' human capital (Fama and Jensen, 1983b). The value of that human capital is sensitive to the auditor's reputation, and the auditor's reputation is tied to the partnership reputation.

The size of the large firm's bond means the large firm is more likely than the single accredited auditor to resist a given manager's pressure to not report breaches (i.e., is more likely to be independent; see DeAngelo, 1981b). The large firm has many clients. The value of quasi-rents lost if a given client does change auditors is more likely to be less than the impact of the failure to report a breach on the firm's brand name and its audit fees.

Mutual monitoring is reinforced by the closer ties between partners' reputations and the greater potential liabilities of the large-scale firm. Each partner is liable for the firm's debts, and his or her human capital varies with the partnership's reputation. Hence, each partner has a large incentive to monitor the other partners' performance and to establish mechanisms for such monitoring. In professional societies, the members performing the monitoring lose if a member fails to live up to the market's expectation about his performance. The society's brand name is damaged. However, the society's other members' reputations and human capital are not as closely tied to the miscreant's behavior as the miscreant's partners'. And the other society members are not liable for the miscreant's actions; his partners are liable.

The importance of bonding via audit firm partnership can be illustrated using the Price, Waterhouse example given earlier. Jones and Caesar were not partners although they were chartered accountants. Their reputations were not as closely tied to Price, Waterhouse's as a partner's and so they were less likely to maintain Price, Waterhouse's reputation. In addition, distance made mutual monitoring by partners difficult.

Industry Specialization

Initial audit start-up costs and economies of scale in information can explain the observed audit firm specialization by industry (see Dopuch and Simunic, 1980a). For example, Arthur Andersen has a greater relative proportion of gas utilities among its clients than do other firms. Eichenseher and Danos (1981), who also find significant industry specialization in auditing, argue that start-up costs are increased by regulation.

The preceding explanations for auditing practices are merely some of the explanations that can be generated from contracting theory. The theory can provide a wider set of explanations for auditing. For example, it should be able to explain why *particular* audit firms concentrate in particular industries and the particular audit procedures employed. However, while these explanations are intuitive, their predictions are not formally tested. Academic acceptance of the theory will depend on formal predictions and tests such as those in the next section.

A STUDY USING CONTRACTING
TO PREDICT AUDITS (CHOW)

The studies summarized in Chapter 11 use contracting and political cost variables to predict and explain the firm's choice of accounting procedures. Chow (1982) uses contracting variables to predict and explain the firm's choice in 1926 between being audited and not being audited by a professional auditor. At that time such audits were not required by law.

Variables Used to Explain Decisions

Chow hypothesizes that external auditing is associated with

1. Firm size (market value of equity + book value of debt)
2. Capital structure (book value of debt/firm size)
3. The number of debt covenants written in terms of accounting numbers

Chow argues that firm size proxies for at least two effects. (1) Managers of larger firms typically own a smaller fraction of the firm's shares and therefore have a greater incentive to transfer wealth from shareholders (i.e., larger firms are expected to have greater demand for audits). (2) If there are significant fixed costs of providing audits (e.g., if start-up costs are less than proportional to firm size), then the audit costs per dollar of sales audited declines in firm size. Therefore, larger firms are more likely to be audited than smaller firms, ceteris paribus.

Chow also argues that firms with higher debt/equity ratios are more likely to be audited. The incentives to transfer bondholder wealth increase with leverage, as do agency costs and the shareholders' incentives to offer contracts (and other monitoring devices including auditing) to reduce these conflicts. Another variable, similar to leverage, is the number of debt covenants written in terms of accounting numbers. Chow counted the number of accounting-based debt covenants for each company as described in the *Poor's Manual*. Firms that were audited had on average 1.5 such covenants, whereas unaudited firms had .9 covenants per firm.

Results

Using data from the 1926 *Poor's Industrial Manual*, Chow selects a sample of 165 firms (100 NYSE firms and 65 OTC firms). OTC firms are included to check if exchange listing affected the frequency of auditing.

Table 13.1 reports the results of Chow's tests. LOGIT regressions estimate a model of the probability the firm has an external audit. The

TABLE 13.1

LOGIT Regressions of Existence of an External Audit on Contracting Variables

Coefficients and Their t-statistics

	Constant	Size ($\times 10^{10}$)	Debt to Equity	Number of Covenants	NYSE Dummy	R^2	χ^2 (significance)
Predicted Sign		+	+	+	+		
Sample							
Entire sample	−.78	7.60	1.52	.40	1.45	.23	29.86
(N = 165)	(−2.34)	(.37)	(1.18)	(2.35)**	(3.81)***		(.005)
NYSE	.25	11.24	2.25	.85		.21	14.26
(N = 100)	(.68)	(.45)	(1.12)	(2.61)**			(.005)
OTC	.05	6.97	3.31	.10		.17	8.91
(N = 65)	(.12)	(1.97)**	(1.50)*	(.43)			(.07)

* Significant at .1, one-tail test.
** Significant at .05, one-tail test.
*** Significant at .01, one-tail test.
Source: C. W. Chow, "The Demand for External Auditing: Size Debt and Ownership Influences," Accounting Review 57 (April 1982), Table 5.

model is estimated for the whole sample and for the NYSE and OTC samples separately. The results are generally consistent with the hypotheses. All the independent variables have the predicted signs. Size is significant only in the OTC sample. In each model, either debt to equity or number of covenants is significant, but these two variables are correlated. This multicollinearity increases the standard errors of the coefficients, thereby reducing their individual significance levels.[4] It also makes discrimination between the effects of the two variables difficult (see Christie, Kennelley, King, and Schaefer, 1984). However, since the two variables represent the same factor (the existence of accounting-based debt contracts) and one of them is significant in every model, the evidence is consistent with the proposition that debt contracts are associated with the existence of a professional outside audit.

These results are generally consistent with contracting theory. They suggest that contracting theory has the potential to predict auditing practice. However, Chow's study is subject to some problems. It ignores the availability and cost of monitoring methods other than auditing. Future studies should consider including variables representing alternative monitoring methods' costs and auditing costs.[5]

POLITICAL PROCESS'S EFFECT ON AUDITING

The political process impinges on, and affects, auditing. Some effects occur through regulation (e.g., the securities acts, state licensing of certified public accountants, and SEC rules). Others occur through

[4] Chow attempts to control for multicollinearity by regressing the number of covenants on the debt/equity ratio and using the residuals from this regression in the LOGIT models. As Christie, Kennelley, King, and Schaefer (1984) discuss, this procedure does not reduce multicollinearity and is equivalent to including both collinear variables in the model.

[5] Single equation regression models (like Chow's and those of Leftwich, Watts, and Zimmerman, 1981) do not represent a simultaneous equations model. The decision to employ an external auditor depends on both supply and demand conditions. Econometrically, such problems should be modeled by considering individual structural equations for demand and supply. These two equations are then estimated jointly. Estimating a single equation can produce incorrect inferences.

Extensions of Chow's tests should consider the problems likely to arise from estimating an incorrectly specified single equation model. One reason the model is not well specified is because there are correlated omitted variables and because the model is not identified. For example, monitoring devices other than auditing may be important (security analysts, outside directors on the board, underwriters, etc.). Data on some of these variables should be included in subsequent extensions. Also, some of these monitoring devices are likely collinear with firm size, which might explain Chow's lack of significance for firm sizes on the NYSE. Other omitted variables for the marginal cost of auditing a given client can be constructed. For example, audits of similar firms in the industry should reduce the costs of auditing other firms in the industry (Eichenseher and Danos, 1981).

threatened regulation. Congressional committees threaten actions against the auditing profession unless audit firms take certain actions (e.g., the Metcalf Report, U.S. Congress, Senate, 1976).

Regulation and threatened regulation affect the nature of the audit. They cause the auditor to perform additional work in the audit itself and may reduce the amount of contract monitoring involved in the audit. Regulation also provides auditors with the opportunity to offer new services to their clients, services that increase both the clients' and auditors' value. Finally, regulation gives auditors the chance to use the political process to transfer wealth to themselves and gives others the opportunity to transfer wealth from the auditors.

Effect on Audit

The 1933 and 1934 securities acts are "disclosure" acts. Their rationale is that corporate disclosure prevents the capital market from "overvaluing" securities as it supposedly did prior to the 1929 stock market crash. The 1933 act requires firms be audited by "independent or certified public accountants." The auditor's intended role is to monitor the manager's disclosure of information that is to be used by investors in their investment decision making (Wiesen, 1978, Ch. 1, pp. 5–19). The imposition of legal liability by the acts increases the auditor's incentive to fulfill that role.

The auditor's role in the securities acts is broader than the contract monitoring role. The contract monitoring role requires the auditor to determine if contracts have been breached. This involves deciding issues such as whether dividends have been paid out of profits. Questions as to the definition of terms such as "profits" depend on what was written and what was intended in the contract (Pixley, 1881, pp. 33–96). Under the securities acts, the auditor's role depends on the investor's decision-making process. Numbers other than those used in contracts can be considered relevant (e.g., replacement costs). This expands the scope of the audit and changes its emphasis.

The securities acts gave the SEC control over accounting procedures used to calculate the numbers in listed firms' financial reports. Given the argument in the acts' rationale that comparable financial statements are required for investors' decisions, the SEC had an incentive to require uniformity in accounting procedures. The SEC pressured the AICPA to form a body to issue accounting standards for that purpose (see Zeff, 1972). That pressure resulted in the establishment of the CAP, which was replaced in time by the APB and FASB (see Chapter 7).

Accounting standards restrict the set of available accounting procedures and cause firms to adopt more costly contracting technology (see Chapter 10). The standards reduce the effectiveness of accounting-based contracts in reducing agency costs and reduce firms' demand for such contracts. This, in turn, reduces the demand for auditing as a contract monitoring device. Hence, while regulation is broadening the nature of the audit and increasing the demand for auditing to meet legal requirements, it decreases the contracting demand for auditing.

Additional Services

The SEC's regulation of disclosure and the formal standard-setting process that has grown up under the SEC's auspices (the CAP, APB, and FASB) provide opportunities for the auditor to offer services in addition to auditing. As we have seen in Chapters 10 and 12, accounting standards can impose costs on the auditors' clients. Audit firms provide their clients with information on new accounting standards in newsletters and on the costs imposed by the new standards in consultations with their technical divisions. Another service the auditor provides in response to disclosure regulation is lobbying. Audit firms lobby for clients in hearings on proposed accounting standards.

Rate regulation also provides the auditor with the opportunity to provide information and lobbying services. Auditors lobby on behalf of clients on accounting issues in rate hearings.

Lobbying and regulation information services are valuable to the auditor's clients even though the clients may not be explicitly charged for them. Potential clients probably consider these services when choosing an auditor and audit fees reflect the services. The services increase both the auditor's and the clients' wealth.

The existence of lobbying services reinforces the auditors' contracting induced industry specialization. The auditor will lobby for a given procedure to be used in an accounting standard and will attract a clientele of firms that prefer that procedure. Since firms in the same industry tend to be affected similarly by accounting standards (accepted accounting procedures vary by industry), industry specialization results. If there are systematic differences in accounting within an industry, one would expect auditors to specialize in clients that use one particular set of procedures.

Wealth Transfers

Lobbying and information services increase client and auditor values. However, the political process also gives auditors incentives to take actions that increase their value at the expense of the clients' value.

Auditors have incentives to lobby with the SEC and FASB for more complicated accounting. Such increased complexity could increase the quantity of auditing and the demand for the auditor's services.

Note, however, that auditors will not necessarily support all standards that increase accounting complexity. The more complex accounting system may be much less useful in monitoring contracts (e.g., replacement costs as the primary accounting system). If the consequent drop in demand for auditor's monitoring services exceeds the increase in demand due to the greater complexity, auditors would oppose the more complex system.

State licensing of auditors is another way in which auditors could use regulation to achieve a wealth transfer for their clients. Licensing has the potential to restrict entry into the audit profession and increase existing auditors' wealth. Finally, some argue (e.g., U.S. Congress, 1976) that SEC regulations and other factors provide the **Big Eight** audit firms (Arthur Andersen; Coopers & Lybrand; Ernst and Whinney; Deloitte, Haskins and Sells; Peat, Marwick and Mitchell; Price, Waterhouse; Touche Ross; and Arthur Young) with an effective monopoly or cartel over audit services for listed corporations.

EMPIRICAL STUDIES OF REGULATION'S AUDITING IMPLICATIONS

In this section we review three types of empirical studies that test hypotheses about regulation's effect on auditing. DeAngelo (1982) represents the first type of study. That study investigates the implications of the auditor's regulation-expanded role and liability for auditor changes and turnover. The second type of study is a lobbying study (Watts and Zimmerman, 1981) that investigates the relation between auditors' lobbying positions on accounting standards and their clients' positions. Auditors are expected to reflect their clients' positions because of the lobbying services they offer. However, auditors will not be in complete agreement with their clients because of regulation's effect on the attractiveness of auditing vis-à-vis other monitoring methods and on wealth transfer opportunities. The third study type attempts to determine whether Big Eight audit firms earn monopoly profits.

A Study of Auditor Turnover (DeAngelo)

DeAngelo (1982) hypothesizes that firms most negatively affected by an accounting standard are more likely to change auditors than are less severely affected firms. The reason is that changing auditors lowers the costs of changing to accounting procedures that mitigate the standard's effects.

In Chapter 11, we argued that managers choose their accounting procedure portfolio to produce a desired time series of reported earnings. If a standard eliminates one of the portfolio's procedures, the manager is likely to want to change other accounting procedures to achieve an earnings series as close as possible to the desired series. In making these procedure changes, the manager is likely to conflict with the firm's auditor. The incumbent auditor certified the previous accounting procedures and is now asked to certify the new procedures. This increases the incumbent auditor's liability under the regulatory rationale that there is an optimal procedure for investors' decision purposes. A new auditor is more likely to certify the clients' new accounting procedures because he is not open to the charge that the new accounting procedures cannot "present fairly" the client's financial position if the old procedure also "presented fairly" the client's position. For these reasons, DeAngelo predicts that auditor turnover is higher surrounding an accounting standard change and that turnover depends on the severity of the change's contracting effects.

SAMPLE AND DATA

DeAngelo investigates the auditor change rates of oil and gas firms around the time of adoption of FASB Statement No. 19. This standard eliminated the full-cost method of accounting and required all firms to write off the costs of dry wells (successful-efforts method). The sample consists of 246 petroleum firms partitioned into three portfolios:

129 Full-cost firms
 80 Successful-efforts control firms
 37 Successful-efforts firms affected by FASB 19

FASB 19 also restricted how successful efforts is applied. Thirty-seven successful-efforts firms in the sample reported a 10 percent or more decline in either earnings or retained earnings due to the accounting standard change. These firms are combined with the 129 full-cost firms to form a sample for which auditor turnover is expected.

DeAngelo argues that clients have incentives to switch auditors before a disagreement occurs that has to be disclosed. Hence, clients switch when the adoption of FASB 19 becomes likely. DeAngelo argues that adoption of FASB 19 became likely in 1976 and 1977. The initial exposure draft of FASB 19 was issued in July 1977, followed by the final standard in December 1977. Thus, DeAngelo predicts an increase in auditor turnover in 1976 and 1977.

RESULTS

Table 13.2 reports the test results. The affected oil and gas firms' auditor turnover rates are compared with the unaffected petroleum firms' turnover rates and with all SEC reporting firms' rates in each

TABLE 13.2

Frequency of Auditor Changes During 1973–1980 by Client Accounting Method

Year	Oil and Gas Firms Percentage of Firms Changing				All SEC Reporting (excluding oil firms)	
	Full-Cost Firms (1)	Successful-Efforts Affected Firms (2)	Subtotal Affected Firms (3)	Successful-Efforts Control Firms (4)	No. of Changes (5)	Percent Changes (6)
1973	1%	0%	1%	3%	534	5.33%
1974	4	3	4	1	621	6.37
1975	5	5	5	3	453	4.75
1976	6	5	6	4	399	4.24
1977	8	22	11	3	411	4.56
1978	2	3	2	3	373	4.13
1979	1	3	1	3	304	3.17
1980	5	0	4	3	300	3.12

Source: L. DeAngelo, "Mandated Successful Efforts and Auditor Choice," *Journal of Accounting and Economics* 4 (December 1982), Tables 2 and 3.

year. The third column in Table 13.2 reports that the affected firms have the highest auditor turnover in 1976 and 1977, 6 percent and 11 percent, respectively. The year when FASB 19 is adopted, 1977, shows the greatest auditor turnover among the affected portfolio. Also, these turnover frequencies are higher than unaffected oil firms and non-oil firms. Unaffected petroleum firms ("successful-efforts control firms") show no increased turnover in 1976 and 1977 (column 4) nor do non-oil or gas firms reporting to the SEC (columns 5 and 6). These differential turnover rates are statistically significant at better than the .05 level, and so DeAngelo's tests are consistent with her hypothesis.

AN ALTERNATIVE HYPOTHESIS—LOBBYING CLIENTELE EFFECTS

Watts and Zimmerman (1981b) advance another auditor change hypothesis that could explain DeAngelo's results. The hypothesis is that firms that take a different lobbying position to their auditors on a standard are likely to change to a new auditor whose position agrees with theirs (i.e., auditors generate a clientele of clients who agree with their lobbying positions). The increase in auditor changes around FASB 19 could be driven by such changes. Note, though, that this hypothesis is not mutually exclusive to DeAngelo's. Both could be descriptive.

DeAngelo tests the clientele hypothesis and tries to discriminate between that hypothesis and her own. To test the Watts and Zimmerman hypothesis, she categorizes all oil firms according to whether they "agreed" or "disagreed" with their auditors. If a client is unaffected by FASB 19 and the auditor supports FASB 19 (i.e., supports successful efforts), the client is placed in the "agree" category. Likewise, if the client is negatively affected by FASB 19 and the auditor opposes FASB 19 (i.e., supports full cost), the client is again placed in the "agree" category. Other combinations are classified as "disagree." A contingency table is constructed, and it is found that only 7.9 percent of petroleum firms whose auditors "agree" with them switch auditors during 1976–1977. However, 19.2 percent of the clients switch auditors when they "disagree." These proportions are statistically significantly different at the .01 level.

To discriminate between her "portfolio adjustment" hypothesis and the "clientele" hypothesis, DeAngelo tests an implication of the "clientele" hypothesis. If the auditor's failure to lobby in accord with the client firm's position (the disagreement) causes the change, the client firm should switch to an auditor who will represent the firm's position.

DeAngelo tests whether clients switch to auditors taking similar positions. Her tests indicate that there is no discernible trend toward auditors who agree with the switching client or are successful-efforts specialists (a majority of their clients used successful-efforts accounting). Nor is there a trend toward any particular audit firm. Hence, the evidence is inconsistent with the clientele hypothesis.

AN ALTERNATIVE HYPOTHESIS—STRUCTURAL CHANGE

As recognized by DeAngelo, one limitation of the study is the switches' timing. Most occur in 1977, the year FASB 19 is adopted (see Table 13.2). DeAngelo argues that 1976 changes occur because clients, anticipating FASB 19, start to undo 19's effects before an auditor conflict arises. But 1974 and 1975 also show a rising number of changes among the full-cost firms. It is unlikely that these firms are changing auditors in anticipation of FASB 19, which was adopted in 1977. (Oil and gas accounting was placed on the FASB's agenda in October 1975).

The rising trend in auditor switches among the affected firms from 1974 to 1977 is consistent with some other structural change also occurring among these firms. A number of oil companies switch to successful-efforts accounting in 1974. This is a period of rapidly changing relative prices for energy, changes in the tax code (depletion allowances), and of regulation. These types of exogenous changes likely affect the firms' optimal size, optimal amount of debt, and optimal contract type.

The firms most affected by FASB 19 are substantially smaller than those unaffected (see DeAngelo, 1982, Table 5). The affected firms' median gross revenues increase about 3.3-fold between 1973 and 1977. The successful-efforts control firms' revenues increase 2.7-fold over the same period. But the market value of the equity of the affected firms doubles, whereas that of the unaffected (successful-efforts) firms increases only 10 percent between 1973 and 1977. However, DeAngelo finds these growth rates are insignificantly different (DeAngelo, 1982, fn. 39).

DeAngelo's results could be due to structural changes in oil and gas firms. Nevertheless, their consistency with her portfolio adjustment hypothesis suggests a potential for a combination of contracting and political theory to explain auditor changes. In combination with Chow's results, they underline the approach's promise for predicting and explaining auditing practice.

A Study of Auditor Lobbying (Watts and Zimmerman)

Watts and Zimmerman (1981b) investigate the combined implications of contracting theory and the political process for auditors' lobbying on proposed accounting standards. They expect the auditors' position on a proposed standard to be positively related to their clients' manager's positions. One reason is that auditors provide such lobbying services to their clients (see the previous section). Another reason is that their audit fees depend on their clients' market value and that provides them with an incentive to argue for standards that increase their clients' market value.

However, the auditors' position will not be determined by their clients' positions alone. The auditors' interests differ from those of their clients. For example, the auditor has an incentive to support, and the clients' managers have incentives to oppose, standards that make work for the auditor. Taking the commonalities and diversities into account, Watts and Zimmerman derive an expected relation between auditors' positions and those of their clients. Their evidence is generally consistent with that relation.

An earlier study (Haring, 1979) on the basis of suggestions that an auditor is controlled by his clients (i.e., is not independent) tested the hypothesis that the auditor's position on a proposed standard is associated with the majority of his clients' positions. The study found no significant relation between auditor and client positions. However, the simple relation tested by Haring does not incorporate the auditor/client relation complexities implied by the combination of contracting theory and the political process.

Watts and Zimmerman (1981b) derive and test a more complex relation between an audit firm's position on an accounting standard and its clients' managers' positions than Haring (1979). They model the audit firm as a single person and assume that both the auditor and the client-manager choose their positions according to the standard's effect on their wealth. If the standard increases wealth, the auditor or client-manager is in favor of it, and if it decreases their wealth, they oppose it.[6]

The client-manager's position is a function of the standard's effect on the firm's value and on the client-manager's bonus. Ceteris paribus standards are supported that increase the firm's value and standards are opposed that decrease it. However, the manager's incentives are not completely in line with the shareholders'. Ceteris paribus managers support standards that increase reported earnings because they may increase executive compensation.

The auditor's position is a function of the standard's effect on his clients' values (because of the audit fees' effect) and two other factors.

---

[6] Watts and Zimmerman assume that the auditors and managers do not "game." For example, they do not support a standard that would decrease their wealth in return for other individuals' support of another standard that would increase their wealth even more. Such a simple assumption is appropriate for an early investigation of the issue. To the event that it is incorrect, the predictive ability of Watts and Zimmerman's model is likely to be reduced. See Amershi, Demski, and Wolfson (1982) for a discussion of gaming in standard lobbying.

One is the standard's effect on the set of available accounting procedures and the other is the standard's potential to transfer wealth to the auditor by making work for him.

Standards that restrict the set of available accounting procedures reduce the attractiveness of the combination of accounting-based contracts and auditing as an agency cost-reducing method. As a consequence, parties to the firm are more likely to use agency cost-reducing methods that do not involve accounting and auditing. This imposes more costs on the auditor than on the manager, and so the auditor is more likely to oppose standards that restrict available accounting procedures.

If a standard increases accounting complexity, it tends to increase audit fees. Simunic (1980) finds that audit fees are higher, the more complex the accounts. Hence, the auditor is more likely than the manager to support standards that increase accounting complexity.

Given the preceding determinants of auditors' and managers' positions, Watts and Zimmerman derive a model in which the auditors' positions on a standard are a positive function of a weighted sum of their clients' managers' positions (because both auditors' and managers' positions depend on the standard's effect on client firm value). In the model, the auditor's position differs from that function to the extent that the standard (1) increases the earnings number used in compensation plans, (2) restricts the set of accounting procedures available for calculating numbers used in debt contracts and compensation plans, and (3) increases accounting complexity.

Because they have a limited number of observations on auditor positions, Watts and Zimmerman estimate the model over a number of accounting standards. All of those accounting standards increase accounting complexity, and none of them increase earnings on average. Hence, apart from the weighted sum of client-manager's positions, the only independent variable that varies across standards is the standard's effect on available accounting procedures. And the model that is estimated across standards incorporates only those two variables:

$$\text{APOS}_{i,s} = c_0 + c_1 (\text{VFAV}_{i,s} - \text{VOPP}_{i,s}) + c_2 \text{TV}_{i,s} + c_3 \text{BDUM}_s \text{TV}_{i,s}$$

Predicted sign (?) (+)   (?)   (−)

$$+ c_4 \text{MBDUM}_s \text{TV}_{i,s} + u_{i,s}$$
$$(-)$$

$$(13.1)$$

where

$\text{APOS}_{i,s}$ = 1 if auditor i favors standard s and
  0 if auditor i opposes standard s
$\text{VFAV}_{i,s}$ = the sum of the values of auditor i's clients whose managers favor standard s

$\text{VOPP}_{i,s}$ = the sum of the values of auditor i's clients whose managers oppose standard s

$\text{TV}_{i,s}$ = the total value of auditor i's clients who lobby on standard s, $\text{TV}_{i,s} = \text{VFAV}_{i,s} + \text{VOPP}_{i,s}$

BDUM_s = 1 if standard s only restricts accounting procedures used in bond covenants and 0 otherwise

MBDUM_s = 1 if standard s restricts accounting procedures used in both bond covenants and management compensation plans and 0 otherwise

The term $(\text{VFAV}_{i,s} - \text{VOPP}_{i,s})$ is the weighted sum of client-manager positions. Its coefficient (c_1) is expected to be positive, because both the manager's and the auditor's position depend on the standard's effect on firm value. The coefficient of total client value (c_2) represents the auditor wealth effect of a standard that doesn't affect numbers used in debt contracts and compensation plans (in this study, a proposed general price-level adjustment standard), and its sign is indeterminate.[7]

BDUM_s is a dummy variable for standards that restrict procedures used to calculate accounting numbers used in debt contracts, but don't affect accounting numbers used in compensation plans (in this study a proposed interim reporting standard). Its coefficient (c_3) is expected to be negative, because such standards make accounting-based debt contracts and auditing less attractive agency cost-reducing devices. As a consequence, the auditor is more likely than the manager to oppose the standard. MBDUM_s is a dummy variable for standards that restrict accounting procedures used to calculate numbers used in *both* debt contracts and compensation plans. Because they have an even greater effect on the demand for auditing for contracting purposes, the auditor is even more likely to oppose these standards than those represented by BDUM_s. Hence, the MBDUM's coefficient (c_4) is expected to be more negative than BDUM's coefficient (c_3).

SAMPLE AND RESULTS

Watts and Zimmerman estimate equation (13.1) on auditor and manager positions on five proposed standards. The standards' topics and the boards proposing them are

1. 1962 investment tax credit (APB)
2. 1971 investment tax credit (APB)
3. Leases (FASB)

---

[7] The effect has two components with opposite signs. One is negative because the standard imposes costs on the client, and the other is positive because it increases complexity and makes work for the auditor.

4. Interim reporting (APB)

5. General price-level adjustments (FASB)

All written submissions to the FASB and APB on those proposed standards were read and classified by position taken. Corporate submissions were further classified by the client's auditor. Auditors usually did not make written submissions to the APB. However, each of the Big Eight firms had a voting member on the APB, and the audit firm's position was inferred from their representative's vote. This process resulted in 41 auditor positions and 645 client positions.

The first three proposed standards restrict procedures used to calculate numbers used in both debt contracts and compensation plans, and so MBDUM takes the value one for positions on those standards. The interim reporting standard does not affect annual earnings and so does not affect earnings numbers used in compensation plans. It does affect debt contracts since numbers in quarterly reports have to meet debt covenant restrictions. Hence, BDUM takes the value one for positions on the proposed interim reporting standard. GPLA does not affect any numbers used in debt contracts or compensation plans.

The estimated equation for the five standards' positions is (with asymptotic t-statistics shown in parentheses)[8]

$$\text{APOS}_{i,s} = .42 + 21.0(\text{VFAV}_{i,s} - \text{VOPP}_{i,s}) + 26.8\text{TV}_{i,s} - 39.5\text{BDUM}_s\text{TV}_{i,s}$$
$$\quad\ (1.33)\ \ (1.69) \qquad\qquad\qquad\quad (1.34) \qquad\ \ (1.80)$$

$$\quad - 29.4\text{MBDUM}_s\text{TV}_{i,s}$$
$$\qquad\ \ (1.53)$$

$$\chi^2 = 15.1$$ (13.2)

No. of observations = 41

All three predicted coefficients (c_1, c_3, and c_4) have the correct signs and are statistically significant at the .10 level or better (one-tail test). The χ^2 statistic indicates that the model is significant at the .01 level. The significant positive coefficient of ($\text{VFAV}_{i,s} - \text{VOPP}_{i,s}$) indicates that the auditor's position is positively associated with the weighted positions of his clients' managers. The significant negative coefficients on the two variables representing contracting effects indicates that the auditor is more likely to oppose a standard if it affects the clients' contracts and, hence, the derived demand for audits. However, the coefficient of the variable representing debt contract effects only is more negative than the coefficient of the variable representing both

---

[8] Various measures of client value were used, including total assets, sales, and both logarithms and square roots of these variables. All these measures produced very similar results and only the model estimated using total assets is reported. The dependent variable in equation (13.1) is dichotomous. For this reason, Probit was used. OLS and LOGIT produced similar results.

debt contracts and compensation plan effects, contrary to prediction. Despite this last inconsistency, in general the results in equation (13.2) are consistent with the simple model Watts and Zimmerman advance to explain auditors' and client-managers' positions on accounting standards.

MANAGERS' POSITIONS

Watts and Zimmerman use their model to generate and test predictions about managers' positions on the five accounting standards used to estimate equation (13.1) and another proposed standard that increases reported earnings (the FASB's proposal for interest capitalization). Manager's positions depend on the proposed standard's effect on the firm's value and on earnings used in compensation plans. Ceteris paribus, managers are more likely to oppose standards that restrict accounting procedures used in contracts (increasing agency costs) and reduce reported earnings than standards that do not restrict accounting procedures used in contracts and/or do not reduce reported earnings.

The proposed lease and the investment tax credit accounting standards restrict the accounting procedures contracting parties can choose for both debt and compensation contracts and so increase agency costs. In addition, these three standards tend to reduce earnings and therefore managerial compensation unless compensation committees make adjustments for the standards.[9] Hence, managerial opposition is expected to be heavy on these three standards. Managerial opposition should be less on GPLA, interim reporting, and interest capitalization. GPLA does not directly affect the primary financial statements whose numbers are used in debt contracts and compensation plans. Interim reporting affects debt contracts but not compensation plans. And while interest capitalization affects both types of contracts, it increases earnings. Hence to the extent that compensation plans are based on earnings after interest and the compensation committee does not adjust for the change, the manager's compensation is increased.

Watts and Zimmerman report the results of a test of the proposition that there is greater managerial opposition to the lease and investment tax credit proposals. Consistent with the predictions, a much greater proportion of client-managers oppose the investment tax credit and lease proposals than oppose interim reporting, GPLA, and interest capitalization. Ninety-one percent of the managers opposed the investment credit and lease proposals compared with the 51 percent who oppose interims, GPLA, and interest capitalization. The results are statistically significant at the .01 level.

---

[9] Almost all firms submitting on the lease standard were lessees.

EVALUATION

The empirical results of the estimation of the predicted relation between auditors' and managers' positions (equation (13.2)) and of predictions that managers are more likely to oppose the proposed standards on the investment tax credit and leasing are generally consistent with the simple model advanced by Watts and Zimmerman. To the extent that the model reflects the contracting and political process effects, these results (like those of Chow and DeAngelo) suggest that the theory outlined in the preceding chapters has some potential to explain auditing practice. However, much more research has to be conducted before we can have confidence in the results.

There are at least three problems in the study that require further attention. First, the tests are based on very small samples (five or six accounting issues), and observations within issues and across issues (especially the two investment tax credit proposals) are not independent. Therefore, the significance levels of the tests are overstated. The study should be expanded to include more issues. Second, estimating equation (13.1) requires the assumption that each proposed standard has the same wealth effect on client-managers. This assumption is likely violated and should be investigated. Third, the tests do not control for differences among client-managers' compensation plans and these differences should be investigated.

A Study of Auditor Competition (Simunic)

Simunic (1980) investigates the charge that the Big Eight audit firms have an effective cartel or monopoly on audits of listed corporations (for an example of this contention, see U.S. Congress, 1976). He investigates whether the Big Eight are able to charge higher fees than their small rivals.[10] A questionnaire was mailed to a stratified sample of 1,207 companies asking for their audit fees and the salaries paid to internal auditors. Three hundred and fourteen usable observations resulted. The sample consists of Big Eight and non–Big Eight clients.

Simunic estimates a regression where the dependent variable is the sum of external and internal audit fees. Internal audit costs are included to control for possible substitution between internal and external auditing. That is, the extent of the Big Eight's monopoly power

---

[10] Other studies (e.g., Dopuch and Simunic, 1980a and 1980b) attempt to determine whether the Big Eight form an effective monopoly by investigating auditing market shares and changes in market shares. However, it is possible to have effective competition with few competitors and large market shares. And patterns of change in market shares are consistent with both monopoly and competition.

depends on the availability of close substitutes (e.g., internal auditing). Excluding internal audit costs from the dependent variables does not alter the results.

Separate models are fitted to small (sales less than $125 million) and large clients (over $125 million sales). Simunic argues that if the Big Eight are an effective cartel, it is only among large clients. The reasoning is that it is only among the large clients that the Big Eight dominate the market (Dopuch and Simunic, 1980a, Table 3.2). Therefore, assuming that the small clients' market is competitive, a test for a Big Eight monopoly is whether the estimated regression differs for the large and small clients.

Two independent dummy variables are used to test for whether the Big Eight is a cartel. These dummy variables take the value of 1 if the auditor is Price, Waterhouse and 1 if the auditor is one of the other Big Eight, respectively. Price, Waterhouse was treated separately after an initial data analysis indicated that its clients and fees are substantially different from those of the other Big Eight. If the Big Eight are a cartel in the large-client market but not in the small-client market, then the coefficients on these dummy variables should be positive and larger for the large-client sample than for the small-client sample.

Several other independent variables in the model are intended to capture cost differences and other omitted variables. The variables include the client's number of consolidated subsidiaries, ratio of foreign to total assets, ratio of receivables to total assets, and ratio of net income to total assets.

In Simunic's regressions, most of the control variables coefficients have the predicted signs in the full and large- and small-client samples and are statistically significant at the .05 level. The two coefficients used to test for a Big Eight monopoly are inconsistent with the cartel hypothesis. The audit fees of the Big Seven (excluding Price, Waterhouse) are not higher than those of other auditors. In fact they are slightly lower, but not by a statistically significant amount. Audit fees for Price, Waterhouse clients are statistically significantly higher than are those of other clients' auditors'. This result holds only among the large-client sample, not the small-client sample. Further analysis by Simunic reveals that Price, Waterhouse clients used more internal auditing. Based on this result, he concludes that Price, Waterhouse clients demand higher-quality control systems and so Price, Waterhouse's higher prices are not evidence of monopoly power.

Simunic also argues that Price, Waterhouse's positive and significant coefficient is not evidence of monopoly because the coefficient on the Big Seven is inconsistent with monopoly. However, these results call into question Simunic's test. If Price, Waterhouse is pooled with the other Big Seven, the combined dummy is probably positive, supporting the monopoly hypothesis. If Price, Waterhouse is separated and the test is that both coefficients must be positive, rejection of the monopoly hypothesis becomes more likely. In the limit, eight separate dummy variables for each of the Big Eight can be included. Then the test would be a joint test that all eight should be significant. In such a regression test of the Australian audit market, Francis (1984) rejects the monopoly hypothesis.

Overall, Simunic's results suggest there is competition in the auditing market. It is unlikely that Price, Waterhouse alone has monopoly power. Simunic's results have two other interesting implications. They suggest that auditors (at least Price, Waterhouse) specialize in audits of different quality as suggested by DeAngelo (1981b). Also, the significance of various cost variable coefficients such as the number of client subsidiaries is consistent with the idea that complexity in client accounts increases audit fees.

SUMMARY

Auditing and accounting are closely related in contracting theory. Effective use of accounting in contracts requires monitoring. The external professional audit is one monitoring method. If contracting theory can explain accounting, it should be able to provide some explanation of auditing. In addition, the political process affects auditing and should be useful in developing a theory of auditing.

Contracting has been used to develop intuitive explanations for the auditor's concern with his independence and reputation, for development of professional societies and large firms, and for the organizational form adopted by audit firms. Further, contracting variables have been used to predict which firms choose to hire a professional audit firm when outside professional audits are not required by law.

Regulation affects the nature of the audit. It expands the audit. The auditor is responsible, and legally liable, for information beyond that used in contracts. This can affect auditing's contracting role and reduce its efficiency as a monitoring device. However, regulation provides the auditor with the opportunity to perform additional services such as providing information on the effect of accounting standards and lobbying on accounting standards on clients' behalf. Regulation also provides the auditor with the opportunity to lobby for increasing accounting complexity because of its audit fee effect.

Empirical studies find that auditor changes, the relation between auditor positions and their client managers' positions on proposed accounting standards, and manager positions on proposed standards are associated with variables suggested by contracting theory and the political process theory. The studies producing those results make very simple assumptions, there are plausible alternative explanations for some of the results, and there have not yet been enough studies to know whether the results are as robust as those reported in Chapter 11. Nevertheless, in our opinion, these results, together with the audit prediction results, suggest that the combination of contracting theory and political process theory has the potential to explain both accounting and auditing practice.

Finally, a study of the determination of audit fees (Simunic, 1980) indicates the audit market is competitive. Regulation does not give monopoly power to the Big Eight.

CHAPTER FOURTEEN

The Role of Accounting Research

Throughout this book, we use science's concept of theory (positive theory).[1] Under that concept, the objective of accounting theory is to explain and predict accounting practice (broadly defined). However, as we note in Chapter 1, the accounting literature includes other views of theory. In many of those other views, the objective of theory appears to be the production of prescriptions for government accounting policy (i.e., for accounting standards and regulation of disclosure). Proponents of those views assume an objective function and, based on assumptions regarding how the world works (an implicit positive theory), deduce accounting prescriptions. The emphasis is on the prescription rather than on the positive theory underlying it. There is typically no attempt to test the underlying theory, and the theory is often contrary to accepted empirical hypotheses (e.g., the efficient markets hypothesis).

On the surface, this prescriptive literature is contradictory. If its proponents are serious about their prescriptions, they would be concerned about the predictive ability of their implicit positive theory. Unless the theory is predictive, the prescriptions are unlikely to achieve their objective. In Chapter 1 we explain the demand for positive

[1] A substantial proportion of this chapter is taken from Watts and Zimmerman (1979).

theories. Individuals demand positive theories to predict the consequences of their actions. That includes individuals in standard-setting bodies (such as the FASB and SEC). Those individuals want to predict the consequences of adopting particular standards or accounting policy prescriptions. So the apparent users of the prescriptive literature want a theory that explains and predicts. Why then do we observe a prescriptive accounting literature that emphasizes prescription and logic, but not the predictive ability of the underlying theory?

We think the answer is that there is a demand for accounting literature in addition to the demand for positive accounting theory. That additional demand arises in the political process described in Chapter 10 and is the demand for excuses.[2] Individuals want accounting policy prescriptions for self-interest reasons (e.g., electric utility managers want an accounting standard so they can argue for use of the required procedure in rate setting). But, in a political process that is a competition for wealth transfers and is characterized by costly information, it isn't optimal to announce publicly that you want the prescription for selfish reasons. The optimal strategy is to argue that the prescription is in the public interest (e.g., maximizes some social welfare concept). Hence, there is a demand for arguments that the desired accounting prescription is in the public interest.

The prescriptive literature's relative share of the academic accounting literature has varied over time. It increased substantially following the passage of the 1933 and 1934 securities acts and came to dominate the academic literature by the 1950s. Since the mid-1960s the prescriptive literature's share has declined, particularly in the leading academic journals (see Dyckman and Zeff, 1984, Tables 2 and 3). On the other hand, positive theory's share of the literature has grown since the mid-1960s. There has always been a demand for positive accounting theory for the reasons enumerated in Chapter 1. Hence we suggest the growth originates from the supply side, not the demand side. By the mid-1960s the cost of positive theory was substantially reduced.

Computers and large machine-readable data bases (CRSP and *Compustat*) became available in the 1960s. And, partially in response to the lowered cost of empirical work, finance and economic positive theories became available for accounting researchers' use. This led to the development of positive accounting research and to researchers trained in the methodology of positive theory.

We do not imply in the preceding discussion that accounting researchers who produce the prescriptive literature intentionally produce excuses or that positive accounting researchers are not influenced by the demand for excuses. As we shall see, the demand for excuses

---

[2] The demand for excuses applies to other academic areas. See Stigler (1976) for an application to economics.

influences accounting research in very subtle ways, and positive researchers are not immune.

This chapter investigates the role of accounting research. Accounting research is viewed as an economic good. Particular attention is given to explaining the influence of the demand for excuses. That explanation helps understand regulation's influence on the accounting literature. It also explains the FASB's role and the role of the accounting research that is produced as part of the standard setting process.

The demand for accounting research is analyzed first, followed by the analysis of supply. To illustrate the impact of regulation on the accounting literature, the history of selected parts of the accounting literature as responses to the demand for excuses is then interpreted. The final section presents a summary.

THE DEMAND FOR ACCOUNTING RESEARCH

This section analyzes the demand for accounting literature in an unregulated economy and the additional demands generated by government regulation.

The Demand for Accounting Research in an Unregulated Economy

Accounting research serves three overlapping functions in an unregulated economy.

INFORMATION DEMAND

This is the positive theory demand that is explained in Chapter 1. There is a demand by managers, auditors, lenders, investors, and financial analysts to understand and predict the effect of accounting choices on their welfare. For example, managers and other parties to the firm want to understand and predict the contracting effects of different accounting procedures on managers' incentives and hence on the firm's value. Also, the demand for a given auditor's services is a function of the auditor's efficiency in the contracting monitoring process. Hence, the auditor has incentives to understand how management's accounting procedure choice affects contracting costs.

PEDAGOGIC DEMAND

Accounting procedures are devised to reduce contracting costs. Since these costs vary across firms, accounting procedures will vary, giving rise to diversity of procedures and formats. However, diversity in accounting procedures increases the difficulty of teaching the practice of accounting. If there is a developed positive accounting theory teachers use it to structure the variation found in practice and thereby assist learning. In its absence, accounting teachers develop pedagogic devices (rules of thumb) to structure practice's variation. In response to this demand, researchers examine existing accounting systems and summarize their differences and similarities. These practice descriptions highlight the tendencies of firms with particular attributes to follow certain accounting procedures. Nineteenth-century accounting texts and articles indicate that accounting researchers at that time recognized the diversity of practice and attempted to distill general tendencies from the diversity.

JUSTIFICATION DEMAND

Early accounting texts recognize that managers argue against depreciation changes to increase "profits" and their own compensation, at the expense of shareholders and/or bondholders (Matheson, 1893, pp. vii and viii). Accounting texts and articles provide the auditor with ready-made arguments to use against the manager's arguments. To the extent that early texts or articles argued against depreciation charges, they also present the manager with ready-made arguments. Both the auditor and manager demand arguments that have the shareholders' welfare as the objective. In the manager's case, at least, that argument is an excuse, since the motivation is to increase the manager's compensation. The manager avoids self-interest arguments since the company's outside directors presumably are more interested in the shareholders' interest than the manager's.

The pedagogic and information demands are for positive theories of accounting—theories that predict and explain extant accounting and auditing practice. The justification demand, however, can include a demand for excuses. Because of information costs, managers are able to argue for an accounting procedure (e.g., no depreciation charge) on the basis of shareholders' welfare when they want the procedure for self-interest reasons.

The Demand for Accounting Research in a Regulated Economy

The previous analysis of the demand for accounting research is now extended to include the effects of government. As discussed in Chapter 10, private citizens, bureaucrats, and politicians are assumed to have incentives to employ the state's powers to make themselves better off and to coalesce among themselves for that purpose. One way coalitions of individuals are made better off is by wealth redistributive legislation.

The rules and regulations resulting from government regulation of business increase the pedagogic and information demands for accounting research. Even beginning accounting textbooks report the income tax requirements of LIFO, depreciation, and so on. Detailed texts for practitioners explain SEC requirements, tax codes, and other government regulations. And there is a demand to explain and predict the nature of future regulations.

The justification demand for research also expands with regulation. The political process is an advocacy proceeding where proponents and opponents of special interest legislation and regulation give arguments for the positions they advocate. If these positions include changes in accounting procedures, accounting writings that serve as justification are useful. These advocacy positions, including accounting arguments, will be based on contentions that the political action is in the public interest, that everyone is made better off, that most are made better off and no one is harmed, or that the action is "fair" (i.e., they will be excuses). Such contentions generate less opposition than arguments based on one's self-interest. Often, those public interest arguments are based on the underlying positive theory that the unregulated market solution is inefficient. The typical argument is that the free market fails and this failure can only be remedied by government intervention (see Chapter 7).

Politicians and bureaucrats demand research not only to inform them of the trade-offs but also for use in justifying their actions to the press and their constituencies. Politicians' and bureaucrats' support is more likely when the prescription is based on public interest rationales instead of self-interest rationales. Consequently, special interests find such rationales useful and the politicians adopt them when they support or oppose legislation. Special interest groups have a demand for prescriptions that claim to maximize the "public interest."

"Public interest" justifications of accounting procedures are often observed in rate-setting hearings for public utilities. For example, Public Systems, an organization that represents municipalities and rural electrification agencies, applied for a hearing on the Federal Power Commission's (FPC) Order 530 that adopted an accounting procedure that generates higher rates. Public Systems did not argue that it is in its self-interest to oppose Order 530. Instead, it argued that the accounting procedure "represents an *inefficient* means of subsidizing the public utility industry" (U.S. Congress, Senate, 1976, p. 683).

The reported objective of the Securities Exchange Act of 1934 is that information disclosure by corporations is required by investors before they can make rational investment decisions. There is the presumption that required disclosure can increase investors' welfare at virtually zero cost (i.e., that there is a market failure).

Government regulation increases the demand for accounting prescriptions employing public interest arguments (for excuses)—that is, for writings demonstrating that certain accounting procedures *should* be used because they lead to better decisions by investors. Further, the demand is not for *one* prescription, but rather for diverse prescriptions. On any political issue such as utility rate determination, there will be at least two sides. In the FPC Order 530 example, Coopers & Lybrand, which opposed Public Systems, wanted an argument that prescribed the debated accounting procedure, whereas Public Systems wanted an argument that did not. Since accounting methods affect taxes, antitrust cases, union negotiations, disclosure regulations, and utility rate setting, there is a demand for a multitude of prescriptions.

The proposition that theories are useful excuses in the political process is consistent with positive information and coalition costs. Chapter 10 argues that it is time consuming for voters to become informed regarding how potential legislation or regulation will affect their welfare. It is also time consuming to form coalitions to lobby elected representatives. Unless voters enjoy spending their time in these pursuits, only those voters who expect the benefits to exceed the costs will become informed and lobby. Those voters who are harmed by the legislation find it rational not to lobby if the time they spend becoming informed and lobbying is worth more to them than the costs they expect to avoid if their lobbying activities are successful.

Accounting research and other justifications for legislation, if they in fact laid out who benefits and who is harmed in a clear fashion, that is, they used a self-interest justification, would lower the costs to the harmed group of becoming informed. With more harmed individuals informed of that fact, the legislation or regulation is less likely to be enacted. Hence, prescriptions professing a public interest rationale for the regulation raise the costs to the potential opponents of the legislation by forcing them to analyze the proposal. As with most economic activity, the more costly the production process, the less produced. Public interest prescriptions raise the oppositions' lobbying costs, thereby reducing the amount of lobbying they produce.

In this model of the political process, everyone is rational. No one is being "fooled" by accounting theories. If people do not investigate the validity of rationales, it is because they do not expect such investigation to be cost effective. If the expected benefits of investigation to an individual are small, only a limited investigation is made.

THE SUPPLY OF ACCOUNTING RESEARCH

As long as there exists a large number of individuals able to supply accounting research at relatively low cost, then supply will respond to demand. Economist George Stigler observes

> consumers generally determine what will be produced, and producers make profits by discovering more precisely what consumers want and producing it more cheaply. Some may entertain a tinge of doubt about this proposition, thanks to the energy and skill of Professor Galbraith, but even his large talents hardly raise a faint thought that I live in a house rather than a tent because of the comparative advertising outlays of the two industries. This Cambridge eccentricity aside, then, *it is useful to say that consumers direct production—and therefore, do they not direct the production of the words and ideas of intellectuals, rather than, as in the first view, vice-versa?* (emphasis added; Stigler, 1976, p. 347)

We suggest that a large number of individuals can supply policy prescriptions at a relatively low cost. The politically uninformed voter (see Chapter 10) has little incentive to discriminate between complex arguments. Hence, we expect to observe a supply response to an increase in demand for excuses. On the other hand, positive accounting research was costly until the mid-1960s, and so there wasn't much supply response to the demand for positive theory for pedagogic and information purposes.

Supply of Excuses

The demand for excuses arises in both the political and the market processes. However, we suggest that the political process's lower incentive to obtain information (see Chapter 10) leads to that process producing most of the demand for excuses. Consequently, we concentrate on the supply of excuses for use in the political process.

The consumers ("vested interests") determine the production of accounting research through their demand for accounting prescriptions. The greater the prestige and articulation skills of an accounting researcher, the more likely practitioners, regulators, and other academics will know the researcher's work and the greater the flow of both students and funds to his or her university. Practitioners, regulators, and those teaching future practitioners are more likely to know of a researcher's work if it bears on topics of current interest. Therein lies the connection to the demands of vested interests. Controversies arise in accounting when vested interests disagree over accounting standards. For example, the LIFO controversy arose in the 1930s when the Supreme Court outlawed the base stock method of valuing inventory for tax purposes and the American Petroleum Institute recommended

LIFO to replace it. The Internal Revenue Service resisted because of the effect on tax revenues. The parties demanded pro and con LIFO articles, which were eventually produced.

Accounting researchers often include policy recommendations as part of their research. Those recommendations, made on the basis of some objective assumed by the researcher, may never have been intended to serve as an "excuse" for the corporate manager, practitioner, or politician who prefers the recommended procedure for self-interest reasons. Nevertheless, the research findings will be favorably quoted by vested interests. The more readable the research, the more frequently it is quoted.

The tendency of vested interests to quote researchers who support their position produces a survival bias. Just as in any market, those who produce what is demanded have a better chance of survival than those who do not. The bias is introduced by the vested interests. This does not impugn the motives of accounting researchers who advocate particular practices. In fact, vested interests' positions are enhanced by researchers with integrity and consistent positions on accounting issues.

Given the rewards for supplying prescriptions on controversial issues, there is competition in the supply of accounting research related to those issues. The prescriptions for an issue are likely to be as diverse as the positions of vested interests. But despite this diversity, accounting researchers are not necessarily inconsistent across issues. Academic evaluation and criticism create incentives for each researcher to be consistent. However, the rationales given by different researchers for observed accounting standards may well be inconsistent across issues and different sections of the same accounting standard.

Rationales differ and are inconsistent across accounting standards because a standard is the result of political action. The outcome depends on the relative costs that the various involved parties are willing to incur to achieve their goals. And these costs vary with the expected benefits. The rationale given for a standard is the successful party's rationale, and if it is a compromise, such as APB Opinion 16 on business combinations, mixtures of rationales are used. The same party is not successful in every issue; indeed, many are not even involved in every issue. Further, vested interests (e.g., an insurance company) are not constrained to give consistent rationales across issues. Hence, a party is observed supporting historical cost valuation in some cases and market valuation in others.

Supply of Positive Theories

The demand for positive theories comes from the participants in both the market and political processes. Bureaucrats want to understand and predict the consequences of their actions just as the corporate manager does. The demand also comes from educators (the pedagogic demand). Business schools compete to produce effective managers and accountants. Hence, they have incentives to provide their graduates with an understanding of, and ability to predict, the consequences of their decisions (including their accounting decisions). Prediction and understanding of those consequences requires a positive theory. Hence, business schools demand positive research. When the costs of positive accounting research was reduced in the 1960s, positive accounting research was forthcoming.

The time series of positive accounting research is influenced by the demand for excuses as well as pedagogic demands. In particular, it is influenced by accounting regulatory controversies. The researcher in positive accounting theory faces incentives to write on controversial topics just like the researcher in the prescriptive literature. For example, consider the relatively large number of studies investigating the stock price effects of the FASB 19 exposure draft (see Chapter 12, fn. 6). Even if the research follows positive research tradition and does not make policy prescriptions, the research is useful to vested interests. It provides evidence on whether claimed effects do or do not exist. For example, at the SEC hearings on oil and gas accounting, full-cost firms claimed that FASB 19 would reduce their access to the capital markets and consequently reduce their stock prices. They cited an empirical study that found a stock price effect (Collins and Dent, 1979). The FASB claimed that their proposal would not have such detrimental effects and cited a study that found no stock price effect (Dyckman and Smith, 1979).

The acceptance of positive accounting research (the type of studies analyzed in this book) at the leading academic business schools and the leading academic journals forces its recognition in the political process. The prestige of the schools involved is recognized in the political process. Hence, the FASB and the SEC recognize the existence of concepts such as the efficients markets hypothesis when discussing regulation (e.g., Securities and Exchange Commission, 1977). However, that recognition has little effect on the political process's outcome. Vested interests can use criticisms of such concepts by academics at other institutions that are prestigious in the public's eyes. And the diversity of empirical results among studies and the information costs of identifying the quality studies enables competing interest groups to find studies with the desired results.

To illustrate the effect of government regulation on the accounting literature via the demand for excuses, we give our interpretations of the effect on the literature of three major pieces of legislation: the laws regulating railroads, the income tax laws, and the securities acts.

THREE EXAMPLES OF REGULATION'S EFFECT ON THE ACCOUNTING LITERATURE

Railroad Legislation

The growth of railroads had an important impact on the accounting literature. The development of railroads both in the United States and the United Kingdom affected the depreciation accounting literature, including the question of charging depreciation as an expense (Holmes, 1975, p. 18).

The railroad depreciation debates began around 1840 in the United Kingdom and 1850 in the United States. Although the debate did not result in depreciation being treated as an expense in either the United States or the United Kingdom, depreciation prescriptions were enunciated. Our theory of the accounting literature raises the question, Why did this depreciation debate arise with the railroads?

Prior to the railroads' emergence, corporations did not treat depreciation as an annual, systematic charge to earnings. Dividend covenants in loan agreements put a lower bound on the shareholders' equity participation. As long as sufficient earnings were retained in the past to cover the depreciation of fixed assets to the current time, there was no necessity to deduct depreciation systematically each year. Depreciation was not treated generally as an expense prior to this century. Instead, it was treated as an allocation of profits.

With the railroads came the first widespread government regulation of the prices railroads could charge and these rates came to be tied to profits. The early U.S. railroad charters contained provisions for the adjustment of their rates based on profits (Dodd, 1954, p. 260).

The private acts of Parliament incorporating the early U.K. railroads fixed the maximum rates explicitly, but, in one notable exception, the Liverpool and Manchester Railway Act in 1826 limited the company's dividends to 10 percent of the capital and required that its rates be reduced by 5 percent for each 1 percent of dividend above 10 percent.

The question of railroad profits and the public interest was raised in the political process in both the United States and the United Kingdom in the nineteenth century (Nash, 1947, p. 3). And along with these questions, the issue of whether depreciation should be charged as an expense was also raised. The accounting methods for capital additions, depreciation, repairs, and renewals affect reported profits and the rates and market values of railroads. Thus, there was a demand for rationalizations of alternative procedures.

This evidence suggests that railroad rate regulation created a demand for rationalizing depreciation as an expense. Furthermore, the more popular of these prescriptions should stress that it is in the "public interest" for depreciation to be treated as an expense. Without regulation, there is no reason for depreciation to be a charge, systematically deducted each year in determining net income. However, because rate regulation was justified in terms of restricting the economic profits of monopolists or eliminating "ruinous" competition, regulation created a demand for justifications arguing for depreciation to be treated as an annual charge to profits.

Income Tax Acts

The influence of the income tax laws on financial reporting practice is well known. That influence is obvious in the practice of charging depreciation to net income, rather than treating it as an allocation of profit (Saliers, 1939, pp. 17–18).

The tax laws also appear to have influenced the accounting literature, particularly with respect to depreciation. Concern with depreciation as an expense existed mainly in the *railroad* accounting literature until the 1880s. In that decade, numerous U.K. journal articles and textbooks were written on the question of depreciation for corporations in *general*. The same concern is not observed in the United States at that time. This raises the question of why the U.K. and not the U.S. interest with depreciation, not just for regulated firms but for all corporations.

A general concern with depreciation for all corporations (and not just railroads) appeared in the U.K. literature in the 1880s and not before because, prior to 1878, the U.K. tax laws made no allowance for depreciation. "In 1878 the law was modified to permit the deduction of a reasonable amount for the diminished value of machinery and plant resulting from wear and tear" (Saliers, 1939, p. 255). Now there was an additional reason for debating the concept of annual depreciation—taxes.

The income tax explanation for the late nineteenth-century depreciation debate also explains the absence of that debate in the United States. The first effective U.S. corporate income tax law was the Excise Tax Act of 1909 (which went into effect before it was declared unconstitutional). Thus, in 1880 there was no federal tax motivation driving a debate over depreciation. In the United States in 1880, the agency problem of monitoring contracts still existed that did not require an annual depreciation accrual.

The tax laws affected not only the timing of depreciation discussions, but also the resulting concepts of depreciation and of accounting income. In the legal cases where dividends could be paid only out of profits, depreciation was regarded as a valuation procedure. Whether the amount of depreciation taken was sufficient would be decided in the event of a dispute. Administering the tax laws is less costly if the periodic valuation is replaced by an arbitrary proportion of historical cost. This saving was recognized in the early literature and was the likely reason that both U.S. and U.K. income tax allowances for depreciation were based on historical cost. The demand for a rationalization of this procedure and other accruals under the tax law eventually resulted in the concept of income based on matching and the realization concept (Storey, 1959, p. 232).

Securities Acts

The 1933 and 1934 securities acts created the SEC with the authority to regulate the financial disclosure of publicly traded corporations and the right to prescribe the accounting procedures used by these regulated firms. The SEC has consistently chosen not to exercise these rights; instead it has relied on the private sector and a patchwork of official pronouncements, *SEC Accounting Series Releases,* to regulate accounting rules.

Between 1934 and 1938, the commission considered the question of how to standardize accounting practice. The commission was split between promulgating a set of accounting standards itself and letting the accounting profession set standards subject to veto by the commission. On April 25, 1938, the commission issued ASR 4, which stated that "financial statements . . . [which] are prepared in accordance with accounting principles for which there is *no substantial authoritative* support . . . will be presumed to be misleading." Although the commission did not, and has not, defined what constitutes substantial authoritative support, something more than conformity to current practice was meant (Zeff, 1972, pp. 133–134).

The commission could not rely solely on current practice since it was alleged to have contributed to the 1929 crash. Most of the commission realized the difficulty of prescribing and trying to enforce a codified set of accounting procedures. Presumably ASR 4's use of "substantial authoritative support" partially shifted the onus of faulty practice from the commission to the profession. If this is the case, the SEC was relieved of some of the cost of actually setting standards.

ASR 4 had an immediate impact on accounting research. The AICPA responded by establishing a research department and empowering a committee to issue pronouncements on accounting procedures (Zeff, 1972, p. 135).

Since 1938 the AICPA and now the FASB have been issuing accounting pronouncements aimed at providing "substantial authoritative support." But in addition, the AICPA and FASB have been searching for an underlying normative theory or conceptual framework to supply "authoritative support." Besides these professional bodies, academics have generated accounting prescriptions that provide "substantial authoritative support."

The majority of the research between 1940 and the mid-1960s is not directed at trying to explain why accounting is as it is, but rather at how it should be. That is, most research following 1940 is prescriptive as opposed to positive. The prescriptive writings are directed toward providing guidance to policymakers, the FASB and SEC, charged with setting accounting standards and with correcting defects in current practice.

SUMMARY

Positive theory is not the only view of theory in the accounting literature. Another popular view is that the objective of accounting theory is the provision of prescriptions for regulation of accounting and corporate disclosure. Papers in that prescriptive tradition assume an objective function and an implicit positive theory and logically deduce prescriptions. The prescriptive literature does not emphasize testing the implicit positive theories to establish their predictive ability.

The prescriptive literature increased its share of the accounting literature after the securities acts until it reached a predominant position in the top accounting journals in the mid-1960s. Since then, the positive accounting theory's share of space in top journals has increased and the prescriptive literature's share has decreased. The earlier predominance of the prescriptive literature and the shift to positive accounting theory is the product of two factors: the demand for excuses and the reduction in the cost of the positive research in the 1960s.

The accounting literature fulfills a pedagogic demand, an information demand, and an excuses demand. The first two demands are demands for a theory that explains and predicts accounting practice (a positive theory). The excuses demand is primarily from the political process and arises because of information costs. Given those costs, it is optimal for individuals to claim regulations are required for public interest reasons when in fact they are demanded for self-interest reasons.

Accounting researchers do not necessarily intend to supply excuses. The supply comes via a subtle incentive process. Researchers have incentives to write on controversial topics. If a researcher writes a prescriptive paper on the topic of a controversial proposed standard or regulation, it is likely to be used by one of the parties affected by the proposed standard or regulation. A positive accounting study on the effects of a proposed standard can also be useful to parties affected by the standard if it finds, or fails to find, an important effect of the standard. Hence, the excuses demand affects the type of research studies produced by the prescriptive literature *and* by the positive theory literature.

In the 1960s the availability of computers, large data bases, and economic and finance theory combined to reduce the cost of positive theory, and it came to prominence in the leading academic journals. That theory's tradition of not choosing objective functions and making prescriptions reduced the prescriptive content of the accounting literature.

CHAPTER FIFTEEN

Positive Accounting Theory: Summary, Evaluation, and Prospects

The first chapter states that a theory's success (as a theory, not as an excuse) depends on its value to users in *explaining* and *predicting* phenomena. This concluding chapter evaluates positive accounting theory's potential value. It begins by briefly summarizing the evolution of the theory and its major empirical findings. Then we evaluate the theory's potential value and its limitations. Finally, we present our opinions on a few of the more promising areas for future positive theory-based research.

SUMMARY

This book's purpose is not just to transmit the current state of research, but also to train students to conduct (as researchers) and evaluate (as managers) positive research. For the latter reason, the book is organized in roughly chronological order. That order elucidates the research process and emphasizes how research evolves from "crude" to more "sophisticated" studies. Early studies, by their nature, make methodological errors that are corrected in later studies. Also, early studies make simplifying assumptions that later studies are able to relax.

As the research process evolves, we discover which assumptions are critical. These are the ones that, when relaxed, open new research avenues thereby providing richer theories. For example, the early positive research assumes that accounting procedures (other than LIFO) have no cash flow effects. Relaxing this assumption required researchers to hypothesize and test possible cash flow effects. This led to the contracting and political cost hypotheses.

The chronological approach also provides an opportunity to discuss methodological issues. We discuss these methodological issues (e.g., inference, sample selection bias, significance testing, the power of a test, and endogeneity problems) in the context of older studies. The methodological problems in the older studies are better understood because we have the advantage of subsequent studies and hindsight.

Chapter 1 describes positive theory's nature, its role, and its methodology. The second chapter explains the efficient markets hypothesis and the capital asset pricing model, both of which led to the introduction of positive theory into the accounting literature. The next four chapters (Chapters 3–6) describe a line of positive accounting research that evolved from the introduction of the EMH and CAPM. That research takes the EMH as given and views accounting's role as the supply of information to the capital markets. Today, researchers still pursue that information supply research line.

The information supply research line provides several important findings. One is that earnings reports supply information to the capital markets (Chapter 3). Another is that other accounting numbers reflect CAPM variables (e.g., risk) and so can supply information on nontraded securities (Chapter 5). A third finding is that annual earnings are well described by a random walk and that quarterly earnings are described by a seasonal process. While security analysts can outpredict time series earnings models, their superiority is not marked (Chapter 6).

Attempts to use stock price reactions to accounting changes to discriminate between the EMH and the mechanistic hypothesis (Chapter 4), while unsuccessful, raised questions about the reasons for accounting procedure changes. Those studies raised the possibility that tax-neutral accounting procedures have cash flow effects. Applications of the EMH to traditional disclosure regulation rationales also led to the realization that tax-neutral accounting procedures can have cash flow effects via the political process (Chapter 7). The existence of cash flow effects makes possible an economics-based accounting theory that explains and predicts accounting practice variations across firms and industries. The development of such a theory is explained in the second half of this book.

The theory of accounting practice is based on and is an outgrowth of two economic-based theories: the theory of the firm (Chapter 8) and the theory of (government) regulation (Chapter 10). The economic theory of the firm conceptualizes the firm as a *nexus of contracts* that reduces the costs generated by the (self-interested) parties to the firm (agency costs). Formal and informal contracts require monitoring and enforcement, thereby giving rise to a demand for accounting and auditing. Two formal contracts are examined in detail: management compensation plans and debt contracts (Chapter 9). Both of these contracts use accounting numbers. Agency costs vary with the procedures used to calculate the accounting numbers, and so procedures have cash flow effects. An optimal (agency cost minimizing) set of accounting procedures accepted for contracting purposes evolves and varies across industries. Managers can select procedures from within that accepted set, and the manager's selection affects the value of the firm's securities because it changes the terms of debt contracts and compensation plans.

The economic theory of regulation conceptualizes the political process as a competition among self-interested individuals for wealth transfers. Accounting numbers, in particular, earnings, are used in the political process to justify corporate regulation and to regulate corporations. Accounting procedures affect the reported accounting numbers and so affect the ability of a corporation's opponents to impose costly regulation on it. In that way, accounting procedures affect the firm's cash flows.

Empirical studies investigating implications of the positive theory of accounting practice find three general regularities in accounting procedure choice (Chapter 11): (1) managers of firms with earnings-based compensation plans are more likely to choose procedures that increase current earnings (bonus hypothesis); (2) the larger a firm's debt/equity ratio the more likely the firm's manager is to select procedures that increase current earnings (debt/equity hypothesis); and (3) the larger the firm, the more likely the manager selects procedures that decrease current earnings (size hypothesis). These three empirical regularities could be due to factors other than those hypothesized. However, a more powerful test of compensation plans' procedure choice effects that employs bonus plan details (Healy, 1985) finds evidence consistent with the positive theory. Less consistent evidence is obtained from more detailed tests of debt contracts' and size's procedure choice effects.

Studies of the stock price effects of accounting changes find that mandated changes (accounting standards) are associated with stock price changes (Chapter 12). However, the various studies use different debt variables. And the debt variables' statistical significance varies from study to study. These variations could be the result of the collinearity and other econometric problems that typify these studies. A study of voluntary changes finds no stock price effects. With hindsight, this result is anticipated because the market should expect the accounting change.

The audit decision is associated with debt contracting variables (Chapter 13). In addition, there is a significant relation between an auditor's position on a proposed standard and his or her client-managers' positions and that relation varies with contracting variables. Finally, changes in auditors are associated with the client-managers' and auditors' positions on accounting standards.

Overall, we find the empirical results encouraging. The cross-sectional associations between procedure choice and management compensation, capital structure and firm size, and audit decisions and contracting variables were unknown prior to positive research. The value of these regularities and the theory in general, as well as the theory's limitations, are addressed next.

EVALUATION

The Theory's Value

Chapter 1 describes two dimensions of a theory's value: explaining the way the world works and the effect of the theory's predictions on the user's welfare. Ultimately the users, who assess alternative explanations' intuitive appeal and bear the costs and benefits of theories' predictions, will determine the success of the theory outlined in this book. This section gives our assessment of the theory's *potential* value.

EXPLANATION

We think the theory is strong in this dimension in both accounting and auditing. To most, accounting is a confusing mixture of methods. We think the theory has the potential to give order to the confusion. The lower of cost or market rule becomes more understandable when cast in light of the manager's debt contract and compensation plan incentives to increase current earnings. The variation in profit recognition rules makes economic sense. Choices between depreciation methods no longer appear arbitrary. In auditing, the importance of auditor independence becomes apparent, and explanations are available for professional accreditation, the development of the large audit firm, and the audit firm's organizational form.

The theory provides a framework for interpreting accounting and auditing that is useful to many individuals. For example, managers and auditors undoubtedly have an implicit understanding of parts of accounting and auditing phenomena, but we doubt if they have an overall picture. The theory provides a framework in which the trees can be seen as part of the forest.

PREDICTION

In its current state, the theory provides some predictions that should be useful to accounting users: investors and financial analysts, lenders, auditors, managers, and standard setters. But its potential in providing useful predictions is much greater, particularly if we are able to generate predictions about the set of accepted accounting procedures. The following discussion provides examples of useful existing, and potential future, predictions.

The theory provides investors and financial analysts with a useful predictive model of the accounting procedures underlying the financial statements. Using the theory, investors or analysts do not interpret balance sheet and earnings numbers as unbiased estimates of firm value and changes in firm value. Instead, they recognize the effect of the contracting and political processes on the calculation of earnings and balance sheet numbers. For example, the manager's incentives to choose earnings increasing/decreasing accounting methods depend on the existing compensation and debt contracts. With knowledge of these contracts, the analyst can adjust the reported numbers. In particular, if Healy's (1985) evidence regarding the effect of compensation plans on accounting accruals (see Chapter 11) is confirmed, an investor or analyst could adjust the earnings number for expected management manipulations in deriving cash flow estimates. This would help the investor or analyst better predict the market value of nontraded stocks or bonds.

The theory also suggests that investors and analysts could use accounting procedure variations to predict earnings. For example, a politically sensitive, profitable firm switching to an earnings-reducing accounting procedure in the absence of any management compensation or debt covenant reason suggests that management anticipates future earnings increases and further government scrutiny.

Lenders and managers will find the theory useful if researchers are able to predict and explain cross-sectional variations in accepted accounting procedures. That would help them to predict how debt contracts' agency costs vary with the use of different accounting procedures. This, in turn, enables lenders and managers to design contracts that reduce agency costs and make both better off.

Auditors can also use the theory's current predictive ability. For example, they can predict more accounting (and transaction) manipulation and increase the audit's intensity when reported earnings are close to a boundary specified in the compensation plan or in debt contracts. Managers' welfare will be increased if the theory is able to predict the effect of reported earnings and other accounting numbers on political costs. Such predictive ability will enable the manager to manage the earnings time series to reduce political costs. This will require a better knowledge of the extent to which political costs vary with size and other factors.

Officials at the FASB are aware that their standards impose costs on firms. The studies in Chapters 11 and 12 provide evidence on the nature of those costs and suggest that the theory will be able to predict the costs imposed by a proposed standard. Such a predictive ability would enable the FASB to predict reactions before exposing a proposed standard.

The Theory's Limitations

The major limitations at this stage in the development of a positive accounting theory appear to be

1. Developing proxy variables that actually represent contracting and political costs
2. Specifying the cross-sectional models
3. Collinearity among the contracting variables

These limitations were discussed in Chapters 11 and 12. The first two limitations result from the lack of a well-developed positive accounting theory (discussed shortly). Further limitations will become evident as the research evolves and methodological problems emerge. The same process that has illuminated the defects in the early positive research will expose the defects in the current work.

The lack of a well-developed positive accounting theory results from the lack of rich economic theories of the firm (including the contracting process) and of the political process. A richer contracting theory that explained variations in debt contracts and compensation plans across firms and industries would explain the use and nonuse of accounting-based covenants and variations in the accepted accounting procedures. A richer political process theory would enable researchers to use more refined political cost measures than size in studies explaining cross-sectional variations in accounting procedure choice or the stock price effects of accounting standards.

Richer theories of the firm and the political process also would enable better specification of the equations explaining accounting choice and standards' stock price effects. Managers choose a portfolio of accounting procedures based on the portfolio's effect on their utility via contracts and political costs. Very little is known about the functional form of accounting numbers' effects on contracting costs and political costs or the trade-off between those costs. Most of the studies in Chapter 11 specify variables as surrogates for those effects and arbitrarily specify a linear functional form. Similarly, an accounting standard affects a firm's stock price via its contracting and political cost effects. Surrogates are used for those effects and a linear functional form arbitrarily assumed. In both the choice and the stock price effect studies, the surrogates measure the costs with error and it isn't obvious that a linear specification is appropriate.

Even if the surrogate variables measure costs without error and the linear specification is correct, the independent variables in studies reported in Chapters 11, 12, and 13 are often collinear. This makes isolation of the effect of any particular variable difficult (see Christie, Kennelley, King, and Schaefer, 1984).

The development of positive accounting theory would be enhanced by the development of related economic theories. But accounting research need not wait for such developments. In the absence of better specified economic theories, accounting researchers should continue to develop proxy variables based on the firm's specific contracts. They should follow the example of Healy (1985) who increases the power of his tests by constructing variables based on the specific details of each firm's compensation plan.

Moreover, the development of a positive accounting theory will place accounting in the mainstream of economics and finance research. Accounting researchers will test hypotheses emerging in economics and finance and so provide a service to researchers in those areas. This suggests that there are important synergies among accounting, finance, and economics.

PROFITABLE AREAS FOR RESEARCH

Some think that accounting research approaches are like fashions; they come and go frequently and are dependent on whim. But this view of the process is superficial. The important ideas of an approach, the ideas that have relevance to explaining accounting, survive. This is reflected in the organization of this book as it moves from the early applications of financial economics to more recent applications.

The application of the EMH to accounting became fashionable and event studies on changes in accounting procedures flourished in the early 1970s. But, when it was realized that it is difficult to construct powerful tests of market efficiency using accounting procedure changes that are not expected to affect cash flows, such event studies became less popular. However, the use of the EMH and event study methodology did not disappear. Instead, researchers applied the EMH and the event study methodology approach to changes for which cash flow effects are predicted (i.e., LIFO switches). When contracting theory (Chapters 8 and 9) and political theory (Chapter 10) suggested accounting changes have cash flow effects, the event study methodology was again applied to accounting changes.

It is doubtful that the contracting and political explanations for accounting practice will be totally supplanted by alternative explanations. The usefulness of the contracting and political explanations suggests that they will survive. We expect profitable research to continue on those explanations.

Given the lack of economic contracting and political theories that can explain how contracting and political costs vary with accounting procedures, the most promising approach is for accounting researchers to investigate those variations themselves. Examples of the way in which such investigations could proceed are given next. Those examples are chosen on the results' usefulness as well as the likelihood of results.

Investigation of Contracting Costs

As described in Chapters 8, 9, 11, 12, and 13, the accounting procedures used in the firm's contracts are an integral part of the contracting technology. Chapter 9 differentiates between (1) the determination of the set of procedures accepted for contracting purposes and (2) managers' choices from among that set. The accepted set evolves as part of the contracting technology and maximizes firm value (i.e., maximizes the size of the pie available to the contracting parties). Managers are free to choose among procedures within the accepted set. Managers choose procedures that maximize their utility, and their choices can result in wealth transfers among the contracting parties (i.e., affect the distribution of the pie).

Tests of the theory have focused on managers' opportunistic behavior (i.e., choices within the accepted set) and not on the choice of the accepted set of procedures. For example, Healy (1985) examines managers' accounting accruals as a function of bonus plans' upper/lower bounds and cash flows. He hypothesizes that managers manage accruals to maximize executive compensation.

However, the prediction and explanation of the accepted set of procedures rather than managers' choices from among the set is likely to be productive. It would enable better design of contracts (see the discussion of the theory's value in the foregoing section). Development of a complex model of the accepted procedure set is difficult since it would involve modeling the demand for contracting as a monitoring device and the cost of alternative methods of monitoring. A simpler and probably more productive approach at this stage of the theory's development is to investigate how debt contracts and compensation plans vary (across firms) with economic variables suggested by finance theory. Any systematic associations can be used to generate hypotheses about the set of accepted procedures. A second simple approach to generating hypotheses is to gather cross-sectional samples of debt contracts, compensation plans, and accounting procedures and look for systematic associations that do not appear to be driven by the manager's opportunistic choice of procedures.

The relations among firms' capital structures, levels of executive compensation, the types of compensation plan, and investment opportunity sets are investigated by Smith and Watts (1984). Their results can produce an alternative explanation for the relation between the debt/equity ratio and the use of earnings increasing accounting procedures observed in Chapter 11. This explanation is an example of the first simple approach and is based on variations in accepted methods, not variations in managers' opportunistic behavior.

Smith and Watts (1984) observe a strong negative correlation between firms' debt/equity ratios and the top executive's compensation level (after controlling for firm size). They hypothesize that the correlation is driven by the firm's investment opportunity set. Firms with growth opportunities (i.e., opportunities to invest at above market rates of return) are hypothesized to have low debt/equity ratios and high management compensation levels. Holding size constant, growth firms with many profitable investment opportunities and a relatively small proportion of their assets in place require more managerial discretion (more managerial freedom to make decisions) than firms with relatively few profitable investment opportunities. Managers' marginal products are hypothesized to be higher, the higher their discretion, and so their compensation is higher. The less discretion managers have over investment opportunities, the lower the agency costs of debt and the higher the debt/equity ratio. Hence, growth firms have lower debt/equity ratios and higher management compensation than mature firms.

Growth firms' assets are less readily observable since they are represented by *future* investments. Contracts based on these less readily observable values provide managers with greater flexibility to behave opportunistically. This suggests that growth firms' accepted set of accounting procedures would restrict the manager's ability to choose earnings inflating procedures. That is, in growth firms, the accepted set of procedures should limit the manager's accounting procedure choice to fewer earnings inflating procedures than in mature firms. Hence, the lower the debt/equity ratio, the greater the firm's growth opportunities and the more income decreasing accounting procedures chosen. This alternative explanation for the observed association between debt/equity ratios and accounting method choice does not rely on ex post managerial opportunism but rather relies on ex ante restrictions on wealth transfers.

There are several ways of examining the association between the accepted set of accounting procedures and contracting variables. One method is a survey of accounting procedures and contracting structures (debt/equity ratio and existence of bonus plans) used in different industries. Firms in the same industry face similar incentive problems and use similar contracting structures and accounting procedures. An example is the tendency for mining and construction firms to recognize profits at production and for manufacturing firms to recognize profits at sale. Also, firms within the same industry should have similar contract *parameters* (times interest earned constraints). Differences across industries in how the contracts constrain the accounting procedure choice (e.g., debt covenants in some industries may constrain the manager to capitalize all leases) again should suggest cross-sectional differences in contracting costs. The observed association among accounting procedures, contracting techniques, and contract parameters should suggest cross-sectional differences in contracting costs.

A second approach is to examine cross-sectional differences in contracts and accounting procedures across countries. International differences in taxation, regulation, contract laws, and contracting costs should affect systematically the accepted set of accounting procedures (Zimmerman, 1982).

Investigation of Political Costs

Firm size is the most frequent surrogate for the political costs in the studies reported in Chapters 11 and 12. As discussed in those chapters, size can be a surrogate for many other variables. This suggests additional investigation of the hypothesized association between political costs and firm size. Zimmerman (1983) finds that effective tax rates, which are one component of political costs, vary with firm size. This evidence is consistent with that reported in Chapter 11. However, the studies suggest that the oil industry dominates the association between size and accounting procedures. This suggests that factors other than size (e.g., industry) affect political costs. One factor suggested by Zimmerman is the firms' recent success. Recent windfall profits are more likely expropriated by the political process than other wealth. Hence, the magnitude of the earnings change (say, over five years) is an alternative, but cross-sectionally correlated, proxy variable to firm size.

Other factors that could affect political costs should also be investigated. For example, consumer products' price increases are more readily observable by voters than producer products' price increases. This suggests that consumer product firms with rapid product price increases are more politically susceptible than other firms and therefore more likely to change accounting procedures to reduce reported profits.

A FINAL WORD

The reader should now be familiar with the evolutionary nature of accounting research and theory development. Theories evolve through competition among researchers. This competition leads to better understanding of extant accounting and auditing practice. This chapter offered our predictions regarding the existing theory's usefulness and our prognostications for the theory's future development. As with all predictions, ours contain errors. However, we have confidence that the methodology outlined in Chapter 1 and used throughout this book will produce a useful positive accounting theory.

References

ABDEL-KHALIK, A. R., AND J. C. McKEOWN, "Understanding Accounting Changes in an Efficient Market: Evidence of Differential Reaction." *Accounting Review* 53 (October 1978), pp. 851–868.

AHARONY, J., C. P. JONES, AND I. SWARY, "An Analysis of Risk and Return Characteristics of Corporate Bankruptcy Using Capital Market Data," *Journal of Finance* 35 (September 1980), pp. 1001–1016.

AKERLOF, G. A., "The Market for 'Lemons': Quality Uncertainty and the Market Mechanism," *Quarterly Journal of Economics* 84 (August 1970), pp. 488–500.

ALBRECHT, W. S., L. L. LOOKABILL, AND J. C. McKEOWN, "The Time Series Properties of Annual Earnings," *Journal of Accounting Research* 15 (Autumn 1977), pp. 226–244.

ALCHIAN, A. A., "Uncertainty, Evolution and Economic Theory," *Journal of Political Economy* 58 (June 1950), pp. 211–221.

———, "Some Implications of Recognition of Property Right Transaction Costs," unpublished discussion paper. Los Angeles: University of California, 1975.

———, AND H. DEMSETZ, "Production, Information Costs and Economic Organization," *American Economic Review* 62 (December 1972), pp. 777–795.

————, AND R. KESSEL, "Competition, Monopoly and the Pursuit of Money," in *Aspects of Labor Economics*, pp. 157–175. Princeton, N.J.: Princeton University Press, N.B.E.R., 1962.

ALTMAN, E. I., "Financial Ratios, Discriminant Analysis, and the Prediction of Corporate Bankruptcy," *Journal of Finance* 23 (September 1968), pp. 589–609.

————, "Statistical Replication of Bond Quality Ratings: A Worthwhile or Futile Exercise," unpublished working paper. New York: New York University, 1977.

————, R. G. HALDEMAN, AND P. NARAYANAN, "ZETA Analysis: A New Model to Identify Bankruptcy Risk of Corporations," *Journal of Banking and Finance* 1 (June 1977), pp. 29–54.

AMERICAN INSTITUTE OF CERTIFIED PUBLIC ACCOUNTANTS, *Objectives of Financial Statements* (Trueblood Report). Report of the Study Group on the Objectives of Financial Statements. New York: AICPA, 1973.

AMERSHI, A., J. DEMSKI, AND M. WOLFSON, "Strategic Behavior and Regulation Research in Accounting," *Journal of Accounting and Public Policy* 1 (1982), pp. 19–32.

ANTLE, R., "The Auditor as an Economic Agent," *Journal of Accounting Research* 20 (Autumn 1982), Part II, pp. 503–527.

————, "Auditor Independence," *Journal of Accounting Research* 22 (Spring 1984), pp. 1–20.

ARCHIBALD, T. R., "Stock Market Reaction to the Depreciation Switch-Back," *Accounting Review* 47 (January 1972), pp. 22–30.

ARROW, K. J., *Social Choice and Individual Values*, Cowles Foundation Monograph. New York: John Wiley, 1963.

————, "Higher Education as a Filter," *Journal of Public Economics* 2 (July 1973), pp. 193–216.

BALL, R. J., "Changes in Accounting Techniques and Stock Prices," *Empirical Research in Accounting: Selected Studies 1972*, supplement to Vol. 10 of *Journal of Accounting Research* (1972), pp. 1–38.

————, "Anomalies in Relationships Between Securities' Yields and Yield-Surrogates," *Journal of Financial Economics* 6 (June–September 1978), pp. 103–126.

————, AND P. BROWN, "An Empirical Evaluation of Accounting Income Numbers," *Journal of Accounting Research* 6 (Autumn 1968), pp. 159–178.

————, AND P. BROWN, "Portfolio Theory and Accounting," *Journal of Accounting Research* 7 (Autumn 1969), pp. 300–323.

————, AND G. FOSTER, "Corporate Financial Reporting: A Methodological Review of Empirical Research," *Studies on Current Research Methodologies in Accounting: A Critical Evaluation*, supplement to Vol. 20 of *Journal of Accounting Research* (1982), pp. 161–234.

————, AND R. WATTS, "Some Time Series Properties of Accounting Income," *Journal of Finance* 27 (June 1972), pp. 663–682.

————, B. Lev, and R. Watts, "Income Variation and Balance Sheet Compositions," *Journal of Accounting Research* 14 (Spring 1976), pp. 1–9.

Banz, R., "The Relationship Between Return and Market Value of Common Stocks," *Journal of Financial Economics* 9 (March 1981), pp. 3–18.

Barefield, R. M., and E. E. Comiskey, "The Smoothing Hypothesis: An Alternative Test," *Accounting Review* 47 (April 1972), pp. 291–298.

Barnea, A., J. Ronen, and S. Sadan, "The Implementation of Accounting Objectives: An Application to Extraordinary Items," *Accounting Review* 50 (January 1975), pp. 58–68.

Barzel, Y., "Some Fallacies in the Interpretation of Information Costs," *Journal of Law and Economics* 20 (October 1977), pp. 291–307.

Bastable, C. W., "Is SEC Replacement Cost Data Worth the Effort," *Journal of Accountancy* 144 (October 1977), pp. 68–76.

Beaver, W. H., "Financial Ratios as Predictors of Failure," *Empirical Research in Accounting: Selected Studies 1966,* supplement to Vol. 4 of *Journal of Accounting Research* (1966), pp. 71–111.

————, "The Information Content of Annual Earnings Announcements," *Empirical Research in Accounting: Selected Studies 1968,* supplement to Vol. 6 of *Journal of Accounting Research* (1968), pp. 67–92. (a)

————, "Market Prices, Financial Ratios, and the Prediction of Failure," *Journal of Accounting Research* 6 (Autumn 1968), pp. 179–192. (b)

————, "The Time Series Behavior of Earnings," *Empirical Research in Accounting: Selected Studies 1970,* supplement to Vol. 8 of the *Journal of Accounting Research* (1970), pp. 62–99.

————, "What Should Be the FASB's Objectives?" *Journal of Accountancy* 136 (August 1973), pp. 49–56.

————, "The Implications of Security Price Research for Disclosure Policy and the Analyst Community," in A. R. Abdel-Khalik and T. F. Keller (eds.) *Financial Information Requirements for Security Analysis,* pp. 65–81. Proceedings of the Duke Symposium on Financial Information Requirements for Security Analysis, Duke University, December 1976.

————, *Financial Reporting: An Accounting Revolution.* Englewood Cliffs, NJ: Prentice-Hall, 1981.

————, and J. Demski, "The Nature of Financial Accounting Objectives: A Summary and Synthesis," *Studies on Financial Accounting Objectives: 1974,* supplement to Vol. 12 of the *Journal of Accounting Research* (1974), pp. 170–187.

————, and R. E. Dukes, "Interperiod Tax Allocation, Earnings Expectations, and the Behavior of Security Prices," *Accounting Review* 48 (April 1972), pp. 320–333.

————, A. Christie, and P. A. Griffin, "The Information Content of SEC Accounting Series Release No. 190," *Journal of Accounting and Economics* 2 (August 1980), pp. 127–157.

————, R. CLARKE, AND W. WRIGHT, "The Association Between Unsystematic Security Returns and the Magnitude of Earnings Forecast Errors," *Journal of Accounting Research* 17 (Autumn 1979), pp. 316–340.

————, P. KETTLER, AND M. SCHOLES, "The Association Between Market Determined and Accounting Determined Risk Measures," *Accounting Review* 45 (October 1970), pp. 654–682.

————, R. LAMBERT, AND D. MORSE, "The Information Content of Security Prices," *Journal of Accounting and Economics* 2 (March 1980), pp. 3–28.

————, AND W. R. LANDSMAN, "Note on the Behavior of Residual Security Returns for Winner and Loser Portfolios," *Journal of Accounting and Economics* 3 (December 1981), pp. 233–241.

BENSTON, G. J., "Published Corporate Accounting Data and Stock Prices," *Empirical Research in Accounting: Selected Studies 1967*, supplement to Vol. 5 of *Journal of Accounting Research* (1967), pp. 1–14 and 22–54.

————, "The Value of the SEC's Accounting Disclosure Requirements," *Accounting Review* 44 (July 1969), pp. 515–532. (a)

————, "The Effectiveness and Effects of the SEC's Accounting Disclosure Requirements," in Henry G. Manne (ed.), *Economic Policy and the Regulation of Corporate Securities*, pp. 23–79. Washington, D.C.: American Enterprise Institute, 1969. (b)

————, "Required Disclosure and the Stock Market: An Evaluation of the Securities Exchange Act of 1934," *American Economic Review* 63 (March 1973), pp. 132–155.

————, "The Baffling New Numbers Game at the FTC," *Fortune* 92 (October 1975). (a)

————, "Accountant's Integrity and Financial Reporting," *Financial Executive* (August 1975), pp. 10–14. (b)

————, *Corporate Financial Disclosure in the U.K. and the U.S.A.* Westmead, U.K.: Saxon House, 1976.

————, "The Market for Public Accounting Services: Demand, Supply and Regulation," *Accounting Journal* II (Winter 1979–1980), pp. 2–47.

————, "Investors' Use of Financial Accounting Statement Numbers: A Review of Evidence from Stock Market Research," unpublished working paper. Rochester, N.Y.: University of Rochester, 1980.

————, AND R. WATTS. "The Market's Forecast of Earnings," unpublished working paper. Rochester, N.Y.: University of Rochester, 1978.

BEN-ZION, U., AND S. S. SHALIT, "Size, Leverage and Dividend Record as Determinants of Equity Risk," *Journal of Finance* 30 (September 1975), pp. 1015–1026.

BERHOLD, M., "A Theory of Linear Profit Sharing Incentives," *Quarterly Journal of Economics* 84 (August 1971), pp. 460–482.

BERLE, A. A., JR., AND G. C. MEANS, *The Modern Corporation and Private Property*. New York: Commerce Clearing House, 1932.

BIDDLE, G. C., "Accounting Methods and Management Decisions: The Case of Inventory Costing and Inventory Policy," supplement to Vol. 18 of *Journal of Accounting Research* (1980), pp. 235–280.

———, AND F. W. LINDAHL, "Stock Price Reactions to LIFO Adoptions: The Association Between Excess Returns and LIFO Tax Savings," *Journal of Accounting Research* 20 (Autumn 1982, Part II), pp. 551–588.

BILDERSEE, J. S., "The Association Between a Market-Determined Measure of Risk and Alternative Measures of Risk," *Accounting Review* 50 (January 1975), pp. 81–98.

BLACK, F., AND M. S. SCHOLES, "The Pricing of Options and Corporate Liabilities," *Journal of Political Economy* 81 (May–June 1973), pp. 637–654.

BLAUG, M., *The Methodology of Economics*. Cambridge: Cambridge University Press, 1980.

BOGUE, M. C., "The Estimation and Behavior of Systematic Risk," unpublished Ph.D. dissertation. Palo Alto, Calif.: Stanford University, 1972.

BOWEN, R., E. NOREEN, AND J. LACEY, "Determinants of the Corporate Decision to Capitalize Interest," *Journal of Accounting and Economics* 3 (August 1981), pp. 151–179.

BOWMAN, R. G., "The Importance of a Market-Value Measurement of Debt in Assessing Leverage," *Journal of Accounting Research* 18 (Spring 1980), pp. 242–254. (a)

———, "The Debt Equivalence of Leases: An Empirical Investigation," *Accounting Review* 55 (April 1980), pp. 237–253. (b)

BOX, G. E. P., AND G. M. JENKINS, *Time Series Analysis: Forecasting and Control*. San Francisco: Holden Day, 1970.

BREALEY, R., AND S. MYERS, *Principles of Corporate Finance*, 2nd ed. New York: McGraw-Hill, 1984.

BRILOFF, A. J., *Unaccountable Accounting*. New York: Harper & Row, 1972.

BROWN, L., P. GRIFFIN, R. HAGERMAN, AND M. ZMIJEWSKI, "A Comprehensive Analysis of the Predictive Ability of Analysts' and Time-Series Model Forecasts of Earnings Per Share," unpublished working paper. Buffalo: State University of New York at Buffalo, February 8, 1984.

BROWN, L. D., AND M. S. ROZEFF, "The Superiority of Analyst Forecasts as Measures of Expectations: Evidence from Earnings," *Journal of Finance* 33 (March 1978), pp. 1–16.

BROWN, P. "The Impact of the Annual Net Profit Report on the Stock Market," *The Australian Accountant* (July 1970), pp. 277–283.

BROWN, R. M., "Short-Range Market Reaction to Changes to LIFO Accounting Using Preliminary Earnings Announcement Dates," *Journal of Accounting Research* 18 (Spring 1980), pp. 38–63.

BROWN, S. J., AND J. B. WARNER, "Measuring Security Price Performance," *Journal of Financial Economics* 8 (September 1980), pp. 205–258.

BURTON, J. C., "Forecasts: A Changing View from the Securities and Exchange Commission," in P. Prakash and A. Rappaport, eds., *Public Reporting of*

Corporate Financial Forecasts, pp. 81–91. New York: Commerce Clearing House, 1974.

CANNING, J. B., *The Economics of Accountancy: A Critical Analysis of Accounting Theory.* New York: Ronald Press, 1929.

CAREY, J. L., *The Rise of the Accounting Profession,* Vols. 1 and 2. New York: AICPA, 1969.

CASSIDY, D. B., "Investor Evaluation of Accounting Information: Some Additional Empirical Evidence," *Journal of Accounting Research* 14 (Autumn 1976), pp. 212–229.

CHAMBERS, A. E., AND S. H. PENMAN, "Timeliness of Reporting and the Stock Price Reaction to Earnings Announcements," *Journal of Accounting Research* 22 (Spring 1984), pp. 21–47.

CHAMBERS, R. J., "Measurement and Objectivity in Accounting," *Accounting Review* 39 (April 1964), pp. 264–274.

———, *Accounting, Evaluation and Economic Behavior.* Englewood Cliffs, N.J.: Prentice-Hall, 1966.

———, "Continuously Contemporary Accounting—Additivity and Action," *Accounting Review* 42 (October 1967), pp. 751–757.

CHEUNG, S., "The Fable of the Bees: An Economic Investigation," *Journal of Law and Economics* 16 (April 1973), pp. 11–33.

CHOW, C. W., "The Demand for External Auditing: Size, Debt and Ownership Influences," *Accounting Review* 57 (April 1982), pp. 272–291.

———, "The Impacts of Accounting Regulation on Bondholder and Shareholder Wealth: The Case of the Securities Acts," *Accounting Review* 58 (July 1983), pp. 485–520.

CHRISTENSON, C., "The Methodology of Positive Accounting," *Accounting Review,* 58 (January 1983), pp. 1–22.

CHRISTIE, A. A., M. D. KENNELLEY, J. W. KING, AND T. F. SCHAEFER, "Testing for Incremental Information Content in the Presence of Collinearity," *Journal of Accounting and Economics* 6 (December 1984).

COASE, R., "The Problem of Social Cost," *Journal of Law and Economics* 3 (October 1960), pp. 1–44.

———, "The Nature of the Firm," *Economica,* New Series 4 (November 1937), pp. 386–405.

———, "The Lighthouse in Economics," *Journal of Law and Economics* 17 (October 1974), pp. 357–376.

COLE, W. M., *Accounts: Their Construction and Interpretation for Businessmen: Students of Affairs* (Boston: Houghton Mifflin, 1915).

COLLINS, D. W., AND W. T. DENT, "The Proposed Elimination of Full Cost Accounting in the Extractive Petroleum Industry," *Journal of Accounting and Economics* 1 (March 1979), pp. 3–44.

———, AND W. T. DENT, "A Comparison of Alternative Testing Methodologies Used in Capital Market Research," *Journal of Accounting Research* 22 (Spring 1984), pp. 48–84.

——, M. Rozeff, and D. Dhaliwal, "The Economic Determinants of the Market Reaction to Proposed Mandatory Accounting Changes in the Oil and Gas Industry: A Cross Sectional Analysis," *Journal of Accounting and Economics* 3 (March 1981), pp. 37–71.

——, M. S. Rozeff, and W. K. Salatka, "The SEC's Rejection of SFAS No. 19: Tests of Market Price Reversal," *Accounting Review* 57 (January 1982), pp. 1–17.

Conference Board, *Top Executive Bonus Plans*. New York: Conference Board, 1979.

Copeland, R. M., "Income Smoothing," *Empirical Research in Accounting: Selected Studies 1968*, supplement to Vol. 6 of *Journal of Accounting Research* (1968), pp. 101–116.

——, and R. D. LiCastro, "A Note on Income Smoothing," *Accounting Review* 43 (July 1968), pp. 540–545.

Daley, L. A., and R. L. Vigeland, "The Effects of Debt Covenants and Political Costs on the Choice of Accounting Methods: The Case of Accounting for R&D Costs," *Journal of Accounting and Economics* 5 (December 1983), pp. 195–211.

Davidson, S., and R. L. Weil, "Inflation Accounting: What Will General Price Level Adjusted Income Statements Show?" *Financial Analysts Journal* 31 (January–February 1975), pp. 27–31. (a)

——, and R. L. Weil, "Inflation Accounting: Public Utilities," *Financial Analysts Journal* 31 (May–June, 1975), pp. 30–34, 62. (b)

——, C. P. Stickney, and R. L. Weil, *Inflation Accounting*. New York: McGraw-Hill, 1976.

Deakin, E. B., "A Discriminant Analysis of Predictors of Business Failure," *Journal of Accounting Research* 10 (Spring 1972), pp. 167–179.

——, "An Analysis of Differences Between Non-Major Oil Firms Using Successful Efforts and Full Cost Methods," *Accounting Review* 54 (October 1979), pp. 722–734.

Dean, J., *Capital Budgeting*. New York: Columbia University Press, 1951.

DeAngelo, L. E., "Auditor Independence, 'Low Balling,' and Disclosure Regulation," *Journal of Accounting and Economics* 3 (August 1981), pp. 113–127. (a)

——, "Auditor Size and Audit Quality," *Journal of Accounting and Economics* 3 (December 1981), pp. 183–199. (b)

——, "Mandated Successful Efforts and Auditor Choice," *Journal of Accounting and Economics* 4 (December 1982), pp. 171–204.

DeMond, C. W., *Price Waterhouse and Co. in America*. New York: Price, Waterhouse, 1951.

Demsetz, H., "Information and Efficiency: Another Viewpoint," *Journal of Law and Economics* 12 (April 1969), pp. 1–22.

Demski, J. S., "Choice Among Financial Reporting Alternatives," *Accounting Review* 49 (April 1974), pp. 221–232.

DHALIWAL, D., "The Effect of the Firm's Capital Structure on the Choice of Accounting Methods," *Accounting Review* 55 (January 1980), pp. 78–84.

————, G. SALAMON, AND E. SMITH, "The Effect of Owner Versus Management Control on the Choice of Accounting Methods," *Journal of Accounting and Economics* 4 (July 1982), pp. 41–53.

DODD, E. M., *American Business Corporations Until 1860*. Cambridge, Mass.: Harvard University Press, 1954.

DOPUCH, N., AND D. F. DRAKE, "The Effect of Alternative Accounting Rules for Nonsubsidiary Investments," *Empirical Research in Accounting: Selected Studies 1966*, supplement to Vol. 4 of *Journal of Accounting Research* (1966), pp. 192–219.

————, AND D. SIMUNIC, "The Nature of Competition in the Auditing Profession: A Descriptive and Normative View," in J. Buckley and F. Weston, eds., *Regulation and the Accounting Profession*. Belmont, Calif.: Lifetime Learning Publications, 1980. (a)

————, AND D. SIMUNIC, "Competition in Auditing: An Assessment," unpublished working paper. Chicago: University of Chicago, 1980. (b)

DOWNS, A., "An Economic Theory of Political Action in a Democracy," *Journal of Political Economy* (1957), pp. 135–150. (a)

————, *An Economic Theory of Democracy*. New York: Harper & Row, 1957. (b)

DUBOIS, A., *The English Business Company After the Bubble Act 1720–1800*. New York: The Commonwealth Fund, 1938.

DYCKMAN, T. R., AND A. J. SMITH, "Financial Accounting and Reporting by Oil and Gas Producing Companies: A Study of Information Effects," *Journal of Accounting and Economics* 1 (March 1979), pp. 45–75.

————, AND S. A. ZEFF, "Two Decades of the *Journal of Accounting Research*," *Journal of Accounting Research* 22 (Spring 1984), pp. 225–297.

EDWARDS, E. O., AND P. W. BELL, *The Theory and Measurement of Business Income*. Berkeley: University of California Press, 1961.

EICHENSEHER, J. W., AND P. DANOS, "The Analysis of Industry-Specific Auditor Concentration: Towards an Explanatory Model," *Accounting Review* 56 (July 1981), pp. 479–492.

ELGERS, P. T., "Accounting-Based Risk Predictions: A Re-Examination," *Accounting Review* 55 (July 1980), pp. 389–408.

ELLERT, J. C., "Mergers, Antitrust Law Enforcement and Stockholder Returns," *Journal of Finance* 31 (May 1976), pp. 715–732.

ELLIOTT, R. K., AND A. KORPI, "Factors Affecting Audit Fees," in *Cost-Benefit Analysis of Auditing, Commission on Auditors' Responsibility Research Study to 3*, by M. Shakun. New York: AICPA, 1978.

ESKEW, R. K., "The Forecasting Ability of Accounting Risk Measures: Some Additional Evidence," *Accounting Review* 54 (January 1979), pp. 107–118.

FAMA, E. F., "Efficient Capital Markets: A Review of Theory and Empirical Work," *Journal of Finance* 25 (May 1970), pp. 383–417.

————, *Foundations of Finance*. New York: Basic Books, 1976.

————, "Agency Problems and the Theory of the Firm," *Journal of Political Economy* 88 (April 1980), pp. 288–307.

————, L. FISHER, M. C. JENSEN, AND R. ROLL, "The Adjustment of Stock Prices to New Information," *International Economic Review* 10 (February 1969), pp. 1–21.

————, AND M. C. JENSEN, "Separation of Ownership and Control," *Journal of Law and Economics* 26 (June 1983), pp. 301–326. (a)

————, AND M. C. JENSEN, "Agency Problems and Residual Claims," *Journal of Law and Economics* 26 (June 1983), pp. 327–350. (b)

————, AND A. B. LAFFER, "Information and Capital Markets," *Journal of Business* 44 (July 1971), pp. 289–298.

————, AND M. MILLER, *The Theory of Finance*. Hinsdale, Ill.: Dryden Press, 1972.

FIRTH, M., "The Relative Information Content of the Release of Financial Results Data by Firms," *Journal of Accounting Research* 19 (Autumn 1981), pp. 521–529.

FISHER, I., *The Theory of Interest as Determined by Impatience to Spend Income and Opportunity to Invest It.* New York: Macmillan, 1930, A. M. Kelley, 1961.

FOGELSON, J., "The Impact of Changes in Accounting Principles on Restrictive Covenants in Credit Agreements and Indentures," *Business Lawyer* 33 (January 1978), pp. 769–787.

FORSGARDH, L. E., AND K. HERTZEN, "The Adjustment of Stock Prices to New Information," in E. J. Elton and M. J. Gruber, eds., *International Capital Markets,* pp. 68–86. Amsterdam: North-Holland, 1975.

FOSTER, G., "Earnings and Stock Prices of Insurance Companies," *Accounting Review* 50 (October 1975), pp. 686–698.

————, "Quarterly Accounting Data: Time-Series Properties and Predictive-Ability Results," *Accounting Review* 52 (January 1977), pp. 1–21.

————, *Financial Statement Analysis.* Englewood Cliffs, N.J.: Prentice–Hall, 1978.

————, "Briloff and the Capital Market," *Journal of Accounting Research* 17 (Spring 1979), pp. 262–274.

————, "Accounting Policy Decisions and Capital Market Research," *Journal of Accounting and Economics* 2 (March 1980), pp. 29–62.

FRANCIS, J., "The Effect of Audit Firm Size on Audit Prices: A Study of the Australian Market," *Journal of Accounting and Economics* 6 (1984).

FRIED, D., AND D. GIVOLY, "Financial Analysts' Forecasts of Earnings: A Better Surrogate for Market Expectations," *Journal of Accounting and Economics* 4 (October 1982), pp. 85–108.

FRIEDMAN, M., "The Methodology of Positive Economics," *Essays in Positive Economics.* Chicago: University of Chicago Press, 1953, reprinted by Chicago: Phoenix Books, 1966.

GAGNON, J. M., "Purchase Versus Pooling of Interest: The Search for a Predictor," *Empirical Research in Accounting: Selected Studies 1967,* supplement to Vol. 5 of *Journal of Accounting Research* (1967), pp. 187–204.

————, "The Purchase-Pooling Choice: Some Empirical Evidence," *Journal of Accounting Research* 9 (Spring 1971), pp. 52–72.

GHEYARA, K., AND J. BOATSMAN, "Market Reaction to the 1976 Replacement Cost Disclosures," *Journal of Accounting and Economics* 2 (August 1980), pp. 107–126.

GILMAN, STEPHEN, *Accounting Concepts of Profit*. New York: Ronald Press, 1939.

GONEDES, N., "Evidence on the Information Content of Accounting Numbers: Accounting-Based and Market-Based Estimates of Systematic Risk," *Journal of Financial and Quantitative Analysis* 8 (June 1973), pp. 407–444.

———, "The Capital Market, The Market for Information and External Accounting," *Journal of Finance* 31 (May 1976), pp. 611–630.

———, "Corporate Signaling, External Accounting, and Capital Market Equilibrium: Evidence on Dividends, Income and Extraordinary Items," *Journal of Accounting Research* 16 (Spring 1978), pp. 26–79.

———, AND N. DOPUCH, "Capital Market Equilibrium, Information Production, and Selecting Accounting Techniques: Theoretical Framework and Review of Empirical Work," *Studies on Financial Accounting Objectives: 1974*, supplement to Vol. 12 of *Journal of Accounting Research* (1974), pp. 48–130.

———, N. DOPUCH, AND S. H. PENMAN, "Disclosure Rules, Information-Production, and Capital Market Equilibrium: The Case of Forecast Disclosure Rules," *Journal of Accounting Research* 14 (Spring 1976), pp. 89–137.

GORDON, M. J., "Postulates, Principles and Research in Accounting," *Accounting Review* 39 (April 1964), pp. 251–263.

———, B. N. HORWITZ, AND P. T. MEYERS, "Accounting Measurements and Normal Growth of the Firm," R. K. Jaedicke, Y. Ijiri, and O. Nielsen, eds., *Research in Accounting Measurement*. Chicago: American Accounting Association, 1966, pp. 221–231.

GRAHAM, B., D. L. DODD, AND S. COTTLE, *Security Analysis*, 4th ed. New York: McGraw-Hill, 1962.

GRANT, E. B., "Market Implications of Differential Amounts of Interim Information," *Journal of Accounting Research* 18 (Spring 1980), pp. 255–268.

GRIFFIN, P. A., "The Time-Series Behavior of Quarterly Earnings: Preliminary Evidence," *Journal of Accounting Research* 15 (Spring 1977), pp. 71–83.

HAGERMAN, R. L., "The Efficiency of the Market for Bank Stocks: An Empirical Test," *Journal of Money, Credit and Banking* 5 (August 1973), pp. 846–855.

———, AND M. ZMIJEWSKI, "Some Economic Determinants of Accounting Policy Choice," *Journal of Accounting and Economics* 1 (August 1979), pp. 141–161.

HARING, J. R., "Accounting Rules and 'The Accounting Establishment,'" *Journal of Business* 52 (October 1979), pp. 507–519.

HARRISON, T., "Different Market Reactions to Discretionary and Non-Discretionary Accounting Changes," *Journal of Accounting Research* 15 (Spring 1977), pp. 84–107.

HAWKINS, D. F., "The Development of Modern Financial Reporting Practices Among American Manufacturing Corporations," *Business History Review* (Autumn 1963), reprinted in M. Chatfield, ed., *Contemporary Studies in the*

Evolution of Accounting Thought, pp. 247–279. Belmont, CA.: Dickenson, 1968.

HAWORTH, H., J. MATTHEWS, AND C. TUCK, "Full Cost Versus Successful Efforts: A Study of Proposed Accounting Change's Competitive Impact," SEC Directorate of Economic and Policy Research. Washington, D.C.: Securities and Exchange Commission, February, 1978.

HEALY, P., "The Impact of Bonus Schemes on the Selection of Accounting Principles," *Journal of Accounting and Economics* 7 (April 1985).

HEMPEL, C., *Aspects of Scientific Explanation*. New York: The Free Press, 1965.

HENDRIKSEN, E. S., *Accounting Theory*, 4th ed. Homewood, Ill.: Richard D. Irwin, 1982.

HINDLEY, B., "Separation of Ownership and Control in the Modern Corporation," *Journal of Law and Economics* 13 (April 1970), pp. 185–222.

HIRSHLEIFER, J., "On the Theory of Optimal Investment Decision," *Journal of Political Economy* 4 (August 1958), pp. 329–352.

———, "The Private and Social Value of Information and the Reward to Inventive Activity," *American Economic Review* 61 (September 1971), pp. 561–574.

HOLMES, W., "Accounting and Accountants in Massachusetts," *Massachusetts CPA Review* (May–June 1975), pp. 18–21.

HOLMSTROM, B., "Moral Hazard and Observability," *Bell Journal of Economics* 10 (Spring 1979), pp. 74–91.

HOLTHAUSEN, R. W., "Towards a Positive Theory of Choice of Accounting Techniques: The Case of Alternative Depreciation Methods," unpublished working paper. Rochester, N.Y.: University of Rochester, June 1978.

———, "Evidence on the Effect of Bond Covenants and Management Compensation Contracts on the Choice of Accounting Techniques: The Case of the Depreciation Switch-Back," *Journal of Accounting and Economics* 3 (March 1981), pp. 73–109.

———, AND R. W. LEFTWICH, "The Economic Consequences of Accounting Choice: Implications of Costly Contracting and Monitoring," *Journal of Accounting and Economics* 5 (August 1983), pp. 77–117.

HORNGREN, C. T., "Accounting Principles: Private or Public Sector?" *Journal of Accountancy* 133 (May 1972), pp. 37–41.

———, "The Marketing of Accounting Standards," *Journal of Accountancy* 136 (October 1973), pp. 61–66.

HORRIGAN, J., "The Determination of Long-Term Credit Standing with Financial Ratios," *Empirical Research in Accounting: Selected Studies 1966*, supplement to Vol. 4 of *Journal of Accounting Research* (1966), pp. 44–62.

HUGHES, J. S., AND W. E. RICKS, "Accounting for Retail Land Sales: Analysis of a Mandated Change," *Journal of Accounting and Economics* 6 (August 1984), pp. 101–132.

IJIRI, Y., *The Foundations of Accounting Measurement*. Englewood Cliffs, N.J.: Prentice-Hall, 1967.

Jain, P. C., "Cross-Sectional Association Between Abnormal Returns and Firm Specific Variables," *Journal of Accounting and Economics* 4 (December 1982), pp. 205–228.

Jarrell, G. A., "The Demand for State Regulation of the Electric Utility Industry," *Journal of Law and Economics* 21 (October 1978), pp. 269–295.

——, "Pro-Producer Regulation and Accounting for Assets: The Case of Electric Utilities," *Journal of Accounting and Economics* 1 (August 1979), pp. 93–116.

Jensen, M. C. (ed.), *Studies in the Theory of Capital Markets.* New York: Praeger Publishers, 1972.

——, "Towards a Theory of the Press," unpublished working paper. Rochester, N.Y.: University of Rochester, June 1976. (a)

——, "Reflections on the State of Accounting Research and the Regulation of Accounting," Stanford Lectures in Accounting. Palo Alto, CA.: Stanford University Press, 1976. (b)

——, "Some Anomalous Evidence Regarding Market Efficiency," *Journal of Financial Economics* 6 (June–September, 1978), pp. 95–102.

——, "Organization Theory and Methodology," *Accounting Review* 58 (1983), pp. 319–339.

——, and W. H. Meckling, "Theory of the Firm: Managerial Behavior, Agency Costs and Ownership Structure," *Journal of Financial Economics* 3 (October 1976), pp. 305–360.

——, and W. H. Meckling, "Can the Corporation Survive?" *Financial Analysts Journal* 34 (January–February 1978), pp. 31–37.

Kalay, A., "Towards a Theory of Corporate Dividend Policy," unpublished Ph.D. dissertation. Rochester, N.Y.: University of Rochester, 1979.

——, "Stockholder-Bondholder Conflict and Dividend Constraints," *Journal of Financial Economics* 10 (July 1982), pp. 211–233.

Kaplan, R. S., "The Information Content of Financial Accounting Numbers: A Survey of Empirical Evidence," pp. 134–173. In Abdel-khalik and Keller, eds., *Impact of Accounting Research on Practice and Disclosure.* Chapel Hill, N.C.: Duke University Press, 1978.

——, and R. Roll, "Investor Evaluation of Accounting Information: Some Empirical Evidence," *Journal of Business* 45 (April 1972), pp. 225–257.

——, and G. Urwitz, "Statistical Models of Bond Ratings: A Methodological Inquiry," *Journal of Business* 52 (April 1979), pp. 231–262.

Klein, R. W., and V. S. Bawa, "The Effect of Estimation Risk on Optimal Portfolio Choice," *Journal of Financial Economics* 3 (June 1976), pp. 215–232.

——, and V. S. Bawa, "The Effect of Limited Information and Estimation Risk on Optimal Portfolio Diversification," *Journal of Financial Economics* 5 (August 1977), pp. 89–111.

Knight, R. F., "The Association Between Published Accounting Data and the Behavior of Share Prices," unpublished doctoral thesis. Cape Town: University of Cape Town, 1983.

KOCKELMANS, J. J., *Philosophy of Science.* New York: The Free Press, 1968.

KRIPKE, H., *The SEC and Corporate Disclosure: Regulation in Search of a Purpose.* New York: Harcourt Brace Jovanovich, 1979.

LARCKER, D., "The Association Between Performance Plan Adoption and Corporate Capital Investment," *Journal of Accounting and Economics* 5 (April 1983), pp. 3–30.

LEFTWICH, R., "Market Failure Fallacies and Accounting Information," *Journal of Accounting and Economics* 2 (December 1980), pp. 193–211.

———, "Evidence of the Impact of Mandatory Changes in Accounting Principles on Corporate Loan Agreements," *Journal of Accounting and Economics* 3 (March 1981), pp. 3–36.

———, "Accounting Information in Private Markets: Evidence from Private Lending Agreements," *Accounting Review* 58 (January 1983), pp. 23–42.

———, R. WATTS, AND J. ZIMMERMAN, "Voluntary Corporate Disclosure: The Case of Interim Reporting," *Studies on Standardization of Accounting Practices: An Assessment of Alternative Institutional Arrangements,* supplement to Vol. 19 of *Journal of Accounting Research* (1981), pp. 50–77.

LEV, B., "On the Association Between Operating Leverage and Risk," *Journal of Financial and Quantitative Analysis* 9 (September 1974), pp. 627–642.

———, "The Impact of Accounting Regulation on the Stock Market: The Case of Oil and Gas Companies," *Accounting Review* 54 (July 1979), pp. 485–503.

———, "On the Use of Index Models in Analytical Reviews by Auditors," *Journal of Accounting Research* 18 (Autumn 1980), pp. 524–550.

———, "Some Economic Determinants of Time-Series Properties of Earnings," *Journal of Accounting and Economics* 5 (April 1983), pp. 31–48.

LEWELLEN, W., *Executive Compensation in Large Industrial Corporations.* New York: National Bureau of Economic Research, 1968.

LILIEN, S., AND V. PASTENA, "Determinants of Intramethod Choice in the Oil and Gas Industry," *Journal of Accounting and Economics* 4 (December 1982), pp. 145–170.

LINTNER, J., "Distribution of Incomes of Corporations Among Dividends, Retained Earnings, and Taxes," *American Economic Review* 46 (May 1956), pp. 97–113.

———, "The Valuation of Risk Assets and the Selection of Risky Investments in Stock Portfolios and Capital Budgets," *Review of Economics and Statistics* 47 (February 1965), pp. 13–37.

———, AND R. GLAUBER, "Higgledy Piggledy Growth in America?" Seminar on the Analysis of Security Prices, Graduate School of Business. Chicago: University of Chicago, May 11–12, 1967.

LITTLE, I. M. D., "Higgledy Piggledy Growth," *Institute of Statistics* (Oxford) 24 (November 1962).

———, AND A. C. RAYNER, *Higgledy Piggledy Growth Again.* New York: A. M. Kelley, 1966.

LOOKABILL, L. L., "Some Additional Evidence on the Time Series Properties of Accounting Earnings," *Accounting Review* 51 (October 1976), pp. 724–738.

LYS, T., "Selection of Accounting Procedures and Implications of Changes in Generally Accepted Accounting Principles: A Case Study Using Oil and Gas Accounting," unpublished Ph.D. dissertation. Rochester, N.Y.: University of Rochester, 1982.

———, "Mandated Accounting Changes and Debt Covenants: The Case of Oil and Gas Accounting," *Journal of Accounting and Economics* 6 (April 1984), pp. 39–65.

MANNE, H. G., *Insider Trading and the Stock Market*. New York: The Free Press, 1966.

MATHESON, E., *The Depreciation of Factories, Mines and Industrial Undertakings and Their Valuation*. (Originally published in London by E. & F. N. Spon, 1893.) New York: Arno Press, 1976.

MAY, R., "The Influence of Quarterly Earnings Announcements on Investor Decisions as Reflected in Common Stock Price Changes," *Empirical Research in Accounting: Selected Studies 1971*, supplement to Vol. 9 of the *Journal of Accounting Research* (1971), pp. 119–163.

———, AND G. L. SUNDEM, "Research for Accounting Policy: An Overview," *Accounting Review* 51 (October 1976), pp. 747–763.

McCRAW, T. K., "Regulation in America: A Review Article," *Business History Review* 49 (Summer 1975), pp. 159–183.

McKEE, A. J., T. B. BELL, AND J. R. BOATSMAN, "Management Preferences over Accounting Standards: A Replication and Additional Tests," *Accounting Review* 59 (October 1984), pp. 647–659.

McNICHOLS, M., AND J. G. MANEGOLD, "The Effect of the Information Environment on the Relationship Between Financial Disclosure and Security Price Variability," *Journal of Accounting and Economics* 5 (April 1983), pp. 49–74.

MECKLING, W. H., "Towards a Theory of Representative Government," presented at the Third Annual Conference on Analysis and Ideology, Interlaken, Switzerland, June 4, 1976. (a)

———, "Values and the Choice of the Model of the Individual in Social Sciences," *Revue Swisse d'Economic, Politique et de Statistique* (December 1976). (b)

MERTON, R. C., "Theory of Rational Option Pricing," *Bell Journal of Economics and Management Science* 4 (Spring 1973), pp. 141–183.

MILLER, M., "Debt and Taxes," *Journal of Finance* 32 (May 1977), pp. 261–275.

———, AND M. SCHOLES, "Executive Compensation, Taxes and Incentives," in W. F. Sharpe and L. M. Cootner, eds., *Financial Economics: Essays in Honor of Paul Cootner*. Englewood Cliffs, N.J.: Prentice-Hall, 1982.

MIRRLEES, J. A., "Notes on Welfare Economics, Information and Uncertainty," in M. Balch et al., eds., *Essays on Economic Behavior Under Uncertainty*. Amsterdam: North-Holland, 1974.

————, "The Optimal Structure of Incentives and Authority Within an Organization," *Bell Journal of Economics* 7 (Spring 1976), pp. 105–131.

MODIGLIANI, F., AND M. H. MILLER, "The Cost of Capital, Corporation Finance and the Theory of Investment," *American Economic Review* 48 (June 1958), pp. 261–297.

————, AND M. H. MILLER, "Corporate Income Taxes and the Cost of Capital: A Correction," *American Economic Review* 53 (June 1963), pp. 433–443.

MOONITZ, M., "Accounting Principles—How They are Developed," in R. Sterling, ed. *Institutional Issues in Public Accounting.* Lawrence, Kans.: Scholars Book Company, 1974. (a)

————, *Obtaining Agreement on Standards in the Accounting Profession.* Sarasota, Fla.: American Accounting Association, 1974. (b)

MORSE, D., AND G. RICHARDSON, "The LIFO/FIFO Decision," *Journal of Accounting Research* 21 (Spring 1983), pp. 106–127.

MYERS, S. C., "Determinants of Corporate Borrowing," *Journal of Financial Economics* 5 (November 1977), pp. 147–175.

NASH, L. R., *Anatomy of Depreciation.* Washington, D.C.: Public Utilities Reports, 1947.

NELSON, C. R., *Applied Time Series Analysis for Managerial Forecasting.* San Francisco: Holden-Day, 1973.

NISKANEN, W. A., *Bureaucracy and Representative Government.* Chicago: Aldine-Atherton, 1971.

OHLSON, J. A., "Financial Ratios and the Probabilistic Prediction of Bankruptcy," *Journal of Accounting Research* 18 (Spring 1980), pp. 109–131.

OLSON, M., *The Logic of Collective Action.* Cambridge, Mass.: Harvard University Press, 1971.

PASSMORE, J. A., "Can the Social Sciences Be Value-Free?" in H. Feigl and M. Brodbeck, eds., *Readings in the Philosophy of Science* pp. 674–676. New York: Appleton-Century-Crofts, 1953.

PATELL, J. M., "Corporate Forecasts of Earnings Per Share and Stock Price Behavior: Empirical Tests," *Journal of Accounting Research* 14 (Autumn 1976), pp. 246–276.

————, AND R. KAPLAN, "The Information Content of Cash Flow Data Relative to Annual Earnings," unpublished working paper. Palo Alto, Calif.: Stanford University, August 1977.

————, AND M. A. WOLFSON, "Anticipated Information Releases Reflected in Call Option Prices," *Journal of Accounting and Economics* 1 (August 1979), pp. 117–140.

————, AND M. A. WOLFSON, "The Ex Ante and Ex Post Price Effects of Quarterly Earnings Announcements Reflected in Option and Stock Prices," *Journal of Accounting Research* 19 (Autumn 1981), pp. 434–458.

PATON, W. A., AND A. C. LITTLETON, *An Introduction to Corporate Accounting Standards.* Chicago: American Accounting Association, 1940.

PELTZMAN, S., *Regulation of Pharmaceutical Innovation: The 1962 Amendments.* Washington, D.C.: American Enterprise Institute for Public Policy Research, 1974.

———, "Toward a More General Theory of Regulation," *Journal of Law and Economics* 19 (August 1976), pp. 211–240.

PERCIVAL, J. R., "Risky Corporate Debt in a Market Model Context," unpublished working paper. Philadelphia: University of Pennsylvania, 1973.

PHILLIPS, S. M., AND J. R. ZECHER, *The SEC and the Public Interest: An Economic Perspective.* Cambridge, Mass.: MIT Press, 1981.

PIXLEY, F. W., *Auditors* (Originally published in London by E. Wilson, 1881). New York: Arno Press, 1976.

POINCARÉ, H., *Science and Hypothesis.* London: Walter Scott, 1905.

POPPER, K. R., *Conjectures and Refutations: The Growth of Scientific Knowledge.* London: Routledge & Kegan Paul, 1963.

———, *The Logic of Scientific Discovery.* (Originally published in London by Hutchinson, 1959) New York: Harper Torch Books, 1965.

POSNER, R. A., "Theories of Economic Regulation," *Bell Journal of Economics and Management Science* 5 (Autumn 1974), pp. 335–358.

PRAKASH, P., AND A. RAPPAPORT, "Information Inductance and its Significance for Accounting," *Accounting, Organizations and Society,* Vol 2. (1977), pp. 29–38.

RAPPAPORT, A., "Corporate Performance Standards and Shareholder Value," *Journal of Business Strategy* 3 (Spring 1983), pp. 28–38.

RAVIV, A., "Management Compensation and the Managerial Labor Market: An Overview," *Journal of Accounting and Economics* 7 (April 1985).

RAYBURN, F. R., "Another Look at the Impact of Accounting Principles Board Opinion No. 16—An Empirical Study," *Mergers and Acquisitions* 10 (Spring 1975), pp. 7–9.

REVSINE, L., *Replacement Cost Accounting.* Englewood Cliffs, N.J.: Prentice-Hall, 1973.

RICKS, W., "The Market's Response to the 1974 LIFO Adoptions," *Journal of Accounting Research* 20 (Autumn 1982, Part I), pp. 367–387.

RO, B. T., "The Adjustment of Security Returns to the Disclosure of Replacement Cost Accounting Information," *Journal of Accounting and Economics* 2 (August 1980), pp. 159–189.

RONEN, J., AND S. SADAN, *Smoothing Income Numbers: Objectives, Means, and Implications.* Reading, Mass.: Addison-Wesley, 1981.

ROSENBERG, B., AND V. MARATHE, "Prediction of Investment Risk: Systematic and Residual Risk," *Proceedings of the Seminar on the Analysis of Security Prices.* Chicago: University of Chicago, November 1975.

ROSS, I., "Higher Stakes in the Bond-Rating Game," *Fortune* 93 (April 1976), pp. 132–142.

ROSS, S. A., "The Economic Theory of Agency: The Principal's Problem," *American Economic Review* 63 (May 1973), pp. 134–139.

—————, "The Economic Theory of Agency and the Principle of Similarity," in M. D. Balch et al., eds., *Essays on Economic Behavior Under Uncertainty.* Amsterdam: North-Holland, 1974.

ROZEFF, M. S., "The Relationship of Bond Betas to Bond Returns and Agency Ratings with a Test of the Capital Asset Pricing Model," unpublished working paper. Iowa City: University of Iowa, 1976.

SALIERS, E. A., *Depreciation: Principles and Applications,* 3rd ed. New York: Ronald Press, 1939.

SALATKA, W. K., "A Study of the Capital Market Reaction to the Accounting Policy Decision Process Relating to Foreign Currency Accounting," unpublished working paper. Tucson: University of Arizona, 1983.

SAVOIE, L. M., "Game Plans and Professional Standards." Address before the Conference Institute, New York City, November 20, 1970. Quoted by Briloff (1972), pp. 13–14.

SCHIPPER, K., AND R. THOMPSON, "The Impact of Merger-Related Regulations on the Shareholders of Acquiring Firms," *Journal of Accounting Research* 21 (Spring 1983), pp. 184–221.

SCHWARTZ, E., AND J. R. ARONSON, "Some Surrogate Evidence in Support of the Concept of Optimal Financial Structure," *Journal of Finance* 22 (March 1967), pp. 10–18.

SCHWERT, G. W., "Size and Stock Returns, and Other Empirical Regularities," *Journal of Financial Economics* 12 (June 1983), pp. 3–12.

SECURITIES AND EXCHANGE COMMISSION, *Report of the SEC Advisory Committee on Corporate Disclosure.* Washington, D.C.: U.S. Government Printing Office, 1977.

SHARPE, W. F., "Capital Asset Prices: A Theory of Market Equilibrium Under Conditions of Risk," *Journal of Finance* 19 (September 1964), pp. 425–442.

SHERWOOD, H. C., *How Corporate and Municipal Debt Is Rated.* New York: John Wiley, 1976.

SIMON, H. A., "Theories of Decision-Making in Economics and Behavioral Science,"*American Economic Review* 49 (June 1959), pp. 253–283.

SIMUNIC, D. A., "The Pricing of Audit Services: Theory and Evidence," *Journal of Accounting Research* 18 (Spring 1980), pp. 161–190.

SMITH, A., *The Wealth of Nations.* New York: Modern Library, 1937. (Originally published, 1776.)

SMITH, A. J., "An Empirical Investigation of the Information Effects of a Change in the Financial Reporting Standards for Oil and Gas Producers: The Proposed Elimination and Subsequent Retention of Full Cost Accounting," unpublished dissertation. Ithaca, N.Y.: Cornell University, 1981. (a)

—————, "The SEC 'Reversal' of FASB Statement No. 19: An Investigation of Information Effects," *Studies on Standardization of Accounting Practices: An Assessment of Alternative Institutional Arrangements* supplement to Vol. 19 of *Journal of Accounting Research* (1981), pp. 174–211. (b)

SMITH, C. W., "Applications of Option Pricing Analysis," Chapter 4, in J. L. Bicksler, ed., *Handbook of Financial Economics.* Amsterdam: North-Holland, 1979.

———, AND J. B. WARNER, "On Financial Contracting: An Analysis of Bond Covenants," *Journal of Financial Economics* 7 (June 1979), pp. 117–161.

———, AND R. WATTS, "Incentive and Tax Effects of Executive Compensation Plans," *Australian Journal of Management* 7 (December 1982), pp. 139–157.

———, AND R. WATTS, "The Structure of Executive Compensation Contracts and the Control of Management," unpublished working paper. Rochester, N.Y.: University of Rochester, 1984.

SPENCE, M., "Job Market Signaling," *Quarterly Journal of Economics* 87 (August 1973), pp. 355–374.

———, AND R. ZECKHAUSER, "Insurance, Information and Individual Action," *American Economic Review* 61 (May 1971), pp. 380–387.

SPROUSE, R. T., AND M. MOONITZ, *A Tentative Set of Broad Accounting Principles for Business Enterprises.* New York: AICPA, 1962.

STACEY, N. A. H., *English Accountancy.* London: Gee and Company, 1954.

STIGLER, G. J., "The Theory of Economic Regulation," *The Bell Journal of Economics and Management Science* 2 (Spring 1971), pp. 3–21.

———, "Do Economists Matter?" *Southern Economic Journal* 42 (January 1976), pp. 347–354.

STIGLITZ, J. E., "Incentives and Risk Sharing in Sharecropping," *Review of Economic Studies* 41 (April 1974), pp. 219–255.

———, "The Theory of 'Screening', Education, and the Distribution of Income," *American Economic Review* 65 (June 1975), pp. 283–300. (a)

———, "Incentives, Risk and Information: Notes Towards a Theory of Hierarchy," *Bell Journal of Economics* 6 (Autumn 1975), pp. 552–579. (b)

STOREY, R. K., "Revenue Realization, Going Concern and Measurement of Income," *Accounting Review* 34 (April 1959), pp. 232–238.

SUNDER, S., "Relationship Between Accounting Changes and Stock Prices: Problems of Measurement and Some Empirical Evidence," *Empirical Research in Accounting: Selected Studies 1973,* supplement to Vol. 11 of *Journal of Accounting Research* (1973), pp. 1–45.

———, "Stock Price and Risk Related to Accounting Changes in Inventory Valuation," *Accounting Review* 50 (April 1975), pp. 305–315.

———, "Properties of Accounting Numbers Under Full Costing and Successful-Efforts Costing in the Petroleum Industry," *Accounting Review* 51 (January 1976), pp. 1–18.

TAUSSIG, F. W. AND W. S. BARKER, "American Corporations and Their Executives," *Quarterly Journal of Economics* 40 (1925), pp. 1–25.

U.S. CONGRESS, SENATE, SUBCOMMITTEE ON REPORTS, ACCOUNTING AND MANAGEMENT OF THE COMMITTEE ON GOVERNMENT OPERATIONS, *The Account Establishment: A Staff Study* (Metcalf Report), 94th Cong., 2d sess., 1976.

URWITZ, G., "Evidence on the Information Content of Market Determined Risk Measures of Corporate Bonds," unpublished working paper. Pittsburgh: Carnegie-Mellon University, 1975.

VATTER, W. J., *The Fund Theory of Accounting.* Chicago: University of Chicago Press, 1947.

VERRECCHIA, R. E., "On the Relationship Between Volume Reaction and Consensus of Investors: Implications for Interpreting Tests of Information Content," *Journal of Accounting Research* 19 (Spring 1981), pp. 271–283.

————, "The Use of Mathematical Models in Financial Accounting," *Studies on Current Research Methodologies in Accounting: A Critical Evaluation,* supplement to Vol. 20 of *Journal of Accounting Research* (1982), pp. 1–42.

WAKEMAN, L. M., "The Function of Bond Rating Agencies: Theory and Evidence," unpublished working paper. Rochester, N.Y.: University of Rochester, 1981.

————, AND R. WATTS, "Introduction to Agency Costs," Chapter 6, in "Notes on Corporate Finance," unpublished manuscript. Rochester, N.Y.: University of Rochester, 1978.

WALLACE, W. A., *The Economic Role of the Audit in Free and Regulated Markets.* Rochester, N.Y.: University of Rochester, 1980.

WARNER, J. B., "Bankruptcy, Absolute Priority, and the Pricing of Risky Debt Claims," *Journal of Financial Economics* 4 (May 1977), pp. 239–276.

WATTS, R., Appendix A to "Information Content of Dividends," unpublished working paper. Chicago: University of Chicago, October 1970.

————, "The Time Series Behavior of Quarterly Earnings," unpublished paper. Australia: University of Newcastle, 1975.

————, "Corporate Financial Statements, A Product of the Market and Political Processes," *Australian Journal of Management* 2 (April 1977), pp. 53–75.

————, "Systematic 'Abnormal' Returns After Quarterly Earnings Announcements," *Journal of Financial Economics* 6 (June–September 1978), pp. 127–150.

————, AND R. W. LEFTWICH, "The Time Series of Annual Accounting Earnings," *Journal of Accounting Research* 15 (Autumn 1977), pp. 253–271.

————, AND J. ZIMMERMAN, "Towards a Positive Theory of the Determination of Accounting Standards," *Accounting Review* 53 (January 1978), pp. 112–134.

————, AND J. ZIMMERMAN, "The Demand for and Supply of Accounting Theories: The Market for Excuses," *Accounting Review* 54 (April 1979), pp. 273–305.

————, AND J. ZIMMERMAN, "The Markets for Independence and Independent Auditors," unpublished working paper. Rochester, N.Y.: University of Rochester, March 1981. (a)

————, AND J. ZIMMERMAN, "Auditors and the Determination of Accounting Standards," unpublished working paper. Rochester, N.Y.: University of Rochester, 1981. (b)

————, AND J. ZIMMERMAN, "Auditor Independence and Scope of Services," unpublished working paper. Rochester, N.Y.: University of Rochester, 1982.

————, AND J. ZIMMERMAN, "Agency Problems, Auditing and the Theory of the Firm: Some Evidence," *Journal of Law and Economics* 26 (October 1983), pp. 613–634.

WEINSTEIN, M., "The Effect of a Rating Change Announcement on Bond Price," *Journal of Financial Economics* 5 (December 1977), pp. 329–350.

WESTERFIELD, R., "Pre-Bankruptcy Stock Price Performance," unpublished working paper. Philadelphia: University of Pennsylvania, 1970.

WHEATLEY, S. M., "The Information Content of Security Prices: Comment," unpublished manuscript. Rochester, N.Y.: University of Rochester, 1982.

WHITTRED, G. P., "Audit Qualification and the Timeliness of Corporate Annual Reports," *Accounting Review* 55 (October 1980), pp. 563–577.

WIESEN, J., *The Securities Acts and Independent Auditors: What Did Congress Intend.* New York: AICPA, 1978.

WILLIAMSON, O.E., "A Dynamic Stochastic Theory of Managerial Behavior," in A. Phillips and O. Williamson, eds., *Prices: Issues in Theory, Practice and Public Policy*, pp. 11–31. Philadelphia: University of Pennsylvania Press, 1967.

————, *The Economics of Discretionary Behavior: Managerial Objectives in a Theory of the Firm.* Englewood Cliffs, N.J.: Prentice-Hall, 1964.

WILSON, R., "The Theory of Syndicates," *Econometrica* 36 (January 1968), pp. 119–132.

WYATT, A. R., *A Critical Study of Accounting for Business Combinations.* New York: AICPA, 1963.

YAMEY, B. S., "Some Topics in the History of Financial Accounting in England 1500–1900," in W. T. Baxter and S. Davison, eds., *Studies in Accounting Theory*, pp. 14–43. London: Sweet and Maxwell, 1962.

ZEFF, S. A., *Forging Accounting Principles in Five Countries: A History and Analysis of Trends*, 1971, Arthur Andersen Lecture Series. Champaign, Ill.: Stipes, 1972, pp. 110–268.

ZIMMERMAN, J. L., "The Municipal Accounting Maze: An Analysis of Political Incentives," *Studies on Measurement and Evaluation of the Economic Efficiency of Public and Private Nonprofit Institutions*, supplement to Vol. 15 of *Journal of Accounting Research* (1977), pp. 107–144.

————, "The Costs and Benefits of Cost Allocations," *Accounting Review* 54 (July 1979), pp. 504–521.

————, "Research on Positive Theories of Financial Accounting," *Accounting Research Conference.* University, AL.: University of Alabama, 1982.

————, "Taxes and Firm Size," *Journal of Accounting and Economics* 5 (August 1983), pp. 119–149.

ZMIJEWSKI, M., AND R. HAGERMAN, "An Income Strategy Approach to the Positive Theory of Accounting Standard Setting/Choice," *Journal of Accounting and Economics* 3 (August 1981), pp. 129–149.

Index